N. Gordon Bechman
Lexington, Ky.
June 1955

CHARLES R. WALGREEN

FOUNDATION LECTURES

THE UNITED STATES AND CIVILIZATION

THE UNIVERSITY OF CHICAGO PRESS · CHICAGO
THE BAKER & TAYLOR COMPANY, NEW YORK
THE CAMBRIDGE UNIVERSITY PRESS, LONDON

THE
UNITED STATES AND
CIVILIZATION

By

JOHN U. NEF
The University of Chicago

THE UNIVERSITY OF CHICAGO PRESS
CHICAGO · ILLINOIS

To
ROBERT MAYNARD HUTCHINS

".... so must I nedes confesse and graunt that many thinges be in the Utopian weale publique, whiche in our cities I maye rather wishe for, then hope after."

—THOMAS MORE

FOREWORD

✵

LECTURES given at the University of Chicago under the Charles R. Walgreen Foundation for the Study of American Institutions are designed to assist students toward an understanding of contemporary life in the United States—its background in history, its ideals, values, and institutions, its present needs and possible future. To foster an intelligent citizenship and patriotism, not narrowly nationalistic in their expression, and with thought and knowledge much more than emotion as their foundation, is a principal purpose of this Foundation.

During the university year, 1940–41, "What Is Democracy?" "Democracy in American Life: a Historical View," "Democracy and National Unity," "Education in a Democracy," "The United States and Civilization," and "Basic Documents of Our Republic" were the several titles of the six series of lectures offered under the sponsorship of the Walgreen Foundation. As groups of addresses they were prepared for delivery to audiences of students. In their published form they represent an effort of the Walgreen Foundation to extend its usefulness beyond the limits of the University of Chicago campus.

Without the gracious co-operation of the authors and the University of Chicago Press, this effort could not have been made. The road through the Press was much the smoother because of the kindly help given at all times by Miss Mary D. Alexander and Miss Mary Irwin.

WILLIAM T. HUTCHINSON

Executive Secretary, Charles R. Walgreen Foundation
for the Study of American Institutions

xi

PREFACE

✹

SOME students at a neighboring college recently invited me to speak to them. Uncertain as to what kind of subject would be appropriate for the occasion, I appealed for advice, through a friend, to one of their professors whom I had met. This was the substance of his reply: In company with many other members of the "lost generation," I obviously felt, he said, that much was wrong with the kind of education we had had and with the civilization of which we found ourselves a part. Two world-wars within three decades had done nothing to dispel our doubts. He suggested that I explain what is wrong, why it is wrong, and what can be done about it!

Those are the questions with which my essay is concerned. I need scarcely say that it makes no pretense at supplying either comprehensive or sufficient answers! I release it for publication with many misgivings, which arise from a deep sense of my inadequate endowment and training. But my essay is not the product of a hasty impulse. It was written before the professor asked me his questions. The argument and structure of Part I took form in my mind at least as early as 1934. I have made use of notes that I began collecting, in odd moments, in 1919 and 1920, when I spent my Junior and Senior years at Harvard following the Armistice. Such inadequate qualifications as I have for my task are a love of art (which I owe to my mother, my father, and my wife) and a study that I have been making of industrial history in relation to the history of civilization since the Renaissance. The present book is in the nature of an epilogue to that study—far the greater part of which remains to be completed, though I have in manuscript sketches for the whole of it. Epilogues should not be printed in advance of the work they conclude, and my excuse for publishing this one is the uncertainty of the times and the apparent relevancy to the issues that confront the United States today of the lessons which history has taught me. They are issues that need to be faced without delay. If, as I scarcely dare to hope, my essay should find a few readers and encourage them to face these issues, its purpose would be attained.

My historical work has kept me rather continually occupied during the past twenty years, so that I have had little opportunity to turn aside from it. Although I published articles on subjects treated in this book as early as 1939, it would not have appeared as soon as it has if Mr. Emery T. Filbey had not done me the honor of asking me to lecture under the auspices of the Walgreen Foundation in the spring of 1941.

My essay might never have been written at all but for the generous and constant encouragement I have received from the distinguished American to whom it is dedicated. Thanks to him, it is at the University of Chicago alone that the important problems with which I have attempted to deal have been seriously and continually raised during the last decade. The essay itself has benefited in many ways, as will be apparent, from his written works and from his speeches. It has been greatly improved, in ways that will be less apparent, by the frequent advice and help that he has given me at various stages of composition. I need hardly add that, like the other friends who have kindly assisted me, he is in no way responsible for the conclusions or the nature of the argument.

My wife has helped me in all manner of ways. My book treats, from a somewhat different point of view, several subjects she has dealt with in a book which she had in hand long before I began this one, and which should soon be published. Suffice it to say that I am indebted to her, not she to me, for the resemblances.

Professor Frank H. Knight has read through the whole essay, either in typescript or in proof, with a care for my interests that I would describe as Christian were I not afraid of offending him. It will be understood that he is in no way implicated in the result by the fact that his criticisms and suggestions have helped me to improve the work considerably. Professor Yves R. Simon has done much for Part II. Professor Quincy Wright and Mr. James Dingwall, both of whom kindly read through an earlier version of the book, when it was in the form of lectures, made several useful suggestions.

I have derived help and encouragement from a number of friends and scholars who have not read the book. My obligations to Professor R. H. Tawney and Professor Jacques Maritain will be obvious. Both of them have gone out of their way to help me. Others whom I should like to thank also are Professor E. A. Duddy, Professor A. L. Dunham, Dr. Earl Harlan, Miss Stella Lange, the late Professor Marcel Moye of the University of Montpellier, Professor Robert E. Park, Dr. Artur Schnabel, Mr. Harrington Shortall, and Rev. Von Ogden Vogt. Parts of several chapters have appeared, in a somewhat different form, in the *Review of Politics*, and I am under special obligations to its editor, Dr. Waldemar Gurian. Parts of two chapters were published in 1939 in the *General Magazine and Historical Chronicle* and the *University of Chicago Magazine*.

I am very grateful to the Walgreen Foundation for putting at my disposal the resources necessary to see the book through the press. My relations with the Foundation were made especially pleasant by the thoughtfulness of its secretary, Professor William T. Hutchinson. The staff of the University of Chicago

Press have provided me with technical assistance in connection with the typescript and proofs which only a person who has published books elsewhere can adequately appreciate. I am indebted to Mrs. Margaret DeVinney for her careful typing, and to Dean Robert Redfield and Miss Diane Greeter for putting her services at my disposal. The Index is largely the work of Mr. George Batruel.

November 19, 1941

TABLE OF CONTENTS

✻

PART III. MEANS OF APPROACH

INDEX

I

INTRODUCTION

✺

HISTORY can teach what has been. It cannot teach what ought to be. It cannot even settle what is possible. For any conception of what ought to be we have to turn to moral philosophy, the science of the good. That is a venerable subject. Like most of man's works which have stood the test of time, it is regarded by those of our contemporaries who recognize its existence—and they are not the majority—with curiosity or amusement or distaste. What seldom, if ever, occurs to them is that the subject of moral philosophy, as expounded by the wisest philosophers of the past, can help them toward a solution of the grave problems they face today as individuals and as members of communities and nations.

On the rare occasions when it is suggested that the study of what is good for man and for mankind is relevant to modern scholarship and modern statesmanship, the suggestion, if it reaches a wide audience, arouses such storms of hasty opposition and suspicion in the American schools, colleges, and universities that all trace of its original meaning has been blown out of it by the time the winds of public and scholastic opinion have died down. It is hardly possible for anyone in the United States today to suggest that Plato, Aristotle, St. Augustine, or Aquinas might to advantage influence the conduct or even the thought of our time, without being called a medievalist, out of touch with modern conditions. If persons treat the wisdom

1

of these ancient philosophers as superior to most current opinion on matters of learning, art, politics, or private conduct, they are suspected of wishing to see all the American institutions of higher learning converted into medieval universities, if not into medieval monasteries and nunneries. They are suspected of wanting to scrap all our industrial machinery and return to the relatively simple economic relationships of the thirteenth century or even the Dark Ages. Their critics see a priest lurking behind every desk in their lecture-rooms.

These nightmares arise in part from the mistaken assumption that moral philosophy is an alternative to the historical, sociological, and anthropological studies[1] of man and of ideas with which university men have been concerned in recent decades. It is assumed that we must either return to the great ancient and medieval philosophers and forget all the analytical studies of the past century and a half or, as is the common practice in the United States at present, regard the works of those philosophers, together with yesterday's analytical studies, as irrelevant to contemporary inquiry, and focus all the attention of scholars on new analytical studies of the immediate, and occasionally of the ancient, past. The believers in the importance of past knowledge and wisdom for the struggle with present-day problems have not always helped as much as they might to dispel the nightmares.

We need a firm grasp of the knowledge and wisdom bequeathed us by ancient sages—not to destroy the work of serious and impartial modern students of society, but to make this work valuable to mankind. It is only with the help of moral philosophy that we can detect the ores of general truth which such studies contain. It is only with the help of moral philosophy that we can distinguish which aspects of these studies are important and which are unimportant. Far from

---

[1] We include under these heads the analytical studies of economists and political scientists.

being alternatives, moral philosophy and history, at their best, are complementary. Moral philosophy shows us both the limitations of historical research and its uses. Recent historical investigations, carried on by "social scientists" and by students of the so-called "humanities," have provided vast mines of information concerning the economic, the political, the religious, the intellectual, and the cultural conditions of different peoples, different nations, and different civilizations. The moral philosopher can use this buried treasure to compose a more concrete picture of the nature of good ends than was possible for Aristotle or St. Thomas Aquinas, with their more meager materials.

By drawing on the knowledge and wisdom of the moral philosopher, a few historians, together with some other students of society, can escape being smothered by the materials which now envelop them. What is lacking today in history, as in poetry and literature generally, is a hierarchy of moral and aesthetic values such as might be derived from philosophy. Such a hierarchy is hardly less indispensable for the writing of great history than for the writing of great literature.

Moral philosophy is a more exalted study than history, in the sense that it is concerned with the whole universe and that it seeks to cultivate the best in man. This does not mean that it diminishes the stature of history. To distinguish is not to diminish. On the contrary, moral philosophy contributes to the dignity and the significance of history, just as the true cultivation of history contributes to the force of moral philosophy. Unlike the quest for private riches, the quest for the true and the just is not a competitive game. If the wise man were asked, "Which is the greater, moral philosophy or history?" his answer would properly be the same that Goethe is said to have given the Philistine who tried to trap him by inquiring, "Who is the greater artist, you or Schiller?" Goethe's reply was, "You had better be glad you have us both."

If a small group of intelligent men, seeking the highest wisdom and the highest good, appeared on earth in the twentieth century, if they took refuge on some lovely island of the imagination, to seek there the ideal state, they would turn to history as well as to philosophy for guidance. They would know that historical, sociological, anthropological, and humanistic researches, by themselves, cannot show us what ought to be, or even what is possible. But they would also see that the study of past experience, together with past wisdom, could help them to establish a goal for suffering and confused humanity. They would see that, once they could establish this goal, the study of past experience could help them to instruct men in methods of working toward it.

What has the ideal state, what has some beautiful island of the imagination, what have wisdom and saintliness to do with the modern world of steel, steam, and electricity? What have they to do with guns, tanks, submarines, and bombing planes? The answer these philosophers could make is this: Upon the vision of the ideal state, upon the vision of a fair realm for mankind, conceived amid the skyscrapers, the noise of turning machinery and of swiftly moving railroad trains and airships, depends the hope of the human race to escape from slavery to steel, steam, and electricity. Upon such a vision depends also the hope of escaping exhaustion or destruction by the barbarous weapons that civilized men have invented and developed to cater to their ferocious instincts.

A study of the rise of machine technology and industrialism suggests that moral philosophy has not been made obsolete by the much-vaunted progress of modern times. On the contrary, moral philosophy seems to have a special relevance for mankind in the twentieth century. If a small group of philosophers considered the history of the Western European peoples during the last four or five hundred years, they would be convinced of the need at the present time for a renewal in a fresh form of moral philosophy in the Platonic, Aristotelian, and Christian sense. History suggests that the great achievements of civilized societies have come when some struggling section of mankind has been carried forward by a magnificent conception of life, expressed for it most perfectly by a few saints and wise men. The formulated conception may precede or accompany or follow the manifestation of it among the people. Such conceptions eventually exhaust themselves, not because they are false, but because the truths they contain, always imperfect and to some extent partial, are warped and debased by lesser men until they no longer conform even remotely to the deeper needs of mankind, with which true philosophers have always been concerned. In order to affect the life of a later and different age the old conceptions have to be discovered all over again in their relation to it. Fundamental truths can be made to play a great role in a civilization only after they have been cultivated by many generations in forms appropriate to it.

The conception that has guided Western civilization in Europe and America since the Renaissance appears to be exhausted in the twentieth century, like other conceptions before it. There has been a disposition all over the world, and not least of all in Russia and Germany, to think that the triumph of the machine marks the beginning of a new era. May it not mark rather the close of an old era? Unless man is able to master the machine and to use it for the highest ends of human existence, what has been heralded in some quarters as the dawn of a better age for humanity may prove to be nothing more, as Spengler has predicted, than the twilight of a civilization that has already run its course.

PART I
CIVILIZATION AT THE CROSSROADS

II

THE RISE OF INDUSTRIALISM

✳

THE extraordinary prosperity of the Western peoples in Europe and America at the beginning of the twentieth century, on the eve of the first World War, was reached after a series of efforts which began at about the time Leonardo da Vinci was born in 1452. In the twelfth and thirteenth centuries Europeans had generally agreed that the highest ideal in human conduct was the renunciation of earthly pleasures, even though the pleasures themselves might be legitimate in the sight of God. Men were disposed to subordinate actual life to certain absolute values, derived, as they believed, from God. Most of these values could be discovered by the human mind without revelation, in so far as men could rise above their human imperfections. It was never supposed that life in this world was actually being conducted in accordance with these values. Men saw evil all about them much more clearly than Americans see it today even when it stares them in the face. But evil was explained by original sin. Its existence in no way led men to question the values themselves. By honoring them, by groping after them here on earth, men felt they were working, however imperfectly, toward the Kingdom of God. The words which the priests and monks repeated, the plain chant in which all men participated in every Christian community from one end of Europe to the other, the orderly statues and the richly designed and colored windows of the recently built abbeys and cathedrals where men gathered—all reminded

9

them of their common end. All reminded them that in the end the wicked would be punished and the good rewarded. All these rites and monuments strengthened their sense of the unity of mankind here on earth, which no war or schism or heresy had been sufficiently devastating to destroy. All these rites and monuments were a constant testimonial to the general belief that what was best in man, his mind and spirit, in so far as they were just and good, did not belong to him as an individual, but to God the Father. As an earnest of that belief, they possessed, through the Church, the knowledge that Christ had appeared on earth, a part of God in the image of a man.

Believing as men did in the eternity of the mind and spirit, both of which belonged to God, they found it natural to work for the good of the individual through the good of each of the many communities into which the Christian world was divided. Artisans labored in common on common monuments. They did not sign their work as individual artists. Philosophers almost never referred in writing by name to their contemporaries.

The Gothic Age was a period of rapidly growing population and remarkable material progress. It lasted longer than any other period of great prosperity the European peoples were to experience until the late eighteenth and nineteenth centuries. During the twelfth and thirteenth centuries hundreds of thousands of peasants were gaining freedom from serfdom, along with a higher standard of living. Townsmen were growing richer. There were many new openings for the amassing of considerable fortunes in trade, finance, and even in industry. Notwithstanding the increasing opportunities for worldly success, wealth was accorded, in the thought and teaching of the age, a place subordinate to wisdom and goodness.

The long and brilliant age of the greatest Gothic architecture and art, when the area of cultivation and pasturage was extended in every direction into wooded, hilly, and even mountainous country, came to an end before the Black Death of 1348–50. The old conception of unity, derived from the subordination of actual life to the absolute values for which the Church stood, however inadequately, lost its force in the fourteenth century. This conception, of which the origins go back to Roman times, had provided the turbulent continent of Europe with a measure of peace and order during the Gothic Age. This conception did not disappear in the fourteenth and fifteenth centuries; its supporters grew more dogmatic in their teaching and writing after the Gothic Age. But, particularly as stated in its increasingly dogmatic form, it proved inadequate as a civilizing force. Its decay coincided with a period of religious, social, political, and economic disorder. The population of most countries ceased growing. The volume of food and of industrial produce turned out each year stopped increasing.

As the older conception of the ends of human existence ossified, a fresh conception began to form in a few men's minds. Its beginnings can be traced to a period of turmoil, bitterness, and bewilderment not unlike that which confronts the Western peoples again in our time. The new conception of the Renaissance gave a greater importance to the physical world, and to the human being as an end in himself, than the Gothic conception had done. It tended to make man the center of the universe. But man's mind and spirit, rather than his power to command material comforts, were still regarded as his first claim to dignity. As conceived by the greatest thinkers and artists of the Renaissance, the highest goals of earthly existence for man were the cultivation of his God-given intelligence, the development to the full of his reasoning powers, and the embellishment of life by art. As conceived by the greatest theologians of the Reformation, the highest religious task was for man, as an individual, to shoulder his moral obligations and strive toward the Christian virtues. The new works of thought and art were guided by a fuller knowledge of classical tradition than those of the Romanesque or the Gothic period. They were modeled more directly on classical examples. They were inspired by a more individualistic interpretation of the Christian faith. They were based to a greater degree upon the world that men saw directly with their eyes and felt directly with their senses. Nevertheless, the thought and art of the Renaissance were created by the light of a vision of human beings, not as they are in their daily lives, but as man in the finest flights of his imagination, with his love of order, beauty, splendor, calm, and joy,[1] would like to have them. Then, as now, the very great majority of the people were concerned first and foremost with gaining their bread. But the goal toward which the industrial laborer, like the artist or the poet, was directed in his work was primarily quality, in the aesthetic sense, rather than quantity. The craftsman got far less in material things, in physical comforts of all kinds, than the workman in a mine or factory today, but he took part far more often than the modern laborer in work that was varied and creative. Its products were generally enduring. They did not disappear as quickly from the scene of the labor as does a piece of coal hewed by a modern miner, or the parts of an automobile on the assembly line after a factory worker has tightened a bolt with his wrench.

I. THE INDUSTRIAL EXPANSION OF THE RENAISSANCE

In contrast to the fourteenth and early fifteenth, the late fifteenth and early sixteenth centuries were a period of prosperity in most districts of continental Europe. The Middle Ages drew to a close in the midst of great movements of discovery, colonization, and economic progress.

---

[1] My choice of these five words was determined by Baudelaire's famous poem, "L'Invitation au voyage."

Between 1450 and 1530 the annual output of silver probably increased at least fivefold in central Europe.[2] There and in other continental countries the production of copper, tin, iron, salt, and cloth grew almost as rapidly as that of silver. Printing was introduced in scores of towns in Germany, Italy, France, and the Low Countries. A number of products—such as paper, soap, glass, and gunpowder—for which the demand had been slight were manufactured for the first time in considerable quantities. All over the Continent the palaces of merchants, and the town halls and municipal law courts representing a flourishing mercantile society, were rising in profusion. Kings and princes, lay and ecclesiastical, were building castles mainly outside the old towns. Many of these castles were placed to dominate bourgs and villages.

One effect of the growth of trade and industry was to pull industrial enterprise away from the old towns. In some districts, particularly in Flanders and Brabant, the textile industries were spilling over beyond the ancient walls within which they had been largely confined. The cloth workers and merchants were transforming many villages into populous settlements, with streets shooting out in all directions—from a central square—"like the rays of a great star" at night.[3]

Elsewhere, particularly in central Europe, thousands of miners and metallurgical workers were forming equally populous centers in the hills, the high valleys, and the mountains. Great horse-driven engines pumped up water from depths of several hundred feet to drain the pits. In at least one case some of the horses were driven to their stations down into the earth

[2] For the calculations on which this statement is based, see my note on "Silver Production in Central Europe, 1450–1618," *Journal of Political Economy*, XLIX, No. 4 (1941), 586.

[3] In Pirenne's picturesque language (Henri Pirenne, *Histoire de Belgique* [3d ed.; Brussels, 1923], III, 236).

along a ramp, which wound about the main shaft like a screw.[4]

These economic changes were symptoms of the great new movement among the Western peoples, which was also reflected in the art and thought of the Renaissance and the religious ideas of the Reformation. The modern movement has been expansive to a degree without parallel in the whole of history, and eventually the emphasis on order and beauty in the products of craftsmanship, for which the Renaissance stood, gave way before the expansive tendencies. The search for new continents and a new celestial world, the development of contrapuntal music and new ways of creating a sense of distance in painting with perspective and color, the use of gunpowder to drive projectiles, the creation of credit money —Oswald Spengler has described these and many other of the expansive characteristics of the Western peoples in his celebrated book.[5] It is not necessary to accept his main thesis—that the only future for Western civilization is in military despotism—in order to recognize the essential truth of the description.

On the economic side, the expansion has taken various forms. The method devised for getting horses into the earth to pump water out of mines was a sort of symbol pointing the way to those ingenious ramps for parking automobiles, typical of the industrial civilization toward which the Renaissance miners and technical experts were inadvertently working. As time went on, the Western peoples aimed to multiply indefinitely, and at an ever increasing rate of growth, the volume of ores and minerals, metal and cloth, and durable goods of every kind produced each year. At the same time, and as a means of

[4] For the description on which this and the previous paragraph are based, see my "Industrial Europe at the Time of the Reformation," in *Journal of Political Economy*, XLIX, Nos. 1 and 2 (1941), 1–40, 183–224.

[5] *Der Untergang des Abendlandes* (2 vols.; Munich, 1922).

increasing the volume, they increased the size and scale of industrial units with the help of more and more powerful machinery, both by combining various industrial processes and by assembling workpeople engaged on the same product in larger and larger establishments.

The industrial expansion of the Renaissance had several modern characteristics, but it did not lead directly to the industrialism of modern times. It was not of long duration. It had spread from the south and east of Europe, from Italy and the Eastern Alps, toward the north and west. It generally petered out first in the countries where it had first started. It was over in Italy earlier than in France, where it lasted until the end of Francis I's reign (1515–47). It came to a close in Hungary in the twenties of the sixteenth century, with the Turkish invasions, before it had begun to wane in Saxony and southern Germany. It culminated there in the thirties and forties, somewhat earlier than in Franche-Comté and the Spanish Netherlands, where it lasted almost until the first sack of Antwerp in 1576.

Eventually the rapid growth in output was followed almost everywhere on the Continent by a long period of industrial stagnation, and even of retrogression. The volume of production actually fell in Spain, the Spanish Netherlands, and above all in the states of central Europe, at the end of the sixteenth century and during the first half of the seventeenth. At the close of the Thirty Years' War, in 1648, the output of silver in central Europe was probably little greater than at the close of the Hussite wars of the early fifteenth century, before the industrial expansion of the Renaissance had begun.

Despotism is not a medieval but a modern ideal of government, as Professor McIlwain has told us. Unlike the constitutional monarch of more recent times, the king or prince in the twelfth and thirteenth centuries had no superior in civil government, but his actual authority did not extend beyond distinct limits defined by tradition and custom. The lack of a generally admitted right to tax the nation's wealth imposed one of the limits. The duties owed by the prince to God and to the Church imposed another, and one of some importance in an age when most men still believed in the Christian God. The local authority of feudal nobles, great churchmen, ecclesiastical foundations, municipalities, and even little mining communities imposed other limits.

In the age of Machiavelli (1469–1527) the despotic principle of government gained strength on the Continent. The bounds set up by medieval constitutionalism gave way as the whole religious, intellectual, and political structure of the Gothic Age lost its hold on the Western peoples. The same countries —Italy, Germany, and Spain—took the lead in fostering despotism that were destined to revive it in our time. The sovereign authority in Italy and Germany was then split up among many princes and other governors, lay and ecclesiastical. During the late fifteenth and early sixteenth centuries, the princes were making the first great bid in Western history for the establishment of unlimited authority. As a part of their effort to control all phases of the lives of their peoples, they set about to regulate industry and to participate in industrial enterprise. They had much success. More and more, large-scale industry was brought under the control of political bureaucracies, able to curb the independence of the private merchants with industrial interests and other investors, and, if necessary, to dispossess them, even though they were guilty of no crime other than that of exercising economic power.

There was a conflict between this rise of despotic government and the aspirations of the Renaissance for a fuller life here on earth for individual man. At a time when the ideal of renunciation to the divine will was beginning to lose its hold over men, princes and their advisers were asking for a new kind of renunciation. They were asking the individual to accept the dominion of civil authority independently of the divine will, to accept the lordship of a man over men. In the early sixteenth century that conception of civil authority seemed about to triumph among the Western peoples everywhere in Europe. Americans were brought up to think of the modern age as an age of liberty. But it was under the auspices of growing authority and not of liberty that the modern age was ushered in.

In a famous generalization, Jean Bodin, the greatest political thinker of the late sixteenth century, laid it down that peoples living in a relatively cold climate—in the north or in mountainous country—were naturally inclined toward popular government, or at least toward elective monarchy.[6] The challenge to absolutism which came after the Reformation came especially in the countries of northern Europe. These countries had participated least in the industrial expansion of the late fifteenth and early sixteenth centuries. The challenge came in the late sixteenth and seventeenth centuries. It came at a time when the torch of commercial and industrial leadership passed from southern Germany, Italy, and Spain to the United Provinces, Sweden, and above all to Great Britain. In regions where the climate is harsh and the problem of wringing a living from the soil is challenging, the Europeans set about to secure comforts and ease never enjoyed by the inhabitants of those parts of the earth where nature is kinder to man.

The new economic development that followed the Reformation differed in fundamental respects from that of the Renaissance. In the north men turned from quality to quantity. They turned from splendor and beauty to plenty and comfort.

[6] *Les six livres de la République* (Paris, 1583), Book V, chap. i (esp. p. 694). Of course Bodin recognized that geographical conditions were only one of a number of factors that determined the inclinations and manners of a people. He recognized that the natural inclinations of a people, as derived from geographical conditions, might be greatly changed, if not completely transformed, by other circumstances.

In mining they turned from silver-bearing ore to coal and iron ore. Especially in Great Britain they turned from warfare and the preparation for warfare to peaceful occupations. In the creation of the new world, with its great emphasis on material values, the learning bred of the Renaissance and the conception of human life in this world as an end were not lost. Until very recent times the intense belief in the importance of right moral conduct, derived from the Reformation and especially from Calvinism, was cultivated. But in Holland, England, and its American colonies, the motives of private profit and individualism, which Calvinism itself and most of the other Protestant creeds were ultimately to encourage, were allowed a freedom that conflicted with the growing despotism of most continental princes.

II. THE EARLY ENGLISH "INDUSTRIAL REVOLUTION"

There have been two industrial revolutions in England, not one.[7] The first is still not given anything like the place in history to which its importance entitles it. It occurred during the hundred years that followed the dissolution of the monasteries in 1536 and 1539, and especially between about 1575 and 1620, in the time of Spenser, Hooker, Shakespeare, Bacon, and Donne. In the century between the Reformation and the English civil war, the output of coal in England increased some tenfold; the output of such products as salt, iron and steel, lead, ships, and glass from fivefold to tenfold. Many new or virtually new industries were introduced, such as the manu-

---

[7] Cf. R. H. Tawney, *The Agrarian Problem in the Sixteenth Century* (London, 1912), p. 403; Thorstein Veblen, *Imperial Germany and the Industrial Revolution* (New York, 1918), pp. 89–95; A. P. Wadsworth and J. de L. Mann, *The Cotton Trade Industry and Industrial Lancashire* (Manchester, 1931), p. 11; J. U. Nef, *The Rise of the British Coal Industry* (London, 1932), Part II; "The Progress of Technology and the Growth of Large-Scale Industry in Great Britain, 1540–1640," *Economic History Review*, V (1934), 3–24; "A Comparison of Industrial Growth in France and England, 1540–1640," *Journal of Political Economy*, XL (1936), 289–317, 505–33, 643–66; "Prices and Industrial Capitalism in France and England, 1540–1640," *Economic History Review*, VII (1937), 155–85.

facture of copper and brass, paper, sugar, soap, alum for dye-ing, tobacco, and the pipes in which it was smoked.

The phenomenal growth in the volume of output in Great Britain, together with the development of industrial tech-nology, changed the economic map of Europe. For rapidity of industrial progress there had been nothing quite like it any-where on the Continent, even in the late fifteenth and early sixteenth centuries. There was to be nothing quite like it again in any country until well on in the eighteenth century. On the eve of the English civil war, which broke out in 1642, England had come to produce at least three or four times as much coal as all the other states of Europe combined. She built more ships than any other country except Holland. Rela-tive to her population, she produced a larger volume of iron, steel, copper, and brass, of finished metal commodities, and of building material—such as bricks and lime—than any conti-nental country. It was only in the making of wares that the very wealthy alone could afford to acquire—such as lace, silks, and tapestries, and works of art modeled in glass, metal, clay, and stone—that continental nations, France in particular, had retained and increased the advantage they had always had over the English. Fostered by the French court, art and artistic craftsmanship consolidated a position in France which they had inherited from the age of Gothic cathedrals as well as from the age of the Italian Renaissance. The French cultivated or-der, beauty, and luxury at a time when English industrial ad-venturers were coming to be interested primarily in inventions designed to lower costs of production or transportation and to increase output. French industry had suffered somewhat less than that of most other continental states in the political and religious upheavals of the late sixteenth and early seventeenth centuries. France was establishing an industrial civilization of her own, which emphasized quality and style. This was des-tined to serve more than English industrial civilization as a model for the Continent until the middle of the eighteenth century.

Foreigners who visited London in the reign of Charles I (1625–42) were astonished by the coal smoke belching from tens of thousands of domestic hearths and kitchen stoves and from hundreds of furnaces, kilns, and ovens in small factories and workshops. To them the city with its breweries, its soap and starch houses, its brick kilns, sugar refineries, and glass manufactures seemed hardly fit for human habitation. There were plenty of Londoners who agreed with them. In 1627 a complaint was brought "full cry" to the privy council that an alum house near the Tower caused great annoyance to the inhabitants within a mile compass. The "loathesome vapour" from the factory was said to poison the very fish in the Thames, and an appeal was made to the college of physicians to pronounce the vapor damaging to the health of the citizens.[8] But in spite of many protests of this kind,[9] the factories grew in number. London had taken her place in Charles I's reign as the leading industrial city of the world.

Unlike the earlier industrial expansion on the Continent, that in England under Elizabeth and the first two Stuarts pointed the way toward the dominance of large-scale enterprise controlled by private capitalists. The attempts of the English crown to regulate industry and participate in it, to make mercantile subsidiary to political interests, after the fashion of most continental princes and kings, were undermined in the seventeenth century. The struggles which culminated in the English civil war and the revolution of 1688 established the rights of the private merchants and landlords to freedom from the arbitrary exercise of royal authority. These struggles did more. They put political authority in-

[8] *Calendar of State Papers, Domestic* (1627–28), pp. 269–70.
[9] Cf. Nef, *Rise of the British Coal Industry*, I, 157.

creasingly at the disposal of economic interests. Thus the English industrial expansion in early modern times gradually created the new conception of the ends of man destined to replace the old medieval conception. Both conceptions aimed to foster the dignity of man, as all great civilizations must. Henceforth that dignity was sought more than in the Middle Ages by efforts of individual men to attain material happiness in this world for the largest possible number of persons. The main objects of existence were to multiply commodities, to diminish physical cruelty and disease, and to leave the individual the greatest possible freedom to lead his own life without interference by political authority.

III. THE WORLD INDUSTRIAL REVOLUTION

The full fruits of the new conception were harvested only in the nineteenth century, after considerable delays. In Great Britain the remarkable industrial expansion during the hundred years preceding the civil war was followed by more than a hundred years during which the volume of industrial production continued to expand, but at a slower rate than between 1575 and 1620. The "industrial revolution," which Americans have been taught in the schools and colleges to regard as the watershed between barbarism and civilization, has been spoken of usually as beginning in 1760. That is a convenient date, because it marks the accession of George III. For the purposes of industrial history, it is not altogether satisfactory. In France a rather striking industrial development had got under way two decades or so earlier.[10] In Great Britain it was not until the eighties and nineties of the eighteenth century that the use of coal in smelting iron ore and of steam power in manufacturing began to tell heavily in the industrial life of the

[10] Cf. Nef, "English and French Industrial History after 1540 in Relation to the Constitution" in *The Constitution Reconsidered*, ed. Conyers Read (New York, 1938), pp. 93-94.

country. By that time canals and improved roads were greatly cheapening the cost of carrying bulky goods. They were opening new markets at home.

The fall of Napoleon in 1815 ushered in for all the European states a century of more peaceful relations than any other in Western history. Years without war between the chief powers on the Continent had been abnormal; they now became normal. As the Napoleonic experience had shown, warfare, if it came, was likely to be far more serious and extensive than the dynastic warfare of the eighteenth century, with its small armies and limited objectives. But except for the short, sharp, and bitter struggle of 1870–71, such warfare was only a threat. Peace in 1815 was followed soon by an era of free trade and by a revolution in transportation produced by the introduction of steam. All the elements necessary for the consummation of a long process of material improvement and expansion, stretching back to the Reformation and even to the Renaissance, were present. The industrial revolution of the Elizabethan Age could now be repeated on a grand scale. It was repeated in the nineteenth century as a movement of the European peoples everywhere, in Europe itself, in America, and eventually even in Asia.

Sir John Seeley's celebrated epigram about the English having "conquered and peopled half the world in a fit of absence of mind" can be interpreted in various ways.[11] What is important to remember here is that the ascendancy of British ideas in modern times was achieved in a considerable measure without force. Much is made by Britain's present enemies of the vast territories which are united under the English crown. But the governing power exercised by England in its colonies and dependencies counted for less in Europe, in the late eighteenth and nineteenth centuries, than the moral and intellectual

---

[11] *Expansion of England* (2d ed.; London, 1904), p. 10; cf. Conyers Read, *The Case for the British Empire* (Philadelphia, 1941).

ascendancy of English civilization in the far more powerful countries of the Continent over which England exercised no political authority. The mercantile conception of life, which the English were the first among the Western peoples to cultivate for its own sake, achieved a bloodless conquest in Europe, because it conformed in a considerable measure to the wishes of the inhabitants and to the views of leading European thinkers. In the eighteenth century foreigners began to admire England's material success and the lofty conceptions which accompanied it of the value, the rights, and also the obligations of the individual. Foreigners set about consciously or unconsciously to copy or adapt to their own countries the English intellectual outlook and political philosophy, especially in its relation to economic and social life. The belief that economic improvement and expansion provided the main keys to general happiness led to a growing admiration for natural science and mechanics both on the continent of Europe and in the New World. Foreigners began to share with Englishmen the further belief that economic improvement and expansion were encouraged by popular sovereignty and constitutional government. Continental Europeans began to think that a minute regulation of economic affairs by the state and a participation by the state in economic enterprise, such as they had been accustomed to, were obstacles to progress. Progress was everywhere becoming the chief object of statesmen and of the people they governed.[12]

The movement to enthrone the precepts of economic liberalism, and the methods of the natural sciences associated with it, as the guiding principles for the whole of civilized existence, did not bring the same response in all countries. In the United States these ideas met almost no opposition. They developed without many of the restraints imposed by older traditions in England. On the continent of Europe they frequently encoun-

[12] Cf. below, chap. x.

tered tough opposition. But admiration for the English conception of civilization began to have an influence on French thought and governing policy even before the Revolution. To many eighteenth-century French writers, who were more materialistic in their thought than their ancestors of the classical seventeenth century, it seemed that the country had mistaken the ornaments for the substance of living. Impatient with his countrymen for their inability to understand Newton, Voltaire wrote in 1735, "In Truth, we are the whipped cream of Europe."[13] For him, the grace, the precision, the sweetness, and the finesse of French culture could not make up entirely for what he called the more masculine virtues in which the English excelled.[14] From Voltaire's time until the beginning of the twentieth century France made one concession after another to these "masculine" ways of thinking, governing, and conducting economic enterprise. In Scandinavia and the Low Countries these ways were more congenial than in France, especially after the middle of the nineteenth century. They had taken root in the north of Europe to some extent independently of English influence. England herself had derived some of them from the Low Countries. No nation in Europe was more American in the welcome it accorded the new industrialism than little Belgium. There, on the eve of the present war, the blaring of loud-speakers in the streets and the gestures of hitchhikers by the roadside made the motorist from the United States feel almost completely at home.

It was in Italy and Germany, where a very different conception of government had been associated with the industrial expansion of the Renaissance, that English economic and political thought made the slowest headway and encountered the

[13] Letter of November 30, 1735, to Abbé d'Olivet (*Œuvres complètes de Voltaire* [Paris, 1880], XXXIII, 556).

[14] Letter of November 11, 1738, to Abbé le Blanc (*ibid.*, XXXV, 41).

stiffest opposition. Germany never welcomed to the same extent as France the doctrine of free trade. But, under the influence of Prussia, a whole series of more liberal laws concerning the ownership of minerals and the conduct of industrial enterprise was adopted in the late nineteenth century. Italy actually set up a constitutional monarchy modeled to a considerable degree on that of England.

Toward the end of the nineteenth century the Western European races, which had expanded since the Middle Ages over a great part of the globe, seemed on the point of agreeing upon a new conception of the ends of life. It may be summed up in the words, "the greatest economic good for the greatest number." Most people found it difficult to see how this conception, and the increasingly humane ways of treating men that had accompanied its spread, could fail to win firmer adherence throughout the world for a very long time to come. The benefits of industrialism were everywhere so obvious that it seemed incredible, particularly to the British and the Americans, that men would ever relinquish so fruitful a conception. The standard of living was rising in every land. Peace was coming to be regarded as the normal condition for mankind. Tourists moved from one European country to another with the most perfunctory examination of their luggage at the frontiers. No American traveler thought of getting a passport unless he intended to visit what were regarded as semibarbarous countries such as Turkey or Spain.

Everywhere unwary people mistook the abnormal for the normal. They were right in thinking that there had never been an age in history when mankind had achieved so great a triumph over matter. They were wrong in thinking that the triumph would ultimately prove other than empty without an improvement in the morals and the intelligence of mankind, comparable to the improvement that was taking place in the knowledge of natural science and technology. They were

wrong in thinking that they had discovered for civilized man
the secret of eternal life in political economy and the natural
sciences. They had forgotten that eras of great material improvement had occurred before and had ended in exhaustion.

The nineteenth century drew to its close in a delicate haze of
hope. The Spanish-American War and the Boer War were ending with little loss of life and with little damage to economic
welfare. Few people in America or Great Britain dreamed that
the time would come soon when all the able-bodied young men
in every land would be bearing arms and facing death on the
battlefield, in the air, and on the sea. Even in nightmares, almost no one imagined that great cities would be bombed and
largely destroyed by hordes of fast-moving planes. 1899 and
1900 were summers full of brilliant sunshine. They produced
some of the most perfect clarets in history. Most influential
people saw the world through the clear ruby colors of those
wines. They mistook twilight for dawn.

It is now evident that this happy hope for a better world
than any which earlier civilizations had created may have
been no more than a dream. The Balkan wars were a prelude
to what was up to then the greatest war in history, in point of
the number of large nations and of persons involved. Rumors
of the coming of such a war had been circulating for years.
But until the cannons actually went off, most of the people of
Western European origin, including many of the best educated
and the most learned, had believed that such a war was impossible. The varying degree of surprise with which it broke upon the inhabitants of the various nations reflected the degree
to which each had absorbed the new beliefs in natural science
and political economy and in the progress they were supposed
to guarantee.

I remember the account of the fatal day for which some few
had hoped, given me not long ago by an elderly American professor of culture and learning. He had lived much abroad, had

written most of his scientific articles in the German language, and had had from his youth a deep knowledge of central Europe. July, 1914, found him, a man in middle life, with his family, in the heart of the European Continent, in a large Swiss hotel, high above Zermatt. Like all good tourist hotels in that happy age, it was crowded. Like most, it had an international clientele of upper-middle-class citizens. There were Germans, Austrians, Frenchmen, British, and Americans. As an emblem of the sympathy between the peoples of Europe, in which so many had put their hopes, some of the children were the offspring of international marriages. They spoke German, French, and English so interchangeably that it was often difficult even for this cosmopolitan American to determine their nationality. Carefree and happy on their vacations, the children and their parents spent their days strolling, climbing, and playing tennis. They spent their evenings at cards and billiards.

August 1 is the Swiss national holiday. At the hotel it was celebrated by a gala dinner. According to the fashion of the time, the ice cream had been made into fantastic shapes— ducks, ocean liners, mountain peaks. Dinner came after a perfect day, such as one always expects in the Alps, but seldom finds. It was one of a succession of cloudless days. They had begun in the middle of July and they were destined to continue, in spite of the flow of blood, until the middle of September. In the midst of conversation and laughter, news terrible but vague began to travel from table to table, for the most part without the exchange of a word. Table after table was emptied prematurely of its occupants. They gathered in little groups in the large reception hall, where they besieged the clerks and other hotel employees with questions.

What struck the American professor, as he moved about among these groups, was that the Germans and the Austrians he had seen in July were missing. He overheard the talk of two Frenchmen. One asked the other what he thought of the unconfirmed report that Germany had declared war on Russia and France. The second was a lithe young man of about thirty, probably an officer. He would remember until his dying day, the American said, this young man's quiet answer: "C'est bon si c'est vrai." It was the French answer of 1914. It was not the French answer of 1939.

The numerous English guests were incredulous to a man. One expressed astonishment when, on appealing to the American for an opinion, he was told that not only had war probably come but that England would not stand aside. Turning to another group the American remembered he talked with an English woman, the wife of a member of parliament, with a bright young son of seventeen on the point of entering Cambridge. They had played billiards together on several occasions, the youth and the middle-aged professor. The professor found his young partner fairly exuding excited amusement. In the morning he had left a pair of shoes with the valet to be fitted with nails. He now discovered that "boots" had been mobilized during the day, and had gone off without leaving the key to the closet in which he had locked the shoes. This struck the young Englishman as ridiculously funny. "All the wretched Swiss are rushing off to join the army," he told the professor, "all so serious, just as if they were really going to fight." Seeing one of the waiters passing, he grasped him by the coat sleeve, forgetting the English etiquette that had been drilled into him from childhood. "Look here, you idiot," he shouted, "don't take all this so hard. What if the Germans do invade Switzerland? Why don't you fellows collect the apples you have been putting on the tables these last days? Nobody could eat them. They are so hard that all you need do is throw them at the Germans!"

So that old world disappeared. Men hurried to get passports and places in railroad carriages, only to find, after a day or two, that no more trains were running from Switzerland. During those warm sunny weeks of August and early September it seemed as if all the European blood that had been spared during a century of virtual peace, with its humane ways, spurted out in forty days over the fields and amid the hills and woods of Belgium, the Rhineland, and northeastern France.

For nearly a decade after the unprecedented slaughter of that terrific four years' war, when men soon learned to fight from trenches and to live in deep underground tunnels such as none but miners had hitherto inhabited, it seemed to Englishmen and Americans that it all had been a mere interlude in the long era of progress. Then the knowledge that had been possessed earlier by some wise men, that all was not right with Western civilization, began to spread. It became apparent that an epoch was ending. Even a few complacent and comfortable Americans living in the Middle West or on the Pacific coast have begun to wonder whether we are all getting better every day and in every way.

The position of the United States, the richest of all countries, isolated as she remains to some extent from the rest of the world, in spite of the new means of transportation and destruction, imposes upon Americans special obligations in the new epoch that looms in front of us. At least for the moment, this country has greater freedom than any other to work out some rational conception of civilization to take the place of those conceptions which made the thirteenth and the nineteenth centuries such glorious periods for the Western peoples. Our future as a nation and even the future of Western civilization may well depend upon our success or failure in carrying through such a reconstruction. The first step toward bringing American opinion to recognize the need for a reconstruction of the world of thought, with which university professors are still ostensibly concerned, is to show that we cannot look forward to an indefinite continuation of the expansive movement of material production to which our fathers and grandfathers and great-grandfathers became accustomed. We can no longer look forward to a continually mounting rate of increase in the national dividend. At the same time we are confronted by a breakdown in the guiding principles, moral and intellectual, which made that expansive movement in the material sphere orderly—which may even be said to have made it possible.

III

THE MATERIAL CRISIS

✳

WHAT marked off industrial organization in Western Europe and America at the end of the nineteenth century from industrial organization in all earlier civilizations was not the existence of large-scale enterprise; it was not even the existence of large-scale enterprise in private hands—it was the dominance of large-scale enterprise in private hands. For the first time in history, the majority of all industrial workers in the leading countries of the world had come to be employed under conditions of industrial capitalism. The typical venture for mining and manufacturing was a plant specially built for industrial purposes, owned and operated for the profit of a capitalist or group of capitalists who took no part in the manual labor, and staffed by wage-earners hired in a free market. The policy of the plant was settled by the owners and the administrative officers they employed, or by those among the owners who secured through their activity or their financial connections a controlling voice in the management. As long as the enterprise broke no general laws, as long as it did not lay itself open to prosecution in the courts, the state had no authority to interfere with it.

The rise of this form of enterprise to a position of dominance in Western civilization was closely related to the triumph of machine technology and the phenomenally rapid increase in the volume of industrial output. What gave this form of enterprise its prestige was, above all, the lightening of manual labor and the rapid decrease in the costs of production which accompanied its spread. We shall get a more intelligent understanding of the probable future of industrial capitalism than would be otherwise possible if we consider the future of some of the factors which have promoted the development of machine technology and the expansion of output. These factors are many and complex. They are all interrelated, and it is probably beyond the power of the human mind to give a perfect description of their operation. This is not the place to attempt a description. But even some rough and general remarks are sufficient to show that the Western peoples in all probability have reached a turning point in their industrial history.

Prominent among the material factors that created modern industrialism have been the widespread use of coal fuel, the phenomenally rapid increase of the population, and the even more rapid growth in the demand per capita for cheap manufactured commodities.

I. COAL AND INDUSTRIALISM

As far back as the reigns of Queen Elizabeth (1558–1603) and her two Stuart successors, James I (1603–25) and Charles I (1625–42), the growth in the volume of the national output and the progress of technology in England were bound up with the burning of coal, a fuel of which no civilization except Western has ever made extensive use. No change in the appearance of the English countryside so struck the seasoned traveler, as he rode from county to county about the year 1600, as the havoc wrought in the fine forests and thick shrubberies which he remembered from the days of his youth. There is a celebrated passage in *Gargantua* where Rabelais explains how the province of Beauce got its name. As anyone who has driven along the roads to Chartres will remember, the country all around is practically bare of trees. Before the present war

Frenchmen who did their military service there in the summer complained that there was never any shade in which to rest. Rabelais explains the want of woods by telling how Gargantua's mare, wandering through the province, full as it was of trees and shrubbery, became infuriated by the stings of dorflies, hornets, and wasps, and struck out with her mighty tail until she had mowed down every tree in the forest. Gargantua was so pleased by this display of his mare's prodigious power that he simply said to his company, "Je trouve beau ce."[1]

Now, if our Elizabethan traveler had read his Rabelais, he may well have imagined that Gargantua's mare had got loose in every English shire since his childhood and had reduced much of the country to a plain field like the province of Beauce. What had actually wrought the destruction was not literary magic, but the expansion in production that heralded the early "industrial revolution." Lumber was wanted to construct new ships, which were being launched in scores in the shipyards of East Anglia and the south of England. It was wanted to build thousands of houses and barns in the newly laid out parks, the rapidly growing industrial villages, the provincial towns, and above all in London, which was sprawling almost daily farther beyond the ancient city limits. Lumber was wanted also for machinery—still made almost entirely of wood except for the gears and axles. Lumber was wanted to build hundreds of small factories for making alum and copperas, saltpeter and gunpowder, sugar and soap, salt and iron, copper, brass, and lead. It was wanted to build the dams to store up water for driving the engines at blast furnaces and forges. At the same time tens of thousands of trees were being turned into charcoal every year and tens of thousands more were being burned as faggots and small logs in these rapidly growing manufactures.

[1] Book I, chap. xvi.

What would have been the outcome of this remarkable industrial expansion if there had been in Great Britain, as in classical Greece and Italy, practically no coal? An answer to this question is provided by what actually happened to the output of iron. While coal was beginning to be successfully substituted for wood in most English manufactures by the middle of the seventeenth century, inventors were unable to find a satisfactory method of using the new fuel in the smelting of ores. Many wagonloads of wood continued to go up in smoke with the production of each ton of iron. As a result, a remarkable growth in the output of iron which began about 1540 was brought to an end after the death of Shakespeare, in 1616, by the scarcity and high price of wood fuel.

The plight of the English iron-making industry after about 1620 would have been the common plight of all English industries if there had been no coal to substitute for wood. Indeed, the result all around would have been much more serious than it actually was in the case of iron, for the substitution of coal for wood in other industries and in the domestic hearths and kitchen stoves of the common people conserved timber which would otherwise have been burned. The substitution of coal for wood in baking bricks and burning limestone conserved timber which would otherwise have been used in building. Without coal, industrial output generally could hardly have gone on increasing. The early "industrial revolution" might have been stillborn. The later world industrial revolution, to which the early expansion ultimately led, might never have taken place.

Coal also played a positive role in the rise of capitalist industry. English travelers brought back from central Europe models of the most elaborate and powerful machinery hitherto used at mines. Similar machinery, with adaptations and some improvements, was installed at collieries in Great Britain. Prospectors seeking coal were aided by the invention, probably between 1600 and 1615, of boring rods.[2] These tools marked a great advance over the old divining rod. Apart from such clews as the nature of the surface was supposed to give, the divining rod was still the only means known to the German miners of searching for ore without sinking shafts, at the height of the mining development in central Europe in the sixteenth century. A few experts in each mining district were believed by some of the local population to possess a mysterious art. They roamed over the hills, holding a forked twig straight out in front of them until it turned or twisted as they passed over a hidden seam of ore.[3] The introduction in England of boring rods enabled the mining prospectors to bring to the surface and examine samples of the underground strata. This showed the growing desire of men to replace fancy and folklore by actual contact with the material world. At about the same time in England new and cheaper means were found for moving coal overland. Wooden rails were fastened to the ground, and wagons, their wheels fitted with flanges and brakes, were fashioned to run on these rails. The new wagons began to roll over rough and muddy country, along bridges and through cuts, down a gentle incline connecting the pits with the wharves beside the river. Horses then drew them empty back to the mine's mouth.[4]

[2] Nef, *Rise of the British Coal Industry*, II, 446.

[3] Georgius Agricola, *De re metallica* (1556), eds. H. C. and L. H. Hoover (London, 1912), pp. 37–41. Agricola himself had no faith in the value of the divining rod.

[4] The idea of the railway was apparently conceived in sixteenth-century Germany. An illustration in Sebastian Münster's *Cosmographia universalis* (1550) shows a workman at a German mine pushing a tiny truck along wooden rails (A. Wolf, *A History of Science, Technology, and Philosophy in the Sixteenth and Seventeenth Centuries* [London, 1935], pp. 511–12). But there is no evidence that the Germans had railways several miles long, suitable for heavily laden wagons, of the sort built and used in England in the seventeenth century. If the Germans had had them, Agricola would hardly have failed to mention this in his extraordinarily comprehensive works on mining and metallurgy. All doubt concerning the novelty of the English railway should be removed by the

The search for more power to drive the drainage machinery at collieries led at the beginning of the eighteenth century to the discovery of the steam engine. Much earlier, kilns and furnaces had been invented to make possible the use of mineral fuel in such industries as the drying of malt, the melting of glass, and the manufacture of steel from bar iron. The new furnaces were generally larger than those which they superseded. The wares produced with coal tended to be cheaper, less elegant, and less beautiful than those made in charcoal fires. As the supplies of coal were localized, the substitution of coal for wood led to the concentration of industry about the mines. For all these reasons, the new fuel encouraged the manufacture of cheap goods in large quantities and at larger plants, requiring more capital than had been necessary in the Middle Ages.

In the eighteenth century the progress of industry caused a timber crisis in France and some other continental countries, comparable to the one which had beset Great Britain in the Elizabethan Age. Before the end of the nineteenth century even the United States, in spite of what had once seemed boundless virgin forests, had begun to experience the problems of deforestation. One Western people after another followed in the footsteps of the English in substituting coal for wood as fuel in every branch of manufacturing, and also in substituting for lumber building materials produced with coal. At the same time the influence exerted by the new fuel in favor of the manufacture of cheap goods in large industrial enterprises was becoming more pronounced, with new inventions and a host of technical improvements which spread through Europe and America and eventually to Asia. The discovery in the eighteenth century of methods of producing, first, pig iron

knowledge that it was introduced into the Ruhr district at the end of the eighteenth century as an "englischer Kohlenweg" (Ludwig Beck, *Geschichte des Eisen* [Braunschweig, 1884–1903], III, 960). Cf. Nef, *op. cit.*, I, 244–45.

from the ore, and later bar iron, with coal and coke, made it possible eventually to turn out iron at something like a fifteenth of the cost that had prevailed at the richest period of Greco-Roman civilization.[5] Construction on a grand scale, with iron and steel, cement and glass, became possible for the first time in history. The application of steam power (first used in draining coal mines) to manufacturing was followed by its application to transportation. Rails, originally devised for carrying coal, combined with steam to cheapen the cost of moving heavy goods overland to a small fraction of what it had been over the finest Roman roads at the height of the Roman Empire. It is no wonder that the growth among the Western peoples in the manufacture of cheap commodities coincided roughly with the growth in the output of coal.

Ever since the late fifteenth century, when the coal mines around Liége and just west of Mons (discovered probably before 1200) were exploited with greater vigor than ever before, the world-output of coal has increased continually, rapidly, and almost uninterruptedly from decade to decade. In the nineteenth century the rate of increase became phenomenal. The movement of rapid increase lasted some four hundred and fifty years, during which the output multiplied two or three thousand fold or more. The rapid increase seems now to have come to an end. Since the outbreak of the first World War the output of coal has grown very little. In the United States the output has declined somewhat. During the two decades, 1914–33, there was no increase in world-production. If world-pro-

---

[5] According to Tenney Frank, a given amount of gold in Cicero's day would have bought only about a fifth as much iron as in the United States in 1910, although it would have bought twice as much wheat, rye, and cheese, thrice as much wine and oil, and four times as much coarse wool. Domestic servants could be had for about a tenth as much as in the United States in 1910. Historians have arrived at the rough generalization that gold in Cicero's day had about three times as great a purchasing power as in the United States at the beginning of the twentieth century (*An Economic History of Rome* [Baltimore, 1920], pp. 80–81).

duction had increased since 1913 at the same rate as from 1864 to 1913, the annual output on the eve of the present war would have been at least 4,000 million tons. In fact it was only about 1,500 million tons.

This great change in the course of coal production has not been caused primarily by the exhaustion of the supplies. Modern scientific and engineering skill has made it possible to estimate with reasonable accuracy the coal resources of the globe. If the annual consumption does not increase in the future, the world's coal supply would probably not be used up for many hundreds of years, though the difficulties of obtaining coal would obviously multiply with the necessity of extracting it at ever greater depths. What has brought the expansion in coal output to such an abrupt end is only partly the substitution of other fuels for coal—for example, oil, and heat generated by hydroelectric power. The main explanation of the change in the course of coal production since 1913 is the virtual halt in the growth of the demand for energy, the striking decline in the rate of expansion in the markets for fuel.[6]

What of the future? The future of oil is more uncertain than that of coal. In its natural state in the earth, oil is an elusive liquid. Most attempts to estimate its quantity suggest that the supplies will be exhausted within a few decades. While vast undiscovered resources may well exist, so far as we are aware no one claims that at the present rate of consumption the reserves of oil will last nearly as long as the reserves of coal. It is generally agreed that if the hydroelectric power throughout the world is fully harnessed to serve industry, it cannot provide, under present conditions of transmission, nearly as much energy as is now supplied by coal.

Further rapid expansion in the use of fuel and power, of the sort to which the Western peoples have grown accustomed, de-

[6] Cf. W. Bowden, M. Karpovitch, and A. P. Usher, *An Economic History of Europe since 1750* (New York, 1937), pp. 667–69.

pends, then, partly upon the development of cheaper methods of generating heat from coal, oil, and hydroelectric power, and partly upon the exploitation of other sources of fuel, such as uranium, which the recent and future discoveries of the natural scientists and the applications of technicians may make available. For a nonexpert to hazard a prediction concerning the possibilities of either of these developments would be presumptuous, especially when the experts themselves are apparently quite uncertain about the future. This much seems clear: If a great expansion in the use of energy were to take place during the next two centuries, it would be an expansion based on different kinds of fuel than those with which the Western peoples accomplished the economic conquest of the world. It might encourage the development of other forms of economic enterprise from those associated with the rise of industrialism.

The probabilities are against an increase in the use of heat during the next two centuries at anything like the same rate as during the last two. A conservative estimate would put the increase since 1740 at something like three or four hundred fold. A similar rate of increase during the next two hundred years would exhaust all the supplies of coal and oil long before A.D. 2140, even if much more efficient methods of burning them were employed. Unless we escape almost altogether for our fuel from coal, oil, and water power, a point will be reached where the limitations of these resources will impose limits upon further industrial expansion.

Almost eighty years ago W. S. Jevons, the eminent English economist, pointed out that the exhaustion of the British coal supplies was bound to bring about a decline in the rate of industrial progress in Great Britain within a century.[7] In spite of the extensive use, since he wrote, of oil and water power as

[7] *The Coal Question* (London, 1865) (see the 3d ed., rev. by A. W. Flux [London, 1906]).

substitutes for coal, his prediction is coming true, though we owe the change less than he supposed to the exhaustion of natural resources and more to a slackening in the growth of markets. The rate of increase in industrial output in Great Britain has slowed down very greatly during the past eighty years. As measured by the volume of production, industrial progress during that time has been much slower in Great Britain than in the other chief industrial nations of the world, though Great Britain had so imposing a lead in 1865 that she has remained ahead of all the other nations except Germany and the United States.

Jevons' generalization can now be applied to these other nations. In spite of possible future improvements in the methods of using all kinds of fuel, and in spite of the possible use of new fuel, the exhaustion of the coal supplies of the world will be likely to bring about a decline in the rate of growth in the output of manufactures during the century that lies ahead. When we think of the fantastic implications of an increase of a hundred fold or so in the use of energy during the next hundred years, among peoples who have not succeeded in improving notably the dignity of their lives with the mechanical devices and gadgets they already have, it may be doubted whether such a probability should be the cause for unmixed regrets.

Heat has been the power behind every kind of manufacturing; during the last century it has become the power behind transportation. Cheap fuel, then, is the foundation stone of modern industrialism. The increase in the nation's or the world's productive capacity probably depends upon cheap fuel more than upon any other single factor. Yet any attempt to account for the rise of industrialism, even in the purely material sense, in terms of cheap fuel alone would be most one-sided. Coal and oil have existed in the earth probably as far back as the time when man first appeared on this planet. But

even in Great Britain it is only in the last four hundred years
that the subsoil came to be the principal source of physical
energy. Among the Western peoples generally it is only during
the last hundred and fifty years that most of their fuel has been
dug out from subterranean passages or pumped up from wells.
It is only in the last century that men have discovered how to
generate heat from rushing water.

What forces have driven man at this late stage in his development to push manufacturing and transportation to such a
point that they could be nourished only by new kinds of fuel
and power? The answer to that question is to be found mainly
in a study of markets, and of the factors that have contributed
to their extraordinary growth during the last five centuries,
and more especially since the era of the Napoleonic wars. The
future of industrial output depends not only upon the supplies
of cheap fuel made available to generate commodities and upon new inventions that reduce the manual labor needed to produce them; it depends also, and probably to a much greater
degree, upon the further expansion of markets. As we have
seen, the chief explanation for the slow growth in the output
of coal since 1913 has been the slow growth in the demand for
energy. Are there limits to the growth of markets which also
impose bounds upon the increase in the volume of production
during the centuries that lie ahead?

II. POPULATION AND INDUSTRIALISM

As far as our present knowledge of history extends, every
age of very rapid increase in commercial activity and industrial
production has been an age of growing population. This was
true of the Gothic Age. Between the tenth and the early fourteenth centuries the population of France is believed to have
increased something like threefold or even more; the population of the newly established Holy Roman Empire probably
grew as rapidly as that of France; the population of England

and Wales perhaps doubled. The same thing was true of the
Elizabethan Age. The early English "industrial revolution"
was accompanied by a remarkable growth in the population,
which had remained more or less stationary during the two
centuries preceding the reign of Henry VIII (1509–47). "The
English nation encreaseth," Englishmen frequently remarked
with pride in the time of Elizabeth and James I. John Evelyn's
grandfather had twenty-four children by two wives. Many
wealthy persons in the merchant class and the rising gentry
were hardly less prolific. There were, perhaps, almost twice as
many Englishmen in the world on the eve of the civil war, in
1640, as at the dissolution of the monasteries, in 1536 and 1539.

As far as can now be judged, there has never been a period of
equal length in the whole history of civilization when the
population of the world increased at anything like as rapid a
rate as between about the middle of the eighteenth century
and the beginning of the twentieth. It was the Western people, the creators of industrialism, who took the lead. Around
1740 the inhabitants of Western Europe probably numbered
not more than eighty or ninety millions.[8] The population of
the whole of Europe was perhaps one hundred and thirty millions. The peoples of European stock in North and South
America numbered perhaps six or seven millions.[9] At about
this time the English and French began to multiply rapidly.
The increase soon extended to all the European peoples. On
the eve of the first World War there were more than five hun-

---

[8] I include in Western Europe the countries included by J. Beloch ("Die Bevölkerung
Europas zur Zeit der Renaissance," *Zeitschrift für Socialwissenschaft*, III [1900], 786).
Beloch excludes Russia and the Balkans. The population of Western Europe was prob-
ably not much larger than in 1600, when Beloch estimated it at 73.5 millions.

[9] A. M. Carr-Saunders, *World Population* (Oxford, 1936), p. 30. Dr. Carr-Saunders
gives the figure 12.4 millions for America in 1750, but this includes, of course, persons
not of European origin. His figure for Europe in 1750 is 140 millions. As he makes
plain, the estimate is based almost entirely on guesswork and cannot be regarded as at
all precise.

dred millions of them in Europe and elsewhere. France was about twice as populous as she had been a century and a half before; Germany probably more than three times as populous; Great Britain almost six times as populous. During the hundred and thirty years from 1790 to 1920 the population of the United States grew about twenty-seven fold, from just under four millions to nearly a hundred and six millions.[10] Today almost all these countries are still more populous. In two centuries the population of European extraction in Europe and America has probably increased more than fivefold, to upward of seven hundred millions. The population of the world as a whole has perhaps tripled. In 1740 there were possibly between six and seven hundred millions. Now there are some two thousand millions.[11]

It needs no sophisticated mind to conclude that one explanation for the extraordinary increase in the volume of industrial output between the late eighteenth and the early twentieth centuries is the rapid growth in the number of persons to be fed, clothed, housed, transported, and entertained, as well as in the number available as workmen. The natural expansion in markets and in productive power afforded by the multiplication of the species was something the like of which no great civilization of the past had ever experienced. Even in those countries where the growth had been least, there were generally two persons to supply in place of one; in many regions there were four, five, and six for one; in some there were thirty, forty, fifty, and even hundreds for one.

How far the growth in population has been a result of the expansion of industrial output, as well as a cause for it, is a question we need not discuss, beyond remarking that the growth has been both cause and effect. A continued expansion of industrial output in the future depends partly upon the con-

---

[10] J. Russell Smith, *North America* (New York, 1925), p. 806.

[11] Carr-Saunders, *op. cit.*, pp. 17, 30, and *passim*.

tinued growth of population. During the last century the increasing wealth and leisure that have accompanied the decreasing labor costs of production have been used for many purposes that contribute to production only indirectly, if at all. One of these is the collection of statistics on a scale that would have bewildered a Frenchman in the age of Louis XIV hardly less than an Athenian in the age of Pericles. It is these statistics which give us a reasonably true picture of the recent growth of the population of Western European origin. For the leading countries fairly accurate data are available concerning the birth rate as well as the death rate over a long range of years. On the basis of trends revealed by these data, several learned demographers have busied themselves computing the possible number of inhabitants of Europe and North America in the future.[12] A few learned historians have examined the history of earlier movements of growth in population. Both the statistical and the historical evidence suggest that the period of phenomenal growth is coming to an end in so far as the population of Western Europe and North America is concerned. It has been freely predicted by statisticians that the Western European races will no longer continue to multiply after a few decades, and that there is a probability of a great decline during the next two centuries.[13]

Neither statisticians nor historians determine the birth rate. Neither of them determine the death rate or the course of migration. The fluctuations that will come over a considerable period of time in the death rate and the birth rate are not

[12] For a tabular view of some of the results, see Carr-Saunders, *op. cit.*, Fig. 26, facing p. 129.

[13] W. S. Thompson and P. K. Whelpton, *Population Trends in the United States* (New York, 1933), pp. 6–7, 316; R. R. Kuczynski, *The Balance of Births and Deaths* (New York, 1928), p. 54 and *passim; The Measurement of Population Growth* (New York, 1936), pp. 226–28 and *passim;* "The World's Future Population," *New Republic*, LXII (May 7, 1930), 315 ff.; Carr-Saunders, *op. cit.*, pp. 129–36 and *passim*. And see the references cited by these authors.

susceptible to prediction; it is therefore more than possible that the careful estimates made by statisticians of the future population of this or that country, of the Western peoples, or of the world, a hundred years or more hence will prove to be wide of the mark.

We have learned from vital statistics that the enormous increase in the inhabitants of Western countries, at any rate after the early nineteenth century, has been due mainly to the saving of life. Improvements in medicine and surgery, improvements in sanitation and diet, the tremendous reduction in the quantity of wine, beer, or ale consumed by the ordinary man and woman, and, above all, improvements in the standard of living—the provision of more food, more time for rest, more artificial heat, cleaner clothes, more soap and water, less crowding of families in stuffy homes used for industrial as well as for living purposes—have made it possible for some two or three children to survive their tender years where one survived before. They have greatly increased the chances for youths to reach middle life. In the late nineteenth and early twentieth centuries the population has gone on increasing in spite of a precipitate fall in the birth rate in the industrial nations. In these the death rate is now hardly a third as high as two hundred years ago.[14] The crude birth rate has now fallen to almost as low a figure as the crude death rate.

A great deal remains to be done by way of saving life, even in countries, like the United States and Great Britain, where the life-expectancy of the inhabitants is highest. The chief opportunities lie with a rise in the physical standard of living among the poorer classes. If warfare between the great nations of the world continues, it is likely to interfere with a further striking increase in the average span of life, if not di-

---

[14] For England, Wales, and Sweden, see Carr-Saunders, *op. cit.*, pp. 59–61. Cf. G. Talbot Griffith, *Population Problems of the Age of Malthus* (Cambridge, 1926), p. 34 and *passim*.

rectly, at least by lowering the standard of living. Even if the peaceful conditions of the late nineteenth century should be restored, it is most improbable that twenty years and more will be added to the life of the average man and woman in the leading industrial countries during the next century, as was done during the last.[15] No one has yet suggested that science will enable men and women to live forever!

A substantial increase in the population of Western European origin during the next two centuries has come to depend, in any case, much less on a further increase in life-expectancy, than upon a rise in the birth rate. Under the leadership of persons who aimed, frequently with the zeal of the crusader, to promote the happiness and welfare of the human race,[16] a knowledge of contraceptive methods was spread among all classes of the population during the last hundred years. Widespread use of these methods has been in all probability the principal cause for the fall in the birth rate.[17] There are some indications that a low point has been reached, although demographers are inclined to think otherwise. It is conceivable that the average size of families might increase during the next decades. But the possibility for a restoration of anything approaching the early nineteenth-century birth rate among the Western European peoples is remote.

While the statisticians may be mistaken in predicting that the inhabitants of the great Western countries will diminish substantially in the next two centuries, it is improbable that, under favorable political conditions, as many persons will be added to the population of these countries as were added during the last two centuries. Anything like the rate of increase that accompanied the rise of industrialism would seem to be almost impossible. Such a rate of increase would give us by

---

[15] Kuczynski, *The Measurement of Population Growth*, pp. 184–85.

[16] For the part played by one of them, see Richard W. Leopold, *Robert Dale Owen: A Biography* (Cambridge, Mass., 1940), pp. 76–77, 79, 83–84, 117.

[17] Cf. Carr-Saunders, *op. cit.*, chap. viii.

A.D. 2140 a population of more than three thousand million people of Western European extraction. One does not have to be a demographer to predict that the actual number will fall far short of that colossal figure. In all probability the pressure exerted by growing population to increase the volume of output in Western Europe and America will be nothing like as great during the next hundred years as in the nineteenth century.[18]

III. DEMAND AND INDUSTRIALISM

The growth of industrial production has not been exclusively, or even predominantly, the function of the growth of population. The output of many materials—such as coal, iron, steel, oil, and glass—has increased a great many times as rapidly as the population. Where, in 1740 or even in 1800, were the railroad cars, the steamships, the automobiles, the airplanes, which enable mankind to get about so quickly and so comfortably? Where were the radiators, the bathtubs, the electric refrigerators, and the air-conditioning devices? Where were the radio sets which some of our contemporaries regard as conspicuous marks of civilized existence?

One of our leading psychologists has recently measured the "General Goodness" of more than three hundred American cities, predominantly on the basis of statistics concerning the wealth and health of the citizens, and to a considerable extent in terms of the quantity relative to population of gas, electricity, telephones, automobiles, radio sets, and of the number of copies in circulation of *Better Homes*, *Good Housekeeping*, *National Geographic*, and the *Literary Digest*. He finds that nothing is more indicative of the "goodness of life for good people" than the abundance of dentists, though whether they should be regarded primarily as cause or as result of the goodness he is unable to determine. According to his exacting standards, Pasadena and, in the Middle West, Cleveland

---

[18] Cf. J. R. Hicks, *Value and Capital* (Oxford, 1939), p. 302 n.

Heights, Oak Park, and Evanston come out on top. Charleston and Savannah come out at the bottom. If our psychologist had analyzed the Paris of Madame de Sévigné and Racine, or even the London of Newton and Boyle, he would have placed these cities far below present-day Charleston and Savannah in "goodness."[19] He would have found them without any "measurable" civilization at all—without gas, electricity, automobiles, or radio sets, without *Better Homes*, even without dentists except for a few itinerant practitioners and barber surgeons who jerked out aching teeth with primitive instruments of torture. Civilization measured in his manner has multiplied in the last two hundred years beyond recognition. However far short many American cities fall of our psychologist's goal, when we compare conditions with the past, the world, and particularly the American world, is now full of cities positively stuffed with the "goodness of life for good people."

As if in anticipation of such remarks as these about the "goodness" of cities of the past, Professor Thorndike writes:

Certain humanists who abominate all efforts to measure human values will object to the list of items and to the scores computed from them. "The Florence of Dante and Benvenuto Cellini would be rated far below some humdrum suburb. The Athens of Pericles would not rate as high as Athens, Georgia, by this inventory," they will complain. "It does not include the important things. Radio sets, free schools, swimming-pools and baby-clinics cannot atone for bigotry and bad taste. What use are free libraries when the people read trash? It is better to live in a city that is mean by your standards if it has men and women sensitive to what is fine and noble."

The appropriate answer to such criticism is briefly as follows: The list of items is imperfect in respect of certain personal qualities in the population, as stated above, but is good as far as it goes.[20]

---

[19] E. L. Thorndike, *Your City* (New York, 1939). I owe my knowledge of this book to my friend and colleague, Professor Robert E. Park.

[20] *Ibid.*, p. 27.

How far that is, our author has not made clear. To determine approximately how far that is we should have to turn to moral philosophy, in the ancient Aristotelian and Platonic sense, and that is a subject which few, if any, American students of man and society recognize as relevant to their work. It is obvious that the tremendous increase in industrial output during the last two hundred years has been brought about by a growth in the volume of production per capita no less phenomenal than the growth in population. While the population of Great Britain has probably increased between sixfold and sevenfold since the early eighteenth century, the volume of industrial output is said to have increased more than forty times over[21]—a growth of at least sixfold per capita. During the thirty years from 1899 to 1929, the per capita output of the manufacturing industries in the United States more than doubled.[22]

Why, then, should the decline in the rate of growth in population impose a limit upon the expansion of markets? All we need to do is to go on improving the material standard of living faster than in the past. Triple and quadruple the number of telephones, automobiles, and dentists in Pasadena and Evanston, and equip the citizens with private airplanes in numbers sufficient to darken the sun. Raise Savannah and Charleston to the same high level of culture. Instal several bathrooms of machine-made tile in the homes of share-croppers. Carry the music and drama which come over the radio, together with the advertisements of new dental creams and cheap cigars, into the wastelands of Africa to edify the Ne-

---

[21] Walter Hoffmann, "Ein Index der industriellen Produktion für Grossbritannien seit dem 18. Jahrhundert," *Weltwirtschaftliches Archiv*, XL (ii) (1934), 396–98 (comparing the average for the decade 1720–29 with the average for the decade 1920–29).

[22] Solomon Fabricant, *The Output of Manufacturing Industries, 1899–1937* (New York: National Bureau of Economic Research, 1940), p. 53. Mr. Fabricant's estimate is "about 100 percent per capita," but this is for the period 1899–1937. From 1929–37 the volume of output increased more slowly than the population.

groes. Inclose whole towns in the tropics under one great roof and, by air conditioning, provide within them the temperature and the humidity which Professor Ellsworth Huntington considers ideal for white people to live in.[23]

It is possible that all these improvements, and many more like them, will be made. It is possible that the volume of industrial output—the production of mines and factories—will increase even more rapidly, relative to population, during the next hundred years than during the nineteenth century. But the statistical evidence suggests that this is most unlikely. Since 1900 there has been a notable tendency in the chief industrial countries—the United States, Great Britain, Germany, and France—for the rate of growth of real income per person gainfully employed to diminish. In all these countries the rate of growth per decade has been markedly slower from 1900 to 1940 than it was from 1850 to 1900. Japan showed an exceedingly rapid upward trend from 1900 to 1930, but since 1930 "there are unmistakable signs of slowing down." It is only in a few much smaller countries—New Zealand, Sweden, and Norway, with a combined population considerably less than that of France—that no tapering off in the upward movement of real income could be detected before the outbreak of the second World War.[24]

The reduction in the rate of growth of real income among the leading industrial nations is partly a reflection of a striking reduction in the progress of industrial output relative to population. In Great Britain per capita industrial production grew more than fourfold during the nineteenth century. From 1800 to 1901 population increased 3.4 times over; industrial production is said to have increased 14.3 times over.[25] Since 1901 in-

[23] Smith, *op. cit.*, p. 811.

[24] Colin Clark, *The Conditions of Economic Progress* (London, 1940), pp. 147–49. Cf., on Great Britain, G. T. Jones, *Increasing Return* (Cambridge, 1933), p. 248.

[25] Hoffmann, *op. cit.*, pp. 396–98. Population figures from J. H. Clapham, *An Economic History of Modern Britain* (1926), I, 53; (1932), II, 29.

dustrial production has hardly kept pace with the growth of population.

In the United States the slowing down in the rate of growth of real income about 1900 was sudden,[26] though the per capita output of manufactures went on increasing until 1929. A recent investigation of the physical volume of output of manufacturing industries shows that the rate of growth was faster from 1899 to 1916 than from 1916 to 1929. From 1929 to 1938, the year before the second World War broke out, there was no appreciable increase in the volume of output, although the population grew.[27] In spite of the efforts made during the last decade to increase the purchasing power of the poorer classes, and thus raise the standards of consumption, a very long period of phenomenal increase in industrial output came, at least temporarily, to an end. While the country was at peace and while no attempt was being made to convert industries from peaceful to warlike purposes, the per capita production of manufactured goods fell slightly, after it had approximately doubled between 1899 and 1929. Between 1869 and 1899 the rate of increase was much more rapid than during the first thirty years of the present century. The per capita output grew approximately fourfold.[28]

Unless there should be a reversal in the near future of what the statisticians have showed to be a marked trend, industrial production per capita will increase much less rapidly during the next hundred years than during the last. While it would be no less of a mistake to make a fetish of statistics concerning output and real income than to make a fetish of vital statistics, even an economic optimist would be hard put to it to offer any convincing evidence, in a world ablaze with wars, that a sharp

[26] Clark, *op. cit.*, pp. 147, 158–59.

[27] Fabricant, *op. cit.*, pp. 43–53. In 1937 output was a shade greater than in 1929, but "according to available monthly indexes" output in 1938 and 1939 "was below that of 1937" (*ibid.*, pp. 44, 46).

[28] Chester W. Wright, *Economic History of the United States* (New York, 1941), p. 707.

reversal of the trend toward slower growth of production is imminent. If the increase in volume of output per capita is to proceed again at anything like the same rate as in the nineteenth century, it can be only by an enormous further increase in the material demands of the Western countries, and by a further penetration of Western (and especially British and American) standards of living among the other peoples of the world. What are the prospects for a reversal of the trend toward diminishing industrial output per capita in the greatest industrial countries?

It is an axiom of political economy that general overproduction is impossible. While an individual or a community of individuals may have more of certain products than they will want to use, human desires, we have been told, are limitless. As expounded by a master like the late Philip Wicksteed, economics does not distinguish between the wants for concrete physical goods and services and other wants. The economist has to take account of every kind of human desire. He has to take account of religious and artistic desires, as well as of the desires for food, clothing, and the comforts of a well-appointed home. It is admitted that in different ages, in different countries, among different peoples, the relative importance of certain desires varies greatly. Does it not follow that there is theoretically the possibility that a community might have a surfeit of all kinds of machine-made goods, or at any rate so large a quantity of machine-made goods that the people would cease to care much for additions to the supply?

If this is theoretically possible, is it not practically absurd? With hundreds of thousands of persons living in poverty, with many living on the verge of starvation, even in the United States, the richest of modern countries, it seems callous to suggest that any community could be burdened with an oversupply of material goods. When one has a comfortable income of one's own, the suggestion sounds smug. Our argument is not that all members of society have enough physical goods and services. Our point is that the emphasis in some countries on machine-made goods and services, on synthetic entertainments, and on the financial structure designed to sell or publicize them, has been carried so far that poor and rich alike are starved for other values which are more inspiring. These are the values of the mind and spirit and the values of creative workmanship with matter, guided by the mind and spirit. The question is whether the future of the Western peoples and even the maintenance of the relatively high physical standard of living that has come to prevail in Great Britain, the British dominions, and the United States may not depend upon a recovery of these other values.

Within the realm of strictly physical goods, it may be doubted whether the markets for machine-made commodities can expand indefinitely. There have been many signs in recent years in Europe and America that Western civilization is beginning to suffer from overindustrialization. The rapidity with which capital has flowed into large-scale enterprises for mining and manufacturing during the last hundred and fifty years, in one country after another, reminds the historian of the flow of capital in Roman times in the Mediterranean world into the large estates known as villas. The primary purpose of the villa economy was to produce wine or olive oil for sale. The driving force behind that economy was the thirst of landlords, the great majority of whom lived in the cities, for profits from the sales. In the first century of the Roman Empire, province after province followed central Italy in converting arable and forest land increasingly to vineyards and olive orchards. While the wants of the classical peoples were no doubt limitless, their desire for wine and olive oil, though much more extensive than that of the Western peoples today, could not be stretched beyond a certain point. Both these liquids became drugs on the market. The price they commanded fell;

sometimes buyers could not be found for them at any price.[29] So the economic system built up about the villa collapsed—partly, perhaps, because the rich men of ancient civilization had unwittingly directed production further in a single direction than human nature could bear.

Equipped with cheap fuel and machinery, and stimulated by a rapid succession of fresh inventions, the Western peoples have managed, in the last four hundred and especially in the last hundred and fifty years, to reduce beyond the dreams of Francis Bacon and Robert Boyle the real cost of producing standardized construction materials, conveyances, furniture, and various kinds of gadgets. Machine-made commodities have assumed in the economy of the modern world a central place, resembling somewhat the place occupied by wine and olive oil in the early Roman Empire. Every kind of progress in physical welfare has come to hinge to a large extent on the maintenance of a great output of machine-made commodities. Is there not a danger that the Western peoples have been unwittingly setting for themselves an economic trap similar to that which, perhaps, contributed, at least in a small degree, to the decay of prosperity in the later Roman Empire?[30] In some Western countries, particularly in parts of the United States, there is a tendency to push the output of heavy manufactures dangerously close to the limit of the population to absorb them at any price. For many years now the purchase of machine-made commodities has been encouraged less and less

[29] Cf. M. Rostovtzeff, *The Social and Economic History of the Roman Empire* (Oxford, 1926), pp. 93–94, 186–90.

[30] The causes for the decline of ancient Greco-Roman civilization were numerous, of course. This is not the place to enter into a discourse concerning an extremely complicated and much-discussed subject. While Professor Rostovtzeff has emphasized the overproduction of wine and olive oil as the cause of economic crisis, he does not regard this crisis as an important explanation for the disintegration of classical civilization ("The Decay of the Ancient World and Its Economic Explanations," *Economic History Review*, II, No. 2 (1930), 207–8 and *passim*). Cf. below, chap. x, sec. ii.

for the sake of the consumer and more and more for the sake of the financiers and the stockholders who control productive plant, for the sake of the wage-earners who depend upon such plant for their livelihood, and for the sake of the enterprises launched to sell the output.

As long ago as the eighties of the nineteenth century, some Englishmen began to feel concern over the problem of markets glutted with machine-made products. Great Britain was still the leading industrial state of the world, though her leadership was already challenged by Germany and the United States. Professor Clapham has just presented us with a monumental history of the rise of the British industrial state. In his discussion of Victorian England he speaks of "some people, and they not poets," who were beginning to think that the world might have too many engines. They were beginning to think, John Stuart Mill notwithstanding, that "general overproduction, or something which might with reasonable accuracy be so described, may after all exist if only in what economists call 'the short period.' "[31] Since the eighties of the nineteenth century the problem presented by the toiling engines has been intensified. It has become a world-problem.

What were the stimulants behind the phenomenal expansion of the markets for machine-made goods in Europe and the United States? Three of the most prominent have been changes in fashion, changes in construction materials, and the spread of advertising.

Our knowledge of the economic and social history of early civilizations is extremely fragmentary, but it suggests that in no earlier civilization was the disposition to change for the sake of change as compelling a motive in economic life as it is in Western civilization. Among the Western peoples these changes in fashion go far back. Even in seventeenth-century England well-to-do persons, merchants as well as courtiers and

[31] Clapham, *op. cit.*, II, 113.

noblemen, had adopted the practice of discarding clothing not because it was worn out, but because new arrangements of dress had become the fad. Ladies who appeared in the robes of previous years felt out of place. In James I's reign, a member of the house of commons protested against a bill which aimed to increase the sale of domestic cloth and clothing. He saw that it would interfere with the sophisticated habits of English ladies of quality, who depended upon the import trade for their finery. "It is hard," he said, "to make a law whereby we shall not know our wives from our chambermaids."[32]

The making of the most fashionable ladies' garments has been one of the last branches of production to be invaded by the machine. But change for the sake of fashion spread in modern times from clothing to almost every kind of product, particularly to more durable and bulky goods. For its influence upon the volume of manufactured output, the most important field invaded by fashion was probably that of architecture. In the late twelfth and thirteenth centuries all the important edifices had been built in a single great style, the Gothic. It is hardly too much to say that the medieval cathedrals and churches and abbeys were built for eternity, in so far as it is possible for mortal men with stone and glass and other materials, that are less mortal than man, to create permanent monuments. Not until the late sixteenth and seventeenth centuries in the north of Europe, with the growing independence of the private merchant from political interference, were many masons, carpenters, tilers, and other building artisans assembled in large groups to put up rich private dwellings of a much less permanent kind than the public and semipublic buildings that had furnished the principal orders in the medieval building trades.

Until the end of the eighteenth century architectural principles derived from the Renaissance offered a barrier in the

[32] E. Lipson, *The Economic History of England* (London, 1931), III, 45.

building trades to the rapid changes in fashion which accompanied the growing wealth of the mercantile classes, especially
in Great Britain. Then, with the nineteenth century, agreement about architectural style (together with the unified principles that spring from agreement) was lost. In the United
States, as the settlers moved westward in quest of land, build-
ers threw up, helter-skelter, new towns and cities. Different
schools of architects, in Europe as well as the United States,
revived and interpreted one old style after another. Some of
them brought in new fashions of their own.[33] Fashions in architecture began to change almost as fast as fashions in clothing. More houses were built than ever before, but the number
built to endure diminished. The opportunities to tear them
down and rebuild in a new fashion increased. What did it matter if the walls sometimes looked like papier-mâché, so long as
orders poured in upon the manufacturers of building materials?

At the same time, the provision of new structural materials
was stimulating the building industry even more than were
changes in fashion. With the spread of coal as fuel in smelting, with the spread of power-driven machinery and the introduction of steam transportation, the Western world was largely rebuilt. Iron and then steel, concrete, and glass replaced
wood, brick, and plaster. Macadam roads were laid, then
railed ways of iron and later of steel, then concrete replaced
macadam. The continual changes in construction materials
stimulated the demand for manufactured products. The drive
to increase industrial output much faster even than the rapidly
growing population became irresistible.

The last of the three great stimuli to the growth of domestic
markets in the industrial countries was the spread of advertising, carried to its highest pitch in the United States during
recent decades, and combined with instalment selling which

[33] For a discussion of the subject see Geoffrey Scott, *The Architecture of Humanism: A
Study in the History of Taste* (2d ed.; New York, 1924).

encouraged men and women to mortgage the future earnings they hoped to receive. By advertising and instalment selling, the natural inclinations among the Western peoples to change styles and materials were artificially whipped up. Men and women were enticed into buying, not as a matter of more or less rational choice and out of a knowledge of the quality of the objects purchased, but because hosts of advertisers were hired to din into the public, by attractive-looking pictures in newspapers and magazines, by radio announcements and telephone calls and house-to-house visits, the alleged advantages of some new kind of residence, or of scrapping old for new brands of the same product. One result has been the creation of markets that are largely artificial. Many of the wants are derived from talk rather than experience. The new wants, together with the talk, serve to divert the attention of the public from intelligent reflection and from the art of living as our ancestors understood it.

It is apparent that the phenomenal growth in the markets for manufactured goods has not been brought about entirely by the imperative requirements of poor people for the necessities of life. In so far as the growth of these markets helped to provide poor people with work at good wages, it enabled them to raise their material standard of living, and permitted them to enter extensively the class of buyers of industrial products. Thus the number of consumers continually increased; the stratum of society from which they were drawn was continually extended. The matter to grasp is that the most important driving force behind industrial production has been the desire of men for material things that they could do without. The line between necessities and luxuries is, of course, impossible to draw, especially as there is a tendency for it to change. "The luxury of yesterday is the necessity of tomorrow," people are fond of saying. There is undoubtedly much truth in the remark. While persons could have foregone most of the improvements that accompanied the rise of industrialism with-

out dying immediately of starvation or exhaustion, the as-
tonishing reduction of the death rate during the last two centuries has been brought about indirectly, in a large measure,
by the tremendous expansion of industrial output.

By its indirect effects in improving health and increasing
comfort, the growth of markets for the products of industry
has provided the Western peoples with greatly increased material opportunities for happiness and for service to humanity.
The increasingly artificial character of these markets—that
has been brought about by the spread of advertising and instalment selling in particular—has interfered with the enjoyment people used to get out of more homely products, whose
composition they understood. As time has gone on the expansion of markets has been based less and less on urgent wants,
and more and more on artificially created ones. A point has
now been reached at which larger and larger numbers of people
get diminishing returns out of products which cater to change
for the sake of change. That is one explanation for the striking decline in recent decades all over the Western world in the
rate of increase in manufactured output.

The demand for machine-made products is no longer sufficiently compelling to elicit manual labor on as favorable
economic terms as in the past. Improvements in mechanical
efficiency and in management have been used in recent decades
much more to reduce the hours of work than to increase output. It is frequently assumed that better management and the
exercise of more inventive skill can be counted on to effect
continual reductions in what the economists call "the average
real costs per physical unit of product." But theoretical considerations suggest that in any industry increasing returns, in
this sense, depend to a large extent on the rapid growth of
output. Recent statistical studies of various industries in
Great Britain and the United States have shown that in the
past hundred years there has been, in fact, a connection between the expansion, not of the individual firm, but of indus-

try and the rate of reduction in real costs.[34] It follows that, if the slackening in the growth of industrial output continues, we cannot look forward confidently to the maintenance for an indefinite time of the increasing returns to which the manufacturing nations of the world have become accustomed. This is not to say that average real costs are likely to increase; but it does mean that they are not likely to diminish as rapidly as during the nineteenth century.

All this evidence suggests that an increase in per capita output in the industrial nations at as rapid a rate as that to which our ancestors were accustomed is as unlikely during the next hundred years as an increase in population at the nineteenth-century rate. The expansive forces in economic, and particularly in industrial, life that have developed since the Reformation seem to be playing themselves out. All intelligent planning for the future welfare of the Western peoples should be based upon an understanding of these conditions. They are not at present widely recognized by men of business, by political or labor leaders, or by the men in charge of the education of the young.

What chances are there for increasing production by stimulating the demand for machine-made products outside the highly industrialized countries, among peoples with a lower physical standard of living? The penetration by Europeans of all parts of the world, civilized as well as backward, has contributed greatly during the past two hundred years to the increase in demand. But the very weakening of the energy which the Western peoples are putting into the production of machine-made products for themselves suggests that they are less, rather than more, likely than in the nineteenth century to expend effort in raising the standards of living in foreign countries.

[34] Clark, *op. cit.*, p. 11, and chap. viii, generally; Jones, *op. cit.*, pp. 250–51, 253–54. The theoretical work referred to is that of the late Professor Allyn Young ("Increasing Returns and Economic Progress," *Economic Journal*, XXXVIII (1928), 527–42).

As a wise colleague has said, it is indispensable for an effective missionary to believe in the gospel that he preaches. If the Western nations are to carry bathtubs into the tropics, where natural bathing is often easy, if they are to spread air-conditioned villages and towns in Africa, India, and Central America, they must persuade hosts of men and women, who possess a different scale of values, of the advantages of an existence to which they are not accustomed and which they would not seek on their own account. The history of the past forty years does not suggest that the Americans are filled with effective crusading zeal on behalf of such a cause.

In all probability the heroic period of expanding industrial output is over. Whether we look at natural resources, at statistics of population growth, or at the conditions governing demand, we are led to the conclusion that, after five centuries of more or less continuous increase in the rate of industrial expansion, the Western peoples are entering an age in which the rate is almost certain to diminish. The chances are that in the decades which lie ahead the volume of industrial output among the Western nations will increase very much more slowly than during the nineteenth century. The hope of the Western peoples would seem to lie in the recognition that the end of an epoch marked by successive increases in the rate of expansion in physical production is inevitable and in many ways desirable. Human needs are not fulfilled merely by the satisfaction of men's physical wants, by the increase in wealth and in life-expectancy. Still less are they fulfilled merely by the increase in the volume of machine-made industrial commodities turned out each year by the factories. The hope of the Western peoples would seem to lie in the recognition that their riches, their leisure, and their health have been purchased in recent years at an increasingly heavy price in intelligence, in the sense of individual responsibility, and in the general love of mankind. Has not the time come to redress the balance?

IV

THE MORAL AND INTELLECTUAL CRISIS

✻

THE last four or five decades have been a period of increasing tension and insecurity throughout the world, especially among the Western peoples. Pessimism, cynicism, and despair have gained the ascendancy over most of Europe; uncertainty and lack of confidence over much of the United States. It would be natural for businessmen and for social scientists, who measure civilization mainly in terms of real income or the volume of industrial production, to attribute this tension and discouragement to the slowing down in the rate of industrial progress, to the material crisis of the twentieth century.

Such an explanation doubtless contains a measure of truth. But it would be a mistake to suppose that poverty is the main cause of the dismay that has come to pervade the Western countries. The absence of zest and enthusiasm which makes our time different from the times of our grandfathers and fathers is not primarily the result of physical want. In the whole of history there has never been a civilization wealthier in the material sense than Western civilization. Thanks to the enterprise of Mr. Colin Clark, we know how immense are the differences between the various nations of the world in respect to wealth. But the correlations between their wealth and their morale are by no means exact. In international units of real income per head of persons gainfully employed, the United States was more than twice as rich as Germany and approximately four times as rich as Japan, Italy, or the U.S.S.R. in the interval between the two world wars. Great Britain and even France were richer than Germany.[1] The richest countries—the United States, the British dominions, and Great Britain—the countries in which the standard of living among the poor and the wealthy alike is highest, have not escaped the uncertainty and demoralization that have been so general throughout the world. The victors in the first World War have taken longer to find themselves than the vanquished. If that is the price of avoiding the forms of totalitarianism which have restored a measure of outward confidence in Germany, it is not too high a price to pay. But it is hardly safe to assume that our riches and our high standard of living, together with our love of peace, are enough to protect us from the threat of totalitarianism from within and from without.

What accounts for the increasing disillusionment which has accompanied the reduction during recent years in the rate of industrial progress, is primarily the exaggerated store which all classes of the population have come to put upon material wealth. It has been made an end in itself, rather than being used as a means of attaining the higher goods—faith, wisdom, goodness, love, and beauty. Any definition of material wealth is arbitrary. We mean what Professor Pigou calls "that part of social welfare that can be brought directly or indirectly into relation with the measuring-rod of money."[2] We recognize, as do Professor Pigou and the late Professor Cannan, that the outline of the territory covered by this definition is vague. It is no less important to recognize that much of concern to the welfare of mankind lies outside this territory. Neither moral nor intellectual qualities can be brought, without straining, into relation with such a measuring rod. To measure either

[1] Colin Clark, *The Conditions of Economic Progress* (London, 1940), p. 41. The figures are for the decade 1925–34.

[2] A. C. Pigou, *The Economics of Welfare* (London, 1921), p. 11.

morality or intelligence in terms of the money they command currently in the market place is to destroy their meaning. The disposition among economists and others to extend the principles of economics to cover all aspects of human life involves a denial of the independent existence of man's mind and spirit. It was an axiom among the wisest philosophers of antiquity that happiness and righteousness in the individual were achieved when a proper harmony was maintained between what Plato called the three attributes of the soul—reason, passion or spirit, and desire or appetite. Harmony could be obtained only when the rational principle ruled both passion and appetite, and the spirit became the ally of reason rather than the slave of desire.

The slackening in the rate of economic progress during the past half-century has been accompanied by an increasing disharmony in this ancient philosophical sense. It is almost as if learning had come to regard it as proper for desire to govern both the spirit and the mind. It is almost as if what the wise men of the past regarded as the order necessary to human happiness had been stood on its head. Almost the only curbs on the appetite which learning now regards as important are those which contribute to man's physical well-being and material wealth, without reference to his mind and spirit. Thus the satisfaction of men's desires has come to be sanctioned as a contribution to the welfare ultimately not of the soul but of the body. The disharmony between the various attributes of the soul seems to be at the root of our distress, much more than the material crisis brought about by the weakening during recent decades of the expansive forces that had developed in economic life over a period of some four centuries. How has this disharmony been produced? What is the significance of the moral and intellectual crisis for those who are concerned with the future of Western civilization, and in particular with the future welfare of the United States?

I. THE COLLAPSE OF STANDARDS

We are faced with the breakdown of established beliefs and traditions concerning religion, conduct, thought, art, and politics. The standards which have fallen have a long history. They can be traced back easily to early Christian and to ancient Greek civilization, as well as to the Middle Ages. As Western civilization seems to have grown up mainly after the tenth century, these beliefs and traditions, confirmed and amplified in the Gothic Age, form an integral part of our heritage. It is not easy to determine when they began to give way. In a sense they were undermined before the Reformation. They were pieced together again in new forms in modern times. Their virtual obliteration is a recent phenomenon. It has taken place during the last fifty years or so.

There is a disposition—now rather less strong, perhaps, than a decade or two ago—to blame our plight on the hypocrisy of our Victorian ancestors. That offers a comfortable means of evading responsibility, one of the cardinal points in the strategy of the generation now in middle life. Laying the blame on the nineteenth century has also the sounder excuse of being justified, at least to some extent.

"Oh triste dix-neuvième siècle!" Stendhal was fond of repeating in one of the incomparable novels with which he ornamented the years that followed the fall of Napoleon. Stendhal wrote in the midst of an industrial revolution that was hardly less violent in France than in England, in the social, political, intellectual, and cultural transformations it produced. Combining more than any French writer of his time the old classical tradition, that was dying, with the new romantic tradition, that was being born, Stendhal felt acutely the disappearance of the powers of reason, order, sweetness, and finesse, which had been cultivated with so much pains and success in the France of Louis XIV. Like Delacroix, the great painter who was his younger contemporary, Stendhal saw

with deep misgivings these qualities swallowed up in a middle-class world. Money, machinery, and natural science were
becoming the arbiters of man's destiny. Taste was disappearing. The change was more shocking in France than in England, not because the actual increase in the volume of output
was as rapid or the progress of large-scale industry in private
hands as striking, but because France was less prepared than
England for the change. The preliminary industrial revolution
had come in the eighteenth century, much later than in England, and after the French had created under Louis XIV a type
of modern civilization different than the English. The change
in France was also more shocking because scientific knowledge and material improvement have always been somewhat
less congenial as objectives to Frenchmen than to Englishmen,
notwithstanding the remarkable originality of some French
scientists and technicians. France has produced a number of
inventive geniuses, but it has been other countries which have
exploited their ideas. Pasteur's development of the germ theory of disease has not enabled the French to reduce their death
rate as much as other great Western peoples. De Gaulle's proposals for a mechanized army, rejected by the French military
leaders, helped the Germans to conquer his country.

In the century of Louis XIV, who died in 1715, France had
made few adjustments to the new commercial spirit and to
scientific thought, comparable to those made by England under the Stuarts. She was less well prepared than England to
harness the new forces effectively for economic progress. Unlike Germany, France had neither the natural resources nor the
traditions to make an efficient use of the new forces for European conquest. The attempt of the French to do so under Napoleon had no sequel.

When we think of the intellectual side of the nineteenth century, it is natural to think of it as the century of economics and
natural science. Yet for all the prestige that attached to eco-

nomic and scientific thought, the methods of inquiry associated with them were not at once allowed to determine the character of other learned disciplines. During the greater part of the century, the attacks on Christianity and the older humanism did not succeed in destroying their autonomous influence in the family, in the churches, in the schools, colleges, and universities. For a time there was a reconciliation of, or at least a balance between, Christianity and humanism and the materialism bred of the new industrialism. However much thinkers like Renan questioned the foundations of Christianity as revealed in the Scriptures, they accepted the code of ethics contained in the New Testament as the only sound basis for conduct. Even Mill spoke, in his essay "On Liberty," of the survival of Christianity in the Roman Empire as an example of the triumph of truth in the face of persecution.[3] While scientific inquiry was beginning to undermine theology, it was seldom suggested that the principles of justice and knowledge associated with the teaching of Catholic and Protestant churches alike were subject to doubt. The humanism of early modern times had freed man to some extent from his dependence upon constant community worship. In its English form it had freed him from the necessity of adhering to the universal Catholic Church. But it had placed upon him, as an individual, the responsibility for maintaining the virtues for which Christ had been crucified. That responsibility had been accepted by Christian learning and incorporated into it. The traditions of Christian learning provided the Western peoples in the nineteenth century with a common bond which took the place of the common bond provided by theology in the thirteenth century. In Christian learning the Western nations found a unifying system of culture which partly offset the tendencies toward division bred of nationalism and economic individualism.

Christian humanism had flowered long before the nineteenth century. It was an expression of the Renaissance, which provided man with a renewed sense of his dignity, at the same time that it provided him with a new conception of government, which, if allowed to assert itself without restraint, was capable of crushing that dignity. Milton has been called the "last and greatest English representative" of Christian humanism.[4] But the values associated with it were not lost with Milton's death in 1674, for they had entered into the discipline of the churches and even more into that of the schools and universities. As John Morley once said, "the substitution of the Book for the Church was the essence of the Protestant Revolt." The reading of the Bible, made accessible everywhere with the spread of printing, was enjoined in the grammar schools and was practiced as a regular part of daily family life. What was especially significant, it was read aloud and was for many children the only book and for nearly all the most important. With this discipline of careful reading there was combined, especially among the Puritans, a tremendous sense of human responsibility for the good life, a responsibility expressed so movingly in *Paradise Lost*.[5] For generation after generation the English-speaking peoples absorbed the Christian ethics, in a pure form, in their early and impressionable years.

The persistence of the moral and intellectual values of Christian humanism, the acceptance by English thought of the responsibility of the individual for the maintenance of Christian justice, are brought out strikingly in the eighteenth century in the novels of Richardson and again in the nineteenth century

[4] *Times Literary Supplement*, January 18, 1941.

[5] Cf. Foster Watson, *The English Grammar Schools to 1660: Their Curriculum and Practice* (Cambridge, 1908), pp. 60–61, 114–15, and chap. iii generally.

in those of Trollope. The great enthusiasm for both these writers in their time suggests that there was widespread admiration for the values they upheld. It is no accident that in our time, when Christian humanism has lost its strength, Milton, Richardson, and Trollope are all less read and less admired than some of their contemporaries who were not, as they were, first and foremost moralists.

During the late eighteenth and most of the nineteenth centuries, much was done to strengthen the practice of the Christian virtues, especially in the English-speaking countries. Partly, perhaps, as a result of material improvement, physical cruelty and—at least in Great Britain—crimes of violence were diminishing. The reformers of the industrial revolution were great humanitarians. They laid their emphasis on the duty of leaders to be charitable, and to diminish the suffering—above all the physical suffering—which men and women either passively or actively imposed on their fellows, and which nature imposed, in varying degrees, on all people. It seemed for a time that, if improvement were left to the individual conscience, good could be counted on to triumph over evil. It seemed that the pursuit of private interests in economic transactions could be counted on to promote the general welfare for centuries to come.

"There must have been a catch in it somewhere; it all seemed to be working so well, yet it ended badly." In those words one of the most distinguished writers of our time, Professor Tawney, summed up the nineteenth century. Why did that century end badly? What was the catch? Surely there was nothing wrong with feeding the poor, with reducing physical cruelty and suffering of every kind, with trying to outlaw war. All these were excellent things, the signs of a civilization in most ways more humane and enlightened than any other in history. The efforts of the humanitarians cannot be dismissed simply as manifestations of Victorian hypocrisy.

Much of the trouble lay in the growing disposition among the reformers to mistake means for ends. Woman suffrage, the spread of contraceptives, shorter working hours, for example, came eventually to be regarded as good in themselves rather than as providing men with opportunities to reach toward the highest standards of conduct and intelligence. The most generous men and women of the Victorian Age were devoting their lives, with their altruism and their love of mankind, to means. Few generous and intelligent persons were left to look out for ends. The opportunities offered by the improved material conditions were gradually forgotten. Progress in sanitation, heating, bathing, and refrigeration became ultimate objectives.

The case of a liberal and successful American professor in one of our leading universities is suggestive of what became a prevalent attitude. In his early years in the profession, he and his wife had campaigned for woman suffrage, for prohibition, for the eight-hour day, and for world-peace. In 1920, when he was hardly on the threshold of what we now regard as middle life, he bemoaned to his colleagues and students that all these objectives had been won. That was, he admitted, a good thing in itself. But it had deprived him of the need of striving for human betterment. Since all the elements that had been lacking for human happiness had been now provided, with the ending of the great war waged to make the world "safe for democracy," there was, the professor explained, nothing more in life for him and his wife to strive after. Such a profession of satisfaction hardly helped him to hand on to the young a torch that would encourage them to labor for human betterment, although the lighting of such a torch was once regarded as the most important function of a great teacher. This professor's students concluded, not unnaturally, that there was no need for them to devote their lives to anything beyond making money or seeking promotion.

The humanitarian movements of the nineteenth century were accompanied by the gradual withdrawal of the training in responsibility and generosity that had done so much to produce the great reforming spirit of the age. The Christian morality and the Christian humanism that had emerged from the Reformation and the Renaissance were the expression in a new form of ancient principles which had piloted the Western peoples throughout their civilized history, however much the actual conduct of mortal men and women fell short of those principles. In their zeal for humanitarianism and gentleness many generous people began, not unnaturally, to distrust the authority and the methods of the principal institutions which had hitherto nourished virtue and had insisted upon the duty of men to fulfil moral obligations to their fellows. These institutions were the church, the family, and the school, with its emphasis upon classical training and upon the discipline of the mind without reference to material ends. As controlled by men and women somewhat less than perfect—priests and clerics, fathers and mothers, teachers and professors—these institutions exercised a tyranny sometimes physical, more often mental, over those confided to their charge. This led many distinguished men to believe that they should free the people from the obligation to serve these institutions. This was to be done, not by abolishing the institutions, but by changing their character. In the past they had been expected to arouse in their members a sense of responsibility, to inculcate in the young good moral and intellectual habits. Henceforth these functions were to give way before the demand for self-development. Family ties were to be loosened. As sharp distinctions between good and evil were no longer recognized, as it was taken for granted that children would find what was best for them if left to themselves, the young were to become the guides of their parents. Women were not only to be treated by men as equals; henceforth there was to be little differentiation between the spheres of activity of men and women. Women were no longer to be tied down to their homes. If women made a bad job of home management, so much the worse for the home. "To hell with the home," became the half-serious slogan of advanced women, some of whom felt a great affection not only for humanity but for their own children. The schools were to turn to so-called "practical" studies. In extreme cases, attempts were made to have the studies conform to the wishes of the children, whatever these happened to be. Needless to say, little had been done to train the children in good mental and moral habits. It was felt to be enough if they had been trained, like dogs and other domestic animals, to take care of themselves physically. That was, perhaps, not the most efficacious way to prepare them to choose wisely how to train themselves in matters of intelligence and morality.

With some notable exceptions, the United States was tributary to Europe in its cultural life and in the development of its thought, especially during the early decades of the nineteenth century. This did not mean that the traditions of Christian humanism were less powerful or influential in the young republic than in the older European nations. In some ways those traditions were more effective than on the continent of Europe, or even in early Victorian England. Theology, moral philosophy, and political economy in America may have been almost completely sterile in so far as original creative thought was concerned—but imitators and followers can hold beliefs with a greater intensity and much more dogmatically than the creators themselves.

The United States of the present has something in common with that of the early nineteenth century. There was then a similar spendthrift attitude toward the economic resources with which the people were blessed, a similar desire for physical change and movement, a similar distaste and even distrust of art and thought (when either was pursued with what

Veblen might call "intemperate enthusiasm"), a similar pressure on citizens to conform in their manners and their morals to the ways of living of their neighbors. But there were then general standards in manners and morals.

In their manners and their moral outlook, the Americans of the early nineteenth century were poles apart from those who now occupy this continent. In the United States a century ago, the people believed fervently in Christianity and in Christian ethics. On all such matters Tocqueville was the shrewdest of observers. He found the Christian faith more generally and more devoutly held by the members of the Catholic and Protestant churches in America than by churchgoers in those Latin countries where the state still countenanced only one form of worship. Nowhere in Europe, he found, was conjugal fidelity so respected. Nowhere was the family as a unit regarded as so sacred. Nowhere were the children brought up in as strict a code of Christian morals. In the schools and colleges great attention was paid to the fundamentals of spelling, arithmetic, and grammar, and to the study of Greek and Latin. The leading writers of classical antiquity and of Western Europe were treated with no less respect than abroad, and in the case of the theologians and moralists with no less reverence. As Van Wyck Brooks has shown, an intelligent renewal of an interest in classical and European culture at Harvard College helped prepare the soil for that "flowering of New England" which gave the United States its first important literary movement.

If, in spite of much bigotry and misunderstanding, Christian faith and schooling were once taken even more seriously in the United States than in Europe, the reaction against both was no less violent when it came. After the Civil War, and especially after the great growth of industry in the 1870's and 1880's, the leaders in American thought and education began to look upon the old conceptions of the family, the church, and the school, not as common bonds but as chains which they had outgrown. The decline of religious belief, the weakening of the sense of family responsibility, the abandonment of schooling in the disciplines of writing and careful reading, have gone on more rapidly during the last fifty years in the United States than in Europe. The emancipation of women from their obligations as sisters, wives, and mothers, the emancipation of most men and women from religious obligations, seemed to progressive-minded Americans to offer a highroad to the freedom of opportunity and the freedom of enterprise which they regarded as essential to progress. At the same time professors of education and college presidents began to advocate the substitution of practical studies for careful drill in the fundamentals of speaking and writing and for the reading of the great books of classical and Western civilization. Elementary schools were founded in which twenty-five-minute lessons in mathematics and English composition were interspersed with twenty-five-minute lessons in cooking, sewing, clay modeling, typesetting, geography, singing, gymnastics, and social relations. If the boys and girls still read any enduring works of literature in their childhood, they did it under the influence of parents whom the neighbors regarded as eccentric, because the task imposed interfered with playtime in the company of normal, healthy children. If the Bible was still read to them, they could not always expect a response from their playmates. "Have you read the Bible?" one of my friends recently asked an excitable seven-year-old boy, to the astonishment of his very well-educated and widely read father, a publisher who has lived with books all his life. "What's that?" the child fired back.

The great increase in the number and the change in the character of immigrants after the Civil War facilitated the collapse of the old standards inherent in Christian morality, learning, and family loyalty. The primary objective of the recent immigrants has been economic improvement. Unlike many of the early settlers, they did not come to America because of the opportunities for freedom to worship as they chose.

Anyone who has had the experience of teaching in an American university, and who has tried to speak of justice, goodness, or truth, will realize that these words have lost almost all meaning, not only for the students, graduate as well as undergraduate, but also for many members of the faculty. Americans still defend the right of the individual to say whatever he may please. It is only with difficulty that they can be brought to extend this principle of free speech to cover the case of men who claim the right to judge what other men say in terms of its contribution to justice or goodness or beauty. It is easy enough to rule out what is said or done on the ground that it is unscientific or inexpedient, but it is nothing less than revolutionary to rule out what is said or done on the ground that it is unjust or evil or ugly in its implications. The case of a writer on social questions who was being considered for an honor in an American university is instructive. In support of his candidacy it was urged that he had devised some new methods of statistical calculation in relation to social conditions. When one of the committee brought forward the information that he had been recently detained on suspicion that he was a secret agent of a foreign government, his supporter was heard to murmur, "What's that against him?" If it had been possible to show that the man's methods of statistical calculation were being used to further the objectives of the totalitarian government, the same question would probably have been asked.

II. THE ENCROACHMENT OF SCIENTIFIC METHODS ON THOUGHT AND ART

The new attitude toward firm standards in thought and art is a product to a large degree of the view that, in affairs of the mind, scientific experiment and observation offer the only reliable paths to knowledge. There are several kinds of rational process, and the exclusive use of methods appropriate for dealing with matter and space leaves no room for beauty, ethics, or wisdom. As a result partly of the "unscientific" assumption that the methods employed in the physical and biological laboratories are exhaustive in so far as the reasoning mind is concerned, almost exclusive emphasis is laid upon the changeable and the fleeting. The existence of anything approaching permanent values is more and more denied. In the exploration of organic and inorganic matter, new theories are continually replacing old. As scientific methods have been extended to social and humanistic studies, the view has become very general in the social sciences and the humanities that today's knowledge exists mainly to be superseded by tomorrow's; that all constructions of the mind are merely scaffolds for scaffolds, that each generation writes a history, a politics, a sociology, or an economics almost entirely irrelevant for the next. In economic science the story of Alfred Marshall's gesture to one of his favorite pupils is suggestive of a viewpoint concerning the study of man in relation to man that is now accepted literally, almost without question. He presented this pupil with a copy of his classic work, *The Principles of Economics*, the fruit of rather more than two decades of thought and labor on his own part and that of his gifted wife. On the flyleaf he inscribed this copy to his student, "in the hope that in due course you will render this treatise obsolete."[6]

The basic emphasis in natural science is different from that in art or thought. Scientific investigations build on the works of previous scientists and often largely or entirely supersede them. The work of a great artist or a great philosopher is complete within itself. It is influenced profoundly by past art or thought, but as a creation it is independent of them. While it can influence and inspire future artists and philosophers, it can-

---

[6] J. M. Keynes, *Essays in Biography* (London, 1933), pp. 253–54.

not be improved on or done over again to advantage by another person, no matter how gifted. It has added something permanent to human riches. As Sainte-Beuve wrote:

Un vrai classique ... c'est un auteur qui a enrichi l'esprit humain, qui en a réellement augmenté le trésor, qui lui a fait faire un pas de plus, qui a découvert quelque vérité morale non équivoque, ou ressaisi quelque passion éternelle dans ce coeur où tout semblait connu et exploré; qui a rendu sa pensée, son observation ou son invention, sous une forme n'importe laquelle, mais large et grande,fine et sensée, saine et belle en soi; qui a parlé à tous dans un style à lui et qui se trouve aussi celui de tout le monde, dans un style nouveau sans néologisme, nouveau et antique, aisement contemporain de tous les âges. Un tel classique a pu être un moment révolutionnaire, il a pu le paraître du moins, mais il ne l'est pas; il n'a fait main basse d'abord autour de lui, il n'a renversé ce qui le gênait que pour rétablir bien vite l'équilibre au profit de l'ordre et du beau.[7]

The ridiculous attempt made some years ago, and now happily forgotten, to finish Schubert's *Unfinished Symphony* brings out the differences between art and natural science. It is frequently possible for a scientist to complete the unfinished experiments of his predecessors. In the one case the material is dominated by the human mind and spirit—in the other the human mind is placed at the disposal of the material. When the mind is mainly a free agent, as in art, it creates a work of

[7] "A true classic . . . . is an author who has enriched the human mind and spirit, who has really added to their treasure, who has led them to take another step, who has discovered an unequivocal moral truth, or captured some eternal passion in the human heart where all seemed to be known and explored; who has conveyed his thought, his observation or his invention in a form which, whatever its nature, is broad and great, fine and subtle, sound and beautiful in itself; who has spoken to all in a style of his own which proves to be universal, new without new words, new and old, easily contemporary with every age. Such a classic may be revolutionary for a moment, may at least seem to be, but is not; it lays hands upon what lies about it and overthrows what is in its way only to re-establish quickly the equilibrium for the benefit of order and beauty" (C.-A. Sainte-Beuve, "Qu'est-ce qu'un classique?" *Causeries du Lundi*, October 21, 1850). I am grateful to Dr. Waldemar Gurian for calling this essay to my attention.

its own which appeals to the world because of qualities common to all men, but which as a work is particular to its author. When the mind is mainly not a free agent, as in natural science, it is dominated by the material. Thus great works of art and all other great constructions of the intellect are not made obsolete in the same sense as theories in the natural sciences or as mere research into the social and intellectual conditions of the past. The reason is that such works are largely dependent on the human mind, which at its best is much the same from generation to generation. In the greatest geniuses the human mind is capable of rising above the circumstances of its age and speaking for all time. That is what Samuel Johnson meant when he wrote, "The stream of time, which is continually washing the dissoluble fabricks of other poets, passes without injury by the adamant of Shakespeare."[8] There is a sense in which Shakespeare is closer to Dante, or to Plato, or to Homer, than any of these great men was to most of his contemporaries. Their works are also more universal than those of lesser poets and of the greatest scientists. It was Goethe who said, "Was ist das Allgemeine? Der einzelne Fall. Was ist das Besondere? Millionen Fälle!"[9] While he speaks as no one else could, the great genius in the realm of art or in the realm of thought speaks to everyone and for everyone as no scientist who is dependent on matter can ever hope to do.

In recent years the methods and outlook of the natural scientist have been extended in the American universities to cover all the activities of the mind. The scientists themselves are less responsible for this extension than the scholars who deal with the humanities and with social and economic relations.

---

[8] Walter Raleigh, *Johnson on Shakespeare* (London, 1908), p. 19.

[9] "What is the universal? The unique. What is the particular? The everyday occurrence!" I am indebted for this quotation to my friend, Dr. Artur Schnabel. It appears in a work of his that is about to be published by the Princeton University Press under the title *Some Aspects of Music*.

We now have scientific theories of aesthetics. Thus what has been called the physical process of "intellection," which belongs in the realm of psychology, has been extended to cover ontology, epistemology, and ethics, which are not subject to scientific analysis as is the physical structure of the brain. The old distinction between science and art, which we have tried to explain and which was readily understood when Victor Hugo wrote his essay on Shakespeare some eighty years ago, has been almost entirely forgotten by American teachers.

The extraordinary change in the outlook of scholars in these matters in the United States can be seen by comparing definitions in authoritative encyclopedias. Let us take, for example, the phrase "natural law." Natural law is indispensable to the whole conception of limited government, a conception of vital interest, as Professor McIlwain has shown, to anyone who wishes to preserve democracy.[10] In Western history the appeal to natural law has been a means of restraining tyrants, of preventing an arbitrary exercise of political power whether by a king or a representative assembly. In the *Century Dictionary*, prepared by American scholars of the 1880's, under the direction of the late Professor William Dwight Whitney of Yale University, the definition of natural law is this: "The expression of right reason or the dictate of religion, inhering in nature and man, and having ethically a binding force as a rule of civil conduct; the will of man's Maker."[11] Since at least the middle of the seventeenth century, and possibly much earlier, the English phrase "natural law" has had another meaning— the scientific. The "laws of nature," in the sense of laws of matter or space, came into frequent use in England after the Restoration of 1660, especially among the ever widening circle

[10] See, for example, his *Constitutionalism Ancient and Modern* (Ithaca, 1940).

[11] *Century Dictionary* (New York, 1895 ed.), V, 3942, 3944. There is, of course, a third meaning, which has had theological implications—the law of human life, to which all human beings are subject (cf. below, chap. vi).

of men and women who were influenced by the publications of the Royal Society and the experiments of its members. But the older meaning retained its importance throughout the eighteenth and nineteenth centuries. It is the meaning given for "natural law" and "law of nature" in the *Century Dictionary*, although the more modern meaning can be found under "law." Only during the last fifty years has the scientific crowded out the humanistic meaning. In the fourteenth edition of the *Encyclopaedia Britannica*, published in 1929, the scientific definition alone is given. "Natural law, in science, means the formulation of some uniform characters or connection of things or events; but it is frequently used for the uniformity itself as it exists in natural phenomena. Any such uniformity may be called a natural law; for example, all laws formulated in physics and chemistry. On the other hand, the term 'law of nature' is sometimes restricted to irreducible or ultimate laws (like the law of gravitation), as distinguished from derivative laws (like Kepler's three laws of planetary motion)."

It is not easy to see how this second definition can be used by free men as a bulwark against dictatorship, or for any moral or philosophical purpose. The contrast between the two definitions reveals the character of the changes that have swept over learning among the Western European peoples and, above all, the Americans, during the last half-century. As the methods of natural science have come to be regarded as the only methods that the mind may appropriately employ in the higher learning, as all procedures of the mind that do not follow the scheme of the natural scientist have been thrown into discredit, the belief that the mind is capable of creating durable values for the guidance of mankind has been lost.

Less than a century ago Cardinal Newman imagined a condition of human society in which the mental and moral sciences would have no place in the higher learning. He regarded this as so fantastic a condition that his listeners could not possibly entertain it. He hoped to lead them, by analogy, to reject the notion that theology had properly no bearing on secular learning. "Henceforth," he said in parading his intellectual horror, "man is to be as if he were not, in the general course of Education; the moral and mental sciences are to have no professorial chairs, and the treatment of them is to be simply left as a matter of private judgment, which each individual may carry out as he will. I can just fancy such a prohibition abstractly possible; but one thing I cannot fancy possible, viz., that the parties in question, after this sweeping act of exclusion, should forthwith send out proposals on the basis of such exclusion for publishing an Encyclopaedia, or erecting a National University."[12] Newman was mistaken. His intellectual horror has become a reality. Without specific enactment and without any serious protest, this exclusion was gradually accomplished in one American university after another.

There is a widespread belief that the change is entirely for the good. It is regarded as one of the most important elements in "progress." By this most people have in mind the tremendous material improvement that has added more than twenty years to the normal life-expectancy of a child at birth. The discredit thrown upon the relevancy for our present problems of the wisdom of great thinkers and artists of the past is supposed to have liberated men. They are supposed to have shaken off those ancient prejudices created by writers who tried conscientiously but unsuccessfully (for want of natural science) to be objective, to rise above their time, and to say something that would endure for all time, or at any rate as long as there were civilized men to see or read it.

Let us apply the pragmatic test to this new progressive view of the methods that are appropriate to the study of man and to the study of his intellectual pursuits. Is it scientific to regard

[12] J. H. Cardinal Newman, *The Idea of a University* (London, 1899), p. 54.

progressive education and modern social science as important causes for the material progress of the Western peoples, and the Americans in particular? The origins of that progress have to be traced back to the early nineteenth and eighteenth centuries. In the case of England they have to be traced back even further, to the early seventeenth and late sixteenth centuries. The fruits of machinery and large-scale enterprise were very striking all over the world during the last half of the nineteenth century. But it was not until the very end of it that the new patronizing attitude toward ancient knowledge, toward the great thought and art of the past, began to have an important influence on scholarship and on the curriculum of the schools and colleges.

We have therefore to admit that there was a great deal of material progress and a very substantial fall in the death rate before the advent of modern social science, which is largely divorced from reason and dependent almost exclusively upon the methods of the natural scientists. The Victorian Age, with what we were brought up to regard as its hypocritical prejudices and its stifling exercise of authority in intellectual and moral matters, does not seem to have made impossible the material progress on which we now feed. Its prejudices and its authority could not prevent the strengthening of constitutional government and democracy all over the world. The torrent of progressive education during the last fifty years or so has been accompanied, not by a speeding-up, but by a slowing-down in the rate of that material progress which is so widely regarded as the chief, if not the only, source of well-being.

Americans may be ready to admit that Europe is going to pieces. But some of them may claim that this is in no way a result of the encroachment of scientific methods on social and humanistic studies. Some may even claim that the decline of taste and the decay of standards have nothing to do with the disintegration of civilization. The United States is the real home of progressive education and modern social science, they will point out. And is not this country better off materially than any other? It is possible to agree that social and humanistic studies have broken even further away from tradition in the United States than in most European countries, and also to agree that the United States is at the moment the richest large country in the world. It does not follow that the break with tradition is a cause for our material well-being. There are a number of obviously very important reasons for our favorable economic position, none of which has anything to do with the adoption of the methods of the natural scientist as the only appropriate guides in social and humanistic studies. The American people started on their career of economic conquest later than the people of most European states. They were armed with all the technical machinery that their European forebears had devised, and with the traditions of private enterprise that had been established in Great Britain. They had at their disposal, and they exploited with great spirit, courage, and tenacity, a vast and sparsely settled continent, extraordinarily rich in the natural resources—coal, iron ore, copper, oil, water power, etc.—that were essential to the triumph of industrialism. They established political unity on this continent. They were protected, largely by geographical conditions, from the danger of invasion by other powerful nations.

The happy conditions which have done so much to create a high standard of living in the United States were not brought about by the exclusion of reason and of moral judgments from social and humanistic studies. It would be more justifiable to attribute the wide acceptance of the new learning to a happy freedom from difficulties and responsibilities that twentieth-century Americans received as their endowment than to attribute the happy freedom to the new learning. The fall in the death rate among the Western peoples and the rise in the standard of living may with justice be attributed in the main to natural science and industrial technology. They cannot with justice be attributed to the almost complete eclipse of faith, reason, and art.

In so far as the actual production of wealth is concerned, even the most enthusiastic admirers of the economists or the political scientists would probably agree that the roles played by these scholars have been secondary to those played by the *natural* scientist and the *mechanical* engineer. Pasteur's contribution to the health of mankind was probably greater than that of all the economists who ever lived. His contribution to the wealth of mankind is easier to establish than that of Alfred Marshall—though not, perhaps, than that of Adam Smith. During the past half-century the greatest contributions of social planning to health and physical comfort have been made not in the production but in the distribution of wealth. They have been the work less of scholars or university professors than of medical men and of social reformers like Jane Addams and Mr. Justice Brandeis. They have been the work, in short, either of persons trained in the natural sciences or of persons whose primary guide in life was not science but ethics. The important social reformers have been able writers rather than "social engineers," for no one would deny that the prose of Miss Addams or Justice Brandeis, while not of as high a quality as that of Jane Austen or Francis Bacon, is respectable, agreeable, and at times delightful.

The scientific approach to social studies bore valuable fruit, especially on the side of method, as long as the ethical and literary standards of society generally were high. These standards were essential to the maintenance of a high level of scholarship in the social sciences—but the social scientists, who were increasingly anxious to be scientific, did little to cultivate them or to emphasize their importance. As the principles of ethical conduct, along with the teachings of Christianity,

lost their influence in the universities, they also lost their influence in society. They were replaced by materialism, individual selfishness, and extreme nationalism. In some countries the social scientists were expected by the government to
promote the power of the nation even at the expense of truth;
in others they were left to seek their own advantage or that of
the groups they found it advantageous to serve. In many
places the result has been a decline in the standards of objectivity and accuracy upon which nineteenth-century scholarship prided itself. Nowhere has the decline been more pre-
cipitous than in Germany, the first home of scientific history.
This suggests that the social scientist cannot help to improve
the relations between man and man, or to hinder these relations from deteriorating, simply by examining the facts with
which he deals in a scientific spirit. Something more is
needed.

It would be unfair to throw all the blame for the present
state of the Western world onto the shoulders of the social
scientists! But it is evident that social science has not done all
it can to resist the currents of extreme nationalism and extreme
materialism that are sweeping Western civilization toward destruction today. The weakness of social science before these
powerful currents is partly the result of its excessive dependence on the methods and objectives of natural science, divorced from the higher objectives of human existence, which
are to live honorably, justly, graciously, and courageously,
whether or not this contributes to greater material abundance
or to greater personal influence and worldly prestige. A great
deal is heard nowadays about the influence of this or that professor. The important questions, What is the nature of his
influence? Is it good or bad? are almost never intelligently
asked. Objectivity and accuracy cannot survive the strains of
recent historical development unless there is a renewed emphasis on the good life as man's primary objective, an emphasis

that we find in the greatest Greek philosophers and the greatest Christian saints.

It is not surprising that economic progress should have added to the prestige of natural science. This would be no cause for regret if economic progress had not been accompanied by the almost complete eclipse of the prestige and authority that were once attached to faith, reason, and art. There is nothing to show that the denial of the independent controlling power of the mind in connection with social and humanistic studies has added substantially to our material wealth, or that it has done much to bring about a distribution of wealth that has contributed to economic welfare.

A sound lesson to derive from recent history would be this. The economic experience of the hundred years from 1815 to 1914, great though it has been in material achievement, has not lifted man above the guidance of past knowledge and wisdom. Those hundred years, historically speaking, were an age of quite abnormal tranquillity and peace between the great nations of the earth. The signs suggest that we may be entering again a period of strain and strife. Great parts of the world have seethed with people and wealth before. For all the material comfort that industrialism has generated, it has not succeeded in creating a new kind of human being, so superior in moral and intellectual qualities to the human beings of the past that he can get along without moral and intellectual training. It is by no means clear that our intelligence and our morality are above those of earlier peoples, though our knowledge of natural science and our command of mechanical technique are obviously superior. We shall need more rather than less guidance from ancient saints and wise men if we are to survive the storms that are now appearing and that we were brought up to suppose would never return. To imagine that American industrialism is basically different in its effects from European industrialism, to imagine that the fundamental characteristics of human beings of the same stock have been greatly altered for the better by crossing the Atlantic Ocean, are errors. Such daydreaming creates illusions that the people of the United States cannot afford in the dangerous times ahead.

III. ECONOMIC WELFARE AND GENERAL WELFARE

There is today a growing recognition in the United States that the world is confronted with a serious crisis, from which America cannot stand aloof. The majority of the persons who are concerned about the crisis think of it almost exclusively in terms of a great war that we must win, or that our friends across the sea must win for us. The deeper problems facing Western civilization, of which the world wars are partly a reflection, are largely forgotten.

On the rare occasions when they are considered, it is taken for granted that the way to meet them is by technical invention and economic planning. It is taken for granted, as it has been for some decades, that all we have to do is to improve the material welfare of the people. We are to look to natural science, to technology, to business administration, to economics, or to economic politics to save us. That is just what we have been doing for the last fifty years or so. That is just what we have been doing ever since the phenomenal material progress of the nineteenth century began to slow down, and men began to distrust economic individualism and to doubt whether material welfare could be counted on to take care of itself. Different medicines have been tried to improve our welfare, but all of them have been directed toward curing the physical ailments of the patient. The medicines have been administered by doctors of very different kinds. Some have been corrupt, some have been stupid, some skilful, many interested primarily in their fees and their fame, but others interested genuinely in the physical condition of the patient. They have disagreed on almost every conceivable matter save one—that if they could only improve the patient's physical condition, his morale, his intelligence, his moral conduct, and his taste would improve automatically.

When we consider the course of real income and of industrial production in the chief countries of the world since about 1900, we are left wondering how far even the patient's physique has benefited by the treatment he has received. The kind of medicine he has taken has not arrested the rapid fall in the rate of material progress. Yet even now the only way that Americans see of meeting the situation is to administer further doses of ingenious variants of the same type of medicine. Is this enough?

In medical practice the intelligent physician knows that the mind and the spirit play a role of some importance in relation to physical health. He knows that if he is interested in making his clients into effective men and women he must work on their minds and spirits as well as their bodies to free them from concern about their bodies. The truly healthy person is free from worry and even from much thought about his body. Such a state of health cannot be achieved without the cultivation of a sturdy mind and buoyant spirit, for, after the flush of youth and young manhood, such a state of health is possible only when the spirit asserts itself independently of the body and when the mind is in command of both the spirit and the body.

Cannot American society derive a lesson from the knowledge of the intelligent physician? If the extraordinary reduction in the death rate, in the incidence of tuberculosis, malaria, and typhoid fever, together with the virtual elimination of smallpox and bubonic plague, have not relieved the good physician from the need of nourishing the morale of his patients, is it likely that the great rise in the physical standard of living during the nineteenth century has relieved society from the need of nourishing the morality, the taste, and the intelligence of its members? Forty years or so ago it was common to believe that people were growing more just and truthful, more honorable and wise, in spite of themselves. It was common to believe that justice and truth, honor and wisdom, and even beauty, were natural by-products of the rapid growth in the national dividend. No doubt wealth does contribute to morality, to intelligence, and to taste, as both Plato and Aristotle pointed out some twenty-three hundred years ago. But neither Plato nor Aristotle made the mistake of thinking that morals and taste were bound to improve and intelligence to increase simply because men and women grew richer. Goodness, beauty, and wisdom cannot increase, even with the growth of wealth, unless they are cultivated for their own sake. The growing sense of disillusionment that has come at the end of an age of rapidly increasing economic expansion has been accentuated by the failure of our society during the past half-century to cultivate effectively morality, taste, or intelligence. With the collapse of standards, men and women have been left with nothing to fall back on save wealth, at a time when wealth seems to have an uncertain future.

The material wealth of society, like the physical health of the individual, is in a measure at the mercy of circumstances. That is no reason why men should not do what they intelligently can to promote the material wealth of society, just as they should do what they can to obey those laws without adherence to which, as science and medicine have shown, physical health is likely to be impaired. But if society devotes itself exclusively to matters of material wealth, the result may actually be damaging to wealth, just as a man who thinks of nothing but his health is likely to end up not only by becoming a useless citizen but by harming his health into the bargain. So the preoccupation with material improvement that has resulted during the past decades partly from the collapse of standards of morality and intelligence, has become a danger not only to man's morals and his intelligence, both good in themselves, but also to his physical standard of living. Men and women are no longer prepared to work as long, as seriously, or as carefully for material improvement as they once were. They expect technical tricks to relieve them from the necessity of hard labor. Materialism threatens to become its own worst enemy.

The doctrine that general welfare follows automatically from economic welfare has been widely taught in American colleges and universities, though it is not a doctrine to which all recent American economists have subscribed. It is held in an extreme form by Professor T. N. Carver, in whose *Religion Worth Having* economic and general welfare are made practically identical. Few other scholars would go as far as he has gone, or would state their position with his honorable bluntness. But most American scholars take a line which is, for practical purposes, the same as Dr. Carver's. One of them writes, for example, "all forces . . . . which impair . . . . productive operations threaten the material and *therefore* the intellectual welfare of mankind."[13] If we assume that intellectual follows automatically from economic welfare, we are bound to concentrate all our thought and action upon the improvement of economic welfare.

The view that increases in economic welfare necessarily contribute to general welfare is one which the wisest economic thinkers of recent times have seen to be false. Professor Pigou is at great pains to show that, even in a peaceful, stable, and progressive society, economic welfare is not only "a bad *index* of total welfare, but . . . . an economic cause may effect noneconomic welfare in ways that cancel its effect on economic welfare."[14] Noneconomic welfare is likely to be modified, perhaps for the worse, both by the way in which real income is

---

[13] N. S. B. Gras, *Business and Capitalism* (New York, 1939), p. vii (my italics).
[14] Pigou, *op. cit.*, p. 12 (his italics).

earned and by the way in which it is spent. What is at least equally important, noneconomic causes—such as war, or moral and intellectual instability—affect economic welfare profoundly. They may easily render a measure which, on purely economic reasoning, would promote economic welfare, harmful even to that. Professor Pigou concludes that it is safe to work for economic welfare without taking account of noneconomic forces only "among nations with a stable general culture."[15] In view of the recent collapse in cultural standards and the world-wide political strife, it would require considerable optimism to think of Western civilization today as exhibiting a group of nations with a stable general culture. Disharmony between nations and even within nations threatens to become the chief characteristic of our time. If we believe that man's spirit and intelligence represent his highest claim to dignity, we should strive toward the establishment of high moral and intellectual standards whether they contribute to economic welfare or not. On Pigou's own showing, it is at least possible that we can do as much indirectly for economic welfare in that way as we can do for it directly through economics, business administration, economic politics, natural science, and technology. The two attacks on the problem are not alternatives. But, following the economists, we should attach a special value to the scarcer of the two, until the supply of it becomes adequate to our needs!

Another economic thinker, whose influence upon the leading English economists of the present day is hardly inferior to Pigou's, gives us a clearer view than he does of what is so sorely needed today to promote and even to maintain the welfare of the Western European peoples both in Europe and the United States. As far as we know, the only things that can be said against the late Philip Wicksteed—and it must be admitted that they are damning things to say in America today—

---

[15] *Ibid.*, pp. 20–21 and chap. i generally.

are that he was drawn to study economics by reading Henry George, that he was by inclination a moralist and by training a medievalist. But as the London School of Economics has put a seal of approval on his work, it has a certain respectability among orthodox American economists. "The enlightened student of political economy and of society," Wicksteed wrote on the eve of the first World War, before devastating blows had been struck at our stable general culture, "will take care to assume nothing as to the economic forces except the constant pressure which they bring to bear upon men's actions and their absolute moral and social indifference. . . . . [He will] no more . . . . take it as axiomatic that they work for social good than we should take it for granted that lightning will strike things that are better felled. . . . ." How, then, are we to know what is socially good? Wicksteed leaves us in no doubt. "The prophet and the poet," he tells us, "may regenerate the world without the economist, but the economist cannot regenerate it without them."[16]

Have the American businessmen, the American political and labor leaders, and the American university men taken Wicksteed's advice to heart? Most of them talk and write as though they knew better, perhaps because they want no truck with a moralist and medievalist. Far from accepting the prophet and the poet as guides, the American university man generally dismisses them as unscientific, if he does not sneer at them. "He's a poet" has become a phrase of abuse in speaking of a colleague. It is felt that there is no place for prophets or poets in universities. What Veblen called the "disinterested pursuit of knowledge," if it is assisted by the great thinkers and artists of the past, is out of date. All reading not directly related to research is regarded as legitimate only as a source of entertainment. In his work the American university scholar is now

[16] Philip H. Wicksteed, *The Common Sense of Political Economy*, ed. Lionel Robbins (London, 1933), I, 191–92, 123–24.

beyond all that is not scientific. As is natural with a generation of professors that was not brought up on poetry or the
great works of literature and past thought, university men
turn in their off-hours not to prophets or poets but to detective
stories and motion pictures. This does not show that they are
poor judges of entertainment. The object of prophets and
poets has never been primarily to entertain; it has been to
warn, to instruct, to delight, and to inspire. Motion pictures
are more relaxing than poetry; they require less mental exertion. Detective stories can be more exciting than the Scriptures, and there can be no possible obligation to take them
seriously. Motion pictures or detective stories may even send
a thrill up the spine, indistinguishable from the sensation
which some American professors of literature tell their students is indicative of a work of art, and which can be obtained
also from a cold in the head!

The doctrine that material improvement is all that is
needed to promote the good life is no less prevalent among the
champions of the wageworkers than among professors and
businessmen. It presents itself, of course, in a different form.
But we search in vain through most books intended to contribute to the welfare of labor, talented and altruistically conceived though some of them are, for any ultimate objectives
for the working people beyond bathrooms with plumbing,
comfortable beds, adequate food, and proper dental and medical care. These are all very good things; it is certainly desirable to provide them for the poor. We are not suggesting that
the economic welfare of the workers ought not to be considered, or that they are always treated with conspicuous
fairness by their employers. We are suggesting only that such
a view of civilized values as we find in most books written on
behalf of labor is essentially the same as that of the well-
known psychologist whose researches led him to conclude
that the "general goodness" of a community bears a close rela-

tion to the number of its dentists and the volume of its tobacco consumption. "All would be well," the writers of books which deal with the modern labor problem seem to say, "if only the government or some other agency would increase the quantity of bathtubs, electrical refrigerators, cigarettes, and dentists in workers' settlements, and thus raise them as near as possible to the cultural level of Pasadena or Evanston." The workers are "good people," these writers might say, if they used the learned language of our psychologist. Why should they not enjoy the same "general goodness" as the citizens of those cities?

Such a conception of the ends of human life, by itself, can at best only lead to a great increase in the number of complacent middle-class people, without taste or a sense of their responsibility for the spiritual or even the material welfare of their neighbors. It may serve the economic purpose of providing more readers for detective stories, larger audiences for motion pictures, and more listeners to radio advertisements. It will not help the common run of men to take joy in their work. It will not enrich their lives. One of the greatest disillusionments experienced by an intelligent friend of mine was to find that the people in the excellently appointed third class of one of the new ocean liners, launched on the eve of the second World War, were no better than those in the first class, either in the ways they employed their time or in their generosity toward their fellow-men. The pressing problems of our age will not be solved simply by inclosing the whole world in a great air-conditioned, third-class cabin—or, for that matter, by inclosing it in a great first-class cabin. One of the wisest, most trusted, and most seasoned socialists alive has written these striking words about the British working class, which is certainly not the least honest in the world, or even the least intelligent. Tawney says of them:

They denounce, and rightly, the injustices of capitalism; but they do not always realize that capitalism is maintained not only by capitalists, but by those who, like some of themselves, would be capitalists if they could, and that these injustices survive, not merely because the rich exploit the poor, but because, in their hearts, too many of the poor admire the rich. They know and complain that they are tyrannized over by the power of money. But they do not yet see that what makes money the tyrant of society is largely their own reverence for it.[17]

If our analysis of the probable course of material production in the decades that lie ahead is at all justified, it is clear that the materialistic doctrines which make the increase in wealth and life-expectancy the only practicable tests of "goodness" contain serious elements of danger even from the pragmatic standpoint. If men are not likely to get richer during the next hundred years as fast as they did during the last, if under the stress of wars which threaten to become again the normal condition among the great nations of the world, they should not get rich at all, the doctrine that makes all the goods of life contingent upon material goods is not likely to offer much consolation to men. It is not likely to strengthen their power to meet the additional ordeals which they may well have to face, and which their ancestors in the nineteenth century, not yet deprived of the strength provided by Christian humanism, were largely spared. It may not even contribute to the economic welfare of the present generation and the generations which follow. In order to meet the future, men need the very values which have been disappearing in the moral and intellectual crisis of the last half-century.

IV. DEMOCRACY AND TOTALITARIANISM

The representative form of government, as Western civilization in modern times knows it, grew up under the aegis of the Christian and the humanist traditions. This is not to say that these traditions account for modern constitutionalism. The history of its establishment in Holland and in Stuart England, as revealed to us by constitutional historians, is exceedingly

[17] R. H. Tawney, *Equality* (2d ed.; London, 1937), p. 248.

complex. Rapid economic progress was one of a large number of factors which contributed to its establishment in the north of Europe. Rapid economic progress helped to strengthen the political power of the private merchants, and to put them in a position to resist effectively the exercise of absolute authority by a monarch. The early English "industrial revolution" strengthened the authority of the house of commons.[18] On the Continent, the Christian and the humanist traditions did not prevent the triumph of royal absolutism. It does not follow that modern constitutionalism can be explained adequately by economic causes. Still less does it follow that the collapse of moral and intellectual standards during the last fifty years is a source of strength to constitutionalism, as those persons who regard as totalitarian every attempt to establish the authority of human wisdom would have us suppose.

The moral and intellectual foundations of modern constitutionalism are more fundamental than the economic ones. Without them democracy would hardly have arisen; unless they are repaired and preserved democracy can hardly survive. Like all great human conceptions, these foundations can be simply explained. Constitutionalism takes for granted the dignity of the individual. It assumes that every individual has within him an element of goodness. In spite of the prevalence of evil, which may submerge this element in some people all of the time and in all people some of the time, constitutionalism assumes that mankind will be best served when men and women have a considerable measure of freedom to cultivate the good. Therefore true freedom is possible only when there is a knowledge of good and evil, independently of the individual. Since the world about us is made up of individuals, it follows that impersonal knowledge of good and evil depends upon the embodiment in customs and traditions of the wisdom

---

[18] Cf. J. U. Nef, *Industry and Government in France and England, 1540–1640* (Philadelphia, 1940).

and saintliness of the past. Christianity in its Catholic form has stood for such customs and traditions, with an institution to cultivate and to enforce them. Humanism, as developed by the greatest classical philosophers and as revived in the Middle Ages and early modern times, has stood for essentially the same customs and traditions, without an institution to enforce them. Modern constitutionalism rests partly on the assumption, as Professor McIlwain has done much to emphasize, that these customs and traditions have an existence, not only independently of individuals but also independently of all political authority. According to a conception which is essentially modern, and which cannot, perhaps, be traced in Western history back further than Bodin, these customs and traditions impose effective limits on the power of any ruler, whether it be a monarch or an assembly, as over against the individuals within the state. Medieval constitutionalism embodied a tradition of natural law,[19] but, as McIlwain has said, "the fundamental weakness of all medieval constitutionalism lay in its failure to enforce any penalty, except the threat or the exercise of revolutionary force, against a prince who actually trampled under foot those rights of his subjects which undoubtedly lay beyond the scope of his legitimate authority." In the late sixteenth and seventeenth centuries, after the rise of Renaissance despotism, political thinkers attempted, with success in England and some other countries, to secure for these rights embodied in natural law, a sanction short of force.[20] Upon such a limitation of political authority rest the rights to freedom of speech and freedom of assembly. Obviously such rights can exist only if the individuals themselves assume obligations to accept the same customs and traditions that should be binding on the state.

[19] Cf. above, p. 79.

[20] C. H. McIlwain, *Constitutionalism Ancient and Modern*, p. 95 and *passim*. Cf. Felix Gilbert, "Political Thought of the Renaissance and Reformation," *Huntington Library Quarterly*, IV, No. 4 (1941), 462–63.

Without the existence of some sort of authority in moral and intellectual matters, there is no check on the authority of political rulers. We come back inevitably to the customs and traditions which Christianity and humanism have fostered. If we assume that there are no such things as good and evil, apart from the economic or political desires of individuals, we destroy the foundations of constitutionalism and democracy. Unless men, when it comes to a showdown, care more for goodness and honor than they care for themselves or for any individual no matter how powerful, they are bound in the end, paradoxically enough, to lose their rights as individuals. And what appears still stranger in a world which has lost its standards, these customs and traditions which are so essential to our liberties have to be created by and based upon that fragile and imperfect instrument, man's reason. They have to be taken on faith. Their truth is not susceptible to scientific proof, in the natural scientist's sense of the word.

Neither the origin of democracy nor its future is bound up with extreme individualism or the exclusive use, in the study of man, of methods derived from natural science. The scientific method and individualism are excellent things in their proper places. They have done much for mankind. But when the scientific method is regarded as the only appropriate method for dealing with man's relation to man and even to art, when individualism becomes solely a right and is divorced from the responsibilities for good which alone can justify it, constitutionalism and democracy are endangered. Democracy's chief claim to glory is not that it has made men rich, but that it has contributed to the dignity of all men. Neither natural science, with its handmaiden technology, nor individualism could have done much for the dignity of man without the conceptions of righteousness and knowledge which both Christianity and humanism at their best have established and affirmed. At a time when standards have broken down, attempts to re-establish wise authority in matters of the mind are to be welcomed. The one thing which a man who aspires to become a successful totalitarian leader must not have, it has been suggested, is a definite program in which he *believes*. Least of all must he *believe* in general principles of good and evil and in the dignity of man. What a successful dictator has to have is an overwhelming belief in himself, and an overwhelming desire for power.[21] No confusion in the present age of confusion is more complete than the common opinion that a belief in principles has something to do with dictatorship. Far from being allies, political absolutism and the authority of independent minds embodied in natural law, are uncompromising opponents. Far from leading us toward totalitarianism, attempts to establish wise authority in matters of the mind may well offer us the only means of challenging it. Such attempts need not destroy either individualism or the scientific method. They provide the only effective way of seeing both individualism and the scientific method in their proper proportions in relation to the economic, the political, the moral, the intellectual, and the artistic life as a whole. They should enable us to recognize that both individualism and the scientific method lose their power for good when they cease to be what they properly are—means, when society tries to erect them into ends. Upon such recognition the future of both individualism and natural science depends.

In a world of independent nations, in any world made up of human beings, neither natural science nor economic science nor realistic studies of facts will be left for long to work out the salvation of the race without interference. If these forms of inquiry are not controlled by faith and reason, they are likely to be controlled by might. The human will and the human mind demand expression in some other forms besides those of laboratory experiments, equations, and factual re-

[21] Cf. *The New Statesman and Nation*, February 4, 1939.

ports. If the men of learning and culture fail to supply such expression, they will seal their own intellectual doom, or at least the doom of their successors. Deprived of the principles of Christian humanism, and the comfort and consolation these principles offered mankind, people after people have been handing over the keeping of their individual wills and such minds as they have left to the capricious wills of absolute rulers. Like a few of the rulers of the small principalities of Italy and central Europe in the age of the Renaissance, the modern leaders acknowledge no responsibility to God or to natural law as built up by men with the help of their saints and sages, their prophets and poets. Scientists and economists can retain their positions only as long as they conform to the wishes of the leader.

It is true that totalitarianism has triumphed first in Italy, central Europe, and Spain, in countries which have had a relatively short experience with the forms of constitutional government created in modern times in Great Britain, France, and the United States. It is true that totalitarianism has triumphed first in the countries to which it is most congenial, the countries which fostered a rather similar conception of government and sovereign authority, on a much smaller scale, in the age of the Renaissance. Who would expect totalitarianism to win out first where fundamentally different governing traditions were strongest? We can derive some comfort from these traditions, but we cannot afford to think that of themselves, and without positive effort on our part, they will preserve our freedom during the century that lies ahead.

It is also true that material want has facilitated the triumph of despotism. Hungry men have no time to think. If they are faced with the choice of starving in liberty or being fed by a despot, they will make the easy choice, unless they are inspired by reason and the faith needed to sustain it.

Neither hunger nor the lack of democratic traditions accounts satisfactorily for the rise of dictatorship in the twentieth century. The most important cause would seem to be the decay of the Christian humanism upon which in different forms the European civilization of the thirteenth and the nineteenth centuries was erected. The collapse of traditional standards in the fifteenth and sixteenth centuries gave the Renaissance despot his opportunity. The collapse of traditional standards in our own time is giving the modern despot his opportunity. What enabled men successfully to combat despotism in Europe after the age of the Renaissance was not the rejection of past customs and traditions. It was their recovery, development, and incorporation in new forms. It would seem to follow that the way to meet the latest wave of despotism is not by the destruction of natural law, but by its recovery, development, and incorporation in new forms. When people generally cease to believe that there are such things as principles of honor, justice, truth, and beauty, independent of the whims of individuals, they have no body of doctrine to oppose to the power of the despot. It is the moral and intellectual more than the material crisis of our times that has nourished the rise of totalitarianism throughout the world. The end of rapid growth in industrial output in the twentieth century has proved a calamity because the objectives necessary to sustain the mind and spirit, to give life meaning and purpose, have been lost. The only ultimate bulwark against absolute government consists in the recovery of impersonal objectives, unrelated to the power or wealth of individuals or worldly institutions—objectives of whose value the people are so convinced that they are willing in the end to risk everything, even their wealth and comfort and their lives, to maintain them.

If we are to save ourselves from totalitarianism and barbarism, it is more important that we should recover these principles than that we should improve or even maintain our material standard of life. Let us do both if we can. But let us put first things first. Let those of us to whom it is possible to appeal only on economic grounds reflect that, in the long run, the chief threat to our material standard of life may come from a lack of principles. Our present disposition is to put material goods first, and even to forget spiritual goods altogether. That disposition threatens in the end to deprive us not only of spiritual but of material goods.

The Christian and humanist traditions are now attacked in Europe by more ferocious forces than any as yet unleashed in our own country. These forces would destroy not only the form of the nineteenth-century beliefs, which must now go in any case, but also the principles, the ideals, which are eternal in so far as man is capable of rising above the beasts and savages. The threat of the totalitarian form of government to Western civilization is not only a military, it is also a moral threat, a threat to those values we associate with Christianity and humanism, values which have been weakened in our country and in Western civilization generally.

In the thirteenth, in the fifteenth and sixteenth, and again in the eighteenth and nineteenth centuries, Germany was drawn into the orbit of peoples whose objectives were Christian and humanist. Germany's contribution to this tradition was great in painting, in poetry, and in thought. In music Germany's contribution was greater than that of any other country. But among the Germans, traditions which are pagan and hostile to both Christianity and humanism seem to be more powerful than among the other great nations of the West. The historical accident that has placed the Germans in the center of Europe, surrounded by other races, has brought the leaders of this great people to put a higher value on military valor and conquest than the other leading peoples of Western civilization. When the pagan and the military traditions are harnessed together, the Germans seem more impelled than other nations to use their remarkable organizing skill for expansive purposes at the expense of civilized as well as primitive peoples.

During the last eighty years these expansionist tendencies have taken a much more formidable shape than ever before. The movement is more formidable than any of the past, partly because the weapons available are much more powerful and long range, partly because the Germans in the last century have united, until during the last decade they have been brought under a single absolute authority. Unity has replaced the divided sovereignty of scores of independent princes, which interfered with the expansion of the German peoples at the time of the Renaissance.

It is not difficult to form a conception of the position of the pan-German movement toward Christianity and humanism, and of the future of these ideals in case the National Socialists should conquer the world.[22] Recent historical inquiry has thrown doubt upon the old nineteenth-century view, fostered by German and to some extent by English historians (like Freeman and Maitland), that the conception of freedom in Western society is derived primarily from the medieval Germans. In mining, for example, it used to be supposed that freedom, the right of the finder of ore to share possession of it with the royalty owner, was of German origin. It now seems that a similar arrangement was common in the Roman Empire in the second century after Christ, and even earlier. The medieval miner owed his free status partly to ancient custom, which had been handed down in certain regions where the digging of ore had never been long abandoned, and partly to new conditions related to the rapid economic and social and intellectual development of Europe in the twelfth and thirteenth centuries. These conditions were common to all the Western peoples and not peculiar to the Germans.[23]

[22] Cf. R. H. Tawney, *Why Britain Fights* (London, 1941), pp. 9–12.

[23] Evidence in support of this view is contained in an essay on "Mining and Metallurgy in Medieval Civilization," that I have contributed to Vol. II of the *Cambridge Economic History*. Its publication has been delayed by the war.

In the wider matter of the general relation of the political subject to his ruler, Professor McIlwain has recently made it more difficult than it once was to accept the thesis that Western civilization owes its conception of liberty to the German tribes. According to the theory behind the Roman constitution, "the people alone are the source of all law." McIlwain has brought out the resemblance between the development of individual liberty in Roman and in English history. He has suggested that the influence of Roman law, before the Italian Renaissance, was exercised even through the legal compilation of Justinian on behalf not of absolutism but of constitutionalism. If McIlwain's tentative conclusions are justified, we have to thank early Rome more than has been supposed, and medieval Germany less, for the political liberties that we rightly hold so precious.[24]

In the light of this recent historical research, as well as of the showing of the German government since 1933, it becomes very difficult to hope for a recognition of the dignity of man, independently of his power to plow, organize efficiently, and conquer, in order to plow and organize efficiently further afield, in the pure Germanic conception of life and civilization. That view of life has its grandeur, but it is not Christian. It is more likely to arouse the enthusiasm of those who participate in it than of those who are rendered subordinate by it. The code of morality which we associate with Christ, and the view that the independent mind should play a part in the establishment of justice and beauty, a view which we associate with the greatest Greek philosophers, are alien to this Germanic conception. They were handed down to us from classical times by the Latins. It is not accidental that the English language (as well as the French and all the other Romance languages) derives much more from Latin than does German. It will be even more difficult to prove, to persons for whom

<hr>

[24] McIlwain, *op. cit.*, pp. 43–44, 48, 53–56, 59, 64–65, 68.

words still retain a precise meaning, that it is the intention of the pan-Germans to help the meek inherit the earth than it will be to prove, as some American writers have recently tried to do, that Christ was pre-eminently a man of business.

What makes totalitarianism and pan-Germanism more powerful than they otherwise would be is the lack of an alternative system that men are capable of practicing, a system that embodies the eternal values of Christianity and humanism, which the thirteenth-century and nineteenth-century European civilizations, with all their faults, embodied to some extent. In his moving address at the University of Chicago commencement in June, 1940, President Hutchins said that if we are to engage in war effectively the people of the United States must have values worth fighting for. The Christian and the humanist values have been undermined by the widely popular view that there are no such things as firm principles, that there is no such thing as right, that there is no such thing as wrong. If principles are denied, the only test of an idea becomes its success. If asked whether the totalitarian or the democratic conception of life is the better, Americans have no more effective answer today than "we like our way of life better," or "our way of life has made us richer."

These are weak answers. Neither of them will fortify us for the hard struggle that lies ahead, whether or not we go to war. Unless we lose that struggle completely, it is not likely to be short. The attitude of most Americans toward the war and toward the larger struggle which it represents and which the United States must enter whether the country fights or remains at peace, is based on a fundamental misconception of the forces arrayed against humanism and Christianity. It has been common to assume that at any time we may see a complete collapse of the totalitarian outlook and of the system of government connected with it. While any system of tyranny is bound to be vulnerable, the danger of a sudden collapse seems to be more on our side than on that of totalitarianism. Totalitarianism has been made possible by weaknesses that Americans, like other opponents of totalitarianism, share with the peoples who have surrendered their liberties. These weaknesses will not disappear with the fall of a conquering tyrant. There seems to be more danger that the world will become totalitarian than hope that it will become democratic. Less imbued than the peoples who have enjoyed a long experience of constitutional government with the illusion that material progress will bring with it all the good things of life, the totalitarians have found it easier to cast out this illusion than have the more democratic countries. Casting it out may well be a condition of our survival as a great power. Casting it out for something better, rather than for something worse (as the totalitarians have done), is a herculean task. Upon its accomplishment, the building of a fresh and more enduring civilization than any in the past depends.

PART II
ENDS OF CIVILIZATION

V

HUMANISM

☼

PREJUDICES," says André Gide, the great French writer, "are the pillars of civilization."[1] Neither Gide's Protestant upbringing nor his predilection in his later years for human freedom and the dignity of man has prevented him from recognizing the fundamental importance of collective beliefs for the maintenance of civilized life. It is the duty of civilized men to hold fast to "prejudices" on behalf of righteousness. Any edifice must have principles if it is to be coherent. As Gide's words suggest, that is no less true of a society than of a building.

What conceptions are offered for a civilization of the future? Broadly there seem to be three—the totalitarian, the materialistic, and what may be called the humanistic. The first two are very much in evidence. Neither is worthy of the best in man. Both are partial. One glorifies the state, at the expense of all other values whatever, and ultimately this is likely to mean that it glorifies that state which is able to triumph by might over all others. The second glorifies material wealth. Both the state and material wealth are necessary to civilized human welfare. Neither is properly an end in itself.

On the only ground that ought to count, on the ground of humanity, the materialistic is greatly superior to the totalitarian conception of civilization. That is because it aims, however one-sidedly, to serve man, while totalitarianism leads

[1] *Les Faux-monnayeurs* (Paris, 1925), p. 17.

to the enslavement of man. But, in its present weakened form, a materialistic conception does not offer an adequate defense against totalitarianism. It is no longer at its best. Its chief grandeur consisted not in the opportunity it offered men to improve their economic welfare, important though that has been, but in the independence it allowed the mind, and in the sense of individual responsibility for the general welfare that it fostered. Its weakness today has come about partly because these qualities of reason and responsibility have been almost entirely submerged by selfishness. Too many men are now out exclusively to serve themselves or their groups rather than to serve man. Selfishness has always been, alas, the dominant motive behind the actions of most human beings. But the disposition in the world of knowledge to make self-interest or group interest the final principle of judgment in all aspects of human affairs is more novel among the Western peoples. Matters of politics, culture, and even morality and religion are no longer judged according to whether they are true, or right, or beautiful; they are judged according to whether they will help "my" business, "my" trade-union, "my" university or special subject, "my" racial group, "my" church, or "me." With the decline of reason and of the sense of responsibility to mankind, with the collapse of the cultural traditions of Western civilization, the vulgarity, inherent in a materialistic view of the end of life, has come more and more into the foreground. The power of the materialistic conception of civilization has also been weakened because the economic and social, as well as the moral and intellectual, circumstances of the twentieth century have made it much more difficult than it was in the eighteenth and nineteenth centuries to satisfy men's economic ambitions. Men now expect to get much more with much less effort than their ancestors. What are needed today to meet the threat of totalitarianism are affirmations, based on deep thought and belief, and supported by enthusiastic, tireless action. What we have had are negations, and occasionally superficial appeals on behalf of ancient catchwords, such as "freedom," "liberty," "equality." Such words have lost their reality and hence their power to move us.

The third—the humanistic—conception of civilization might offer mankind a way of surmounting the catastrophe which threatens it. Such a conception might even offer hope for a world better than any in past history. Toward such a conception mankind can be said only to be groping. Attempts to move along the road indicated by such a conception are either misunderstood and misnamed or dismissed as utopian. That reproach—if it be a reproach—is justified. When one sets foot on this road, one is at once beset with a consciousness of one's unworthiness for the task of even sketching in roughest outline the way mankind ought to travel. One is reminded also of the words Thomas More is said to have spoken, in merriment, as he was about to mount the scaffold. Seeing that it had been hastily and flimsily built, he turned to the lieutenant from the Tower of London who had accompanied him. "I praye you, Maister Lieftenante," said he, "see me safe upp, and for my cominge downe let me shifte for myselfe."[2]

I. THE CONTROL OF APPETITE AND PASSION BY THE INTELLECT

Any suggestion that agreement should be sought concerning the ends of life arouses widespread misgiving. With the kind of education that has gained the ascendancy in the United States during the past half-century, the view has become deep rooted that democracy consists in leaving every person free to do whatever he likes. Now it is obvious that no person is actually free to do what he likes. His freedom is limited in almost every instant of his existence, if in no other ways than by

[2] William Roper, "The Life of Sir Thomas More, Knight," in *The Utopia of Sir Thomas More*, ed. George Sampson (London, 1910), p. 271.

his mental equipment, his physique, and his income, and even by the fact of his freedom, which forces upon him the obligation to decide between means, without reference to a few supreme ends. Without the guiding principles provided by religion and moral philosophy, and by customs which are in basic accord with religion and philosophy—principles which are independent of the individual yet binding on him in advance of his choice—the liberty that is one of the most precious gifts conferred on man becomes a chore. It may even become a burden. When a man chooses between means for their own sake, without any impersonal and firm ends to aim at, he is likely to be overwhelmed by the possible choices. He is befuddled by his inability, lacking any hierarchy of values, to fix an appropriate weight to each of the choices open to him, such as would enable him readily to reject most of them. "Must I do what I want to?" a little boy is said to have asked his teacher after some months in one of our progressive schools, where the children are left to follow their own inclinations.

The view that man should be free to do whatever he pleases for the sake of doing what he pleases has been accompanied by another view—which seems to be in sharp opposition to it —that he is completely bound by material circumstances over which he has no control. This relieves him to some extent from the necessity of making an effort and thus contributes in a way at once paradoxical and treacherous to his sense of freedom. Like the modern conception of freedom, determinism helps to divest him of all responsibility to serve higher ends. Under the frequently unsuspected influence of these two views, which complement as well as contradict each other, the custodians of education in the United States have been led to the conclusion that the only possible roles for the individual mind, even among persons whose lives are ostensibly devoted to the higher learning, are two. The first is for the mind of each man to assert his own ego. This can be done in various ways. For example, it can be done by exercising the power of selection on such momentous questions as a choice between the various varieties of manufactured breakfast foods, washing machines, electric refrigerators, and cigarettes. Another role left to the individual mind has much greater value, especially if scholars realize that its results should never constitute the sum of knowledge. That role is to carry out investigations which will supply the world with additional knowledge, and help to reveal the processes by which the lives of men and of societies are determined.

What is denied is the role of the trained, disinterested mind, impelled by a love for mankind, to help in determining the nature of the prejudices without which, as André Gide has suggested, civilization is impossible. At a time when the old prejudices have broken down, the place for such a mind ought to be expanded. Instead it is being contracted until almost no room remains. The fostering of prejudices is left to untrained, undisciplined minds, and to the charlatan. It is left partly to persons like the late Billy Sunday and Aimee Semple McPherson, or to their more recent and rather less spectacular, but hardly less influential successors. The motives of such persons are material gain and publicity. They appeal to these motives in their public. They appeal not to reason or to the spirit of devotion, but to the emotions and the passions, divorced from every rational principle and made the slave of the appetites. The prejudices they produce are somewhat less inspiring than those which the wise men of the past have transmitted to society. While the "message" of a particular charlatan is soon forgotten, along with its author, there is no lack of charlatans to take his place and to dispense a new "message" of the same genus.

It will be asked again, in spite of the argument in the previous chapter—How can we give men authority in matters of the mind without setting up a dictatorship? Such a question would hardly be raised if the mind were still generally regarded as independent. The question itself is a reflection of the mind's weakness, of its feeling of impotence in the modern world. The answer is that the establishment of authority, which arises not from the kind of position a man holds in politics, in business, or in the professions, but which arises from the simple power of the intellect itself, not swayed by the utterances of either political leaders or newspaper editors, or by facts when facts can offer no guidance, could provide a formidable barrier against dictatorship, if channels could be opened through which it might transmit its conclusions accurately and effectively, and thus influence the people who vote, the parents and teachers who train the young, the churchmen whose duty it is to look after men's souls, the business, political, and labor leaders who direct the economic life of the nation. Unless there is such a thing as trained authority within the country on moral, intellectual, and aesthetic questions, there is little to restrain unscrupulous people from making the central government the only arbiter on moral, intellectual, and even aesthetic questions. This is what has been done in Germany and Italy. If dictatorship does not result from the lack of trained authority on these matters, then values will be at the mercy of the rich and prominent or of persons chosen by the rich and prominent for reasons unrelated to the intellect. This is already to a very considerable extent the situation in the United States.

Trained authority on moral, intellectual, and artistic questions cannot be obtained either by a process of voting or by leaving the guidance in the hands of businessmen, politicians, newspaper editors, and professors of current events. It can be obtained only by giving the wisest, the best endowed, the best trained, and the most disinterested philosophers, theologians, writers, and artists a prestige and power of leadership that our American civilization would now make it difficult for such persons to obtain even if they existed. So philosophers, theologians, writers, and artists should strive to establish for their ideas a place of authority. They cannot gain such a place by compromising their convictions, if these convictions are based on reason. They cannot gain it if they are moved by self-interest. They will have to gain it by the independence and the force of objective and impersonal thought, assisted by historical and scientific research and by the wisdom of ancient sages.

Now we hear a chorus of objections from our contemporaries. "Who is to decide which minds are powerful and which minds are disinterested?" "What tests have we of truth?" "Do not André Gide's words prove that there is no such thing as truth, that there is nothing but prejudice?"

In attempting to answer these legitimate questions, we must begin by invoking the guidance of the greatest minds of the past. By doing so we shall invoke the other of the twin bogies that stand in the way today of the cultivation of the intellect. These bogies are authority and the past. What justification, then, is there for seeking guidance in past thought? In what ways shall we seek it?

During the fourteenth and early fifteenth centuries Western civilization entered a period which resembles our own in certain respects. An age of great prosperity and phenomenal economic progress, that had probably begun in the eleventh century and had lasted through the thirteenth, drew to a close. The traditions and principles—the "prejudices"—that had bound the European peoples together in the Gothic Age no longer served their purpose. As is the case today, one conception of civilization was breaking down, and no new one had been found upon which the Western peoples could agree. The decaying conception had solidified into a bigotry and a tyranny no less intense, and no more recognized by the intellectual bigots and tyrants, than the bigotry and tyranny that have grown up in our own time around another decaying conception of civilization.

Perhaps the greatest difference between the later Middle Ages and the twentieth century, in matters of the mind, is in the attitude of the institutions of learning toward the thought of the past. It is scarcely too much to say that at the end of the Middle Ages orthodox opinion in the Continental universities, as well as in the abbeys and priories, could see little virtue in an idea that had not been precisely stated by some great authority of the past. As late, even, as the early seventeenth century, when Kircher, the celebrated German physicist, expounded his views concerning the newly discovered sunspots to a provincial Jesuit professor, the man would not bother to look through the recently invented telescope as Kircher suggested he do. "It is useless, my son," he told the learned scientist, "I have read Aristotle through twice and have not found anything about spots on the sun in him. There are no spots on the sun. They arise either from the imperfections of your telescope or from the defects of your own eyes."[3]

The authority of Aristotle had become a tyranny. A great English poet, in celebrating the growing scientific enlightenment in which his countrymen were taking the lead, described the situation in these lines.

> The longest tyranny that ever sway'd,
> Was that wherein our ancestors betray'd
> Their free-born reason to the Stagyrite,
> And made his torch a universal light.
> So truth, while only one supply'd the state,
> Grew scarce, and dear, and yet sophisticate.[4]

[3] B. Hessen, "The Social and Economic Roots of Newton's 'Principia,' " in *Science at the Cross Roads* (London: Kniga, 1931[?]), pp. 167–68.

[4] John Dryden, "Epistle II. to Dr. Charleton (1663)," in *The Miscellaneous Works of John Dryden* (London, 1767), II, 117.

If Dryden were here now he might conclude that the scientists, whose efforts he so greatly admired, had done their work too well. One extreme has given way to its opposite. The most persuasive and effective champion of the mean in the whole of history, Aristotle himself, has been the sufferer. If students now read Aristotle at all, they have learned from their teachers to dismiss his principles (including, no doubt, the one to the effect that murder, theft, and adultery are wrong altogether) as an example of the special mores of the Greeks. The *Ethics* and the *Politics* are interesting to modern readers; but these readers seldom think of them even as rough guides to the solution of modern problems. Aristotle's remarks are regarded as no less irrelevant to the learning and the conduct of our progressive age than the telescope seemed to the science which interested Scholastic scholars. Who today would think of condemning an erring husband or wife for unfaithfulness by citing Aristotle?

In the realm of the intellect we have come to nourish, unwittingly, a tyranny hardly less complete than that exercised by Scholasticism at the close of the Middle Ages. The opinion of the pragmatists and some other social scientists that by testing all theories by facts we can escape from preconceptions, from all the idols of the tribe, is an illusion. The view that the empirical methods of the natural scientist are sufficient for the study of social and intellectual problems is itself an idol of the tribe.[5] There is a great realm in which the intelligent mind finds it necessary to move, where the principles of conduct and of understanding cannot be determined by scientific experiments and objective tests. In this realm the only weapon is man's reason—his intuition and his powers of logical construction, as these are cultivated in the most intelligent beings

---

[5] Cf. Frank H. Knight, "Social Science," *Ethics*, LI, No. 2 (1941), 127 ff.; Robert E. Park, "Social Contributions of Physics," *American Physics Teacher*, VII (1939), 327, 329.

by a long process of training and constant exercise, a continuous communion with the experiences of life and science,
and also with those experiences as they have been distilled for us by the great minds of the past. The schools,
universities, and churches of the later Middle Ages and early
modern times made a great error when they allowed little
room for experiment or even for observation. We are in danger
today of falling into the equally serious error of allowing no
room for the independent mind. It is not a want of science on
which despotism has fed as much as a want of balance in
matters of the intellect. There has been no lack of science in
Germany during the past century. When the balance is overweighted, as it is today, on the side of natural science and
the empirical methods of investigation derived from it, the
freedom of the mind is no less threatened than when the balance is overweighted on the side of past authority, as it was
at the end of the Middle Ages. It is the social scientists today
who are playing the role of the followers of the Scholastics
in early modern times. Today the champions of reason and
past authority in matters of the intellect and the arts are no
less the champions of human welfare than were the champions
of natural science during the sixteenth, seventeenth, and eighteenth centuries.

This historical digression has put us in a position to answer
the question which turned us into it. How are we to decide
which minds are powerful and which are disinterested? The
answer is that the great works of the past—in philosophy, in
literature, in history, and in the arts—provide us with standards in the light of which it is possible to estimate the achievements of our contemporaries. It is not that in matters of
thought and art the wise men of the past were always right. It
is not that conditions never alter in such a way as to make
their statements on particular matters inapplicable to the
present. We shall not advance the cause of the disinterested

mind by repeating, parrot-like, the precepts of the greatest ancient philosophers or by copying slavishly the models of the greatest artists of the past. What it comes to is this: When we find ourselves in disagreement with the wise men of the past on moral, intellectual, and artistic issues, the burden of proof is on us. We must have really relevant new knowledge with which to refute their conclusions. We must be certain that they were wrong or that the differences between our times and theirs have made their statements obsolete. We must be sure we understand their position. It is common to say that they were prejudiced because of their want of scientific knowledge. It is necessary to recognize that the spread of scientific knowledge has brought with it new prejudices from which they were free. We must realize that they did not have our prejudices any more than we have theirs. Until their ideas are proved inapplicable, they should be treated as relevant to our problems rather than as mere curiosities and adornments of a world that has disappeared. Their strength rests in the fact that, while they worked in their time, their faith, their disinterestedness, their love of truth enabled them to go beyond it. We cannot be sure that we share their strength. We should welcome all the light their works can give us.

The most original achievements in historical scholarship, an intelligent historian recently remarked, are made by proving, with the help of documents, what a wise and learned man's common sense or intuition tells him in advance must be so. The same thing is true to some extent even in the natural sciences, as is shown by the work of such great physicists as Lord Rutherford and Einstein. If we take away the role of intuition in learning, the study of past wisdom which nourishes it, and the training in orderly logical reasoning that alone can produce a disciplined mind able to convert its intuitions into enduring forms, documents and other data, by themselves, will not enable us to discover the truth. Still less will the data, by themselves, enable us to state the truths derived from social and humanistic studies in an intelligible and memorable way, worthy of the attention of men generally, now and in the future.

II. THE THREAT TO CHRISTIAN AND HUMANISTIC VALUES

The existence of the values for which Christianity and humanism, at their best, have stood, is threatened, not only by marching armies, tanks, warships, and bombing planes, but by the widespread denial among learned men of the existence of truth apart from verifiable experiments and observations of documents and of the physical world. By their denial of truth, the Western peoples have been preparing a gift for the powers of evil. The way has been paved for the triumph of error. It is as certain for society as a whole as it is for each individual that, without a continual striving toward what is right, society will become a prey to what is wrong. The way of truth, the way of beauty, the way of honor, is always the hard way. Did not one of the greatest of American teachers and philosophers, William James, tell us that the only successful method for overcoming a bad habit is never to permit one's self to indulge in it? Yet we have been schooled—if such an absence of teaching can be called schooling—to imagine that the good things of life will fall into our laps if we follow the line of least resistance, if we do what will bring the biggest immediate reward with the minimum of effort, and particularly with the minimum of thought.

The task of defending civilization in the United States, the least insecure among the nations of the West by its size and its geographical position, would seem to require a renewed recognition of the existence of truth. In the difficult years that lie ahead, Americans, if they are to survive as a Christian people, or if they are to retain the humanist tradition, will have to turn their backs on the lazy habits that the last two

generations have acquired. One important step in the defense
of civilization, and the one with which the universities and
the schools, as well as the churches, should be primarily concerned, is to strengthen the moral fiber and the intelligence of
our people. It is difficult to strengthen either if the only ends
of life are material improvement and private advantage. Now
it may be objected that, as one English liberal put it some
fifteen years ago, "you can't eat moral values." While it is
obvious that one cannot think or act without eating, what is
apparently less obvious (though it is difficult to understand
why) is that one cannot measure moral, intellectual, or artistic values in terms of wealth. Western civilization is suffering
today (as the most distinguished of my colleagues has frequently pointed out) from a disproportionate emphasis upon
material values, from a disposition to judge things that cannot yield an economic profit in material terms. Since there is
no such thing as truth, since art is simply a matter of individual taste regardless of whether or not the persons who
judge it have any taste, we are inevitably thrown back on material standards for judging values of a higher order. A man's
merit and his gifts are measured by the income he receives, the
worldly position he occupies, and the publicity he manages to
obtain. The value of a book is determined by its circulation,
the value of a painting by its price. The important matters are
not the ideas or the art, but the way in which books and paintings can be exploited for the personal advantage of the author
and his sponsors, in a world of mass production and mass consumption.

Many say that the end of American civilization, the promise
of American life, is not material wealth, but equality of opportunity. Equality of opportunity is excellent—but is it not,
after all, a means rather than an end? The question that is of
moment for the future of civilization is—Equality of opportu-

nity for what? In practice, the phrase frequently means equality of opportunity to get ahead in a material and worldly way, regardless of the methods employed or the consequences. Less frequently it means equality of opportunity for all to share in material goods. Again it means equality of opportunity to increase the material income of the nation. In the first case, the effects are mainly bad, even when ruthless methods of getting ahead have been camouflaged to appear harmless. "Do not be reconciled to dishonesty, indecency, and brutality because gentlemanly ways have been discovered of being dishonest, indecent, and brutal."[6] In the second case, the effects are good in so far as they contribute to the spirit of charity, bad in so far as they deny the obligation of man to suffer and to labor even for a small material reward. In the third case, the effects are mainly good, but insufficient.

Why do we say they are insufficient? While material improvement has contributed and can contribute to the highest ends of man, in so far as it becomes for the individual, for a class, or for a nation the end of life, there is nothing basically to differentiate men from animals. The object of animals is to live as long as they can and as comfortably as they can. In so far as men exist to eat and sleep, to turn on the radio and go to the movies, there is nothing specifically human in their conduct.[7] Man's nature is not distinguished from the beast's

[6] R. M. Hutchins, *No Friendly Voice* (Chicago, 1936), p. 4.

[7] It is not suggested that the better radio or motion-picture programs could have been devised without intelligence or that the listeners and spectators never derive any ideas from the programs. The point is that the mere transmission of programs, even on the rare occasions when they are genuinely artistic, does not necessarily improve the taste of the population by increasing the size of the audience. It is participation that counts in forming taste, and a radio audience is less likely to participate in a concert than a concert-going audience (cf. below, pp. 250–51). On the other hand, the time wasted listening aimlessly to the great majority of programs, which are from the aesthetic standpoint bad or indifferent, deprives the American people of a great amount of energy which they might otherwise use in cultivating their minds—for example, by reading good books.

merely by the fact that his intelligence has enabled him to command food, houses, conveniences, and diversions in larger quantities than tigers or birds of prey can do. Nor is man's nature distinguished from the beast's by the fact that his intelligence has enabled him to command murderous weapons to kill others of his kind and take territory from them by making war. There is nothing to distinguish human beings from other forms of life in either mere eating or mere fighting, though the one is always necessary and legitimate, if wisely indulged in, and the other may become so for purposes of self-defense and for enforcing justice and right.

It is significant that Sir William Bragg, one of the most eminent scientists of our time, can regard the experimental achievements of the leading scientists as in some ways less noble, less excellent, than the lives of the noblest among them. In his address two years ago to the National Academy of Sciences, he put the philosophy and the conduct of Pasteur and Faraday on an even higher plane than their scientific discoveries. Their lives offer the world models of disinterestedness and goodness, of which it stands in greater need today than of new scientific knowledge. "The spirit in which knowledge is sought and the manner in which it is used are more important, more real than knowledge itself."[8]

What are the ends of man, if material progress and armed might are properly not ends but means, which should be governed by the principles of taste and the principles of justice and truth? How can material progress and armed might best be ordered to contribute to the higher ends of man? Those are problems that American philosophy must face if the United States is to help in preserving civilization from the forces that threaten to destroy it.

[8] "History in the Archives of the Royal Society," *Science*, LXXXIX, No. 2316 (1939), 452–53.

III. A PHILOSOPHICAL JUSTIFICATION OF HUMANISM

The ends of man, it may be suggested, are to be found in those attributes of his which are specifically human, which he does not share with the animals, and the cultivation of which gives him a place of special dignity on this planet. These attributes are common to the Christian religion and to the works of the greatest philosophers and artists, before as well as since the time of Christ. They consist in a refusal to accept the actual world of human beings, however improved by science, mechanics, and medicine, as worthy of the best in man. They consist in man's capacity to create with his mind a world of his own better than the world about him, or to describe the weaknesses, the shortcomings, and the sufferings of the actual world in relation to the standards of the ideal world that the mind alone can create. They consist in bringing comfort to human beings through the spirit and the mind independently of the body. Such attributes of man lose the qualities that give them dignity and force in so far as they are ordered to the material or the political life of man. In so far as the material and political life of man is ordered to the higher ends of religion, moral philosophy, and art, it approaches that perfection of which man alone, unlike the animals, obtains glimpses. "We are all monsters, that is, a composition of man and beast," wrote Thomas Browne, "wherein we must endeavour to . . . . have the Region of Man above that of Beast, and sense to sit but at the feet of reason."[9]

Such a view of the ends of man is to be found both in Christianity and in the humanism that goes back at least to Plato. "Humanism is not the exclusive possession either of those who reject some particular body of religious doctrine or of those who accept it," Tawney has said. "It is, or it can be, the possession of both. . . . . Humanism is the antithesis not

[9] *Religio medici* (reprint of 1643 ed.; Oxford, 1909), p. 125.

of theism or of Christianity . . . . but of materialism."[10]
Understood in this sense, humanism is the possession of both
Catholics and Protestants, in so far as they are concerned with
man's mind and spirit, exercised for the disinterested benefit
of qualities that are specifically human. It is the possession
also of those who have not found a place in the churches, but
who are striving, both as individuals and as members of
society, for the values with which Christianity has been always identified.

What, it will be asked, is the justification for putting religion, moral philosophy, and art in a higher category in the
order of goods than material improvement, if they are the
creation of the few? The answer is that while they must
necessarily be conceived by the few independently of the
many, there exists in nearly all men, to a greater or lesser
degree, a need for moral, intellectual, and aesthetic standards,
which cannot be satisfied by the multiplication through mass
production of commodities and of entertainments. Great
works of religious thought and of moral philosophy serve as a
pattern. They help to guide men toward the good in their
everyday living. Great works of art help many men besides
the artist toward a higher fulfilment than can be obtained from
material comforts and entertainment. The contemplation of a
great painting or a great cathedral, the reading of a great
book, the performance of a great work of music, enable a
wide circle to participate to some extent in the experience of
the artist. Even though the circle capable of benefiting directly from a work of art almost always represents a small minority of the population, the participation of this minority, like
the participation of churchmen and teachers capable of understanding the great works of religion and moral philosophy,
serves as an example to a larger number. The people generally,

[10] *Equality* (3d ed.; London, 1938), p. 83. Cf. Jacques Maritain, *Humanism intégrale*
(Paris, 1936).

in so far as they are impelled to reach upward toward perfection, obtain a sense of the importance of standards of conduct, knowledge, and art unrelated to private advantage. They obtain a sense of the importance of quality independent of quantity.

It is an error to suppose that people benefit by having the theologian, the philosopher, or the artist stoop to meet them. It is only when people have to reach, have to exert themselves, that they benefit by religion, philosophy, or art. Civilized life, to be worth living and worth fighting for, must be a perpetual striving toward what is good. The "realizable ideals" which Americans have been told to work for are no ideals at all. To be valuable, the goal we set ourselves must remain beyond our grasp. An answer to those persons who object to the counsels of perfection contained in great works of moral philosophy or literature is to be found in one of the sermons of John Tillotson, archbishop of Canterbury from 1691 to 1694:

There is no manner of inconvenience in having a pattern propounded to us of so great perfection, as is above our reach to attain to; and there may be great advantages in it. The way to excel in any kind, is, *optima quaeque exempla ad imitandum proponere;* to propose the brightest and most perfect Examples to our imitation. No man can write after too perfect and good a copy; and tho' he can never reach the perfection of it, yet he is like to learn more, than by one less perfect. He that aims at the heavens, which yet he is sure to come short of, is like to shoot higher than he that aims at a mark within his reach.

Besides that, the excellency of the pattern, as it leaves room for continual improvement, so it kindles ambition, and makes men strain and contend to the utmost to do better. And, tho' he can never hope to equal the Example before him, yet he will endeavor to come as near it as he can. So that a perfect pattern is no hindrance, but an advantage rather, to our improvement in any kind.[11]

[11] As quoted by Samuel Richardson in the concluding note to *The History of Sir Charles Grandison* (1753).

The philosophical justification for making religion, moral philosophy, and art the primary ends of man is that they are indispensable if a nation is to reach the highest moral, intellectual, and cultural stature of which it is capable.

Religion, moral philosophy, and art can also be justified as the primary ends of civilized existence, on the ground that they have greater powers of endurance than other efforts of men. Those Americans who think of civilization in terms of bathtubs, washing machines, electric refrigerators, air-conditioning plants, radios, automobiles, and dentists' equipment, might meditate on the brittle character of these devices. Some men have the ambition, apparently peculiar to human beings, to leave their trace long after they are dead. Highly civilized societies have a similar ambition. No one who reads Pericles' funeral oration can suppose that, when he spoke with such moving faith in the civilization of Attica, he was speaking only for the people of his time. The civilizations of the past are remembered above all for their art, their philosophy, and their moral teaching. The exploits of great military captains are brought to us by great historians. The works of Homer, Aristotle, and Plato, and the magnificent Greek temples, had a powerful influence upon Western civilization for centuries before modern archeologists dug up Roman baths and hypocausts and constructed their uncertain picture of classical material civilization. We remember the civilization of the Gothic Age mainly by the *Divine Comedy* of Dante, the *Summa* of St. Thomas Aquinas, the paintings of Giotto, and the wonderful cathedrals, the embodiment of a collective artistic effort which few other ages have rivaled.

The United States can hope to defend civilization only by working toward other ends from those which have gained the ascendancy and guided the actions of Americans during the last fifty years, since we ceased to be a nation with a moving frontier. The United States can defend civilization only if virtue, wisdom, and beauty can secure places for themselves independent of material standards of value—only if they can make an impression of their own upon the life, the thought, the art, the architecture, and the decorations of this North American continent.

History suggests that societies disintegrate unless they have unifying beliefs. If we are to have a world-society, or even a stable and enduring American society, it cannot be founded on administrative machinery or voting, though both good administration and popular suffrage are indispensable. Enthusiasm for ends does not interfere with improvements in the means. It spurs men on to make such improvements. The stuff of belief is old. It has not changed. What collapses is the form. In order again to find a form there will have to be an honest striving on the part of men to recapture the ancient values of religion, philosophy, and art, which have been so freely discarded with the triumph of industrialism, and largely, no doubt, as a consequence of the sweeping economic and social changes that have accompanied it. These ancient values are needed by the people. Their lives can derive meaning and direction from wise, independent minds. Such minds are not the private property of their possessors. They are the glory of the human race.

VI

RELIGION

✳

A BALANCED view of the world, and of the place of human beings in it, is the chief mark of wisdom. It is the task of the philosopher, with infinite care and with supreme disinterestedness, to find a place for every aspect of human life and to arrange all aspects in a scheme where each is given a weight suitable to its importance for human welfare. The difficulties in the way of success in such a task may well seem insuperable. So pre-eminent a contemporary authority as Professor Gilson tells us that we need only three fingers to count the philosophers who have actually possessed the wisdom, the reasoning powers, and the detachment to approach perfection as metaphysicians. They are Plato, Aristotle, and St. Thomas Aquinas. "Their ambition was not to achieve philosophy once and for all, [which is not possible for any man] but to maintain it and to serve it in their own times, as we have to maintain it and to serve it in ours."[1]

In spite of the difficulties—or, to put it more truly, because of them—it is the proper task of civilized men to strive, according to the means each has at his disposal, toward a philosophical view of life, in the sense of a view that is at once just and balanced—balanced because it is just, just because it is balanced. Even though only a few men are capable of attaining to the dignity of philosophers, such men are the ex-

[1] Etienne Gilson, *The Unity of Philosophical Experience* (New York, 1937), pp. 316–17; cf. Jacques Maritain, *Les Degrés du savoir* (Paris, 1932), pp. viii, xiv–xvii.

pression of a very high general level of thought in the country that breeds them. They speak for, as well as to, their fellow-countrymen. The study of social and cultural history has not disproved the truth of Themistocles' answer to the Seriphian, as reported by Plato. The Seriphian was abusing Themistocles and saying he was famous, not for his own merits, but because he was an Athenian. "If you had been a native of my country or I of yours, neither of us would have been famous."[2] The most civilized nations have been those which have achieved, like the Athenians for a brief period in the fifth century B.C., an almost perfect harmony between all the goods of life. No nation which champions one side of life, to the exclusion of others that history has shown to be important to civilized growth, can hope to offer the peoples of the world the harmony which, if it were open to them and their eyes were open to it, they would embrace in preference to force. If we ever have, as some persons today hope we shall, a civilized world in which the various nations and races are in essential agreement, in which no single nation dominates the others by armed might, it will be only after all the nations have adopted a philosophical view of life that will bind them together closely enough to outweigh their individual economic, social, and political differences. While the history of Europe shows that a measure of common culture does not insure political agreement between independent states, it does not follow that complete cultural diversity helps to prevent disagreement! Without agreement concerning the goal of human life, and the sympathy which such agreement would create among the peoples, it is doubtful whether any political treaties, no matter how ingenious, can endure. If the true goal should be found, every country of the West could make contributions toward it, determined by its special needs, subordinate to the general need common to all nations.

[2] *The Republic*, ed. Jowett (3d ed.; Oxford, 1888), i. 329E.

With balance and reason such scarce commodities as they are today, their value for human welfare has become greater than at any time in a thousand years of Western civilization. No disinterested student of history, free from the modern idols of the tribe, would argue that the present American scene offers a conspicuous example of balance in the philosophical sense. The extreme division of labor in economic life, the extreme division of thought in religion, in education, and even in the higher learning, the almost exclusive use of scientific methods of inquiry in attempts to deal with subjects for which reason and art are primarily appropriate, the disposition to determine all values entirely in material terms—these are the most characteristic features of American life and activity to-day. All of them tend to make men narrow in their outlook, partial in their judgment, and violent in their expression, when the great need is for restraint, breadth of vision, and all-embracing humanity.

The extent to which human beings in the United States have had their existence weighted in the direction of some specialty, at the expense of the cultivation of the mind and the spirit, becomes still more apparent when we reflect upon the want of any binding force, in the philosophical sense, to hold the innumerable separate occupations and disciplines together, to show how all are related to the great common problems of human existence. The coming of industrial civilization has brought the different parts of the world closer together with the fantastically rapid speed of the express train, the automobile, the airplane, and, finally, the waves of sound that are caught by radio sets. At the same time, by both greatly complicating and greatly simplifying the problem of getting a living, industrial civilization seems to have reduced the instinctive sympathy and understanding among men and women. The division of labor has tremendously increased, while the kind of labor actually required of the common run of men and women demands far less ingenuity. Almost every worker is a specialist, and the specialties which occupy the great majority give almost exclusive scope to the single gift for routine, mechanized labor, the form least stimulating to the faculties of the mind and least satisfying to the longings of the spirit. Are not our inner lives more separate than those of our ancestors? Are we not more alone than they? Viewed superficially, the railroad, the automobile, the airplane, the telephone, and the radio have united us; in a day most men can see more faces, hear more voices, than most peasants in the Middle Ages saw and heard during a lifetime. But what common ground for genuine understanding have a workman in a Ford factory, a western cowboy on a visit to the city, a laryngologist, a bank clerk, a business executive, a professor of philology, and a poet, who meet on the platform of the central station? It is not mere travel, still less is it mere hearing, that creates understanding; it is participation in the same experiences, the same thought, the same faith, and the same kind of tasks, especially when these tasks call for the exercise of the mind and spirit. In the twelfth and thirteenth centuries, medieval society all over Europe was bound together by the firm ties which such participation provides and strengthens. The remarkable increase in travel and in trade spread the consciousness of these similarities and helped to give the Western peoples a deeper sense of unity than they have ever felt since. Extreme specialization undoes those knots that the performance of common and creative tasks tightens. If men are hungrier today for companionship than their Gothic ancestors, it is partly because the great majority have less.

The principal work that confronts the mind in the United States is that of restoring the balance that has been lost, by revealing to men and women all that they have in common, by reaffirming the value of faith, reason, art, and creative craftsmanship. By the performance of this work, learning and the arts can help to revive the sense of companionship that has largely disappeared in the modern impersonal, industrialized world. Advance along the winding and difficult way, with formidable barriers and deceptive bypaths, that alone can reveal the vision of our common humanity, has now become the promise of American life.

I. RELIGION AND SCIENCE

The position of religion as the first of the ends of human existence toward which we are drawn in striving to bring out the best in man requires justification. Of all man's activities, are not religious observances the least balanced and scientific? If orthodox religion is partial and narrow, as scientific and liberal thought during the last hundred years have taught us to suppose, what business have we to invoke it or even to speak well of it, when our object is a balanced view of the world? Of all the learned disciplines that our ancestors inherited, none, some of us were led to suppose, has so warped the intelligent minds of past generations as theology.

The relation of men and of nature to their Maker is the principal subject matter of theology. Newman called it "the Science of God, or the truths we know about God put into a system."[3] If the rise of natural science has led to a weakening of Christian religious belief, this has been contrary to the wishes of many of the greatest scientists. As it developed in early modern times, especially in seventeenth-century England, natural science, with its increasing interest in observation and its new interest in experiment, was frequently regarded by the great scientists, though seldom by the Catholic Church, and in the beginning not even by the fathers of the reformed churches, as an important ally of theology. By wresting the secrets from matter and from the living bodies of animals and human beings, the scientists thought they would

[3] J. H. Cardinal Newman, *The Idea of a University* (London, 1899), p. 61.

increase the wonder felt by men in the presence of the works of God. Observation and experiment were to be means of adding to "the truths we know about God."[4]

Such scientists failed to take account of the fundamental difference between the objectives of natural science and those of the Christian religion. The one aims to show what is, the other what ought to be. The one confines itself to the finite physical world, the other rises into the infinite world of the mind and spirit which transcends the matter visible through the most powerful microscopes and telescopes. Unless the objectives of natural science and religion are distinguished and reconciled, the emphasis on science is bound to breed disunity and confusion among the human family, harmful to religion, and in the end to natural science.

Two developments in more recent times go a long way toward explaining why the hope of some of the early devout scientists that experiment and observation would strengthen Christian belief, has proved deceptive. As knowledge of bodily processes and of the composition of matter increased, both the body and the physical world were robbed to a considerable degree of their mysteries. This was not because, in actual fact, the power behind the behavior of the body and of matter was less mysterious after the scientists had probed further and further into them. Depths beyond depths and heights beyond heights always remained. But, as was natural, men came to be fascinated by the bodily and the material processes themselves, to the exclusion of the power behind them.

Science has supplied the ordinary run of men and women with a vast number of new toys to occupy their leisure time, in an age when the need for steady, continuous labor has diminished. When they become ill they learn from their physicians all about some new virus. While the physician does not always understand it, it provides him with a con-

4 See below, pp. 162–63.

venient subject for talk beside the bed. The patient becomes absorbed in speculating on the way in which this virus develops and moves about within him. His body takes on the aspect of a battlefield, and he envisages with fascination, as a spectator, the reserve forces that he is able to throw against the enemy. When he recovers, the defeated virus provides a fertile topic of conversation. Conversation is an important need of a generation starved for it, but left without the materials necessary to make it. How many women's luncheons and tea parties have been saved from silence, if not from boredom, by one guest's talk about her peculiar form of allergy and another's description of her recent bout with diverticultis!

Science and medicine have helped many people to think of their bodies and their lives almost altogether in physical terms. Love, birth, and death have become physiological matters—to be analyzed in the laboratory and presented to the public in museum exhibits or in ten-minute talks over the radio. They are no longer subjects for meditation in the church or the cloister, or on some quiet countryside.

For the accuracy of the early supposition that scientific inquiry would strengthen orthodox religious faith, the extension of scientific methods beyond the realm of natural science, for which they were originally devised, has been even more serious than the diversion of the mind from the deeper problems of existence that we all have to meet. This extension was seldom brought about directly by the scientists. But eventually the new scientific methods, derived from the study of the natural sciences, came to be applied to the ancient science of theology itself. Since revealed theology rests ultimately on faith, the application of scientific criticism to the miracles of the gospel and to the history of the world as explained in the Old Testament, together with the application of scientific textual criticisms to the gospel, undermined faith itself. From the conclusion that there was no scientific proof of the truth of the New Testament, it was a natural step to the view that revealed theology was an impediment to knowledge. Theism remained. But the weakening of the faith in the divinity of Christ, possible under theism, made room for a far larger number of sects and forms of religious belief than the Reformation had admitted.

It is difficult to dispute the view of Bossuet concerning the effects of the Reformation on faith. "On énerve la religion quand on la change, et on lui ôte un certain poid, qui seul est capable de tenir les peuples."[5] The multiple religions which grew up with the triumph of natural science and industrialism in the nineteenth and early twentieth centuries have much less in common than Catholicism and the various branches of Protestantism had after the triumph of religious toleration in the north of Europe in the lifetime of Bossuet (1626–1704). The condition described by John Donne, in one of the most celebrated of his poems, has become a reality for the modern world in respect to religious belief.

> 'Tis all in peeces, all cohaerence gone;
> All just supply, and all Relation:
> Prince, Subject, Father, Sonne, are things forgot,
> For every man alone thinkes he hath got
> To be a Phoenix, and that then can bee
> None of that kinde, of which he is, but hee.[6]

During recent decades there has been, especially in the United States, a remarkable abandonment of articles of faith once regarded as essential to Christian belief among Protestant

---

[5] "One enervates religion by changing it, and takes from it a certain weight that alone is able to hold the peoples" ("On the death of Henriette-Marie de France, November 16, 1669," *Oraisons funèbres*). Cf. W. K. Jordan, *The Development of Religious Toleration in England, 1640–1660* (London, 1940), II, 481–82, 487–88.

[6] "An Anatomie of the World. The first Anniversary" (1633), ll. 213–18 (*The Poems of John Donne*, ed. H. J. C. Grierson [Oxford, 1912], I, 237–38).

clergymen. An inquiry was made in Chicago and its environs in 1929 into the views of five hundred ministers in service and two hundred students in Protestant theological seminaries. They all answered the same questions covering the chief elements of Christian faith as historically defined. Only one-fourth of the students maintained "that Jesus was born of a virgin without a human father," as compared with nearly three-fourths of the ministers, most of whom belonged to an older generation. There was an even sharper drop from one generation to the next in the number who held that a belief in the virgin birth was necessary for the Christian. Of the ministers, 46 per cent, as compared with 3 per cent of the students, regarded it as essential.[7]

The decay of Christian dogma among the Protestants is partly a reflection of compromises induced by scientific inquiry. The clergymen's own beliefs were shaken, and they gave way to the illusion that they could fill half-empty churches by watering the stock of dogma to fit in with the discoveries of natural science, which changed the prevailing view of matter and physical processes from decade to decade, if not from year to year. They gave way to the illusion that this was the way to win over the professors and teachers alienated by the bigotry and harshness of American Fundamentalism and Puritanism. By hitching their cause to natural science the Protestant clergy were abandoning religion, which is concerned with the right and the eternal, for the actual and the fleeting. If religion is to adjust itself to each important new scientific discovery, there is no end to the changes that will be made and no limit to the number of sects that will be formed.

Persons who were not committed by their parents to any sect, and others who withdrew from the church in which they

[7] *Recent Social Trends in the United States* (New York, 1933), II, 1013. I am grateful to Fr. Cyril N. McKinnon for calling this reference to my attention.

were brought up, reached the conclusion that men are better off without theology and even without any religious belief whatever. That was a logical result of the attempt to make religion scientific, in the natural scientist's sense. Such a conclusion became so prevalent that thousands of the most prominent members of the generation now in early manhood and middle life in the United States were brought up by their parents and most of their teachers to regard all references to scripture, to theological matters, and even to God as evidences of a depravity in the human mind from which the enlightened twentieth century was happily to be delivered. Though perhaps somewhat extreme, the training of a scientist's daughter is nonetheless revealing of a common attitude toward religion in American education and society since the beginning of the present century. This young woman had been continually exposed at home and school to the new doctrines derived from scientific knowledge by some of the pragmatists. She had always felt a distaste for mathematics. In her early twenties she lived in France. There she frequently saw references to Pascal in the writings of eminent men of the time. One day, out of curiosity, she bought the recently published third series of the massive Brunschvicg edition of Pascal's works and began to read the remarkable opening paragraphs of Les Pensées. There Pascal sets forth with great clarity and economy of words the difference between two kinds of reasoning—the geometrical, which can only proceed logically from principles artificially created by the trained mind and consequently difficult to comprehend, and the esprit de finesse. As Pascal explains, the latter enables the mind, "at one bound," to grasp by intuition something of the meaning of the infinitely complicated delicate relationships of the actual world in which human beings move. She could hardly believe that these subtle and illuminating distinctions had anything to do with mathematics, which she had always regarded as a singularly dry and mean-

ingless subject, irrelevant to anything human. Pascal at once
gave it meaning and explained why it had repelled her. She
concluded that the French were right in claiming him as a
genius.

Leading the life of continual social activity to which Americans of her class gave themselves up in the 1920's even in
France, she found no time to pursue her reading beyond the
first twelve pages. But several years afterward an illness gave
her an opportunity to turn back to the writer who had made
such a singularly favorable impression upon her. In the meantime she had acquired the small Massis edition, easier than
the heavier Brunschvicg volumes to manage in bed. It opens
with *Les Provinciales*. Imagine her astonishment, as she began
to skim the pages, to find Pascal talking about theology and
faith with the same assurance, the same clarity, discrimination, and scientific spirit which she had found in his discussion of the nature of reason. She was a woman of considerable
intelligence. She had come to trust her own judgment in
matters of art and thought. Here she was confronted with a
mind which her experience, like all the most respected French
authorities, told her was of the highest order. Her early life in
the United States gave her the not erroneous impression that
none of her American contemporaries could have distinguished
between geometrical reasoning and the far more human *esprit
de finesse* nearly as effectively or convincingly as Pascal, or have
shown with such skill as he why the great mind must employ both in order to arrive at truth. With the ascendancy of
modern science, scientific methods had almost crowded out of
existence these essential elements in the rational process, and
were about to make the word "reason" in the American academic world another name for experiment and the observation
of measurable data and concrete documents. Recognizing the
truth of Pascal's analysis, which differentiated the *esprit de
finesse* from the methods of the natural scientist no less than

from those of the mathematician and the logician, she had no doubt that he was the intellectual superior of anyone she had met in the flesh. Was it possible that intelligence and faith could exist in the same being? Could it be that Pascal was right about theology and religion, and that the persons who had brought her up were wrong? Was Pascal prejudiced or were they?

I do not know whether she ever answered these questions, for I lost touch with her. The answers are difficult for the members of her generation and for those of the one that follows, who are even less inclined than hers to believe in the divinity of Christ. If you have faith, then theology must be the most important subject in the whole realm of learning. If you have faith, and if you have also genius and the highest reasoning powers (as Pascal and Richard Hooker had, and, to an even greater degree, Thomas Aquinas), then theology becomes, not only the most important, but the most all-embracing subject in the realm of learning. Its inquiries illuminate every other subject, particularly philosophy. Once the initial step of belief in the divinity of Christ is made, there is unlimited scope within the properly restricted subject matter of Christian theology to reinforce faith by reason, to reinforce revealed by natural theology. As this young American woman observed, when Pascal wrote about dogmatic theology and Christianity, he wrote no more like a charlatan than when he distinguished between the geometrical and a more subtle kind of reasoning.

What is needed in the twentieth century is the pursuit of good ends which will show mankind the essential unity of all branches of learning and all aspects of human existence. Nothing is better designed to do this than Christian theology, though the danger that it will be abused by theologians is very great. It treats of the whole of existence, even as philosophy does. It has an advantage which philosophy lacks. It emphasizes man's dependence on a Superior Being, who is infinitely good, above all human passions and weaknesses; it emphasizes man's imperfections, his sins; it brings into the foreground the problem of evil. Thus it teaches humility, and that is of particular value in an age when pride (if not downright boastfulness) has come to be regarded as an essential part of a creditable career on earth. Theology covers much the same territory as philosophy; potentially it has far greater power to bind men together in sympathy for each other. As conceived by the greatest theologians, it not only strengthens faith—it exalts and fortifies the mind.

Some persons today admit that theology and religious belief are not, and have not been, as hostile to genuine scientific inquiry as was once assumed. We do not lack eminent scientific colleagues who speak on behalf of religion. They suggest that the discoveries of modern science are in no way incompatible with theism and even with Christianity. As is not surprising in the light of the religious views expressed by theological students, these scientists seldom discuss fundamental matters of Christian dogma, such as the divinity of Christ. It is not suggested that the scientist has, in fact, any special insight into such matters, denied to other people. The question of the possibility of two natures, the one human and the other divine, existing in the same individual lies beyond the range of positive science. It is a philosophical question. The modern tendency to seek the guidance of natural scientists in a realm alien to their special training and knowledge is another manifestation of the prevalent disposition to assume that positive science is capable of solving all the problems of existence. But the pronouncements of scientists on religious matters, however malapropos, also suggest that the scientists themselves are aware that science is not enough.

In spite of the views of scientists that the discoveries of modern science have not destroyed the grounds of Christian belief, in spite of the movement of the intelligence in France toward religious thought—as manifested recently in men like Péguy, Du Bos, and Maritain—Americans now in middle life are always reminding each other of the practical difficulties that stand in the way of a renewal of faith. Whether we like it or not, whether it is desirable or not, whether it is scientific or not, we are told, Christian theology and religion are not going to resume the central place they held in Western history before the eighteenth and nineteenth centuries. That is possible. Without a renewal of belief in Christ, it is inevitable. Is it desirable? Looking at the matter purely from the point of view of life on this planet in the centuries before us, the eclipse of Christianity, if it should be complete, would not seem to provide a cause for rejoicing, as many men who deal with education in the United States have taken for granted. They have not shown us anything that can replace it. By its very nature, natural science, dealing as it does with material evidence, cannot occupy the territory which properly belongs to theology. If Christianity suffers an eclipse, that territory might conceivably remain vacant. In all probability it will be occupied by false gods. Signs are not lacking that the occupation has begun.

II. RELIGION AND THE STUDY OF SOCIETY

The discoveries of historians, archeologists, sociologists, and anthropologists are frequently represented as obstacles in the way of the establishment of any common belief. These discoveries are represented as disproving the existence of such a thing as general truth. The university generation now in middle life was educated in the colleges and universities on works like Sumner's *Folkways* and Westermarck's *History of Human Marriage*. These books were part of a liberal education. They were regarded by students of society as perfectly scientific, not least because they reached no conclusions and applied no moral or intellectual values to the conditions their authors discovered. Impartiality, in the sense of perfect neutrality on all moral and intellectual issues, was coming to be regarded as the final mark of scholarship in connection with the study of man. It was almost as if man's relations to man were placed by the scholar in the same category with the organic and inorganic matter of the biological and physical sciences. Indeed, Jacques Loeb was busy trying to demonstrate that human behavior might be analyzed into the same simple elements that he found in the behavior of the lower animals. It would be in accord with his general mechanistic philosophy to explain the manifestations of the human mind exclusively in terms of the structure and physiology of the brain. In the 1890's such mechanistic views as his revolutionized biological studies in the United States. They have had much influence on the work of every branch of American scholarship.

The new attitude toward the study of man and his history contributed to the decline of Christian faith. It even undermined the Christian ethics, which theists, deists, and agnostics, for the most part, had accepted as sound during the eighteenth and most of the nineteenth centuries. The study of human marriage revealed no uniformity in customs among human beings. Some primitive tribes were found to be monogamous, others polygamous, still others polyandrous, etc. The study of primitive peoples in the flesh, and the fresh information concerning ancient civilizations derived from newly found documents, inscriptions, and archeological remains, brought to light a host of different manners, customs, and religious beliefs. Of course Herodotus had written about this diversity more than 2,300 years ago, but it was no longer common in the United States for university men to study Herodotus. So they took up the subject with all the enthusiasm of the mountaineer who thinks he is making a first ascent. University men in Western Europe and even more in the United States concluded that man's salvation lay in acknowledging the relativity of all values. They not only claimed that neither truth nor virtue exists in an absolute sense—they denied that reason, whether geometrical or intuitional, can help men to edge closer to either truth or virtue. How was one to determine scientifically which system of marriage, which set of political institutions, which religion was the best? Justice, honor, and beauty cannot be made the subjects of quantitative analysis. What was not susceptible of measurement, or precise proof through observation and experiment, was not worth the attention of the social scientist. The deductive method, by itself, was regarded with increasing suspicion. Deductions from revealed theology became scientifically impossible. New students recruited to the new studies were taught to explore new tribes and peoples, to collect and classify more facts concerning them.

Most American social scientists and professors of philosophy take it for granted that Christian dogma, together with the moral and intellectual values that many Western poets, philosophers, and scholars once accepted, have now been rendered obsolete by research in the social sciences and the humanities. They seldom notice that their elders—including that dangerous saint, Thomas Aquinas—did not live or study in complete ignorance of the diversity of beliefs and values which are now regarded as so damaging to the existence of faith and moral or intellectual convictions of any kind. They generally forget that ancient sages did not regard such diversity as an insuperable barrier to a general philosophical synthesis and a consensus of religious belief.

Aristotle pointed out long ago that the subjects of investigation in ethics and political science "exhibit so great a diversity and uncertainty . . . . [that] we must be content to indicate the truth roughly and in outline."[8] Shall we evade sub-

[8] *The Nicomachean Ethics*, Book I, chap. i.

jects simply because they are difficult? That would seem to be a poor reason. But it is not an uncommon one, particularly in an age when men have become accustomed to following the line of least resistance. One is reminded of the French economic historians who send their students to study the French Revolution instead of the wars of religion because so many of the documents relating to the late sixteenth century are in a handwriting hard to decipher!

Once it is admitted that the disinterested mind has an independent part to play in dealing with social data, a role not directed or determined primarily by experiment or scientific observation but by reason, then it is inevitable that ethical judgments concerning the value of different customs and traditions should be regarded not as a mere diversion in connection with the subject but as the most fundamental aspect of it. If, therefore, the mind is again given a place of its own in the higher learning, the approach to history, archeology, sociology, and anthropology will be very different from that hitherto regarded as alone appropriate.[9]

When an ethical attitude toward the study of society is adopted, what impresses men is less the differences between the various religions than the fact that all civilized societies have had religion. This suggests that human nature is bound under all circumstances to be concerned with the power behind the material world that is revealed to it. As far as history is a guide, it would seem that civilized men cannot exist without faith. Such a conclusion is startling for the numerous university men who assume that an absence of faith is an evidence of a superior education. Such a conclusion is bound to lead the intelligent to wonder whether, even if religion were a prejudice, we could free the human mind from all prejudices. They are likely to agree with André Gide that "prejudices are the pillars of civilization." Such minds may even conclude

[9] Cf. below, chap. ix, sec. i.

that it is the supreme duty of learning to try to guide mankind toward good prejudices. They will find nothing in the Constitution of the United States or in the thought of our great statesmen to support the proposition that all prejudices are equal.

If learning were to take this course, wise scholars would be bound to treat the diversity of religions among mankind as something more than a matter for curiosity. They would be impelled to raise the question: Which of all the religions known to history is the best for man? An inquiry into that matter could do nothing directly to restore faith. "Prejudice" can never serve as a sound basis for faith which is a gift that reason has no power to offer. But the inquiry could do much to restore respect. It is conceivable that the growth of respect may make mankind more susceptible to faith.

Unlike the study of comparative religions as mere curiosities, such an inquiry would almost certainly increase our admiration for Christianity. Whether we consider religions from the standpoint of their doctrines or from the standpoint of their universality in history, Christianity rises above the others.[10] Even a person to whom faith has been denied can recognize that the counsel of Christ concerning human conduct is the most sublime advice ever given to man. He can recognize that the advice contained in the works of great writers before and since the time of Christ is in essential agreement with His advice. Men can recognize that the more closely they are able to follow Christ's precepts, the more they are able to put their trust in everything which, according to the gospel, He preached, the nearer they will attain to spiritual happiness, the easier it will be for them to suffer and ultimate-

---

[10] Professor Hocking has, in fact, undertaken an inquiry of this kind. Cf. W. E. Hocking, *Living Religions and a World Faith* (New York, 1940), pp. 228, 230, 232, 235–38, 240–41, 249, 268. For the matters on which he thinks Christianity needs to learn from other religions, see pp. 242–43, 254 ff.

ly to die when their time comes, and the more they will be inclined toward humility and love of their fellow-men here on earth.

Man is born not to serve himself but "to love his neighbor." This was the counsel that the greatest surgeon of the sixteenth century prefixed to his treatise on surgery. Shall we say that this advice was simply a matter of Ambroise Paré's personal bias? Shall we say he was indulging in propaganda? Paré managed to cover his tracks so well that no historian (and few, if any, of his contemporaries) was able to determine for certain whether he was a Huguenot or a Catholic. He concealed his religion for reasons of safety in an age of religious warfare. His admonition could not betray him, for it is no monopoly of Catholicism or Protestantism. It transcends both. It is older than Christianity,[11] but fundamentally Christian. In proportion as it serves to guide surgeons, doctors, and men in every walk of life, human existence is enriched.

By faith in Christ men are consoled for suffering and death. As Madame de Sévigné remarked in 1689: "Un retour à la volonté de Dieu, et à cette loi universelle ou nous sommes condamnés, remet la raison à sa place, et fait prendre patience."[12] This is not the advice of a mystic but of a lady supremely endowed with common sense, with *savoir faire*. The word "reason" is well chosen. The will of God is the only perfect insurance that man can hope to find against excess and insanity.

The ideas are prevalent in the United States today that we are born with a right to escape suffering and unhappiness, that the world owes us a living. Such ideas cause misery. They lead us to spend a large part of our lives trying to avoid suffer-

[11] Cf. Sigmund Freud, *Civilization and Its Discontents* (New York, 1930), p. 81.

[12] "A return to God's will, and to the universal law that condemns us all, puts reason back in its place and makes us patient" (*Lettres de Madame de Sévigné*, ed. M. Monmerqué, IX [Paris, 1862], 334).

ing and trouble, or denying their existence. We spend our time
trying to arrange life instead of living it, without ever reaching a satisfactory solution, because the problems presented by
illness, death, and evil are not soluble, not at any rate by men.

Christianity makes untenable the prevalent idea that we are
put here to indulge in a sort of perpetual good time. According to Christianity, men suffer not only for their own faults
but for those of the human race, for which the Almighty bears
no responsibility. Once the dogma of original sin is accepted,
the reason and patience of which Madame de Sévigné spoke
are always at man's disposal in the face of every difficult and
terrible event. How often have we heard the men of what has
been called the "lost generation" say, when confronted by the
premature death of a companion more virtuous than others
who continue to live: "There is proof that God does not
exist. If he did exist, how could he let men like Joe or Dave
die in their youth like this?" They are deprived of that hope
of which Milton spoke so movingly in his poem consoling a
mother on the death of her infant daughter.

> O fairest flower no sooner blown but blasted,
>   Soft silken Primrose fading timelesslie,
> Summers chief honour if thou hadst out-lasted
>   Bleak winters force that made thy blosome drie;
> .   .   .   .
> Then thou the mother of so sweet a child
>   Her false imagin'd loss cease to lament,
> And wisely learn to curb thy sorrows wild;
>   Think what a present thou to God hast sent,
>   And render him with patience what he lent;
> This if thou do he will an off-spring give,
> That till the worlds last-end shall make thy name to live.[13]

Here we find Milton using the same word, "patience," that
Madame de Sévigné used. Next to conviction, which needs to

----

[13] "On the Death of a fair Infant dying of a Cough," *Poems, etc., upon Several Occasions* (London, 1673).

be tempered by it, patience is, perhaps, the quality in which
modern Americans are most deficient. Such a faith as Milton's, rugged and harsh, no less than the refined faith of
Madame de Sévigné, calls us back to common sense. Is it not
more in accord with reality than the doctrine of man's per-
fectibility in a godless world? As Tawney has said, ". . . . in
order to be at home in this world, it is not sufficient, unfortu-
nately, to disbelieve in another."[14] Is such disbelief even the
best preparation for improving this world? No less esteemed
a modern thinker than Freud has suggested that the sense of
guilt has been one of the great forces in the development of
civilization.[15] With human nature what it is, this sense of
guilt alone can make effective the admonition to love one's
neighbor. Freud would almost certainly have rejected the use
of his thesis on behalf of the Christian religion; he traces the
sense of guilt to the Oedipus complex.[16] Yet it is difficult to
deny that the Christian religion fostered this sense of guilt by
its dogma of original sin, by its emphasis on man's limitations, his imperfections.[17]

"All that a man hath will he give for his life." These are
the words of Satan in the Book of Job. They are also the words
of irreligion and materialism in the modern United States.
Life becomes so supreme a good, it is so much the only good
of which we have any scientific proof, some of the young men
and women of this country have come to say in recent years,
that anything and everything are worth sacrificing merely for
the sake of survival. Such is hardly the road to the true love
of life. Since life in this world must go for all, since love of
life in the fullest sense is impersonal rather than individual,
only those who are willing to lose life can know its full mean-

---

[14] *Equality* (3d ed.; London, 1938), p. 83.

[15] *Op. cit.*, chap. vii, esp. pp. 108-9, 111, 121-22.

[16] *Ibid.*, pp. 103, 118.

[17] Cf. T. E. Hulme, *Speculations* (London, 1924), *passim*.

ing and the infinite love that it has revealed to humanity. In
the end there is only one answer to the words of Satan if the
test comes. That answer is their rejection. To most men the
test of their truth does not come in so crucial a form. It comes,
nevertheless, in a multitude of minor forms, almost every day
of their lives. For example, men are forever being called on to
give up what their conscience tells them is right, for the sake
of personal advantages of one sort and another. The measure
of the power of man's spirit and of the strength of the civilization that has bred him consists in this: When the test presented by Satan comes, is he able to make the right choice?
Has he the courage to act in accordance with it? Who can
doubt that the Christian faith can help him both to make the
right choice and to act on it?

When we consider, not the doctrines of Christ and their
power, but the history of Christianity, we are also led to the
conclusion that its significance cannot be dismissed as a mere
matter of the mores of a particular tribe, race, nation, or
civilization. Christianity was born among the Jews in Pales-
tine almost two thousand years ago. It established itself in
the Roman Empire as part of the classical civilization in the
Mediterranean area. Western civilization was the product of
natural resources, races, and circumstances other than those
which created Greco-Roman civilization. No classical tradition grew in strength with the decline of the Roman Empire
except the rising Christian tradition. Men ceased to read even
commentaries upon the commentaries on the works of Aristotle and the other great writers of antiquity. But their faith
deepened during the Dark Ages when economic life became
more primitive, as they repeated the plain chant together and
listened to the story of the gospel told them by the priests.
Faith was hardly weakened by the break between the Western
and the Eastern church. With the rise of Western civilization
and the growing strength of the Papacy in the eleventh and
twelfth centuries, the Christian gospel assumed a universality

in the life of the Western peoples, and also in that of the very different Eastern peoples of the Balkans and of Russia, that it never possessed among the Classical peoples into whose world it was introduced. Even if we take no account of the relation of Christianity to the ancient Hebrew religion, it is evident that the Christian faith has provided consolation to a medley of races, living under a great diversity of economic and political systems, and belonging to an almost equally numerous diversity of cultures. An ethical study of sociology and of all the subject matter of the social sciences is capable of raising in the minds of intelligent men the question whether intelligence and faith are incompatible. Such men are faced with the problem whether the sense of reality, which in recent decades men have thought they were achieving through science, is in fact truer and more comprehensive than that embodied in the religious beliefs they rejected. They are led to ask the same question that the young American lady asked when she became acquainted with Pascal. The study of society, if approached philosophically, can hardly enable these men to return with perfect confidence the answer that Pascal was more prejudiced than a modern atheist or positivist.

III. RELIGION AND WEALTH

Thus far we have limited our discussion of Christianity to the religion itself. We have omitted all reference to the churches and to the ecclesiastical foundations that have made it their business to teach religious doctrines and to look after men's souls. Such a treatment of the subject may be said to resemble, not the play with Hamlet left out, but Hamlet with all the other players and all the scenery left out. When we are concerned with the ends of human existence, Christianity itself rightly seems far more important than its propagators. But as students of civilization, it is impossible to separate ecclesiastical history from the faith.

Nearly two centuries ago that busy clergyman, Dean Josiah

Tucker, of whom it was said that religion was his trade and trade his religion, sought to reconcile the new doctrines of political economy with the teachings of the Anglican church. One of his efforts was an analysis of conditions favorable and unfavorable to material prosperity, as these were revealed by a comparison of France and Great Britain.[18] In the case of France he found arbitrary and despotic government[19] the first disadvantage to freedom of trade, which he and Adam Smith, among so many others, regarded as the primary objective of civilized existence. The second disadvantage was "the Romish Religion; which has added to its many other Absurdities, a Spirit of Cruelty and Persecution, so repugnant to the Scope and Tendency of the Gospel."[20]

During the last forty years or so, few subjects in economic history have received as much attention from eminent scholars as this one of the influence of religion upon material progress. There is hardly an economic historian who has not touched on the matter since it was reopened, first in the 1890's by a chapter on "the canonist doctrine" in Sir William Ashley's *Introduction to Economic History and Theory*, and then in 1904 by Max Weber's far more celebrated and elaborate essay, which took a line different from Ashley's.[21] Brentano, Cunningham, Sombart, Troeltsch, Coulton, Tawney, Hauser, Sée, Fanfani, and many other writers in several countries have made valuable contributions to the controversy.[22] The main problems

[18] *A Brief Essay on the Advantages and Disadvantages Which Respectively Attend France and Great Britain with Regard to Trade* (2d ed.; London, 1750).

[19] For a historical inquiry into the relation between government and industrial development, see J. U. Nef, *Industry and Government in France and England, 1540–1640* (Philadelphia, 1940).

[20] Tucker, *op. cit.*, p. 24.

[21] *The Protestant Ethic and the Spirit of Capitalism*, trans. Talcott Parsons (London, 1930).

[22] Any list is almost certain to leave out some useful essays or articles on the subject. For helpful references to some of the chief contributions, see R. H. Tawney, *Religion and the Rise of Capitalism* (2d ed.; London, 1936), Preface.

have remained much the same as those suggested by Tucker. First, how far has Catholicism discouraged, and how far has the rise of Protestantism encouraged, the growth of the capitalist spirit and of large-scale enterprise in private hands? Second, how far has the Catholic Church interfered with the increase in economic welfare; how far has the rise of Protestantism promoted it? The two questions are not quite different aspects of the same question, for it does not appear that under all circumstances increasing freedom for the private capitalist promotes economic welfare.[23] In spite of the intelligence of much of the reasoning that has been directed to the subject, many aspects remain unsettled. There are facets which have been hardly examined.[24]

There is a certain unreality in considering the reciprocal relations of religious and economic history, since both religious and economic factors obviously influence and are influenced by political, constitutional, and intellectual factors, and also by geography and natural resources. The human mind has not yet managed to deal satisfactorily with the causal relationships of history as a whole, though a promising beginning has been made in the works of Spengler and Toynbee. When religious and economic history are considered separately, as has been the practice in connection with this controversy concerning religion and wealth, it becomes fairly clear that during much of Western European history the existence of religious institutions, and especially of the Catholic Church, has served as something of a restraint upon the accumulation of riches in the hands of private capitalists, upon the increase in the volume of production, and in particular

[23] Cf. below, chap. x, sec. ii.

[24] The soundest, most balanced treatment of the part played by Protestant doctrine in the growth of private enterprise seems to me that of Tawney, in the volume just cited and also in his *Introduction to Thomas Wilson's Discourse upon Usury* (London, 1925), pp. 105–72.

upon the growth of large-scale privately owned enterprise. Does it follow that a strong Christian church always hampers the increase of what Professor Pigou calls the national dividend?

We look back on the twelfth and thirteenth centuries as a great age for the Christian faith. Notwithstanding all the religious ardor, all the time and thought spent in developing the science of theology; notwithstanding the vast amount of labor which was devoted to the building and the maintenance of monasteries, churches, and cathedrals, designed to glorify God and to teach the people the lessons of history as they were interpreted by Christians, the population grew rapidly, serfdom diminished, towns thrived, and the standard of living rose among most classes nearly everywhere in Europe. In every country economic welfare was very greatly improved. Not until the late eighteenth and nineteenth centuries were all the European nations again bathed as frequently with comparable increases in prosperity. Whether economic progress would have been even more striking than it was without the Church, or if the Reformation had come three or four centuries earlier than it did, are questions that cannot be answered with assurance. The historian is unable to experiment with a civilization by leaving out one of its compounds as the chemist can so often do in his analyses. It is impossible to think of any side of European civilization in the Gothic Age without the Church. When religion formed so integral a part of life, we may reasonably suppose that it helped infuse into the people the consolation and confidence that presumably had something to do with their material development. The passage of the year A.D. 1000, which tradition had set for the possible end of the world, is thought to have produced a fresh interest among the Western peoples in economic improvement. It did not prevent the strengthening of ecclesiastical institutions. The power and influence of the Papacy increased during and after the lifetime of Hildebrand (1020–85).

The ecclesiastical foundations, which controlled a considerable part of all the land in Europe, did little to hinder and a good deal to encourage the clearing and use of land for pasture and arable farming and for the mining, metallurgical, and salt-making industries. By its success in persuading rich men who had amassed their wealth in worldly careers to atone for their sins of greed by making large gifts or bequests for the glory of God, the Church dissipated many, if not most, of the large private fortunes which would have been available for investment in industry and trade. But in the Gothic Age investments of capital in large blocks were much less essential to industrial progress than they became at the end of the Middle Ages. The great income of the Church was used in large part to command labor that produced no consumable commodities. But the hundreds of majestic buildings, which the Church alone was rich enough and powerful enough to undertake, provided work for the growing population, without interfering seriously with the labor and skill devoted to agrarian, commercial, and industrial pursuits which ministered to physical needs. Even when we recognize that Catholic historians have greatly exaggerated the direct part which priests and monks took in manual labor, and the part which ecclesiastical foundations played in supplying capital for productive purposes, it is still difficult to show that all the construction which the Church financed held back economic progress from the time of Abelard to the times of St. Thomas and Dante. The medieval cathedrals, churches, and monasteries built in the twelfth and thirteenth centuries cost a sum equivalent to several billions of dollars,[25] in terms of modern American money, at a time when the yearly dividend of Western Europe probably ran into a few hundreds of millions instead of tens of billions, as in the early twentieth century. Some mod-

---

[25] Cf. Henry Adams, *Mont-Saint-Michel and Chartres* (Boston, 1913), p. 94. Adams speaks of a thousand million dollars as the estimated cost in 1840 of replacing eighty cathedrals and five hundred churches built in France alone between 1170 and 1270.

ern economists take the view that there are circumstances which render a program of public works beneficial to economic welfare, even though the works themselves are of no use in the production or carriage of commodities. May not this have been the case in the late twelfth and thirteenth centuries? Work had to be found for the rapidly increasing inhabitants. As a result of improvements in economic technique and management, it was not necessary to employ all of them in producing, transporting, and selling consumable goods, in order to supply the people generally with a higher standard of living than that to which their ancestors had been accustomed before the Gothic Age.

At the end of the Middle Ages the conditions of economic progress had changed, together with the place of the Church in civilized life. Mining and metallurgy, for example, could be carried on effectively in the thirteenth century by small partnerships of manual workmen. In the late fifteenth and early sixteenth centuries these industries had come to require, in many cases, capital running into the modern equivalent of tens of thousands of dollars. The effective development of economically indispensable industries had come to require a freedom in the use of land and money seldom needed in the Gothic Age. At the same time ecclesiastical foundations seem to have become, speaking generally, rather less enterprising in economic matters than they had once been. The strength, together with the prestige and influence, of the Papacy declined.

Through its control over property and through the doctrines that it taught concerning science and economic and political life, the Church stood, at the end of the Middle Ages, in the way of the kind of economic development that led to the triumph of industrialism. Ecclesiastical foundations were not prepared to invest large sums in enterprises within their own lands. They were seldom willing to lease their lands on as favorable terms as lay landlords to persons who wanted to invest large sums. Land belonging to the Church, unlike land in private hands, was almost never for sale. So the ecclesiastical ownership of landed property interfered with its use for large industrially productive ventures of all kinds.

The dissolution of the monasteries and other ecclesiastical foundations in sixteenth-century England was accompanied and followed by the transfer of a vast amount of land, rich in minerals, from the Church to the Crown and to laymen. This transfer facilitated the exploitation of the coal mines[26] and the introduction of large, efficient plant for smelting iron ore.[27] As the early "industrial revolution" was based in a measure on coal, and the later more famous one on the union of coal with iron, the Reformation played a part of some significance, through the confiscation of religious property, in promoting the progress of all the heavy industries.

In France ecclesiastical foundations retained until the French Revolution—for two and a half centuries longer than in England—almost as much landed property as they had held during the Middle Ages. We catch a glimpse of the attitude of French churchmen toward the use of water-driven machinery and the development of heavy industry in connection with the famous abbey of La Grande Trappe, in the now unimportant iron-making district of Orne Department to the west of Paris. The Trappist monks closed down their metallurgical plant when they found that the noise of the falling hammers at the forge and of the machine-driven pincers pulling out the metal wire interfered with their solitude.[28] Is it not safe to

[26] Nef, *The Rise of the British Coal Industry* (London, 1932), I, 133–56.

[27] The great development in Sussex of the blast furnace (then in its infancy in Europe) came directly after the dissolution of the monasteries in 1536 and 1539, and many of the new iron works were erected on land, formerly the property of the Church, most of which had not been used for smelting iron ore, even on a small scale, before its confiscation (Ernest Straker, *Wealden Iron* [London, 1931], pp. 32, 49, 292).

[28] M. Leroux, *L'Industrie du fer dans le Perche* (Paris, 1916), p. 107.

say that, on monastic estates, economic had frequently to give way to religious considerations when there was a conflict between the two? A rather comprehensive survey was made of the iron manufacture in France in 1789.[29] This survey shows that in Church lands the furnaces for smelting iron ore were much smaller and less modern in equipment than most of those in lands belonging to laymen. In the departments of Côtes du Nord, Cher, Indre, Nièvre, Moselle, Haute Saône, and Saône et Loire, only a negligible proportion of the furnaces for which we have records were in Church lands. The average annual output per furnace in these departments was about 475 tons.[30] In the departments of Ardennes, Meuse, Haute-Marne, Côte d'Or, Isère, and Savoy, something like a third or more of all the furnaces recorded were in lands still held by ecclesiastical foundations. The average annual output per furnace in these departments was 320 tons. There can be little doubt that it was the furnaces in Church lands which brought down the average. There are two departments—Isère and Ardennes—for which it is possible to separate the furnaces on Church lands from those in the lands of laymen. In Isère the former produced on the average about 180 tons a year, as against an average of about 320 tons for all the furnaces in this department. In Ardennes they produced about 75 tons, as against about 380 tons for all those in that department. The output of the French iron furnaces in territory held by the ecclesiastical foundations appears to have been much smaller in 1789 than that of the average furnace in England and Wales on the eve

[29] H. and G. Bourgin, *L'Industrie sidérurgique en France* (Paris, 1920).

[30] I have worked out these and the other figures of production at the French furnaces from data in the book of the Bourgins. My figures are not precise for several reasons. The survey does not include all the iron-making enterprises; most of the statistics actually given are approximations; the exact weight of some of the units in which production was measured (e.g., the *quintal* and the *millier*) is not always clear.

of the English civil war,[31] a hundred and fifty years before. While the greater scale of iron-making in England cannot be explained exclusively or even mainly by the dissolution of the monasteries,[32] the Reformation had something to do with the differences.

Apart from the influence exercised by the Church over the use of land, the expense of maintaining large armies of priests and monks, engaged mainly in devotional rather than in economically productive activities, imposed something of a handicap in early modern times upon the progress of large-scale industrial enterprise and the growth in the output of cheap commodities, made with the help of horse- and water-driven machinery. The Church no longer played the leading part in financing building operations, as it had done in the Gothic Age. Like the French nobility, the French clergy largely escaped the payment of direct taxes, which fell almost entirely on the common people. Like the nobility, the clergy was much less interested than the mercantile class in investing large sums in the heavy industries, or in the sale and purchase of cheap conveniences. When the ecclesiastical foundations as institutions wanted ornaments, hangings, and furniture, they looked more for the beautiful and the lasting than for useful commodities, such as were in demand among the middle class everywhere, and in England, to some extent, even among the best-paid manual workmen.[33] The use which the Church made of its immense income did not stimulate the demand for the products of heavy industry as much as the equivalent income in the hands of the mercantile and the laboring classes would

[31] Nef, "Iron Production in England, 1540–1640," *Journal of Political Economy*, XLIV, No. 3 (1936), 401.

[32] For some of the other causes, see the series of essays that I have published since 1933, and that have been already referred to in these pages. Eventually I hope to bring the matter contained in the essays together in a book.

[33] The influence of royal absolutism was similar, as I attempted to show in my *Industry and Government in France and England, 1540–1640*, esp. chaps. iv and v.

have done. In 1676 Sir William Petty, one of the fathers of economic thought, passed on an exaggeration that we hear with a little surprise from this meticulous statistician. It serves, nevertheless, to bring out a point which is of concern in connection with economic welfare. "The Hollanders," he wrote, "observe that in France and Spain . . . . the Churchmen are about one hundred for one, to what they use or need; the principal care of whom is to preserve Uniformity, and this they take to be a superfluous charge."[34] The maintenance of a far more numerous clergy and of far more costly religious institutions in France and most other continental nations than in England, during the two hundred years following the Reformation, helps to account for the slower progress of capitalist enterprise and the slower expansion of the heavy industries.

In most discussions of religion and the rise of capitalism much less emphasis has been laid upon the influence on economic history of ecclesiastical institutions, with their wealth, than upon the influence of Christian dogma. By emphasizing a side of the problem which has not received as much attention as it would seem to deserve, we do not suggest that the doctrines and teaching of the churches have been unimportant for economic welfare. The bigoted opposition to scientific experiment and observation that was so prominent in late Scholastic thought at the end of the Middle Ages[35] was encouraged by the Catholic Church, and in the beginning by the founders of the new Protestant sects as well, although the early Protestant writers broke with Scholastic thought at many points.[36] As President Conant has pointed out, the mine and factory have helped the laboratory just as the laboratory has helped the mine and factory. There has been in modern

[34] *The Economic Writings of Sir William Petty*, ed. by C. H. Hull (Cambridge, 1899), I, 263.

[35] See above, pp. 119–20.

[36] Cf. T. B. Macaulay, "Lord Bacon," *Essays* (London, 1866), II, 376.

times a sort of symbiosis between scientific inquiry and technological improvements of every kind.[37] Over and over again each has stimulated and encouraged the other. Both have been indispensable to the rise of industrialism. The decidedly tepid enthusiasm of churchmen—and particularly Catholic churchmen—for both perhaps interfered with the introduction of labor-saving devices and other improvements in industry and transportation. Finally, while the doctrines of the Catholic Church imposed restraints upon political power, they were generally unsympathetic to popular sovereignty. The authority of an absolute prince under God, which the Church indorsed in early modern times, was no more favorable to the freedom of private capital and to the unrestricted rights of private capitalists in their business operations than the authority of the Church itself.

In a variety of ways, the doctrines of Christianity, as expounded by churchmen, interfered with the accumulation of capital in private hands and with the intemperate pursuit of profit by communicants. It was only by means of compromises, made invariably with reluctance, that the taking of moderate interest on loans could be brought into any sort of accord with the dogma of the Christian fathers. Priests and monks were in no position to offer a wholehearted indorsement of the careers of men whose rise in the world was brought about principally by their skill and success in amassing fortunes, such as were needed for launching large private industrial and commercial enterprises. The extent to which private accumulation and freedom for private business enterprise promoted economic welfare is impossible to estimate, because those countries (of which Great Britain was the foremost) in which large-scale privately owned enterprise made the greatest headway were countries where, besides religion, other

[37] J. B. Conant, "Lessons from the Past," *Industrial and Engineering Chemistry*, XXXI (1939), 1215-17.

conditions—such as peace and easily accessible mineral resources—were favorable to material prosperity. There were some ways in which the discipline of the Catholic Church stimulated production. It encouraged diligence among owners of businesses, technical experts, and workers, and it accustomed the workers to accept without question orders given them by foremen and managers. Dean Tucker was of the opinion that French workmen were much more thrifty, obedient, and industrious than English workmen.[38]

There has been a disposition on the part of the religious authorities, at least since the twelfth century, to come to terms with the world on those issues where dogma has interfered with economic progress and even with the making of money.[39] The influence of capitalism upon the power of churches, upon religious thought, and upon the doctrines expounded by the clergy has been, in a sense, more striking than the influence of religion upon capitalism. The former influence is positive, the latter for the most part negative. Religion has tended to hold back capitalism. Capitalism has tended to change the nature and even the meaning of religion. In facilitating the change the Reformation was of much importance.

Though it was not the intention of their founders, the Protestant churches were in many ways better adapted than the Catholic Church to make compromises with the mercantile conception of life, and to permit the private capitalist freedom in the pursuit of profit. Before the middle of the seventeenth century the Protestants generally, and the Puritans in particular, welcomed empirical scientific studies and even made reason subservient to empiricism. They began to

---

[38] *Op. cit.*, pp. 36–37. Tucker called the "Want of subordination in the lower Class of people . . . . the first and *capital* Disadvantage" of Great Britain with regard to trade, as compared to France. On this point his testimony is at variance with the more recent view of Max Weber, who thought that Protestantism encouraged diligence among the workers as well as the capitalists.

[39] Cf. Tawney's remarks in Weber, *op. cit.*, p. 8.

see in new scientific discoveries an important means whereby men could glorify God. The Catholic atmosphere was somewhat less favorable than the Protestant to scientific inquiry, because the Catholics clung more to the view that experiment and observation, while desirable if pursued in moderation, were a source of vanity, contrary to the true Christian spirit, when they were regarded as more important than faith or even than reason.[40] By the beginning of the seventeenth century, if not considerably earlier, doctrines of popular sovereignty were treated with greater favor by many of the Protestant sects than by most Catholic writers. As Weber showed, Protestant doctrine, especially in its Calvinist forms, encouraged the view that salvation for the layman lay less in renunciation and resignation, as the priests taught, than in intense worldly activity. Such activity came to be directed, particularly after the middle of the seventeenth century, to the development of industrial, commercial, and financial enterprises. In this way, as Tawney expresses it, certain aspects of later Puritanism provided the capitalist spirit with "a tonic which braced its energies and fortified its already vigorous temper."[41] The pursuit of riches for their own sake by men of business was given religious support which had been lacking.

After the middle of the seventeenth century, if not before, Protestant doctrine, especially in its Calvinist manifestations, looked with less disfavor than Catholic doctrine on most kinds of interest and on private accumulation in general.[42]

[40] Cf. R. K. Merton, "Puritanism, Pietism, and Science," *Sociological Review*, XXVIII, No. 1 (1936), 1–20; B. Hessen, "The Social and Economic Roots of Newton's 'Principia,'" *Science at the Cross Roads* (London: Kniga, 1931 [?]), pp. 167–68; F. Engels, *Socialism, Utopian and Scientific* (Chicago, 1918), p. 25; G. N. Clark, *Science and Social Welfare in the Age of Newton* (Oxford, 1937), pp. 79–84.

[41] Tawney, *op. cit.*, pp. 226–27.

[42] Henri Hauser, "Les Idées économiques de Calvin," *Les Débuts du capitalism* (Paris, 1927), pp. 78–79; cf. Tawney, *Introduction to Wilson's Discourse upon Usury*, pp. 118–21. For a somewhat different view of the matter which has not been widely accepted, see

Even earlier, in the sixteenth century, when there was little to choose between Protestant and Catholic teaching on economic questions, the reformed churches had at their disposal for the enforcement of dogma neither the strong sanctions nor the elaborate ecclesiastical organization that the Church of Rome retained.[43] Even though the views of a few reformers were more orthodox on some points than those of the Catholics, it is by no means certain that they carried as much weight.[44] What mattered was not simply the nature of the doctrine, but its effectiveness. So there were many ways in which the rise of Protestantism helped to release brakes that tended to hold back the progress of capitalism.

Yet it is easy to exaggerate both the influence of Protestantism in facilitating economic progress and that of Catholicism in holding it back. The Protestant sects generally gained their chief strength in countries, like Holland and Great Britain, where the pressure on religion to adjust itself to new economic developments was much stronger, for many reasons that have little to do with religion, than in countries like France, Italy, and Spain, which remained Catholic. War, despotism, and a want of accessible mineral resources are among the important factors which hindered industrial, commercial, and scientific development on the Continent in the late sixteenth and seventeenth centuries. The want of enthusiasm for natural science and for new labor-saving devices in industry was common among Protestants as well as Catholics in most countries of Continental Europe, while in England the enthusiasm can be explained only very partially as an indirect result of the Reformation. If economic progress in the Catholic countries

---

H. M. Robertson, *The Rise of Economic Individualism* (Cambridge, 1933), pp. 120–29. See the reply to Robertson by J. Brodrick, S.J., *The Economic Morals of the Jesuits* (London, 1934).

[43] Cf. Weber, *op. cit.*, pp. 104–5; Tawney, *Religion and the Rise of Capitalism*, p. 97.

[44] Cf. Tawney, *op. cit.*, p. xii.

had been more rapid at this time than it was, Catholic thought would undoubtedly have made greater concessions to economic progress.

History does not prove that a strong church organization and a numerous clergy, together with the widespread ecclesiastical ownership of property and the maintenance of economic doctrines that discourage materialism and the private accumulation of wealth for its own sake, are a handicap to economic welfare under all circumstances. The experience of the last four centuries of religious history is not necessarily the best guide for the future. The conditions of economic progress appear to be changing again, as they changed at the end of the Middle Ages. Is it not possible that the relation of Christianity to material welfare in the Gothic Age is more relevant to the present turning point in Western history than the relation of Christianity to material welfare at another turning point in early modern times?[45]

The assumption that underlies some of the discussion of religion and capitalism since the time of Dean Tucker would seem odd to the early Christian fathers and to medieval churchmen. It has been widely taken for granted that churches justify their existence primarily by their contribution to economic welfare or even to the rise of capitalism. It was hardly for the benefit of rich men or even for the end of material improvement that Christianity was founded. As a result of Western history during the last four centuries, an age like our own, which tends to value all things in terms of material wealth, often looks at religion from points of view that the wise men of the past would find some difficulty in recognizing as religious. These points of view may, perhaps, be divided into two types. There is, first, the disposition to regard religions of every kind as the enemies of economic progress, and to turn away from the churches altogether on that account.

[45] Cf. below, chap. x, sec. iv.

There is, second, the disposition to try to reform religion. The object in this case is to make religion the ally of economic progress. The end of religious services becomes material improvement, and it is assumed that every increase in "economic welfare," in Professor Pigou's sense,[46] will bring about a corresponding increase in general welfare. Naturally, it is the sects which have already made the most compromises with wealth which lend themselves most readily to such a reform of religion.

Neither of these positions is likely to be of great help to mankind in the age that lies ahead. If materialism is becoming its own worst enemy, salvation hardly lies in making materialism the principle upon which one chooses or rejects a particular form of religious worship. Still less does salvation lie in making over religion for the sake of materialism.

Much of the life of mankind may properly be devoted to material improvement, but that is not the object of the religious life. We do not condemn the Christian faith in modern times simply by showing that economic welfare would have increased more than it has during the last four centuries if the Catholic Church had been abolished in the age of the Renaissance, or if it had never existed. That begs the question whether Western Europe could have reached the state of civilization it achieved during the Middle Ages without the Church, and whether, if it could not, such a state of civilization was a prerequisite for the rise of industrialism. It also begs the question how far Christian ethics, through the contribution that they may have made in modern times to constitutional government, to peace, stability, and honesty within the various nations of Europe, may have helped to provide conditions that were a necessary foundation for economic progress since the Reformation. It is not possible without an answer to these questions, and simply on the basis of a discus-

[46] See above, p. 63.

sion of the reciprocal relations between religious and economic history, to say that the Western world would be as well off as it is today, even in a material sense, if the Christian churches had never existed.

In any case the justification, in a worldly sense, for an ecclesiastical polity and state lies not in making men rich, but in their contribution to the love, the goodness, the beauty, and the wisdom of mankind, to which material improvement is properly only a means. In a religious sense, the justification for an ecclesiastical polity and state lies primarily, not in the contribution they make to temporal perfection, even of a moral and intellectual character, but in the belief in a divine life which they cultivate, through grace, faith, and mystical experience.

It is possible to argue that a church devoted primarily to the increase of material wealth would be desirable. That is precisely what Dr. Carver has done in his *Religion Worth Having*. It is not possible to argue, as Dr. Carver is aware, that such a church would be Christian. It is difficult to argue, according to the meaning given the word in all previous societies of which we have record, that such a church would be religious. At the present turning point in history, it may even be doubted whether a church devoted to economic progress will actually do as much for material welfare as a church devoted to religion.

IV. RELIGION AND CIVILIZATION

Faith, a belief in eternal life, is the primary object of a Christian church. As students of civilization, we are concerned not with faith, but with the contribution which Christianity has made, by cultivating faith, to the general welfare of human beings here on earth.

From the worldly point of view, which cannot be the final test for a Christian believer, the greatest contribution of the

Christian religion to the welfare of mankind is that it enlists on the side of the mind and spirit forces that are supernatural and all powerful. In all civilized societies the best in man has lifted him toward the supreme human values of honor, truth, love, goodness, wisdom, and beauty. The best in man has made him long for impersonal, disinterested agreement concerning the nature of these values. As their nature can never be settled by algebraic formulas or by the discoveries of natural science, they must always remain elusive. Eternal vigilance by persons who recognize their existence is the price that has to be paid if there is to be any approach to an understanding of them, or much action in fundamental accord with them. As set forth in the gospel and in the books of the greatest saints and theologians, the Christian religion puts the existence of these values beyond the realm of debate.

Christianity is, therefore, the ally of the good life. It teaches men and women that honesty and charity are right whether they lead to worldly recognition or not. Even if, in a world that is losing its balance and is also losing the meaning of words, the qualities of honesty and charity are called selfishness, they ought still to be cultivated. Why should it be assumed that there is, in our present irreligious world, any close connection between goodness and popularity? Were not the acts of the Savior the cause of his persecution and crucifixion? Did not the Jews protest when Pontius Pilate referred to Christ as their king? When we falter in our duty to honor and truth out of fear of any kind, nothing can sustain us so much as the belief that we are following, however humbly and inadequately, in Christ's footsteps. Nothing can sustain us so much as the belief that we are striving to act here on earth according to the light He has provided for us, and not out of any desire to advance ourselves according to the transient and fragile fashions of this world.

As St. François de Sales says in his benign way, devotion is a sort of sugar for the spirit. It takes some of the bitterness from the difficult acts of life—those which we make in response to duty rather than to self-interest. It infuses into such acts and into all the experiences of life an element of pleasure even when they are painful. "Elle sert de feu en hiver, et de rosée en été; elle sait abonder et souffrir pauvreté; elle rend également utile l'honneur et le mépris; elle reçoit le plaisir et la douleur avec un coeur presque toujours semblable, et nous remplit d'une sauvité merveilleuse."[47] At a time when the people of the Western countries, and most of all of the United States, are suffering from an unwillingness to assume responsibilities, when most people in their public and private relations think mainly in terms of what they can get in a worldly way and very little in terms of what they can give in effort and honesty and sweetness, there is a tremendous need for a renewal of the sense of obligation. Nothing helps men so much to assume obligations, to take a course that is difficult and unpopular, as the belief that an all-wise Being is looking on with approval when they turn away from the course that is easy or popular or likely to save their skins, but that is unjust or unwise or cowardly, if not actually wicked.

The Christian faith is the ally of reason as well as of virtue. Reason has fallen into discredit in recent decades, until even in supposedly learned circles the distinction between reason and opinion has ceased to have meaning. An eminent American astronomer has recently divided all learning into the scientific and the nonscientific. The first, he says, "is the public domain of positive knowledge," the second, "the private domain of

[47] "It serves for fire in winter and for dew in summer; it knows how to abound and how to suffer poverty; it renders equally useful honour and contempt; it receives pleasure and pain with a heart almost always the same, and fills us with a marvelous content" (*Introduction to the Devout Life*, trans. Allan Ross [London, 1937], p. 7). I have changed several words in the translation, in order better to fulfil the meaning, as I see it.

personal judgments." "Each man," he adds, "acquires his own wisdom from his own experience."[48]

These views have been recently cited with approval by a well-known American historian.[49] They ignore the power of the trained and richly endowed mind, in dealing with problems of morality, knowledge, or beauty, to form objective judgments in essential accord with those of wise men in past ages and to go beyond them. These views ignore the whole rich world of the mind to which Pascal introduces us in the opening paragraphs of *Les Pensées*.[50] The admission that there is a realm of human experience to which positive science is inapplicable is good. Dr. Hubble seems to identify this realm with what he calls "humanism." But to leave it to the tender mercies of radio commentators, motion-picture directors, newspaper reporters, and other professors of current events, by inadvertently giving their pronouncements and those of persons even less qualified to reason than they the same weight as those of a disinterested, richly endowed, and well-trained mind, is to belittle a region which is, from the point of view of human welfare, even more important than the scientific. It is a region upon which the scientist depends. If men should cease to cultivate it, science itself would eventually cease to flourish.

Truth is in the intellect, St. Thomas tells us. According to the Christian theology generally accepted in Western history, there is a very simple explanation of the inability of the mind to reach perfectly true statements in this realm. Man attains his power of reasoning from God. By cultivating reason all his life he may in a few rare cases almost overcome his prejudices,

---

[48] Edwin Hubble, "Points of View: Experiment and Experience," *The Huntington Library Quarterly*, No. 3 (April, 1939), p. 243.

[49] Max Farrand, "The Quality of Distinction," *American Historical Review*, XLVI, No. 3 (1941).

[50] See above, p. 138.

his appetites, his faulty education, his material circumstances, and his limited experiences. He may approach wisdom. But he can never attain it, because perfect knowledge, like perfect goodness, is an attribute only of the Supreme Being. What a few wise men (among whom Plato, Aristotle, and Aquinas are the outstanding examples in philosophy) have managed to discover through reason about human life is almost flawless as far as it goes. It has never been and never can be exhaustive. But the opinion so widespread in the United States that, since men can never attain complete wisdom, each man should begin over again from scratch, without the help of the knowledge and wisdom that human beings have captured by reason in the past, is a serious danger to every kind of knowledge. If such an opinion prevails it is bound to reduce further and further the level of learning. Such an opinion is rejected by traditional Christian theology.

Thus the Christian faith provides reason with a shield. As the Christian faith has been weakened, as the churches have made compromises to meet material standards, this shield has grown rusty. The modern world has denied the existence of wisdom because it has seen in the work of the wisest men of the past flaws which they would be the first to recognize. No truly wise man, like Thomas Aquinas, ever claimed that he had found wisdom. Christianity offers an explanation for the flaws. At the same time, it shows how unimportant they are in comparison with the disaster involved in denying the existence of reason. For one does deny reason when it is claimed that every man is equally equipped to reason, regardless of his natural endowment, his circumstances, his training, his character, and his effort.

The Christian faith is the ally of art as well as of reason. No work of art, whether it involves the alteration of matter, like a statue, or is abstract, like a musical composition, is possible without the exercise of the mind in ways that are largely irrelevant to the problems of the natural scientist but are closely related to the ways of faith.[51] At least since the time of Socrates, and consequently long before the advent of Christianity, philosophers have suggested that great poets and other great artists are divinely inspired. The natural scientist is concerned with unraveling the secrets of material things. When he uses matter, the true artist uses it in accordance with principles related to a lofty purpose evolved in his own mind with the help of the minds of fellow-artists of the past as they have revealed their secrets in their works. Unlike the scientist and the technician, he is concerned with achieving a result that is unique.[52] In order to rise above technique, the artist has to impose on his material, whether it be actual matter or simply ideas, a lofty conception derived from his mind, and his spirit at the service of his mind. This conception is suggested by the actual world but transcends it. Whether the artist is a Christian or not, this conception takes him into a realm closely akin to that visited by the Christian believer.[53] Like the true Christian in the act of faith, the true artist in the act of art rises above the world as he sees it with his eyes and feels it with his senses. Thus Christianity strengthens art, by keeping alive belief in a world of the mind, and more especially by making the unseen the principle which actually controls the world about us.[54]

As has been suggested, the authority of the disinterested and cultivated mind alone can provide an adequate bulwark against totalitarianism in the age that lies ahead. By identify-

[51] Cf. Jacques Maritain, *Art et scolastique* (3d ed.; Paris, 1935).

[52] Cf. above, pp. 76–78.

[53] Cf. Von Ogden Vogt, *Art and Religion* (New Haven, 1921), esp. chap. iii.

[54] In the previously mentioned work soon to be published by the Princeton University Press, under the title *Some Aspects of Music*, Dr. Artur Schnabel makes the interesting suggestion that the spirit behind modern absolute music, for which we have no equivalent in the music of past civilizations, is the same as that behind the most inspiring examples of Christian saintliness.

ing this barrier against the exercise of arbitrary power with the Supreme Being, who is wholly good, as Christianity has done, it is given a firmer foundation and the subjects have better protection from a tyrant. The ancient Greeks believed that jealous gods would punish civil tyrants and conquerors when they usurped to themselves a power which does not properly belong to men. The Christian explanation of the fate that awaits such cruel men is far nobler. Their punishment comes not as vengeance—for God is not subject to human passions—but as the consequence of sin; it comes not because they have acted in place of God, but because they have acted in a way that is completely alien to his nature. Sin makes it impossible to use as an instrument of creation a creature who insists upon alienating himself from the life of his Creator.[55] Thus the Christian belief, if widely and profoundly held, acts as a restraint on tyranny and conquest. John Donne has explained the situation in a few lines.

> That thou mayest rightly obey power, her bounds know;
> Those past, her nature, and name is chang'd; to be
> Then humble to her is idolatrie.
> As streames are, Power is; those blest flowers that dwell
> At the rough streames calme head, thrive and do well,
> But having left their roots, and themselves given
> To the streames tyrannous rage, alas, are driven
> Through mills, and rockes, and woods, and at last, almost
> Consum'd in going, in the sea are lost:
> So perish Soules, which more chuse mens unjust
> Power from God claym'd, then God himselfe to trust.[56]

What is still worse than trusting "power from God claimed" is something of which men in Donne's time had no experience, but which we are beginning to feel. It is to trust power

[55] Cf. A. J. Toynbee, *A Study of History* (London, 1939), IV, 256–57.

[56] "Satyre III," ll. 100–110, *The Poems of John Donne*, ed. H. J. C. Grierson (Oxford, 1912), I, 158.

claimed not from God, but from the mob. In the Middle Ages, and to a much smaller extent in early modern times, Christianity was the intellectual foundation on which the limitation upon the authority of the absolute prince rested. In those days governing power passed mainly by inheritance. That differentiates it sharply from the modern governing power of dictators, which in many other respects resembles it. The earlier form of dictatorship in Western history goes under the name of "royal absolutism." There is some justification for calling the new form "democratic absolutism." Totalitarianism operates in the name of democracy. The people put their individual wills in the will of a leader, and have none left. As Tocqueville warned us more than a century ago, this new absolutism, if it came, was likely to be more arbitrary and more cruel than any Western society has known. If totalitarianism ever takes possession of this country, we have been told, it is likely to masquerade as democracy. The most hopeful means of preventing this is to reaffirm the meaning of words, which is being lost, and at the same time to resurrect the power of the disinterested and gifted mind, trained by unending hard work. In so far as religion can strengthen the mind, and invest the principles of democracy with a greater validity than mere opinion, it will be the strongest ally of true democracy.[57]

It is doubtful whether in the whole history of mankind the worldly case for religion has ever been stronger than today. The trouble has been and is that in spite of its origin, the Christian religion is necessarily placed in the keeping of mortal men. Again and again, the churches have disappointed the hopes that one reasonably puts in the followers of Christ when one is familiar with the gospel. However we view church history, we are bound to admit that the millions of mortal men who have had charge in various capacities, ex-

[57] See also Hocking, *op. cit.*, p. 246.

alted and humble, of the administration of ecclesiastical discipline, have fallen somewhat short in their stewardship of the
ideals expressed and the life lived by the Founder here on
earth. They have sometimes made use of the Founder and his
words as a sort of cloak behind which to commit the very sins
which He condemned.

In any discussion of the relation of Christianity to civilization, account has to be taken of the shortcomings of the
Catholic Church and of the Protestant churches. The Catholic Church, in particular, has left some scars on the pages of
history that no impartial inquiry can neglect. The fact that
wicked churchmen may be expiating their sins in the inferno
which Dante painted does not permit us to ignore these sins
in a worldly essay like this one. The question whether the
Church has interfered with economic progress is of far less
concern than the question whether it has, on many occasions,
interfered with virtue, intelligence, and beauty, which are
the ultimate values that justify wealth in civilized societies.
Doubt on this point should make the most ardent Catholic
hesitate, in so far as he has the temporal good of mankind at
heart, to advocate a revival of the power exercised by the
Church in medieval times.

A scholar who has been regarded as an opponent of the
Catholic Church is said to have remarked on one occasion that
his position had been misunderstood. He was quite prepared
to admit that, taken together, those who have professed the
Catholic faith have been, from the temporal point of view,
roughly five per cent better than the rest of the Western
peoples. But, he added, "only five per cent better; no more
than that." This scholar is known for a readiness to meet his
critics half way. His interlocutor, another scholar who, unlike
him, is regarded as friendly to the Catholic Church, expressed
the view that five per cent was much too liberal an allowance!

No doubt our eighteenth- and nineteenth-century ancestors,

with their horror of the excesses of the Church, painted a one-sided picture of its iniquities. Some of our contemporaries even embellish that picture. It remains true that many of the acts of church bodies and of individual churchmen during the Middle Ages and in early modern times stood in the way not only of scientific advance and material progress, but also in the way of art and humanistic inquiries of every kind. Church bodies also stood in the way of virtue. The Catholic Church set itself up to judge, to excommunicate, and to burn thousands of persons who believed themselves to be the better Christians for disregarding certain details of Church ritual. This was bound to horrify the enlightened men of a later era. Whatever their faults (and they have been grave), these men helped to diminish physical cruelty, to establish toleration for persons who chose to worship God in their own way, and to lessen the fear of Hell, which has sometimes tormented young minds groping toward the good. The achievements of the great humanitarian movement of the eighteenth and nineteenth centuries should be husbanded today. The greatest saints, it may be suggested, are those who have insisted that an indifference about the ethics of this world is not the best preparation for life in the next. Mankind can be forgiven for not feeling indifferent to the fact that tens of thousands of persons protected by the cloth have exercised their power unintelligently, and not a few wickedly.

The object of the Reformation was to remedy these evils. Mankind was to be relieved of its dependence on mortal men for its religious knowledge. The object was to bring men into more direct and, it was hoped, closer communion with the gospel, and through the gospel with Christ and with God. In so far as the change was consistent with the maintenance of faith, there was much to recommend it. Benjamin Franklin would hardly be regarded as a good judge by a religious man. There is truth, nevertheless, in his words, "I think vital religion has always suffered when orthodoxy is more regarded than virtue."[58] When a practicing Christian becomes so enamored of orthodoxy that he refuses to recognize morality except among persons who go through the motions required by his church, he in effect rejects those impulses toward good which exist in men independently of Catholicism and even of Christianity, and which are themselves, as the true Catholic and the true Christian are the first to agree, gifts of God. The reforming sects were not altogether misguided when they set out to diminish the emphasis on form and ritual.

Yet, paradoxically, in a world peopled by millions of common men, institutions of a kind which often lend themselves to unintelligent orthodoxy, and even to violence and downright corruption, are apparently necessary to keep vital the knowledge of Christ and his teachings, the most powerful influence on behalf of virtue that humanity has ever been offered. As Richard Hooker pointed out, perhaps more tellingly than anyone else, the Reformation contained seeds which were ultimately to create grave religious weaknesses. Pursued to its logical conclusion, the rise of Protestantism, particularly in its Calvinist forms, left every man free to adopt his own individual interpretation of the truth. This made it relatively easy to alter dogma. It encouraged the disintegration of Protestantism into an ever larger number of sects, at the cost eventually of conviction about the importance of religion itself. Speaking of Henry VIII and the Reformation, a great English historian who was not insensible to the cruelties of religious persecution has written these words:

Then, now, and ever, it was, and remains true, that in this great matter of religion, in which to be right is the first condition of being right in anything—not variety of opinion, but unity—not the equal

---

[58] As quoted by Conyers Read, "The English Elements in Benjamin Franklin," *Pennsylvania Magazine of History and Biography*, July, 1940, p. 321.

license of the wise and the foolish to choose their belief—but an ordered harmony, where wisdom prescribes a law to ignorance, is the rule which reasonable men should most desire for themselves and for mankind.[59]

James Anthony Froude was not a Catholic, but an Anglican who eventually broke with the high-church movement. In his historical writings he never laid himself open to the charge of prejudice in favor of the Catholic Church.

When one comments upon the weaknesses and corruption of churches and ecclesiastical foundations, it is necessary to balance against these weaknesses and this corruption the preservation of the Christian faith itself, with its exaltation of the qualities of humility and love as opposed to the doctrines of force. The question of the worldly value of the Catholic Church would not be settled against the Church even if it were possible to show that professing Catholics have been only five per cent better in their temporal lives than the members of the Protestant sects and the Western peoples who have left the churches altogether. The question would not be settled against the Church if it could be shown that they were no better. It could not be settled even by showing that they were worse. All such comparisons beg the question whether the non-Catholics among the Western peoples may not be better than they would otherwise be through their knowledge of the faith and the ethical traditions associated with it, which the Church has done so much to preserve in its original spirit for nearly twenty centuries. This faith could never have been kept alive in the Roman Empire, and extended during the Dark Ages that followed, without a great Church organization. Few men who consider the Christian religion as we still have it today can feel as confident as some of our eighteenth-

[59] J. A. Froude, *History of England from the Fall of Wolsey to the Defeat of the Spanish Armada* (London, 1870), III, 62.

and nineteenth-century ancestors that the price was too high to pay. Unlike them, we have lived to see men tortured and extinguished, without even the honor of martyrdom often permitted by the Church to heretics. They have been tortured and extinguished for the sake only of worldly power. Without in any way condoning the Church for its treatment of heretics, we are forced to admit that the end for which the religious persecutions were carried on was less ghastly than the end of modern political persecutions. Churchmen at least believed that by burning heretics they were saving a much larger number of the human race from the same fate after death.

Let us hope that such barbarism as theirs may never be the price that our descendants pay for the return of religious faith. But let us not feel sure, as men like Gibbon and Buckle did in the eighteenth and nineteenth centuries, that the Reformation, the victory for religious toleration, and the decay of Christianity provide us with perpetual insurance against the return of such barbarism. Let us not even feel sure that without the Church we should have escaped the barbarism of medieval and early modern times, which the thinkers of the eighteenth and nineteenth centuries so justly censured. Who knows whether, without the Church, medieval men might have been, for some far less worthy cause than Christianity, at least five per cent more cruel than they were?

Today the Protestant churches and the Church of Rome are faced with a more critical task than any that has confronted the custodians of the Christian faith since the Reformation. The Protestant churches, especially in America, have become more and more compromised, by their efforts to adjust themselves to the teachings of natural science and to the material standards of the modern world, at the very time when the Western peoples need more than ever nonmaterial standards and a return to the principles for which Christ spoke through the gospel. The Catholic Church has not altogether escaped such compromises. What is more serious, it has not, in the face of the terrible political crisis of our times, offered any really effective resistance to the growing power of the arbitrary state. One waits in vain for a theologian who will read lessons to a dictator even in terms as strong as those Bossuet used in his funeral orations before the greatest prince in Christendom, Louis XIV. It is all very well to say that politics is of no concern to the Church. No Christian church which makes peace with anti-Christ on anti-Christian terms can remain a Christian church. There is widespread suspicion in the world that the totalitarian forms of government, in some of their manifestations, are fundamentally anti-Christian. Were the words "Render unto Caesar the things that are Caesar's" meant to cover the case in which Caesar claims powers which do not belong to him? If mankind today is to regain its soul, churchmen in high places need to show even greater courage than some of them have shown. Their courage will have to extend to criticism of the Church itself.

It often seems as if the actions of modern Catholics were based on the principle that the object of Christianity and religious beliefs is to maintain the Church, instead of on the principle that the purpose of the Church is to maintain faith and provide consolation for suffering men. If the churches are to reclaim a considerable proportion of the multitudes who have lost faith, they will have to provide leadership on a higher plane than has been revealed in recent years.[60] They will have to show themselves to a credulous and little-believing people, in whom the sparks of virtue and love nevertheless exist, as the true children of Christ. It may well be that this is beyond the power of the churches as they are at present constructed and organized. Their very organization some-

[60] Cf. below, chap. ix, sec. iii.

times prevents them from acting on critical issues on behalf of Christ.

The peoples of the West are in need of religion. They are in need of religious unity, in an age full of fads and fake religions. But, if we are not altogether mistaken, they need neither materialism nor a compromise with political persecution in the guise of religion. Whether or how the great need for faith can be filled is something no man can foresee. It can be filled only if religion succeeds in rising above the human limitations of our time, and in convincing men everywhere who are groping toward the good that it is at once true, divine, and eternal. It must lay emphasis more on substance than on form. It must welcome men into the faith less as a means of saving their souls and more as a means of saving the well-being of suffering and ill-guided humanity. Religious leaders will have to be, as the early Christians were, on the side of the humble and disinterested rather than on the side of the politically strong and of those whose interest in religion is to gain salvation for themselves. A church must come forward in the United States not primarily as a political but as a religious power, strong enough and courageous enough to re-create, with the help of Christ, that spiritual freedom for which Christianity at its best has stood. It will have to reconsider, not only the world, but church organization and power itself, in relation to the words, "Many that are first shall be last; and the last first." This is a hard doctrine to stomach in a country where the only test is worldly success.

The United States was not born a Catholic country. It is not today a Catholic country. The future of Catholicism here depends upon its making concessions, as well as in asking others to make them. There would seem to be a need for a Reformation, not only of the reformed churches but of the Catholic Church as well. Is it to come from within or from without? Is it to come at all? We cannot bring it about by recognizing the need for it. Purification and unification are only to be obtained from some higher mountain than that which the human intellect enables man to ascend.

The advice of the Savior to his disciples, as reported by St. Luke, is not perhaps irrelevant in concluding these remarks on religion. May not the words, "he that is not against us is for us," be applied to religious organization, to the Church? What He required was not fidelity to the Church or even to His disciples. What He required was fidelity to Him. "He that is not with me is against me; and he that gathereth not with me scattereth."[61]

61 Luke, 9:50; 11:23. Cf. Hocking, *op. cit.*, pp. 231–32, 234–36, 253, 269, 281.

VII

MORAL PHILOSOPHY

✺

FAITH is a gift, independent of and superior to wealth. It is not an enemy to material well-being here on earth in so far as such well-being is consistent with the good life of the individual, of the state, and of humanity. The Christian faith is an end in itself, because it holds out to mankind the hope of an ultimate society free from evil. It is also a means, in the sense that when it is genuine and pure it is bound to help human beings toward the attainment of goodness, wisdom, and beauty—the ultimate ends of man here on earth. Christianity provides a superhuman sanction for labor toward these ends.

Even if it comes about, the revival of faith as a civilizing force is bound to take time. It cannot solve our problems or restore reason to its proper place suddenly. For good or ill, neither the hope of a heaven nor the fear of a hell after death is very real in the English-speaking countries today. With the doubt which exists among some honorable people, especially in the United States, concerning the capacity of men to cultivate the good life on earth by working directly for religion,[1] with the doubt which exists among others concerning the capacity of any church worthily to represent Christianity, it would be discouraging—and let us hope untrue—to claim that labor toward the good life cannot be carried on without

[1] Cf. Frank H. Knight, "Religion and Ethics in Modern Civilization," *Journal of Liberal Religion*, III, No. 1 (1941), 4, 7.

faith. The road to faith may well be indirect. It is a comfort to know that the highest worldly ends are in no way hostile to the teachings of Christ.

Three hundred and fifty years ago, when the Christian religion was a matter of much more vital concern to men than it is now, the greatest English theologian wrote: "While riches be a thing which every man wisheth, no man of judgment esteems it better to be rich than to be wise, virtuous and religious." Richard Hooker's words suggest that even as profound a believer as he could regard wisdom and virtue as objects separate and distinct from religion, though complementary to it. No wise theologian has ever claimed that faith and revealed knowledge, by themselves, are adequate to meet all the problems of society or all those of the individuals who compose it. No wise theologian has claimed that faith makes reason, observation, and experiment unnecessary. Before the coming of Christ, the greatest Greeks did not regard it as futile to strive toward the objectives of virtue, wisdom, and beauty. The study of the nature of wisdom and virtue, the study of the conditions that are likely to make them less scarce commodities than they are today, are the province of moral philosophy. Philosophy could provide all men who devote themselves to the advancement and the transmission of knowledge with guideposts and a map, which would make possible the diffusion among mankind of the lofty, ideal conceptions of both knowledge and virtue.

Moral philosophy is properly concerned with the fullest happiness of the individual, of the state as a collection of individuals, and of humanity. Such happiness depends upon the establishment of the most perfect harmony possible between the needs of the body, the spirit, and the intelligence, with reason and its more humble companion, common sense, the master over both the body and the spirit. This is what Plato meant by happiness, and Aristotle was in agreement with him.

The ideal state would be one in which the needs of all the citizens for material comfort and security from violence are satisfied in the ways most compatible with the happiness of the citizens, in this Platonic and Aristotelian sense. In our time the ideal state need not involve slavery, as it did with the Greeks. It would be achieved by bringing the citizens into those occupations they were fitted to perform with the greatest happiness to themselves and to the community of which they form a part.

The word "happiness" should not be misunderstood. Like most words, it has no precise meaning for most people today. Contemporary Americans generally suppose that happiness means having a good time. Everyone, we are told, has his own way of having a good time. "One man's meat is another man's poison" is a generalization that applies not only to diet but to everything man has to do with.

Happiness has had a different meaning for philosophers, at any rate until very recently. In the Aristotelian sense, happiness is not a matter of individual whim. It consists not in seeking pleasure for its own sake, but in gaining it from doing the right things or behaving in the right way, according to the accumulated wisdom of the human race. The concept of happiness, therefore, takes for granted the existence of certain absolute values; it takes for granted the existence of good moral, intellectual, and artistic habits. As everyone who understands words and who has read Aristotle's *Ethics* should know, the existence of good habits does not depend upon the establishment of fixed rules of conduct that will fit every situation. There are certain actions—such as murder, theft, and adultery—which Aristotle regarded as wrong altogether. The "happiness" which some modern psychologists might claim is obtained from committing such acts is counterfeit happiness. It is not happiness in the Aristotelian sense, which is based upon a moral code. But Aristotle saw that morality generally consists in the most appropriate response to a given situation, the action that is most perfectly in accord with wisdom under the circumstances. Circumstances differ greatly. They are obviously not the same now as in Aristotle's time. This does not mean that a man is made "happy" at any time by doing what he pleases without regard to common principles. Since the rise of Christianity, happiness for Christians is related to the practice of the Christian moral virtues—humility, liberality, chastity, gentleness, temperance, patience, and diligence. These virtues do not differ fundamentally from the good habits set forth in the works of both Plato and Aristotle. Happiness consists in effort, not in the absence of effort. It does not consist in the effort to please someone for your own advantage; it consists in the effort to do right.

It will be obvious that, unlike the economic science of Adam Smith and most of his English followers through Alfred Marshall, moral philosophy does not concern itself exclusively or even primarily with material happiness. Unlike the newer economic science, moral philosophy does not take the wants of human beings, whether they are material or not, as given, and then concern itself with the conditions which would enable men to satisfy their wants to the fullest possible extent regardless of the consequences for goodness, wisdom, and beauty.

History shows us that the nature of men's wants is continually changing. In Elizabethan England, for example, ale and beer were regarded as, after bread, the mainstays of nourishment. A passage in *Othello* suggests that the Elizabethans regarded the drinking powers of Englishmen as superior to those of other peoples. Iago shouts: "Some wine, ho!" and sings a drinking song. "'Fore Heaven, an excellent song," says Cassio, his lieutenant. "I learn'd it in England, where (indeed) they are most potent in potting; your Dane, your German, and your swag-belli'd Hollander . . . . are nothing to your English . . . . he drinks you, with facility, your Dane dead drunk; he sweats not to overthrow your Almain; he gives your Hollander a vomit ere the next pottle can be fill'd."

The statistics which moderns love show that this was no idle boast. According to Mr. Colin Clark, the Englishmen gainfully employed were, on the average, approximately three times as well off in international units of real income on the eve of the present war as at the end of the seventeenth century.[2] At that time one of Clark's intellectual fathers, Gregory King, estimated that almost a sixth of the national income in England was spent on alcoholic drink in various forms, as compared with about a ninth in France and about a tenth in Holland. In England the expenditure per head on drink was about twice as great as in France and much greater than in Holland.[3] The beer and ale consumed per capita was at least four times what it is in modern England; perhaps twenty times or more what it is in the United States. In Shakespeare's day the real income of the English worker was probably somewhat less than in the late seventeenth century. But the per capita consumption of alcoholic drink was probably even greater.[4] The Elizabethans were not only capable of wonderful feats in drinking bouts; drink formed, after bread, the chief element in the diet of the common man. He consumed nearly as much in a day as the modern American ordinarily does in a month. For all that, the wits of the Elizabethans were not conspicuously inferior to ours.

[2] *The Conditions of Economic Progress* (London, 1940), p. 83.

[3] Gregory King, *Natural and Political Observations and Conclusions upon the State and Condition of England* (1696) (bound with George Chalmers, *Estimate of the Comparative Strength of Great Britain* [London, 1804]), pp. 47, 64–65, 67. Cf. Colin Clark, *National Income and Outlay* (London, 1937), p. xvii.

[4] J. U. Nef, "Industrial Growth in France and England, 1540–1640," *Journal of Political Economy*, XLIV, No. 5 (1936), 647–48; "Prices and Industrial Capitalism in France and England, 1540–1640," *Economic History Review*, VII, No. 2 (1937), 165, 168–69, 172–73.

Another comparison between the two periods also shows how wants change, though the physical benefit of the change in this case is less apparent than in the first. In the sixteenth century the European workman regarded religious worship as hardly less essential to his well-being than food and drink. When large industrial establishments were laid out for the manufacture of alum, metal, or salt, the owners—whether they were princes, nobles, or laymen—always built chapels for worship as part of the plant. They provided priests or pastors to conduct the services. Such wants as these are far less urgent among the modern workers. The industrial entrepreneur in America who included religious facilities as part of his costs of production would be regarded as somewhat eccentric.

From the point of view of learning there are, broadly speaking, two possible attitudes toward changing human wants. It is possible to say that the changes are not the concern of learned men. Wants should be determined by private taste. The historian, the sociologist, or the anthropologist may collect data on the wants of different peoples at the same or different periods of history. They may compare them as a matter of scientific curiosity. They may discuss the effect of indulging them, in so far as the physical and the biological sciences seem to warrant tentative conclusions on that subject. If, for example, it can be shown that constant drinking shortens the average length of life, it follows that men in a society where drink is used as a food will have a shorter life-expectancy, *if other things are equal*, than men in a society where little beer or wine is drunk. That seems obvious enough. In the study of man, the application of scientific methods sometimes does little more than emphasize the obvious. But any judgment concerning the moral or aesthetic or even the social value of different wants for the individual or for society lies outside the province of the learned man. Such is the first position that can be taken in this matter of human happiness.

What other general attitude can learning adopt? It can attempt to discover what is good for man and for mankind—morally, intellectually, and aesthetically. It can set about to decide tentatively, with reason as a guide and experience as its helpmate, what wants and what combinations of wants contribute most to the happiness of the individual, the nation, and humanity.

The second attitude toward wants is properly that of the moral philosopher. Like religion, moral philosophy is concerned with values. For the moral philosopher, happiness need not be left entirely to chance. If it were possible for wise men to agree to some extent on the order of goods in a world full of riches and people as never before, and brought into contact with one another to a greater extent than ever before, then something might be done to guide mankind, intelligently and disinterestedly, in the direction of their better desires. Something might be done to cultivate in them a love of the best things in life for themselves and their fellow-men. By indicating, however imperfectly, the nature of the ideal, as moral philosophy should try to do, it might enable the world to fall less far short of the ideal than it would otherwise fall. It might light a beacon for the guidance of future generations, as Plato and Aristotle did some twenty-three hundred years ago.

One objection frequently raised today to the study of moral philosophy in this sense is that there is no possible way of distinguishing sharply between good and evil. Yet perhaps human values have not been so completely lost that the ordinary man would consider $5,000 spent in the white-slave traffic equally desirable with the $5,000 or so that were probably required to feed, clothe, and house Hogarth while he painted his famous pictures of "The Rake's Progress" and "Marriage à la Mode," depicting the consequences of earthly indulgence. The fact that people are willing to pay for prostitutes, no less readily than for paintings which strive to drive home moral lessons, does not prove that the choice between the two is a matter of indifference for society. It is true that the philosophical value of the same want is not necessarily the same in different places or at different periods in the same place. It should be possible, nevertheless, to work out tentatively the relative merits of different wants, in terms of moral, intellectual, and aesthetic values. It should also be possible to determine tentatively how far to give priority to such values as over against the purely material values of increasing the volume of production and consumption. It should also be possible to determine tentatively how the production and distribution of economic goods and services can be made to contribute to the higher values. All this should be more easily possible now than ever before, with the vast amount of data put at our disposal by the natural and the biological sciences, as well as by the humanities and social sciences.

The very fact that human wants change shows that these great philosophical questions of the relative moral, intellectual, and aesthetic value of different kinds of wants, judged in terms of human happiness, are a part of human experience. It shows that moral philosophy should not be divorced from life, that it should aim to guide wants in directions that will contribute to human happiness. In the ideally ordered society, all branches of learning and all departments of education would be allied with moral philosophy in this aim. Thus the realm of moral philosophy is only less extensive and less important than that of theology. It will no more remain vacant, if wise and virtuous and disinterested men cease to cultivate it, than will the realm of theology. In the United States, and in the Western world generally at present, this territory which is of such great importance to mankind, this territory which might be of supreme importance for the future of civilization, is not being cultivated by the learned world at all effectively. It is denied that problems of value, in the moral, intellectual, and aesthetic sense, are proper subjects of impartial inquiry and study. Each person, it is said, is the best judge of his own wants. When there is a conflict between the desires of various persons, it can be resolved by a vote of the majority. That is the only way to avoid dictatorship.

Let us consider the consequences of such a position. Leaving aside any question of the morality of most persons (leaving aside the common assumption that all persons are equally intelligent or foolish, equally good or bad, unless they are put in asylums or locked up in jails), we are assuming that in the modern world everyone knows what he wants. We are assuming, further, that everyone is in fact free to choose without the intervention of any external interested influence.

It is enough to state these assumptions to see that they are unwarranted. No man, no matter how strong and wise he feels himself to be, is prepared to act on every issue that confronts him without advice or guidance. In view of the decrease in moral, intellectual, and aesthetic training, fewer persons have a genuine and decided preference one way or another today than a century or more ago. With the decrease in the knowledge most people possess of the way in which the commodities they eat and use are produced and prepared, they have no basis for judging even material values. So they seek advice. There is no lack of "experts" to supply them with it on special subjects, though a man does not always find the perfect agreement that would be reassuring if he takes the trouble to consult more than a single expert.

But where are we to seek guidance when it comes to a choice involving matters of morality, social justice, wisdom, or beauty? The natural place to turn is to a priest or pastor, if one belongs to a church, or to a professor or teacher, or to one's father or mother, brother or sister, or intimate friend. Yet most of these persons, not excepting the pastor and even the priest, have been trained in the modern doctrine (if it can be properly called a doctrine) that there is nothing approaching philosophical standards. Disagreement on philosophical issues is now frequently regarded as beneficial to society. This is not the disagreement of reasoned argument, which contributes to knowledge because distinctions are made in the interest of greater truth, with the object of reaching better, deeper, and more comprehensive generalizations. This is disagreement for the sake of disagreement, disagreement for the sake of the ego. Americans take pleasure in saying that there are a great many sides to every question. That enables anyone to say and do just what he likes with a completely free conscience and with an almost completely empty mind. The lack of any firm judgments which people respect, in matters of morality, intelligence, or beauty, is not surprising when we remember that moral philosophy in the Platonic or Aristotelian sense—the field of human values—has been almost entirely abandoned by learning. We go to doctors and surgeons to find out how to keep well. We go to investment counselors to find out how to invest our money. We go to interior decorators to find out how to furnish our flats. When the advice we obtain from the three experts creates a serious moral or intellectual issue, as it often does, we have only our own principles to fall back upon—those of us who retain any. It rarely occurs to us that books written by wise men of the past might help us. When it does, we realize that we have wasted our lives without reading them for this purpose and that we cannot make up overnight for an ill-spent childhood and youth. There can be no index to wisdom, but we find ourselves in an age where indexes and other short cuts (useful as guides to information) are wrongly regarded as substitutes for culture. We have experts in every field except the supremely important one which encompasses all the others. In that alone are the decisions left to private tastes and eccentricities.

It is a mistake, nevertheless, to assume that the individual's predilections—his "own philosophy" as he is fond of calling them—are in fact determined without outside influences. We all take advice without knowing it, much as Molière's famous would-be gentleman talked prose without discovering what he was about until he hired a teacher to instruct him in the manners of polite society. In matters of morality, intelligence, and aesthetics, pressure is brought to bear on us from the time we are born. It is brought to bear on us by the mores of our schoolfellows and playmates, by the very lack of judgment concerning these great problems which we generally find in our parents and our friends, our teachers and the ministers in the churches we visit, if we happen to go to any. More interested pressure comes, as we grow older, from advertisers and from the business men they represent. These persons are eager to enlist us as consumers and, less frequently, as workers. Politicians seek our votes—sometimes for purposes that are lacking in the finer shades of ethics. The very fact that no one has referred us in early life to principles, or led us to saturate ourselves with books where they can be found, enables any person with sufficient money or publicity to give advice and to gain influence concerning current issues. Such advice is full of philosophical implications. In a society which recognizes no special competence except in the limited cases susceptible to scientific proof, such advice masquerades frequently as knowledge. Men use it "to make friends and influence people" on matters of morality, social justice, and aesthetics, not always with the best motives and almost never with the best thought.

Moral and even intellectual and aesthetic issues are often placed at the mercy of anyone who finds it advantageous to direct them for purposes of business, politics, or graft. In the universities the learned man, if he is also a good man, because of his very modesty is made to regard any "prejudice" he may have in favor of impersonal and durable standards as a private matter, if not an idiosyncrasy. He is allowed to try to guide his own life by these "prejudices," but if he speaks of them in public or adjusts his learned activities to them, his efforts are dismissed as "evangelical." A pastor tells him that he should not speak on behalf of goodness unless he joins the local church. If he joins it he must leave matters of morality to his pastor, who has usually ceased to have any firm judgments concerning them. If he happens to mention his "prejudices" to his colleagues and suggests that it might be worth while for others to act on them, he is told that he takes life too seriously.

Is it better for man to have matters of morality, intelligence, and beauty settled exclusively by the give and take of the market place and by the improvised daily relations between men and women—sometimes moral, sometimes amoral, and at least occasionally immoral—or is it better to have a few gifted men who devote their whole lives to these questions, who are passionately seeking to benefit mankind, with no hope of private gain beyond a competent salary, exercise an influence in the realm of moral philosophy? Some of those who take the first view have been saying that time will repair all the evils which seem to flow from it. They are like the people in a pacifistically minded country who hope and say that time will take its enemies off its hands. Time is neutral. Unless wise men grasp its opportunities and work for good, evil will gain the day. On the whole, time worked in favor of morality and justice in the nineteenth century. This was largely because ancient Christian and humanist traditions influenced men to try to make it work that way. Now that standards have broken down, is there not danger that bad money will drive out good? In the natural sciences we rightly take it for granted that special gifts, training, and study, together with special enthusiasm for the subject, confer on a man a particular competence. Is it only on behalf of human welfare generally that the scholar is to be prohibited from showing enthusiasm and from exercising to the full the powers of his mind, tempered and fortified by his love of humanity? Is it only in the department of human happiness that the universities are to hang up a sign, "To Let"?

Whatever answers the United States gives to these questions, it is hardly possible to claim that affirmative answers are the best means of protecting us from dictatorship. If there are no skilled and impartial judgments on matters of morality, intelligence, and beauty, what is to prevent a political leader whose only object is power from moving into the empty house? As Gilson has said, "The problem of philosophical unity is in itself an essentially philosophical problem, and unless philosophers tackle it, somebody else will solve it for them, and probably against them."[5]

I. MORAL PHILOSOPHY AND SCIENCE

Some persons may say, of course, that, notwithstanding his great reputation and notwithstanding what happened in June, 1940, M. Gilson was talking nonsense. It is one of the charms of the "freedom" we enjoy in all affairs pertaining to the mind that every person, whether learned or not, is free to berate any learned man, living or dead, no matter how eminent, who makes a judgment independent of scientific data, without examining his case at all, let alone paying him the compliment of studying and reflecting upon it. If we are not to fall into this error of what Mr. Hutchins once called "freedom from thinking," it is incumbent upon us and upon M. Gilson to consider the case that is presented against him.

Modern learning has, it is said, at least two ways of determining whether wants are desirable, at least two ways of measuring values. One is the pragmatic test of seeing whether a set of propositions emanating from scholars works. In the

[5] Etienne Gilson, *Medieval Universalism* (New York, 1937), p. 14.

minds of the pragmatic philosophers this meant asking the question, Do these propositions contribute to the welfare of the community? But, since that question is exceedingly difficult to answer and since it was coupled with the idea that the experience of communities, as distinct from the judgment of the trained mind which cannot be simply a mirror of that experience, is the best judge of what will benefit them, the question asked by social scientists is generally a far simpler one. It is this: Does the public take up the propositions or are they rejected?

The other and closely allied method of determining values is to subject these propositions to scientific examination. This can be done by making experiments or by the application of some kind of objective tests.

Let us consider, first, the pragmatic test. It is perfectly true that in the long run ideas, to be effective, must influence a considerable number of persons. This does not mean that other ideas, which do not catch on, might not benefit the human race more than those which are successful. Still less does it mean that the ideas which benefit mankind most are those which are immediately popular. In the modern United States, the test of popularity, or "influence" as it is frequently called, is generally that what is right is what pays or what a majority supports. This assumes that the current public view of moral, intellectual, and aesthetic values is the best possible view. Now this is a proposition for which we have no scientific proof whatever. Unless moral philosophy is cultivated in relation to the whole of knowledge, unless the impartial, wise, carefully trained mind, impelled by a love of the human race and a love of beauty, is encouraged to work according to the needs which it finds in this field and to make such uses of special studies as are appropriate to its purpose, no evidence of value can be offered either for or against the proposition. Experience, as John Stuart Mill suggested, is against it. "No government, by a democracy or a *numerous* aristocracy," he wrote, "either in its political acts or in the opinions, qualities, and tone of mind which it fosters, ever did or could rise above mediocrity, except in so far as the sovereign Many have let themselves be guided . . . . by the counsels and influence of a more highly gifted and instructed One or Few. The initiative in all wise or noble Things, comes and must come from individuals; generally at first from some one individual."[6] It is just this lesson which the sovereign "Many" in the United States today have forgotten. Is it an undemocratic lesson? Mill, at any rate, has not been usually regarded as a champion of totalitarianism or of any form of despotism. In view of his judgment, it would be of help to those persons who are interested in getting at the truth, and who believe that human wants work out for the best if left to take their course, to offer their opinion as a hypothesis to the moral philosopher, if and when he appears.

Objections will be raised to such a course. The first is that moral philosophy cannot be scientific. "The true," writes John Dewey, "means the verified and means nothing else."[7] The second is that the propositions which scholars offer the public already have scientific validity. This leads us to the experiments and objective tests which are supposed to justify laissez faire in the realm of moral philosophy. The propositions have already been tested in the social laboratory or by one of the many new "techniques" (as they are called) which "social scientists" have been devising. It is the special virtue of several modern philosophies that, unlike the ancient philosophies which (to the great benefit of the human race) they have replaced, they rest not on opinion but on "science." The public and the economic and political leaders are not mak-

---

[6] *On Liberty* (New York, 1898), p. 119.

[7] *Reconstruction in Philosophy* (New York, 1920), p. 160. Cf. John Herman Randall, *Our Changing Civilization* (New York, 1929), p. 338.

ing a choice without guidance. They are offered a great number of packages. Many of these packages are stamped with a scientific trade-mark. The public are free to decide what weight to give to the various brands which bear it. If they are foolish enough to turn to one which bears no scientific trade-mark, the scientists are not to blame.

Now the answer to these objections is that both are true, and that both illustrate the need for treating moral philosophy, along with religion and art, as one of the principal ends of civilized society. Aristotle pointed out that ethics could never be an exact science. But what should determine the value of a science is not the degree of precision possible within it, but its importance for human welfare. We have attempted to show that methods derived from natural science for the investigation of human societies are insufficient for the solution of every problem that confronts the humanities and the social sciences.[8] Let us offer one further example of the misdirected use of scientific methods.

I recently listened to a discussion between two foreign and two American university men. All four were both scholars and also what is at present called by the rather inelegant name of "educators." The word always reminds one of those crackers that as children we were encouraged to eat. It is apparently hoped that the "educators" will have a wholesome effect upon the students of the same material kind claimed for the crackers. The subject of this particular discussion was the training of students in the reading, writing, and speaking of foreign languages. One of the Americans referred to the economy of teaching people languages in long stretches early in childhood, if possible by putting them into situations where they had to carry on all their studies and even amusements in foreign tongues. The second American objected. One of the educational foundations, he said, had recently sponsored a scientific inquiry into the question of the best age for

[8] See above, chap. iv, sec. ii.

teaching languages. Research had shown that a person could generally learn better and with less expenditure of time and labor at fifty than at ten. To his surprise, the two foreign scholars, both of whom had been trained in the classical tradition, threw up their hands. In unison they exclaimed: "It simply isn't so!"

It is quite possible, of course, that for the purpose of acquiring a vocabulary in connection with some specialty the conclusions reached after this "scientific" research are correct. A child would have much less knowledge of the specialty than a person who had worked at it all his life. But if the man of fifty had learned the language as a child, he could have got up the vocabulary of his specialty at fifty in a small fraction of the time that would be required if he had not. The statement the learned American made on the basis of the scientific research is not only misleading but entirely unscientific. This illustrates the mistake of trying to apply so-called "scientific methods" to matters where the observation and, above all, the judgment of wise, experienced, and well-read men are better guides.

Even in matters where scientific investigations are appropriate, where they provide a fruitful way of adding to our knowledge, the results obtained are always extremely partial from the standpoint of a unified philosophy. As almost all wise scientists are ready to admit, scientific conclusions are morally, socially, and aesthetically neutral. So we cannot be sure that the stamp of approval which learning at present puts on a package of propositions, connected with the ordering of society, is actually scientifically valuable. Should we, on the basis of the research sponsored by the foundation just referred to, abandon all teaching of foreign languages until men and women reach upper middle life? Even with the increase in life-expectancy, can we assume it will be more useful for a man or woman to learn a language at fifty than at ten?

The view that moral philosophy is not a science in the

sense that chemistry or physics is a science is a sound one. The attempt to make moral philosophy into this kind of science can end up only by confusing it with logic or psychology or some other branch of knowledge more closely related to the natural sciences. While the results of scientific, historical, and anthropological research can be of great importance to philosophy, philosophical inquiries themselves cannot be conducted primarily under the direction of methods appropriate to the study of the natural sciences. Moral philosophy cannot be partial, as any particular science must be, any more than it can be indifferent to problems of good and evil. It can never take anything for granted. It can never say, as some other disciplines so easily can, "other things being equal." In reaching their results, moral philosophers must strive to take into account all aspects of matter and of human beings as individuals, as members of an institution, of a community, of a nation, and of the world. They must attempt to command the essentials of all the learned disciplines. For such labor scientific method has to be a servant, not a master. What is required above all in philosophy, as in art, is genius, together with a long and disciplined training in the thought and culture of the race. The philosopher must have complete freedom, in so far as a human being can attain it, from every kind of partiality, save partiality for the good, the true, and the beautiful. The philosopher makes use of logic and of the results of scientific experiments and of the observation of measurable data when he finds them appropriate to his philosophical problems. He also uses intuition and the wisdom of the past. The more perfectly he can use all these instruments in their proper places, the better for his results. But the vital matter is that he should use them all as philosophy demands and not allow any to take the place of philosophy as a guiding principle beneath the edifice that he builds. The very attitude of scientific individualism, which has come to pervade learning, takes away that breath of humanity indispensable to philosophy. The doctrine of the market place—"every man for himself"—should have no influence on philosophers. The attitude now widely regarded as a mark of the sound scientist —"I cultivate my own field without relation to the rest"— is no better than a somewhat sophisticated version of that doctrine.

Few men, it may be said, could possibly live in so rarefied a realm as that of moral philosophy as we have pictured it. This is true. It does not follow that its reclamation for learning would be of no benefit to mankind. It does not follow that even persons who have not the endowment to find themselves at home in it cannot do something, however small, to lead wise men to cultivate it in the future. A philosopher who succeeds in moving in that high realm cannot do so without taking into account the results of the scholarship to which so many tens of thousands of conscientious workers have contributed during the past two centuries. It is equally true that if scholars recognized the real meaning and high purpose of moral philosophy, enriched by recent scholarship, it would make possible in many separate branches of knowledge the creation of works of greater benefit to mankind than most of those which at present issue from American universities. Scholars would come gradually to understand that the moral and intellectual purpose and the artistic skill and meaning, behind a work destined for publication, are of the first importance. Thus they might be able to reorganize the whole study of man according to an intelligent, orderly, and philosophical plan.

Facts are necessary to a book; but a collection of facts is not a book. Any book worthy of the name has an inner necessity that develops in the mind of its author as he writes it, and can develop only when he is gifted with reason, spirit, and a sense of beauty. If a collection of facts were a book, there would be nothing to prevent the multiplication of master-pieces as rapidly as radio receiving sets or electric refrigerators. It follows that no books worthy of the name will be written in the future if reason and art are effectively denied.

Natural science today has little to fear from the revival of a genuine metaphysics. The true metaphysician will always welcome and make use of new scientific knowledge, just as the true scientist will always derive inspiration and help from the sound restatement of metaphysical truths that is now so greatly needed. But neither the true metaphysician nor the humbler scholars who wish to help him on his way will regard natural science as a substitute for philosophy and theology, as do most of the writers of the hundreds of books and thousands of articles on philosophical and theological subjects that appear every year in the United States. The chief dangers today are not, as American university men seem to fear, that natural science and the scientific method will be stifled by philosophy as in the later Middle Ages, or that philosophy will be solidified in a single system of what our contemporaries describe as "absolutes." The chief danger is that ethics in the ancient Aristotelian sense will die from lack of cultivation. For civilized man that would be, as an Englishman in Shakespeare's time might have said, a "sore alteration."

II. MORAL PHILOSOPHY AND WEALTH

The true moral philosopher looks with favor upon the increase in material wealth, for individuals or for nations, only in so far as riches contribute to general happiness. In dealing with the relation of wealth to general happiness, as in all philosophical subjects, the philosopher has to establish himself in the high kingdom of generalization and remain there. Only there is it possible to make statements of truth that will endure. It is not for the philosopher, as a philosopher, to take a position on controversial and transient issues.

Action has to be left to the statesman, the legislator, the judge, the administrator, and other men of affairs. The philosopher's task is to formulate and develop principles that can guide and fortify in each and all of his acts the public man seeking the good of his country and humanity. While these principles have no specific relation to a particular action—such as a senator's vote on a piece of child-labor legislation or a bill raising the income tax—they can infuse into public men (and likewise into scholars and teachers who deal with narrower subjects than philosophy) the spirit in which they should make each of their practical decisions. The philosopher can show them the ends toward which all their actions should be directed. With the present poverty of philosophy, the denial of the existence of truth, and the confusion over the nature of democracy, most public men in the United States have no guide but opinion—expressed in hastily written newspaper editorials and in petitions and telegrams fired at the governing authorities under the aegis of pressure groups. Such opinion is designed to affect the action of public men in choosing between means. Shall the tariff be raised? Shall money be appropriated for another battleship? If the public office-holder knows his job he will be a far better judge of the technical matters that are of primary importance in a choice of means than the pressure groups and most of the organs of publicity that presume to tell him what to do and vie with each other to push him this way and that.

What the public man needs is guidance concerning ends. He can find it only in the wisdom of the past, kept alive by disinterested philosophers and thinkers of the present. Today the statesman who is seeking the good of the United States and of mankind will do far better to devote most of the time he now spends examining petitions or telegrams and reading newspapers or magazines, to Plato and Aristotle, Herodotus and Thucydides, or even to Dante and Shakespeare. He can be sure that the motives of such sages and poets in guiding him are not suspect, that they are not seeking to drown him in information or misinformation. Their counsel will help him to rise above the heat of the moment. It will help to arouse in him the inner voice that is present to some degree in all sensitive persons and that is no person's private property. In these ways the public man will be helped to order his acts to a great purpose. He will have a firm basis for choosing between means.

In formulating principles for economic and political life, the moral philosopher's objects should be clear. They are to promote the production of wealth and to encourage its distribution in ways that will contribute to goodness, wisdom, and beauty. Philosophy alone can relate all human activities to these ultimate worldly ends. Each of them is independent of the other two, but not in fundamental conflict with them. Philosophy must not starve one for the sake of the others, for happiness depends upon the cultivation of all three.

As happiness is the end sought by moral philosophy, power and influence should be granted to individuals, parties, and institutions only if they are likely, according to the impartial views of wise men, to contribute to happiness. This does not mean that all men should be treated as equal in intelligence, knowledge, administrative capacity, or artistry. They are not so. Only a society lacking in intelligence will fail to recognize it. As Pascal wrote in his notes, "A mesure qu'on a plus d'esprit, on trouve qu'il y a plus d'hommes originaux. Les gens du commun ne trouvent pas de différence entre les hommes."[9] Will these remarks be attributed to their author's bias? Will it be said that Pascal was indulging in propaganda? The difficulty in the way of establishing such

[9] "In proportion as one has intelligence, one finds there are men of originality. It is common men who cannot discover any difference between men" (*Les Pensées*, ed. Adolphe Espiard [Paris, n.d.], I, 59).

contentions would be considerable. By general acknowledg-
ment Pascal was a wise as well as a saintly man, one who
possessed the very highest reasoning powers. There is not a
shred of evidence that he hoped the notes which he jotted
down in his seclusion at Port-Royal, where he went to await
death, would bring him any sort of worldly advantage.

In so far as possible, the body politic should be so constructed and the body economic so ordered that each individual will be given weight proportionate to his power to
contribute to the happiness of the community. The moral
philosopher should occupy a place apart. He should stand to
gain in no way personally from the adoption of any of the
measures he advocates. He is concerned with impartial inquiry, with ideas, and with values. From such a vantage point
he is in a unique position to advise and to guide mankind.

What was done to some extent, especially in the English-
speaking countries, from the seventeenth until the twentieth
centuries, was to give men an influence within states com-
mensurate to their contribution to the material welfare of the
community. The part played by Hobbes, Descartes, and especially Francis Bacon, together with their successors, in producing a state of mind among the people favorable to material
progress and thus in shaping laws and political institutions in
a manner likely to contribute to riches, health, and long life,
is not adequately appreciated. Our age has become obsessed
with the view that a man's mind is a powerless victim of circumstances. It is well to remember that, as a shrewd Frenchman has put it, "there is no historical fatality except when one
believes in such a thing." Our ancestors in the sixteenth and
seventeenth centuries were far from thinking that the mind
was incapable of independent action. One should allow for
the conditions of their time, for the part played by the remarkable economic progress in Great Britain and Holland at
the beginning of the seventeenth century in nourishing the

philosophies of Hobbes, Descartes, and Bacon. After that has been done, it is still impossible to resist the conclusion that their minds, together with those of less prominent men who thought as they did and impressed their fellows, were positive factors in building up the modern industrialized world, with its exceedingly high material standards of living.[10] The philosophical movements that these men helped to start came to bear tremendous fruit only many generations after they were dead. They derived no personal advantage from the ideas they propagated. If they had felt, as Uncle Joe Cannon is said to have felt, that they need do nothing for posterity because posterity had done nothing for them, they would hardly have written as they did.

Bacon's philosophy, like the much more subtle philosophy of some of his successors who were in essential agreement with him about health and wealth, was one-sided. It made man's material well-being the primary, and almost the exclusive, end of human existence. This led eventually to the popular view, so widespread in the United States, that economic and general welfare can be regarded for all practical purposes— and thought has been largely lost in practical purposes—as identical.

In spite of its partiality, the philosophy of material improvement has been of great benefit to man. It grew up at a time when the orthodox philosophy, derived from the classical and medieval schools, often raised singularly unintelligent opposition to advances in the natural sciences and to improvements in the material side of life. As a reaction against a philosophical outlook that was also partial, the "new philosophy" was pulling, however violently, in the right direction.[11] It was pulling the mind away from error, although as a

[10] I hope to offer evidence on behalf of this conclusion in an essay that I have in hand on philosophy and civilization in France and England, 1540–1640.

[11] Cf. above, chap. v, sec. i.

doctrine it never contained anything like a perfect statement of truth. By focusing the attention of men on the opportunities for material improvement opened to them by new continents, abundant new natural resources, and freedom from the almost continual warfare that had been waged between the peoples of Europe, the new philosophy helped the Europeans, led by the British, to create a world far richer in the volume of commodities produced than any achieved by earlier civilizations.

For a number of generations, the one-sidedness of the "new philosophy" was offset, to a considerable extent, by the persistence of ancient humanistic traditions and by the continued power of the Christian religion. Tradition and religion stressed the value of wisdom, goodness, and beauty. The one-sidedness of the "new philosophy" was also offset by the influence of other philosophers who did not share its prejudices. In spite of the enthusiasm which he expressed in one of his works for material improvement, Descartes' influence was thrown mainly on the side of elegance. He overstressed the independent power of the mind, particularly what Pascal called the geometrical side of the mind, and denied the speculative value of natural knowledge. While this led him into another kind of philosophical error from that of Bacon, an error such as never marred the thought of Plato, Aristotle, or Aquinas, Descartes' philosophy provided something of an antidote to the growing materialism inherent in the thought of Bacon and Hobbes. In the seventeenth century French civilization made the most of this antidote, at a time when Englishmen were more easily seduced than Frenchmen by the promises which natural science held out for material improvement. France used the Cartesian philosophy in the cause of beauty, balance, finish, and sweetness. At the same time France drew on the thought of the great Jansenist philosophers, Pascal and Nicole, who exalted the highest moral conduct as the primary end of existence. The proper position of natural science in the realm of learning was explained in these words by the greatest French philosopher of the late seventeenth century, Father Malebranche:

Les hommes peuvent regarder l'astronomie, la chimie et presque toutes les autres sciences, comme des divertissements d'un honnête homme [he wrote in his *Search after Truth*], mais ils ne doivent pas se laisser suprendre par leur éclat ni les préférer à la science de l'homme. ... La plus belle, la plus agréable et la plus nécessaire de toute nos connaissances est sans doute la connaissance de nous-mêmes. De toutes les sciences humaines, la science de l'homme est la plus digne de l'homme.[12]

As built up in the seventeenth century, French civilization had a tremendous influence in Europe. Its influence was by no means negligible in England and even in America. It helped restrain the excesses in thought to which the "new philosophy" of the English naturally led. The values for which French civilization stood were not altogether neglected even in Victorian England. Newman, Ruskin, and Arnold, each in his own way, helped to remind Englishmen that, although economic pursuits are, as their younger contemporary, Alfred Marshall, defined them, the "ordinary business of life," this does not justify learned men in measuring civilization in terms of the volume of production or the quantity of real income, or in making economics, in Marshall's sense, independent of philosophy. Still less does it justify learned men in making economics, in Marshall's sense, a substitute for philosophy. To do so is to identify thought with the ordinary business of life when, to have any substance, thought

[12] "Astronomy, Chymistry, and most of the other Sciences may be looked on as proper Divertisements for a Gentleman. But Men should never be enamour'd with their Gayety, nor prefer them before the Science of Humane Nature. . . . . The finest, the most delightful, and most necessary Knowledge, is undoubtedly that of Our Selves. Of all Humane Sciences, that concerning Man is the most worthy of Man" (T. Taylor, *Father Malebranche His . . . . Search after Truth* [London, 1700], Preface).

must be extraordinary. To do so, consequently, is to destroy thought and to make what is dressed up to resemble it as transient and fleeting as changing economic conditions. Against this destructive process Newman, Ruskin, and Arnold did what they could. Tawney has carried this humanistic tradition into the twentieth century.

During recent decades the defenses provided, both by the ancient traditions and beliefs in which Western civilization was reared and by philosophers who emphasized the importance of reason and morality, have broken down. While France and England have not lost altogether the general culture that nourished European civilization since the early seventeenth century, this culture has been weakened in both countries. What is perhaps still more serious for the faith in man as a rational being, striving toward the good, the true, and the beautiful, the authority of French and English culture in the Western world has dwindled since the middle of the nineteenth century as the two countries have lost their economic and political ascendancy to Germany and the United States.

In neither Germany nor the United States were the ancient Christian and humanist traditions and beliefs as deeply rooted in the experience of creative minds as in France and England. In neither was the emphasis on reason and goodness as ends of human existence as intense. Germany shared in and contributed to the Gothic civilization, with its important classical ingredients, during the twelfth and thirteenth centuries. She borrowed copiously from Italian civilization at the time of the Renaissance and from French and English civilization in the eighteenth and nineteenth centuries. But in Germany the characteristics of classical civilization and Christian culture were eventually fused with a more ancient German tradition in which efficiency and force were dominant. That tradition has now subordinated all the other ingredients derived at home and imported from abroad. A doctrine of force has been made the instrument of national policy. For the time, at least, more moderate doctrines have been denied the right to live. The cult that man exists for the state has been embellished by the claim that the human race is divided into masters and slaves and that overlordship is the mission of the Germans.

In so far as the United States can be said to have developed a characteristic philosophy, it is one which measures the happiness of the community in terms of the physical health, the length of life, and the quantity of material wealth of its citizens. Moral and aesthetic considerations are almost entirely ignored, because it is taken for granted that there can be no firm standards in connection with either. The intelligence is denied a role independent of scientific inquiry. Experiment, together with the examination of measurable data, controls the intelligence—not the intelligence, observation and experiment. As Dewey explains in one of his books, pragmatism is the logical development of the Baconian philosophy, purged of all the mystical and transcendental elements present in the European philosophies which followed Bacon. According to Dewey, Bacon's great achievement consisted in his denial of the value for philosophical truth of independent reason and literary art.[13]

The success and influence of the pragmatic philosophers were not caused mainly by any elements of leadership toward the good life which their doctrines contain—sincere believers though they were in goodness, when it could be obtained (as it could be in the nineteenth century) at no great cost. Their success was brought about, rather, by the fact that their views fitted into the conception of civilization that was coming to please Americans, particularly Americans of wealth and power. Some of these Americans were altruistically inclined —as is shown by their enormous gifts to medicine and educa-

[13] Dewey, op. cit., pp. 28 ff.

tion. But, as they would have been the first to admit, they were not thinkers, certainly not philosophers. They were not even scientists. Pragmatic philosophy came to mean—to a considerable extent in spite of the pragmatic philosophers, most of whom were disturbed by the tendencies they observed in recent American life—giving the public what it wants, or what businessmen, publicity men, and politicians tell it that it wants. The pragmatists and their associates can hardly be regarded as a university sect willing to face martyrdom for their ideas. Those who think otherwise would do well to read the letters of Henry Castle, the brilliant young editor of the *Honolulu Advertiser*, who met a premature death in the North Sea at thirty-two. His early thought does not suggest that he would have become a pragmatist. But, like many of the pragmatists, he had studied philosophy in Germany in the eighties and was a close friend of one of the men who later became a leader in pragmatism. In 1889, he tells us, this man decided to start his career not in philosophy but in physiological psychology. In reaching this decision he was guided by the fact that "he has [here] a harmless territory in which he can work quietly without drawing down upon himself the anathema and excommunication of all-potent evangelicism."[14] Such a choice was hardly the portent of a career destined to lead education in an unpopular direction. "What did any of us have," said another less famous pragmatist, "except a great deal of ambition to succeed?" Of course he was not fair to his distinguished and gifted associates, most of whom were disinterested searchers after truth. They actually derived little personal gain in money or even in position or fame from their labors. Except in educational circles the role they have played in American life has been hardly recognized. But they were swimming with the current, for all that. As the busy people rushing after money and worldly success had little or no re-

[14] Henry Northrup Castle, *Letters* (London, privately printed, 1902), p. 579.

spect for the mind, it was not likely that the persons whose work with their minds helped to justify the current would be noticed, or treated with respect if they were. Pragmatic philosophy, in a corrupt form alien to the hopes of the best pragmatists, took possession of the country with no serious opposition. It became part of the everyday life of millions who had never heard of pragmatism. It offers another glorious American success story, fit to set beside the rise of poor boys to great riches as portrayed by Horatio Alger, except that in this case it was not the poor boys but their ungrateful companions who got most of the riches. The element of tragedy, to which American social scientists have closed their eyes, cannot be kept out of a true history of pragmatism.

The *partial* nature of Baconian philosophy, justifiable philosophically in the beginning as a reply to another philosophy no less partial, has been left in the United States without any effective philosophical force to balance it. When deprived of their function of striving to arrange the various goods of life in an order that will contribute to the general happiness of mankind, philosophical speculations lose their independence. Philosophy becomes the mere handmaiden, at best of science or of economics, at worst of publicity men and the seekers after political office. As a result partly of the emphasis on natural science and on the study of man in the "ordinary" and changing "business of life," the distinction between reason and opinion, so vital to cultural and scholarly life, has been largely lost. It is hardly more possible to draw a definite frontier between reason and opinion than between the economic and the noneconomic aspects of life. That does not justify us in extending the economic to include the whole realm of existence; nor does it justify us in extending opinion to cover the whole realm of speculation, as social scientists have done under the influence of statements that "the true means the verified and means nothing else."

The special need of moral philosophy occasioned by the partial character of modern political economy is brought out strikingly by the words of one of its most intelligible exponents. They were written before the outbreak of the first World War, when economists still had much cause to be optimistic concerning the future of industrial civilization. According to Wicksteed:

Inventions and discoveries of every kind steadily tend to place mankind in fuller control of the powers of nature, and to give them larger means of accomplishing their desires. But this enlarged power has no direct or inevitable tendency to make those desires wise or worthy, or to correct the inequalities that have historically emerged between the powers possessed by different men to direct the resources of others toward the accomplishment of their own desires. The network of interchanges created and sustained by the economic forces is, morally, socially and esthetically, absolutely indifferent. . . . . Economic forces never have been, never can be, and never should be left to themselves. . . . .[15]

How are economic forces to be guided in the interest of general happiness? The task of the economist, as Wicksteed goes on to say, is to understand these forces better, in the hope that it may be more easily possible to control them. The task of the moral philosopher is to consider the nature of happiness; to consider how the constantly changing desires of men can be guided in directions that are morally, socially, and aesthetically beneficial to mankind. Moral philosophy is concerned, among other matters, with the choice of wants, economics with the means of attaining wants that are given. It should be a function of the moral philosopher to show society what wants are beneficial, and thus to provide the economist with a basis for favoring those that are worth attaining. The future of economics depends upon the development of a moral

[15] Philip H. Wicksteed, *The Common Sense of Political Economy* (London, 1933), I, 395, 397.

philosophy, in the Platonic and Aristotelian sense, and upon the collaboration of economists and philosophers. The two subjects can be studied independently. But, in their higher reaches, the one cannot be treated to advantage without reference to the other. Without moral philosophy the economist may conceivably show us how to control economic forces— but only under its guidance could he learn to control them for the benefit of humanity.

III. MORAL PHILOSOPHY AND CIVILIZATION

As the resources and conditions which invited the growth of a Baconian and partial philosophy of material improvement are ceasing to exist in the world of our time, the need for a renewal of a more comprehensive moral philosophy than any offered in the American universities today is compelling. It is doubtful whether there was ever in history a civilized country materially better and intellectually worse endowed than the United States today to make its philosophers kings. For a fraction of the money spent every year in subsidizing research in the social sciences, often valuable in a limited way for the data it provides, we could nourish genuine philosophers. There is no question that we could afford them. The trouble is that wealth cannot create them.

The conditions of our mores, our business life, and our politics are all hostile to their appearance. More than one hundred years ago Tocqueville noticed the special obstacles which confront the free mind in the United States and make it hardly less difficult for men to take an unpopular position on behalf of truth than in a totalitarian state. He wrote:

En Amérique la majorité trace un cercle formidable autour de la pensée. Au dedans de ces limits l'écrivain est libre, mais malheur à lui s'il ose en sortir! ... Avant de publier ces opinions, il croyait avoir des partisans; il lui semble qu'il n'en a plus, maintenant qu'il s'est découvert à tous; ceux qui le blâment s'expriment hautement, et ceux qui pensent comme lui, sans avoir son courage, se taisent et s'éloignent.

The majority says to him, in effect:

Vous êtes libres de ne point penser ainsi que moi; votre vie, vos biens, tout vous reste; mais, de ce jour, vous êtes un étranger parmi nous. ... Il cède, il plie enfin sous l'effort de chaque jour, et rentre dans le silence, comme s'il éprouvait des remords d'avoir dit vrai.[16]

The situation has changed little since the words were written. A man who tells an unpopular truth today finds himself no less an outcast than he did a century ago. Meanwhile the need for the independent mind has increased. There is today an overwhelming need for a balanced view of the world, such as can be secured only with the help of an accurate knowledge of past experience and a just sense of the present structure of society in relation to the constitution of the ideal state. It is necessary to provide for all the needs of man that are legitimate in the sight of God, and not simply for his desire to become wealthy and to exercise authority and dominion over his fellows. It is necessary to provide a place for all the races and all the nations on the globe, and not to accord them especially good or especially bad treatment because they are Aryans, Negroes, or Jews, or because they are Argentines, Portuguese, or Greeks, but to see that they get recognition for the contribution they are making and can make to the common cause

[16] "In America the majority raises very formidable barriers to the liberty of opinion. Within these barriers an author may write whatever he pleases, but he will repent it if he ever steps beyond them. .... Before he published his opinions he imagined that he held them in common with many others; but no sooner has he declared them openly than he is loudly censured by his overbearing opponents, while those who think like him, without having the courage to speak, abandon him in silence. .... " The majority says to him, "you are free to think differently from me, and to retain your life, your property and all that you possess; but if such be your determination you are henceforth an alien among us. .... He yields at length, oppressed by the daily effort he has been making, and he subsides into silence as if he were tormented by remorse for having told the truth" (Alexis de Tocqueville, *De la démocratie en Amérique* [Paris, 1888], II, 154–55). I have changed slightly the standard English translation.

of mankind as this is determined not by might but by philosophy.

Moral philosophy might offer a corrective for those excesses in teaching, expression, and action into which the people of the United States have drifted, and for which we are justly censured by foreigners. Moral philosophy might offer a comprehensive, balanced view of life, such as is especially difficult for a nation with large cities, many races, innumerable separate occupations, and separate branches of study to acquire. Moral philosophy exalts the place of the intellect in human affairs, at a time when Americans have denied that the mind has a role to play in civilized existence independent of either private interest or scientific experiment and observation. Moral philosophy calls attention to the fundamental importance of goodness, at a time when it has become almost a creed to deny that there are any standards of morality. Moral philosophy, properly cultivated, becomes an ally of art, the third of the three great ends of civilized existence.

It may be said that in a world of many races and nations, each with its own special view of life, in a world of changing conditions and changing human wants, any definite scale of values, such as moral philosophy sets about to supply, is impossible.[17] The widely held opinion that there is something peculiar to our time in changing conditions, that the world today is dynamic whereas in the past it was static, is of course mistaken. It would be idle to deny that the social and economic changes of the last half-century have done much to undermine the traditional conceptions of morality among the Western peoples. But the disappearance of ethics is not a necessary part of change, as so many American university men have come to assume. Change is not new. Every civilization of which we have record has been in process of change. In the past, moral and intellectual standards have survived changes

[17] Cf. *ibid.*, Vol. III, Part III, chap. xviii, for an answer to such a contention.

no less cataclysmic than those of the nineteenth and early twentieth centuries. It is true that people's desires and wants are different from those of past peoples, but that has always been true of every society with which philosophers have had to deal. The things that mark off the world today from the worlds of earlier philosophers are not the elements of change. The differences are that the stage is a bigger one, involving a much larger territory and a much larger population, and that the machines and weapons in man's hands are vastly more powerful both in a productive and a destructive sense than they ever were in the past. The task of the moral philosopher is doubtless more complicated than it has ever been, but let us not imagine that his task was ever simple. The few approaches made in the past to a true philosophy have been made in the teeth of overwhelming difficulties. They have always involved a grasp of the essentials of many disciplines and occupations, in which the philosopher himself was not and could not be an expert or an actual worker, as the participants in special disciplines and special occupations must be. The few approaches that have been made to a true philosophy have always involved a reduction of the enormously complex to clarity, harmony, and unity. "Much more would be done if people believed less was impossible," wrote Malesherbes. This is especially true today. Moral philosophy has always involved, as it involves now, an attempt to influence the changing wants of man in the direction of human needs which have a greater permanence.

Let us distinguish further between wants and needs. Apart from the desires for food, warmth, and sleep, sex, comfort, entertainment, and display, satisfied in very different ways, there are the needs for faith, for love, for security (both against death and the evils of life), for justice, for good moral and intellectual habits, and for art. The satisfaction of human needs may not be necessary for life, but their satisfaction, at least in a measure, is indispensable for higher life. It is only when wants are tempered and guided by needs that they can be satisfied in ways that are distinctively human, that fortify the soul. Values that exist in connection with needs are eternal in so far as human beings are concerned. The recognition of them, still more the partial satisfaction of them, draw people together. They are not satisfied at the expense of other men and women to the same degree as wants. The fulfilment of wants, without regard to needs, is almost certain to breed envy. The fulfilment of needs is inclined to breed altruism. Riches cause jealousy, when they are possessed by individuals, groups of individuals, or nations, to a far greater extent than fair play or affection. Wants are inevitable. Many of them are indispensable. Without them, life cannot go on. The satisfaction of some is always harmful to mankind, the satisfaction of others is always helpful. But the satisfaction of the great majority of wants is now harmful and then helpful. With changing conditions and with different societies, it is desirable now to encourage the increase of certain wants, now to discourage their increase. That is notably the case in connection with the desire for material comfort and riches.

It is mainly accurate in one way and mainly false in another to say that absolute truth exists for the moral philosopher. His objective is always the same—human happiness in the highest sense, in the sense of the satisfaction of human needs. But the means of working toward human happiness vary.

The task of the moral philosopher is by impartial inquiry— and with the vast new supply of data now at his disposal—to help mankind to guide their changing wants in the direction of their far more permanent needs. Even a partial philosophy can help, if it is based purely on disinterested inquiry and if it exerts a pull in the right direction. There is a place for philosophers whose thought falls considerably short of the wisdom of Plato, Aristotle, or Aquinas. But it is indispensable that, as Aristotle might have said, the emphasis should not be laid on increasing the errors of emphasis that already exist. The modern exponents of the Baconian philosophy, the pragmatists in particular, for all their merits, were inclined to fall in with the current which, if our analysis is not completely wrong, is taking man farther and farther away from truth and happiness, away from those aspects of human life which need now to be nourished if civilization is to survive. In so far as pragmatism seeks the happiness of the individual everywhere, its aim is sound and desirable. Its exponents have rendered a service to man by emphasizing the importance of happiness. The mistakes that are so widely made by the pragmatists, and even more by the logical positivists and most other present-day philosophers, are likely to defeat their own aims. The mistakes are these. They divorce happiness from principles of wisdom, virtue, and beauty, and deny that reason can be the guiding principle in the study of man's relation to man. They assume that their philosophy is universal rather than partial and—since they themselves tell us it is a philosophy of means, not of ends—that means can be allowed to develop in our mechanized and crowded world without any direction. In its popular form, and even to a considerable extent in the writings of its leading exponents, such as James and Dewey, pragmatism emphasizes human wants and neglects needs. It emphasizes the material side of life and neglects the spiritual and intellectual. It encourages drifting at the expense of order and direction. Far from being the best philosophy for our times, as its exponents and followers have assumed, it is in many ways the worst.

To help mankind now and in the immediate future, the philosopher will have to emphasize needs rather than wants. He will have to emphasize the permanent rather than the fleeting. He will have to emphasize the spiritual rather than the material, unity rather than diversity, reason rather than experiment and observation for their own sake. A place for a moral philosophy which pulls in the necessary direction is required not only for the welfare and the health of philosophers and writers, but for the welfare and the health of man. Unless moral philosophers and writers cultivate the general welfare they will give us neither philosophy nor literature.

The Renaissance taught the Western peoples to exalt the value of man. In the greatest Renaissance thought, this meant the fulfilment of all the good sides of man's instincts. During modern times the two chief civilizations in Europe—the French and the English—came to emphasize different sides of man's aspirations. The French emphasized his aesthetic and intellectual, the English his material and moral, aspirations. There was enough interchange of ideas between the two countries so that the overemphasis of the one did something to offset that of the other, especially in the eighteenth century. In more recent times the balance has been weighted more and more exclusively on the side of man's material aspirations. Can the United States, as a relatively young and fresh nation, in spite of its almost exclusive concern with material improvement and activity, restore the balance that has been lost? Can we cultivate all the good sides of man's desires? Can we realize the dream of Renaissance humanism, which has never been fulfilled?

The answer to these questions lies to a considerable extent in the hands of moral philosophy. It depends upon the place which this wealthy nation is intellectually able to accord the subject, and the influence which wisdom is allowed to have in the remaking of American society. We cannot answer these questions the right way unless we are prepared to recognize our faults and shortcomings. Self-criticism is generally a sign of strength, not of weakness. No one would deny the English patriotism. It is significant that they can criticize themselves. A recognition of weaknesses when and where they exist is an essential step toward wisdom. Let us hope that this great nation will recognize its weaknesses and rise above them.

VIII

ART

☼

NEVER in the history of the world have so many people been writing books as in our time. What city dweller today would be likely to feel his pulse quicken if he were introduced to an "author"? Almost everyone, at any rate in learned circles, is an author. If anything gives a man distinction nowadays it is not that he has written a book or even many books. What distinguishes a man who moves about in colleges or universities or in society is that he has not written a book. The "man of letters" has been lost in a world of hastily improvised words—printed, spoken, and hurled over the radio into houses and apartment buildings, barber-shops, automobiles, and once quiet parks and shady hillsides.

Among modern Americans it is widely believed that anyone can write. Were we not told in our youth that every man or woman had it in him or her to compose a single great book— presumably an autobiography in one form or another? The disposition to act upon this assumption seems to be widespread. Recently a man of fifty, who had made a small fortune in business, presented himself to a learned colleague of mine. The man announced his intention of writing a Doctor's thesis on an ambitious subject, for which few data could have been obtained. After warning him of the difficulties likely to be caused by the want of materials, my colleague asked to see a sample of the man's written work. "But I've never written anything," came the reply. "What, not even a theme or term paper in college?" "No, I can't remember that we were ever asked to write term papers at the college I attended." "What makes you think you can write, then?" "Anybody can learn to write," he replied, "and I can learn anything." The implication was that a person who had made a million dollars could hardly fail in a matter requiring so much less talent.

What we have today is a writing public. If there are to be again "men of letters," there will have to be a reading public. Although the literacy tests are high, nobody has the time or the patience to read. So the very great majority of books are hardly read at all. The fact that they are bought proves little. If some of my learned colleagues in the graduate library school are right, a large portion of the books widely purchased have mainly what they elegantly call a "snob sale." The books find their way onto the living-room table, where visitors and guests will see them and, it is hoped, will regard their owner in a higher light than would otherwise be the case—but they find their way no farther.

Regret over the lack of a reading public is somewhat tempered when we consider the caliber of most contemporary books. They fall roughly into two great categories. There are, first, those written to sell. There are, second, those written to give the world new facts and ideas of a scientific nature.

There is no doubt that a fair number of the authors of books written for the market attain a high level of technical competence. This has been true notably of novels written in England during the last thirty years. Never have so many neatly constructed, polished novels been published before. Some are smooth and slick to the last degree. One trouble is that great works of art are neither smooth nor slick. They are authentic. Like most authentic things, they are often full of roughness. Like real jewels, they have flaws. Few who battle genuinely and deeply with the problems of life—as the true artist must— can avoid flaws. Nothing that is merely smooth and pretty can inspire a deep and lasting affection. When Montaigne expressed his profound love for Paris, he could find no words better than these: "[Paris] a mon cueur dés mon enfance; et m'en est advenu comme des choses excellentes: plus j'ay veu depuis d'autres villes belles, plus la beauté de cette-cy peut et gaigne sur mon affection. Je l'ayme par elle mesme, et plus en son propre estre que rechargée de pompe estrangiere, je l'ayme tendrement jusques à ses verrues et à ses taches."[1]

It is much easier to learn to write in a style that is smooth and slick than it is to say something important even in a style that is crude and labored. The inner voice with a power to move mountains cannot be acquired with the same ease as good technique. The catch in the work of authors who write books perfect in the technical sense is that they have nothing important to say. They have the foreign and acquired embellishments; they have little else. Their authors have no message to give the world, no conviction about life they are bursting to state. They are not writing because of any inner necessity. They are writing for money, because they have a talent for writing and find they can make a living more easily in this way than in some other. While the arrangement of their plots and the technical form of their paragraphs leave little to be desired, their books have little warmth or depth. Their words and images lack power and even beauty, such as is given only by a sense of humanity, an inner elevation of spirit, and a distinction of thought. Some of their books are amusing. A few are sidesplitting. But nearly all lack the quality of wit which comes from an audacious imagination, creating comparisons at once surprising and apt enough to lift both

[1] *Essaies*, Book III, chap. ix: "That city has ever had my heart from my infancy; . . . . the more beautiful cities I have seen since, the more the beauty of this still wins with my affection. I love her for herself, and more in her own native being, than in all the pomp of foreign and acquired embellishments. I love her tenderly [to the point of loving] her warts and blemishes" (Cotton trans., ed. W. C. Hazlitt [London, 1902], IV, 97). I have changed somewhat the last line of the translation.

the writer and the reader out of the actual world in which they live.[2] The force and the dignity of words and phrases that characterized English literature in Milton's time, hardly less than in Shakespeare's, are no longer popular.

Not long ago I overheard, between acts at the theater, the conversation of a young man accompanied by a woman of his own age, whom he was apparently taking out for the first time. Katharine Cornell was appearing in a little play called *No Time for Comedy*. At one point the play contained some unimpeachable sentiments, but it could hardly be regarded as an important work of art. The young man told his companion this was his idea of a good play. He would go to such a play any time rather than listen to Shakespeare. *Hamlet* was being given uncut in a neighboring theater. The young man explained that on no account would he waste an evening there. Frankly, Shakespeare bored him. "It's easy," he remarked, "to get too much of Shakespeare. I teach English literature at the junior college, you know."

He was not exactly the kind of teacher one would select if the object of teaching were to fire young people with a love of literature. Persons who see the absurdity laugh or shrug their shoulders. It does not occur to the large number of teachers, and the far larger number of laymen, who feel as he does to ask whether the fault is theirs. They assume that, without a cultural tradition, without serious training in literature, without a love of art, and without an intellectual effort, they are competent to pass judgment on any plays, books, paintings, or works of music. If Shakespeare bores them, they take it for granted the fault is his. They find the majority feel as they do, and the two traditions that most of them have learned are that everyone should be free to say anything he pleases and that the majority is always right.

[2] For the disappearance of "wit" in modern literature see T. S. Eliot, *Homage to John Dryden* (London, 1924), pp. 42–46.

Under these conditions, how can we feel confident that the public for whom writers now publish their works has the right judgment about present-day literature? Can we assume that there is any connection between the sale of a book and its value? Even in the seventeenth century, Milton was paid only a few pounds for *Paradise Lost*. Had it not been for the income he received from his father, who had made a fortune as a scrivener in London at the turn of the sixteenth and seventeenth centuries, Milton might never have found the time for writing poetry.

Not all books written in the modern world are expected to sell. The authors of those which fall into the second of the two broad categories we have mentioned aim at technical perfection of a different kind. Some are contented with little or no perfection of any kind. They generally hope to have their books reviewed favorably in a few learned magazines, which deal with a special field of scholarship. They write to fit into this groove. If they are successful, their book is purchased by the chief libraries. It is also purchased, but seldom read, by a few dozen or so scholars in the field. Writers of such books are able to bear the expense of preparing and publishing them, either because they have private means or because they are financed by rich universities or colleges, by business houses, or by the educational foundations established by wealthy men in the interest of knowledge and instruction.

The object of the best of these learned works is to present new explanations and information concerning the behavior of matter in the physical and the biological world, new explanations and information concerning the nature and history of man in his relations with other men. The rewards sought are scientific reputation, academic promotion, and various kinds of distinctions.

Many of these scholarly works contain much that is of value for mankind. It is no disparagement of them to suggest that, from the point of view of art or creative thought, most of these writings are useful mainly as materials. The subject matter of great works of literature, whether it is presented in the form of poetry or prose, is chosen not primarily because of its novelty but because of its importance. Neither art nor thought is ever achieved by letting one's materials do most of the work. A mountain of facts, even when they are carefully arranged in categories, has no power to speak to us. In one of his letters, written in 1760, Diderot, who was a champion of science and of industrial technology, refers to a long survey of French economic life that had been recently published in three bulky volumes by a Frenchman named Ange Goudar.[3] Of Goudar and his work Diderot writes, "Il a un monde de choses dont il ne sait rien faire; et le génie sait faire un monde de rien."[4] The words contain a lesson of which American scholarship is in need. No quantity of materials can take the place of genius, even in the study of society. While genius is partly determined by birth, even that very rare human being, a born genius, will be lost without training in reason and in culture. The object of the artist and the thinker is less to say something for the first time than to say something that matters with greater power and meaning than ever before. It is easier to say something "original" on subjects that are small and insignificant than on subjects that are profound and of great consequence for human welfare. According to the criterion sometimes applied in the social sciences, a person who determines from old timetables how many car miles were probably covered by the Baltimore and Ohio Railroad in the year 1857 makes an "original contribution" to knowledge no less than a second person who says something fresh about the problem

---

[3] *Les Intérêts de la France mal entendus* (3 vols.; Amsterdam, 1756).

[4] "He has a world of facts and doesn't know how to do anything with them; and genius knows how to make a world out of nothing" (*Œuvres complètes de Diderot*, ed. J. Assézat and M. Tourneux [Paris, 1876], XVIII, 480).

of meeting death. It is always easier (and safer) to say something entirely new about a subject that is of no concern to
anyone than about another which has been of vital concern to
everyone since the beginning of human experience.

When the scholar, who has made his reputation by what
are called "original contributions" to knowledge, turns away
from his specialty to write a textbook or some other kind of
book for sale or publicity or both, he is generally guided by
the agents of publishing houses, by magazine editors, and
others whose business is to make money. It is from such persons that the scholar finds out, either directly or indirectly,
what the public wants. As he is not brought to his labor by a
desire to supply the public with what it needs, as he makes a
virtue of leaving questions of that kind to the give and take
of the market place, he is generally no less anxious to supply
the public with what he learns to think it wants than is the
professional writer. In the not very numerous instances when
the scholar has talent for writing, he is capable of achieving
in his popular works a competence, a smoothness, and even a
slickness little short of that exhibited by the best professionals. What he almost never succeeds in creating, any more than
the professional of the present day, is a work of art. What he
almost never succeeds in making, any more than the professional, is a contribution to thought. He is no more impelled
to speak out by the deep inner necessity common to all great
artists (and which is quite separate from the desire for worldly renown) than the professionals who, if successful, are hand-
somely paid for their labor. Very often he is told that the way
to sell his wares is to "talk down" to his audience. He falls in
readily with the suggestion, which generally coincides with
his own views, derived from teaching. When he can talk
down he is relieved from the necessity of probing his own
materials deeply. Instead he dilutes the stock of information
and ideas which he commands. It is not always a very large

stock. He is likely to confuse this process of dilution with the clarification and simplification that are a part of art. His confusion and the results of it hardly contribute to the education of his audience or even of himself.

The results both of so-called "scholarly writing" and of the attempts by scholars to popularize their knowledge are sometimes unrelated and often harmful to art and creative thought. The net effect is to detract from the intelligence and the beauty of American society. Neither kind of work hits the mark that counts in forming a cultural tradition. A certain American writer was recently spoken of with enthusiasm in a group of our so-called "intelligentsia." His merit, it was said, was that he wrote in plain language that the common man could understand. He was not, it was said in his favor, "at all learned."

Now all great writers have put their thoughts in plain language, understandable to any person with a genuine education, who has the time and inclination to make the effort of understanding them. But this result has never been obtained by weakening their thought or evading difficulties that arise as it develops. The slur on learning implied in the remarks about the American writer was not justified. It is a much greater achievement to put complex and learned than to put commonplace thought or to put no thought at all into simple language. Simple, plain language has no great merit unless it has valuable content.

In an age like our own, when technique is regarded as the principal kind of labor which calls for skill and training, when there is little recognition of the need for special competence and drill in connection with the higher play of the intellect, the difficulties of learning to paint or to compose music naturally seem much greater than the difficulties of learning to write. To the ordinary person, the technical problems of painting and composing appear far more complex and mysterious than those of writing. So in numbers neither the painters nor the musical composers can compare with the writers. Composers, and especially painters, are exceedingly numerous nonetheless.

The smoothness and slickness so characteristic of much recent writing are not so apparent in modern paintings and musical compositions, though they are apparent in many musical performances. The smoothness and slickness are there all the same. Balzac said of Raphael's famous "Spozalizio," or "Marriage of the Virgin," in Milan, "Ce n'est pas le comble de l'art, c'en est le bonheur."[5] Few critics of painting would be likely to disagree that in the purity and smoothness of his effects, Raphael was unequaled among the painters of the Renaissance. Is it not partly this characteristic of his works that makes them less moving and profoundly beautiful than those of Rembrandt, Leonardo, and Giotto?[6] Pictures are painted today that might almost be mistaken for Raphael's were it not for their subjects. No pictures are painted today that could be mistaken for Rembrandt's, Leonardo's, or Giotto's—except, of course, when a deft attempt is made to copy them. Fine though some recent French paintings have been, they do not approach those supreme heights.

The best-informed and most intelligent students of music and painting tell us that technical proficiency is the long suit of the most accomplished artists of recent years. Lacking convictions, most modern artists resort to tricks. At these they are often exceedingly skilful, and many of them get results on a canvas or in an orchestral work that are technically superb. Like the writers, the painters and composers are seldom drawn to their labor because they have something of overwhelming

---

[5] *La Cousine Bette* (1847), Part I. "It is not the apex of art, but its happiness."

[6] Balzac gave a higher place to Raphael's works in general than the best critics of the last half-century would do. His remark was made in comparing the "Marriage of the Virgin" to other paintings of Raphael's, which he considered greater.

significance to communicate. It is true, of course, that the subject matter of music is far less literal than that of literature, even of poetry. The convictions of the musician, especially of a very great musician like Beethoven, Mozart or Bach, are distilled into a medium that is highly abstract. It does not follow that the convictions of the musician are of no importance, that it is a matter of indifference whether or not he is drawn to his art by a tremendous inner necessity which comes from his mind and spirit. Such inner necessity is of no less importance in great music than in great writing. A sense of humanity, a deep belief and faith, as well as the highest order of intelligence in connection with artistic labor, are essential ingredients of all very great art. Without them no one is blessed with what the Greeks called "divine inspiration." Without them no one can rise above the smooth and talented. Technical competence is indispensable in all art. It is no substitute for higher qualities, which have become more and more scarce in the painting and music of the Western peoples during the last half-century.

I. ART AND MORAL PHILOSOPHY

If our analysis of the condition of modern art contains an element of truth, it follows that literature, painting, and music are suffering from the same kind of weaknesses which have been causing the disintegration of religious faith and of ethics. Art should not be confused with faith, with goodness, or with knowledge. Each has a realm of its own that must be cultivated for itself. But all have this in common—they alone among the goods of life have the capacity to lift man completely out of himself, to escape from self-love. Just as Christianity is the ally of moral philosophy, it is also the ally of art. Art has need of both Christianity and moral philosophy. Moral philosophy and religion both have need of art. All three of them are expressions of the same combination of exaltation and intelligence. All three are supreme expressions of the human spirit. As long as one of them is alive there is always hope for a revival of the others.

If our analysis contains an element of truth, the future of art depends upon a renewed recognition that its main purpose is to treat of the deeper meaning of human existence. Its object cannot be to add to the artist's income or his popularity in the open market. If art is to help mankind, true artistic inspiration and conviction must again rule the market for their own ends. These are never personal. They control the artist; they may lead him in ways that are against his private advantage.

It is true, of course, that the inspiration of the artist must be met with comprehension and recognition by some of his contemporaries if his work is to survive, if it is to have an influence on others besides himself, and if he is to develop to the full his potential powers. But what is important is not that he should be in tune with current values. What is important is that at least a tiny public should be in tune with great art; able to recognize it and to respond to it when it is presented to them. The relationship of the artist to the public has been well explained by one of the greatest contemporary musicians, Artur Schnabel. The artist's inspiration is no more the creation of the public, than a man's voice on some high mountain side is the creation of the rocks, crags, and peaks that rise about him. Yet the extent to which that inspiration is used depends, in a measure, like the use of the voice seeking an echo, upon the surroundings. If the echo comes, the mountaineer is encouraged to go on calling and to try out his voice in new ways. If he gets no response, he will relapse into silence sooner. So with the inspired artist.[7] In the modern world, in the United States, the echo seems to be growing fainter and fainter.

The Christian faith and the study of moral philosophy, as it

[7] Cf. Artur Schnabel, *Reflections on Music*, trans. César Saerchinger (Manchester, 1933).

has come down to us from the greatest Greek philosophers, can be of assistance to art. Faith and moral philosophy each help to create among the vast stretches of hills and valleys formed by human societies—among the population as a whole, rich and poor alike—the conditions that make possible an echo. If faith and moral philosophy are to make an impression upon the future, both must be revived in a new form. The old forms of the thirteenth and nineteenth centuries no longer have a hold on mankind, but the principles contained in them are not dead. As long as civilized societies exist, these ancient principles provide, however imperfectly, for the deepest human needs. Can those needs be met in the decades and centuries which lie immediately ahead, unless these ancient principles of Christianity and ethics are cultivated in relation to the industrial world that has grown up during the past four or five centuries?

By cultivating religion and ethics we shall strengthen true artistic inspiration. Religion in its basic Christian form, as set forth in the New Testament, teaches us that the test of a man's mind and spirit, as of his moral conduct, cannot possibly be worldly success. No message is of greater importance for art today than this one. Religion also shows us that man's mind and spirit cannot be at the command merely of a worldly despot, that they belong in an independent realm subject to the dictation of no mere man. By showing the heights to which man's mind and spirit are capable of reaching, religion helps to reveal to men their powers as artists. How can poets be "divinely inspired" unless there is a Supreme Being of the kind revealed to us by Christianity?

Moral philosophy, in its true sense, exalts the intellect and emphasizes its importance as the controlling factor in the study of man. It demonstrates the autonomy and the value of the trained, independent mind, with its power to reason both geometrically and by intuition. Thought and art have much more in common than either has with natural science or technical invention. Both order their materials for ends determined by the mind, whereas the investigations of the natural scientist and the inventor are governed by their materials, though the aims they serve range all the way from the lofty one of alleviating human suffering to the base one of destroying as many lives as possible. Art and thought strive to create works that are unique—that are valuable as subjects of contemplation and reflection. Science and invention aim to establish temporary general laws and mechanical principles, valuable chiefly because of their widespread usefulness. Thought is indispensable to science and invention, just as correct knowledge of matter and of facts is indispensable to thought, but the emphasis is very different. Any attempt to deny the importance of this difference leads to the absorption and diminution of science and technology in favor of thought and art, or of thought and art in favor of science and technology. The great danger in our time is not the disappearance of science and technology. It is the denial of the independence of thought and art. If it were possible to lay down hard and fast rules and laws governing art as it is to lay down tentatively laws governing mechanics, then it would be possible to turn out works of art by mass production. It is precisely the fact that a work of art is not mechanical, but is the product of man's independent mind and spirit, which gives it a permanence denied to products of the laboratory as well as the factory. As art today, together with social and humanistic studies, suffers from an overemphasis on purely scientific and technical aspects, the lessons which moral philosophy has to teach are of great importance to the future of art. What is needed is a combination of the indifference to sales, characteristic of the best research work done by scholars, with art as well as with science.

Moral philosophy is also of importance to art because it

seeks to establish, tentatively at least, a hierarchy of values concerning knowledge and also concerning moral conduct. In the realm of the intellect, moral philosophy is concerned with distinctions of every kind at a time when men have forgotten that there are any important distinctions save those imposed by material necessity. The question of material necessity can be properly given only minor importance in art. So the success of art as well as of moral philosophy depends upon the establishment by impartial minds of the right intellectual values.

It is frequently supposed that art and moral virtue have nothing in common, or even that they are opposed. In the period immediately preceding and following the first World War, the public came to regard artist colonies as hotbeds of moral laxity. Their view was not entirely without foundation. A good many persons who obtained temporary renown as artists did little by their personal conduct or their work to prove that it was false. In some quarters persons who aspired to become artists felt that they were establishing their artistic reputation almost as much through their irregular hours and their powers as drinkers as by the quality of the poetry they wrote or the pictures they painted.[8]

What has not been recognized is that these activities were no less irrelevant, and possibly even more harmful, to the pursuit of artistic objectives than the confusion of technique with art and the encroachment of science upon thought. All these aberrations were an evidence of the growing materialism which was bound to damage art by submerging it under material values with which it has nothing in common.

In so far as moral philosophy can help to teach the artist just proportions in the conduct of life, in so far as it can help him to acquire good moral habits, it is bound to help him as an artist. It will help him to put his body at the service of his mind and spirit; not to make his mind and spirit the slaves

[8] Cf. Malcolm Cowley, *Exile's Return* (New York, 1934).

of his body. True inspiration, as Plato suggests in some of his Dialogues, is a divine madness. It is not the madness produced by worldly drunkenness.

What is of far greater importance to the artist is the significance of moral philosophy, not for his personal conduct, but for the treatment of his materials. Recent art has suffered greatly, as M. Ramon Fernandez and later Mr. T. S. Eliot have pointed out, from the lack of any hierarchy of values. Quite independently of the artist's conduct of his own life, he can only be inspired to the intensity of conviction woefully lacking in recent art by a consuming love of beauty, justice, and truth. If the existence of absolute values in connection with beauty, justice, and truth is denied, as it has come to be so largely in recent times, then a great source of artistic inspiration is removed. No one can look at the wonderful scenes carved on medieval abbeys, churches, and cathedrals without realizing that the artists who created them had a compelling sense of the difference between right and wrong conduct, and that they could count on the audience who came to worship to share their "prejudices," as modern social scientists would call them. The artists had a compelling sense of the difference between justice and injustice, as these were conceived in the mind, with the help of faith, and not as they were laid down arbitrarily by a despotic ruler in order to increase his own power. In a more recent age, what gave such strength to the works of Balzac or Dostoevski was the deep sense of moral values felt by their authors, combined with the detachment with which as artists they could write. The standards of right and wrong are essentially the same in two writers of such completely different temperament and background as Balzac and Trollope. Their work is equally dependent upon the existence of these standards. It is of little or no significance that Balzac's personal habits as a writer were exceedingly irregular and excessive, while Trollope's were a model of methodical balance, annoying to persons who take for granted that art can thrive only on eccentricity of conduct. Balzac and Trollope were united in this—both were concerned in portraying, in different ways, the overwhelming value of goodness and the overwhelming iniquity of evil. On this vital question there is no room for two opinions in connection with art.

Unless the modern world can re-create a moral philosophy which agrees upon the nature and the order of both the intellectual and the moral virtues, the future for art is not hopeful. Art without a sense of justice, without a belief in truth, is hardly more possible than art without beauty. Much criticism has been leveled at Keats's celebrated line identifying truth and beauty, and not without cause. It remains true that beauty without aesthetic truth is no more conceivable than truth without beauty. A society which denies either ultimately denies both.

II. ART AND WEALTH

Some historians have been struck by the apparent association of exceptionally rich artistic achievements with periods of remarkable material advance. One of the most striking examples is the flowering of Greek culture during the short sixty years between the Battle of Marathon in 490 B.C. and the outbreak of the Peloponnesian War in 431 B.C. During those six decades there worked at Athens, a town hardly as populous as Sinclair Lewis' "Zenith," at least seven of the very greatest figures in the entire history of art and thought. If any competent judge since the Renaissance had been asked to name the hundred leading artists and thinkers of all time, he could hardly have omitted Aeschylus, Phidias, Sophocles, Herodotus, Euripides, Thucydides, or Socrates. All of them, except Aeschylus, were born between 500 and 470 B.C. All of them, except Aeschylus, who died probably in 456, were seen by most Athenians during the two decades 450–431. In those twenty years the Parthenon, the Erechtheum, and the Propylaea, with their monumental embellishments, were all going up on the Acropolis under the direction of Pericles (*ca.* 495–429), to form one of the most perfect groups of buildings ever conceived by man. There they still stand, after twenty-four centuries. The events of the present year show that men retain enough sense of civilized values not to destroy them lightly.

The years between the Persian and the Peloponnesian wars were a time of prosperity for the Greek city-states, and above all for Attica. The population was growing, new colonies were being founded overseas, the imports of grain and timber were mounting rapidly. Attica had almost as many inhabitants as she had before the German invasion of this year. Her increasing wealth was swelled by vast supplies of silver won from the recently discovered mines of argentiferous lead ore on the mountain of Laurion. There some of the shafts went down three hundred feet, an uncommon depth in those days at which to make a livelihood. The slopes and valleys were full of men washing, breaking, and preparing the ore or separating the silver and lead. It is natural to assume that economic progress had something to do with the culture of the Athenians.

Similar associations between a rapid increase in the volume of production and wonderful artistic achievements are to be found in the Gothic Age in France and Italy, in the Renaissance of the late fifteenth and early sixteenth centuries in Italy and southern Germany, and in the Elizabethan and Jacobean periods in England from about 1580 to 1640. The first of these periods gave us Albertus Magnus, St. Thomas Aquinas, Roger Bacon, Giotto, Dante, and the greatest cathedrals. The second gave us Michelangelo, Leonardo, Giorgione, Titian, Dürer, and the architecture of humanism. The third gave us Shakespeare, Spenser, Donne, Milton, Hooker, Francis Bacon, and the most delightful English music. Like the Athenian period in Greek history, each of these ages of giants was an age in which population grew and with it the command of men over matter in agriculture and industry. In the time of St. Thomas, in the time of Michelangelo, in the time of Shakespeare, the merchant could look forward with confidence to a rapid growth in his traffic from decade to decade and almost from year to year. During the great reign of St. Louis (1226–70), the production of silver and copper in Europe may well have increased threefold or more. During the lifetime of Leonardo (1452–1519), the output of iron in Styria, the leading center of the industry, grew at least fourfold. During the lifetime of Francis Bacon (1561–1626), the coal imports of London mounted from less than ten to more than a hundred thousand tons a year.

A superficial historical observer might conclude that rapidly increasing industrial output is indispensable to great art, or even that it leads inevitably to great art. If he were a natural scientist, he might conclude that there is a symbiosis between a remarkable increase in the volume of material production and the development of a very rich culture.

History hardly supports such theses. Greece was probably not conspicuously more prosperous when Plato died in 347 b.c. than on the eve of the Peloponnesian War, a few years before his birth. Neither he nor Aristotle (384–322), who was his junior by some forty years or so, apparently lived in what the economists would call a rapidly expanding economy.

It may be objected that Plato and Aristotle were the fruits of a creative movement that developed originally because of exceptionally prosperous conditions. But it would not be possible to show that the so-called "classical period" in French art coincided with a rapid increase in the national income, such as occurred in Greece in the fifth century b.c. It has been often said that France, more than any other Western country, is heir to the Greek cultural tradition. No period in French history—except, perhaps, the thirteenth century—has been as rich in artistic achievements as the seventeenth. Descartes and Pascal, Poussin and Claude Lorrain, Racine, Corneille, Molière, La Fontaine, Bossuet, Lulli, Couperin, and Mme de Sévigné all were born between 1594 and 1668. Couperin was the only one to survive Louis XIV, who died in 1715.

The seventeenth century was an age in which Frenchmen learned to write poetry, music, and prose, to paint, to build, and to decorate with reason, harmony, balance, grace, and finish unknown to their ancestors. But it was not an age in which the population of the French provinces, or the volume of their agrarian and industrial output, grew rapidly, as the agrarian and industrial output of England grew during the reigns of Elizabeth and James I. There were only two periods of striking prosperity: the first two decades of the century, when France recovered from the religious wars, and the sixties and seventies, when Colbert controlled the national economy. Both were followed by long periods of depression. While France had acquired some new territory, few of the French provinces were much more productive at the beginning of the eighteenth century than at the beginning of the seventeenth, or even the beginning of the sixteenth. The last three decades of Louis XIV's reign were a time of great economic suffering. The output of several industrial products, such as coal and many varieties of cloth, was on the decline. Vauban, the famous fortress-builder, who Voltaire tells us was the only general who preferred the welfare of the state to his own, has painted a picture of the material distress at this time. It is hardly less gloomy than the one painted by the Scotchman, John Law, who came forward with an offer to put things right by reorganizing the national finances and developing credit. Law was a special pleader, so we might expect him to exaggerate. But the same exception cannot be taken to Vauban's description. Michelet's remark that the reign of Louis XIV finished many things but began nothing is nowhere more applicable than in the economic sphere.

If a reduction in the labor costs of production and an increase in the volume of this world's goods were the chief conditions necessary for a flowering in the arts, the sixty-five years from 1865 to 1929 in the United States should have been their greatest period in the whole of history. The population almost quadrupled. The railway, the automobile, and finally the airplane spanned the country. Nearly all industrial work came to be done by machines. The output of manufactured goods increased about twenty-eight fold.[9] Scores of populous towns, many much larger than ancient Athens, were growing up on a continent nearly a hundred times the area of Greece, with natural resources more than a hundred times as abundant. Judged by the material standards of the fifth century B.C., most of the inhabitants of these American towns were well off.[10] Judged by the less modest standards of modern America, there were in every town a good many rich and a good many more about to become rich. The fancies of material abundance, published three centuries ago by Francis Bacon in his *New Atlantis*, seemed on the point of becoming a reality in dozens of communities.[11] Young men full of enthusiasm and energy professed a desire in their off-hours from football, baseball, or business to make culture hum. Millions of children were sent to school. Thousands of wives joined hundreds of clubs in the hope of exposing themselves to every

[9] Chester W. Wright, *Economic History of the United States* (New York, 1941), p. 707.

[10] But the differences in standards of living can be easily exaggerated. A recent comparison suggests that toward the end of the fourth century B.C., at about the time of Aristotle's death, the free wage-earner in Athens could command about as large a quantity of the necessities of life as the modern British wage-earner (Colin Clark, *The Conditions of Economic Progress* [London, 1940], pp. 164–67).

[11] As President Hutchins pointed out in his convocation address at the University of Chicago in 1931 ("The New Atlantis," *University of Chicago Record*, XVII, No. 3, 145–50).

variety of intellectual improvement. They anxiously asked celebrated foreigners whether it was proper to consider their town the modern Athens. If an expanding volume of output were the key to art and thought, the cultural drama of fifth-century Attica should have been repeated in a hundred cities. America should have added seven hundred or more men and women to the hundred greatest artists in the history of the world.

Yet, for all its wealth, this period in American history created no great artistic style. It is questionable whether it produced a single artist in literature, painting, or music fit to place in the same category with those whose names have been mentioned. Mark Twain and Henry James would be the only possible exceptions,[12] and James put the United States behind him to become a British subject. A few striking and permanent, if scattered, works of literature appeared—of which the most perfect in artistry, perhaps, was young Stephen Crane's *Red Badge of Courage*. A few brilliant intellects lighted up the American scene—Thorstein Veblen, Frank Lloyd Wright, Justice Holmes, and Henry Adams—though Adams fled the country almost as often as his fellow New Englander, Henry James. If many Americans of taste and talent went abroad, it was partly because they found there a higher level of aesthetic judgment than they could discover at home. It was in France, where wealth was increasing more slowly than in any other Western nation, and where the population was increasing hardly at all, that they found the greatest painters and the greatest writers. It had been in Germany and Austria, the least progressive of the chief European countries on the industrial side during the eighteenth century and at the beginning of the nineteenth, that the greatest flowering of music had taken

[12] Other American writers—Poe, Emerson, Melville, Whitman—who might also be included were the products of an earlier period, though it is possible to regard Whitman as the forerunner of a later school (cf. V. L. Parrington, *Main Currents in American Thought* [New York, 1927], Vol. II).

place, with Bach, Gluck, Haydn, Mozart, Beethoven, and Schubert. So it was France, the least progressive of European countries on the industrial side in the late nineteenth and early twentieth centuries, that gave us the best Western art of the period.[13] Paris and the south of France became a mecca for artists from America, Germany, England, Italy, Holland, and Belgium.

As we come down to modern times in Western history, it is no longer true, as it was until the Renaissance, that the most prosperous countries, those in which the population and the volume of production grow most rapidly, are also the leading cultural centers. The change seems to be connected with the change in philosophical doctrine that is generally and rightly associated with Francis Bacon and Hobbes, and hardly less generally, but rather less rightly, with Descartes.[14] With the rise of the philosophy of material improvement, it became the first object of the mind to understand natural phenomena, to increase wealth, and to prolong life.

Until the appearance, at the beginning of the seventeenth century, of what John Donne called the "new philosophy," and more especially until the rise of "classical economics" with Adam Smith, it was taken for granted that philosophers and artists should be concerned in their labors with truth and beauty in relation to man's welfare as a whole. While it was no less true then than now that philosophers and artists had

[13] It is debatable, of course, whether the art of Russia belongs properly to Western civilization. If it does, then Russia shared with France leadership in the art of literature in the late nineteenth century.

[14] I say "rather less rightly" because Descartes' philosophy was based not primarily on man's need for material improvement, but on his power to reason, and above all to reason mathematically. Material improvement, as an object of philosophy, came to Descartes somewhat as an afterthought (cf. E. Gilson, "Descartes, Harvey et la scolastique," *Etudes de philosophie médiévale* [Strasbourg, 1921], pp. 191–245). I hope to return to this subject in a chapter on the history of philosophical thought in a book that I have in hand dealing with industry and civilization in France and England from 1540 to 1640.

to be fed, clothed, and housed by the manual labor of other persons, it never occurred to anyone that this imposed on them an obligation to contribute to production. It is only in recent times, and especially in the United States, that it has come to be sometimes assumed that economics is not simply the science of wealth, but that the standards set up by economists are applicable to all aspects of life, including philosophy, art, and politics. So we get, occasionally, the novel doctrine that the work of the poet, the painter, and the musician can properly be judged by the extent that they stimulate the business administrator to arrange land, labor, and capital in such ways as to provide a larger output. Or, much more frequently, we get the hardly less novel doctrine that they can be judged by the extent that they provide work for ushers, bookbinders, publishers, art dealers, and motion-picture officials. Instead of being led by the artist, the artist's public (through the often unrepresentative agents who manage entertainment and art, and confuse the two to the great damage of art) has come to insist that the artist be led by persons whose purpose is almost exclusively the making of money.

A historian of civilization, who considers the history of art in relation to wealth, is in a position to reach certain tentative conclusions. The late Geoffrey Scott has explained the relationship very well. A relative of the most distinguished newspaper editor of modern times (C. P. Scott, of the *Manchester Guardian*), young Scott struggled with tuberculosis during most of his adult life and succumbed to it at a comparatively early age. But he managed to write a work on architecture which is of more general interest than any other book on the subject that has appeared in the last fifty years, with the possible exceptions of Henry Adams' *Mont-Saint-Michel and Chartres* and Emile Mâle's *L'art du treizième siècle*. In his book, Scott says: "Prosperity is a condition of great achievements [in architecture]; it is not their cause. . . . . Rich and flourishing societies have not seldom grown up, and are growing up in our time, without [making architectural history]. . . . .''[15] The same thing is true of art generally, as our short excursion into its history suggests. Circumstances which increase the command over nature possessed by any civilized society are generally favorable to art, in so far as they free men from the necessity of working to provide for the material side of life. Whether or not this freedom is used for purposes likely to lead to true art depends on the maintenance of a proper balance between the desires of the body and the needs of the mind and spirit. In so far as art is made a servant to the material wants of society it ceases to be art.

It is fortifying to find that these conclusions, reached from a study of history, agree with the view of one of the wisest men who ever lived. "There seem to be two causes of the deterioration of the arts," Socrates tells Adeimantus in *The Republic*. "What are they?" he is asked. "Wealth," he says, "and poverty."[16]

III. ART AND CIVILIZATION

Archdeacon Cunningham, one of the fathers of economic history, remarked that the Parthenon was sheer waste from the standpoint of the economist. While a large number of workers, craftsmen, and artists were once employed in its construction, this temple and all the other public works built on the initiative of Pericles were unproductive. Athenian treasure "was locked up in forms that are artistically superb, but economically worthless."[17] The same thing could be said of the Gothic cathedrals and of all edifices, which, unlike shops, dwelling-houses, and factories, are not lived in or used for

[15] Geoffrey Scott, *The Architecture of Humanism* (2d ed.; New York, 1924), p. 26.

[16] *The Republic* iv. 421 (Jowett trans.).

[17] W. Cunningham, *An Essay on Western Civilization in Its Economic Aspects* (Cambridge, 1898), pp. 119–21.

purposes of production, commerce, or finance. Since the object of all genuine art must be to appeal to the mind and the spirit, it follows that art (together with religion, philosophy, and knowledge generally in so far as it is disinterested) is bound to remain largely parasitic in Cunningham's sense.[18] If the concepts and the precepts of economics are extended to cover the creative labor of the artist, or its products, they enter a realm in which they have properly no place, and in which they are bound to do harm. What is essential to the artist is a world of his own. That does not mean that art should be divorced from life. It does not mean art for art's sake. It does mean art for the sake of man, not for the sake of those perfectly legitimate, but incomplete, sides of man's aspirations that he has in common with the animals. To the extent that truth, beauty, and justice permeate the animal side of man, he is always fortified. To the extent that the animal side of man dominates the human, he is always weakened.

If civilization is to survive, or if it is to be revived in the future, it is essential that the mind and the spirit should lead, not follow. It is essential that art, and also religion and philosophy, should be independent of material ends. The ends of religion and philosophy can only be materialistic in so far as a better body contributes to a better mind and a more honorable spirit. What gave the Christian religion much of its force was the view that it is necessary to do right whether or not it pays. Honesty can never be made a matter of policy without a loss to honesty. If material reward comes with doing right, that is always a cause for rejoicing, but it is the duty of society to see to it that material reward conforms to right and not right to material reward.

[18] I am aware that there are modern economists—notably Professor Frank Knight and his school—who do not expound the kind of economic doctrines reflected in Dr. Cunningham's remarks. His view of what is economically productive is widely accepted nonetheless, especially in popular thinking in the United States.

Like moral philosophy, art rests on the belief—frequently held among civilized people—that it is possible for man, with his mind, or with his hands at the service of his mind, to create a world better and more beautiful than the actual world in which he lives. That need is present to a greater or lesser degree in all men. It does not disappear with the increase in material wealth. However rich human beings become in worldly goods, their experience here on earth will always remain incomplete, if not unhappy. Nothing is more depressing, and even tragic, in modern America than the efforts made by men and women to prolong their childhood, and to drug themselves by the radio and other forms of entertainment into a denial of old age and suffering. The inevitable result is to unfit them for life, to unfit them to defend even the material civilization, for which they often express such enthusiasm. Pascal once wrote that it is the knowledge of his sufferings, of his unhappiness, that distinguishes man from the animals. That is why true art, even comedy, is always basically sad. When Count Almaviva asks Figaro, "Qui t'a donné une philosophie aussi gaie?" he answers, "L'habitude du malheur. Je me presse de rire de tout, de peur d'être obligé d'en pleurer."[19] It is the unsatisfied aspect of man's nature, the needs of his spirit, and not his capacity to produce more wealth with the help of science and technology, which constitute his highest claim to dignity. The reason great poems and great novels are almost always sad, as well as beautiful, is because the human experience falls short of the vision of it granted to the poet and the artist. If human experience does not fall short of a man's vision of it, he is not an artist. That is why men squeeze art out of a society when they succeed in making the artist conform to the wishes of men whose vision is limited to material ends. The utility of art, as distinguished

[19] "Accustomed to Misfortunes, I laugh at every Event, lest on consideration I should find myself more disposed to cry" (*The Barber of Seville*, Act I, Scene 2).

from production, is that by helping us to rise above our fate it prepares us to meet it. While it is good to keep the body young as long as we can, this is only of great value if the mind also stays young. As Lord Sankey, the distinguished English judge, once suggested, what the Greeks meant when they said "whom the gods love die young," was that the good die young in mind and spirit whatever their age.

The partial opposition between the ends of art and the ends of production can be seen in striking relief in connection with architecture. No architect can proceed without relation to the economic purposes of the building he constructs. But the architect who is governed primarily by economic purposes is not an artist. One of the weaknesses of American architecture has been an overemphasis on such purposes. When he saw Monticello, a French marquis remarked that Jefferson was "the first American who had consulted the fine arts to know how he should shelter himself from the weather." Jefferson's example has not been widely followed, though the achievements of some American architects—notably the late Louis Sullivan—in solving, with the help of the fine arts, engineering problems raised by the skyscraper have been important. To be great, the architect, like all artists, has beyond a certain point to proceed according to principles of his own, which are not determined by economic ends or even by technical rules relating to the materials he uses or the problems of support. These principles can never be precisely stated, for they arise out of the inner necessity for the architect to solve particular problems as they present themselves. The problems are invariably new and individual, as in all the arts. What is indispensable is that, as the problems arise, the artist or architect should be free to solve them according to the demands of art rather than according to the demands of mechanics or comfort. If the requirements for heat, refrigeration, for gadgets and material conveniences of all kinds, or for large profits, take precedence over the requirements of beauty in the construction of a building, architecture is bound to suffer. Similar conflicts present themselves in the other arts as a result of the attempts to commercialize them.

How can these conflicts be satisfactorily solved? They can be solved only by admitting that there has to be a distinction between economic ends and artistic ends, and by providing, as many far less wealthy societies of the past have done, the means to enable art, philosophy, and religion to be cultivated for the good of man, rather than exclusively for the sake of those aspects of man's instincts which he shares with the animals. It is not suggested that there is anything wrong with these instincts, or that they should be suppressed. But they should not be allowed to devour art, as they are tending to do at present. Instead, art should be given a place of its own, where it can sweeten and embellish life.

There is a widespread feeling in the United States that material civilization is threatened by any activity which has not as its objective an increase in material wealth, by any activity which does not yield a return in money. It is questionable whether this materialistic attitude, by depriving the mind and the spirit of that sustenance once supplied—however imperfectly—by religion and by the reading of good books, has not weakened the moral fiber of our people to a point where they are incapable of defending even the material civilization that our ancestors have built up. While we put a special store upon material things, we are more prodigal of them than any people of the past. We are ready to waste everything save time. Every waking moment must be filled, no matter how. Americans are escorted by bands of jazz music (brought to them by the cinema and the radio), by teas and cocktail parties, into a world of make-believe and artificial excitement, until many of them are so drugged with unreality that they are no more capable of a genuine human experience than a person saturated with morphine. For the trained intellect, time is the one thing that can be wasted fruitfully. The mind has sometimes to lie fallow if it is to achieve the full fertility of which it is capable.

The choice before us is not between the cultivation of art and the promotion of a higher material standard of life. The material sacrifice we shall have to make in order to cultivate genuine art is small. Art depends upon quality, not upon quantity. There is no danger that all men, or even a large minority, will become artists. Nor is there any danger that the artist, like the despot, will aim to dominate the world. The artistic success of the artist is never at someone else's expense.

All the costs required for endowing genuine art and allowing it to flourish, regardless of its capacity to please the dealers in art, would be more than covered by the enormous waste which takes place in the United States. The difficulty is that modern Americans are disposed to think with disapproval of everything that does not command a market, and with approval of everything that does, even if to the uninitiated it seems to perform no useful function. Many Americans apparently see less waste in the action of a housewife, who throws a large part of the food she buys at the local retail store into an incinerator, than in the labors of an artist, who writes a work of creative literature that represents a contribution to human understanding but does not sell. I recently listened to a discussion among a number of learned economists dealing with waste. They brought up the fictitious case of a farmer, who made his living, not by tilling the soil, but by hauling out automobiles which skidded into the ditch beside a road near his house. To improve business he kept the road muddy by watering it every night. Was this waste? The candidate for the Doctor's degree in economics, who handled himself better than most other candidates I have known, was at a loss to explain why it was waste. If he and other American students of economics were less heavily committed than they are to the notion that value is related altogether to services for which the public will pay, they might feel tolerant toward the creative artist whose works do not happen to please the publisher or the dealer, or to lend themselves readily to advertisement.

As Milton's experience suggests, great artists have seldom prospered by the sale of their works in the public market. They are not likely to do so in the future. The idea that it is easier now than in the past to train a large portion of the population in genuine artistic taste is illusory. In many ways it is much more difficult. The encroachments of the methods of business and the ways of thought associated with business upon the administration, the teaching, and the research in colleges, universities, churches, and schools for art have left little or no place for the cultivation of artistic values. The multiplication of machines and conveniences has done more to dull than to sharpen the natural impulses of men to appreciate and to understand true works of art. The need for making commodities individually, with the hands, teaches good craftsmanship, an essential element in art. As this need has diminished, the understanding of craftsmanship has diminished. Even the widespread distribution of works of art, made possible by mechanical improvement, has contributed, in some ways, to the deterioration of taste. It has reduced, for example, the number of persons who participate in music, and the attention which listeners pay to it. A century ago Eugène Delacroix, the distinguished French painter, suggested that the physical effort of going out to a concert and finding a seat among others who had made the same effort enhanced the charm and the meaning of great music. After hearing Beethoven's pastoral symphony in a large auditorium one Sunday afternoon, he noted in his diary that he would not have had so rich an experience if the orchestra had played for him in his studio.[20] If he had lived to listen to the gramophone, or to radio concerts introduced by an advertiser of cigarettes, and sandwiched between the hasty remarks of a news commentator and the hasty account of a prize fight, he would hardly have changed his mind.

As the work of musicians, painters, and writers has got into the hands of dealers and businessmen, there would seem to be only one way to foster true art. It is to provide the few who have inherited a sense of the great artistic traditions of the past with the opportunity to build on these traditions and to cultivate the arts without debasing them. All great movements in human history have had small beginnings. They have been the work of a handful of indomitable men with firm convictions. That is true of art as well as of politics. It will be true in the future as it has been in the past.

IV. THE FUTURE OF CIVILIZATION

If there is truth in our analysis of the relation of wealth to art and of art to civilization, it is the tendency we observe in modern Europe and America to deny the need of man for a more perfect experience than physical life can give him, that largely explains the meagerness of our recent artistic and cultural history, in spite of our tremendous wealth. The situation with respect to art is similar to that with respect to religion and to moral philosophy. Whether Americans like it or not, the United States is faced with a choice of ends. We can continue to regard it as the main objective of private and public life to make ourselves and the public rich in material goods. Or we can regard material wealth as a means, important for the contribution it makes to physical health and to the sense of well-being, but valuable ultimately only in so far as, through the improvement of physical health and com-

[20] *Journal de Eugène Delacroix*, ed. André Joubin (Paris, 1932), I, 275–76.

fort, it contributes to the dignity of man—only in so far as it increases the esteem in which faith, righteousness, wisdom, and beauty are held by our people. If we follow the latter course we shall have to find an honorable place for genuine religious leaders, for true philosophers, and true artists—if and when they appear. We shall have to make conditions more favorable to their appearance than they are at present. We shall have to accord them an influence in the life of the United States. This does not mean that they should be granted large material rewards. It does mean that the present disposition to judge every man by his income, by the administrative position he holds, or by the publicity he receives, cannot prevail. In place of those standards, there will have to be a revival in a new form of the standards associated with the teachings of Christ and the greatest philosophers and artists of history.

Various objections can legitimately be raised to making faith, righteousness, wisdom, and beauty ends of civilization. It can be said, for example, that Americans prefer to go on with "their way of life," directing all of their professional energies exclusively to the advance of their private fortunes, to the further progress of natural science, to an increase in physical comforts. They prefer to go on devoting all their leisure time to entertainment, to dabbling in painting, music, and poetry, and to absorbing bits of information here and there, presented in forms which frequently resemble boxes of assorted cigars.

In his recently published recollections, the Pennsylvania Quaker, Logan Pearsall Smith, tells us of a letter he received in 1921 from a person whom he calls "the wisest man I know." Having lived the life of an American *émigré* in Europe in the age of Henry James and Edith Wharton, Smith had been obliged by his need for an operation to return for a brief stay in the United States. He was concerned to find that

America was according almost no place to culture. His friend agreed that there was little room in the United States for the "mind," which, he said, "in our lips means, I suppose, the liberal or aristocratic life, the mind turned to pure reflection and pure expression and pure pleasure. But why," he added, "need all the tribes of men sacrifice at our altar?"[21]

The way in which the mind was defined betrays the weakness of the tradition in these men's hands. "One thing is certain," writes Roger Hinks, "great art is never a feat of escapist virtuosity."[22] With Smith and his friend, art and thought were divorced from life; they had become mere decorations, pleasant but unessential.[23] Their potentialities for good had been forgotten.

A similar attitude in relation to learning is widespread in the American universities. When I was an undergraduate at Harvard, I listened to a conversation between two graduate students preparing for the Doctor's degree in philosophy. One expressed concern to the other. He was thinking seriously of abandoning his studies. "I can't see any earthly use for this subject," he said. The other student, who was somewhat older and who later became a prominent and influential philosopher, reassured him by telling him, "it hasn't any use." Once he had divested himself of the "prejudice" that learning should have a purpose, the younger student, like the older one, felt free to devote his life to it as a sort of pleasant game, demanding rather more skill and time than bridge, crossword puzzles, or even chess.

Both these students of philosophy and Smith's friend were under the influence of Francis Bacon and his successors, who see no use in any thought unless it contributes directly to

[21] *Unforgotten Years* (Boston, 1939), pp. 283–84.

[22] *The Criterion*, XVIII, No. 70 (1938), 68.

[23] Cf. R. H. Tawney, *Equality* (3d ed.; London, 1938), pp. 77–82; Arthur Clutton-Brock, *The Ultimate Belief* (New York, 1916), pp. 102–3 and *passim*.

physical health or to wealth. If the philosopher had meant that the search for truth is an end in itself, he would have been in agreement with the greatest philosophers; but what he apparently meant, and what others hearing him would certainly assume that he meant, is that it is a matter of indifference to mankind whether philosophy is cultivated or not. As Tolstoy pointed out, art in modern times (like philosophy) has become more and more escapist and obscure, more and more a hothouse plant. So Smith and his friend assumed that art must be inevitably escapist and obscure, that for a wholesome democratic society it must remain parasitic.

Yet, even if we recognize that great art and philosophy must not be confused with feats of escapist virtuosity, even if we recognize that they are of benefit to mankind, the question remains, "Why need all the tribes of men sacrifice at the altar of the mind?" Our answer must be that there is no such necessity. We cannot force men to cultivate the mind and spirit. That is not what philosophers mean when they speak of absolute values. They mean that the mind and spirit exist and have a need for these values.

The American people have a right to choose their destiny. But they should know what they are doing. They should not imagine they are now cultivating the intellect. That is make-believe. They should frankly admit they are trying the experiment of starving the intellect by denying that it has needs of its own independent of man's physical needs and desires. While excellent things in themselves, scientific observations and experiments do not by themselves, and without the help of philosophy and art, insure the future of the mind. Still less does the widespread dissemination of information by the newspaper and the radio contribute, by itself, to the intelligence of the population. As long as the mind is treated as a sponge it does not increase its powers. It is only by exertion directed toward concrete objectives that the mind can increase its powers. These objectives are righteousness, wisdom, and beauty. Nor should we make the mistake of assuming that the information now purveyed by newspapers and radio commentators exceeds in accuracy or value that of the past. It is doubtful, for example, whether any of our contemporaries could, with the help of all the modern improvements, form so precise and judicious an impression of the military and material forces engaged, or the diplomatic objectives envisaged, by the nations in the present war as Thucydides was able to form, without foreign correspondents and radio commentators, during the Peloponnesian War in which he participated as an Athenian admiral. Even if the information possessed by that mysterious and abstract creature—the average man—is superior now to what it was in Greece twenty-four centuries ago, it is impossible to claim that we have acquired principles that make us better able to act upon our information than were the people of that time.

No one has the authority, no one should have the authority, to prevent the United States from attempting to build a society for the future in which there is no place for the trained, independent, disinterested mind. But it is to be hoped that if the attempt is made, it will be recognized that no society in the past has discarded the intellect and retained even its material civilization for any great length of time. The Romans tried it after the second century A.D., after the time of Juvenal, Galen, and Lucian. There is now general agreement among historians that material welfare in the Empire began to decline in Italy early in the third century and in most of the provinces by the end of the third or the beginning of the fourth century. It does not follow, of course, that the disintegration of the intellect was an important cause for the economic decline of the Empire. We cannot be certain that if the Romans had cultivated the intellect classical civilization would have flowered anew. But the historical evidence, for what it is worth, does not support the view that our present treatment of the human mind and spirit in the United States offers a highroad to the progress which most Americans believe in almost as an article of faith. Americans are fond of claiming that they have a special willingness to experiment. They should recognize that the experiment of discarding the intellect has been made by earlier civilized societies. It is the experiment of cultivating it after the symptoms of disintegration have appeared that would be new.

Another argument can be brought against an attempt to establish righteousness, wisdom, and beauty as the ends of civilization. It can be said that the attempt is bound to fail. As a Western people, the Americans have their culture behind them, in their European past. Ours is a materialistic age, and materialism, many learned men have thought, is always a late rather than an early phase in the civilization cycle.

It would be idle to minimize the force of this argument. A great mass of historical evidence can be marshaled to support it. All earlier civilizations have proved mortal. In the past an existence of great comfort and luxury has almost invariably heralded a decay. What reason is there to hope that the United States can escape from what a distinguished American called the law of civilization and decay?[24]

There is little hope, unless we are able to change the ancient pattern. But what man at his best can do always remains to be determined. If the researches of historians, archeologists, anthropologists, and scientists are reliable, millions of men lived on this planet for tens (if not for hundreds) of thousands of years before they succeeded in creating a civilization. Contrary to all historical experience, men were able eventually to create civilizations with great cities, with wealth, and with art and philosophy. Is it not conceivable, then, that civilized men may eventually succeed, contrary to all historical experi-

---

[24] Brooks Adams, *The Law of Civilization and Decay* (New York, 1896).

ence, in creating some new, more enduring, and more humane and enlightened type of human society, with a pattern of its own different from any pattern of the past?

The dead civilizations strew the deck of the ship of human fortunes. . . . . By the Law of Chance the odds are certainly sixteen to ten, and possibly twenty-five to one that Death the Leveller will lay his icy hand on us likewise. . . . . Yet, even in our forlorn and melancholy plight, our deliverance from the incubus of the pre-destinarian creed should put us in better heart; for if this creed is non-proven, then even in Life-in-Death there is still Hope-against-Hope. The dead civilizations are not "dead by fate"; and therefore a living civilization is not doomed inexorably in advance *migrare ad plures:* to join the majority of its kind that have suffered shipwreck. . . . . The divine spark of creative power is instinct in ourselves; and if we have the grace to kindle it into flame, then the stars in their courses cannot defeat our efforts to attain the goal of human endeavours.[25]

Is that to be America's destiny? In spite of all our intellectual and cultural disadvantages, the United States has open to it this possibility of leading Western civilization into the Promised Land. Most of our ancestors in the nineteenth century supposed that land would prove to be the natural fruit of the unprecedented material progress they saw about them. They were mistaken. The price of a more enduring human society than any known to history is the rejuvenation of man's mind and spirit.

If the United States is to show civilized people the way, it will not be by cultivating either materialism or military despotism. Those are ancient conceptions. Where they lead is obvious. Is it illogical to suggest that the hope for a new type of society lies in refusing to be bound by past experience and in cultivating the aims of life defined for us by religion, by moral

[25] A. J. Toynbee, *A Study of History* (London, 1939), IV, 38–39. On the whole subject of the genesis and disintegration of civilizations, see this great work, now in process of publication.

philosophy, and by art, with the help of the enormous material wealth and leisure with which we are endowed? These aims alone can provide the guidance that is so sorely needed when mankind has lost its compasses and its rudders. The late Thorstein Veblen once suggested that the Western peoples are not naturally adapted, physically or spiritually, to the mechanized industry and the mechanical civilization which have now taken possession of them.[26] If he is right, it may be possible for us to turn away from our present ways of thinking and behaving more readily than we suppose. Struggle and labor, inspired by the drive and hope that are human, are what created civilizations. It is only by making a superhuman effort to establish the ideal state that a new form of human society might be brought into being.

[26] *The Instinct of Workmanship* (New York, 1914), esp. pp. 320-21.

PART III
MEANS OF APPROACH

IX

EDUCATION

✲

THE final end of civilization is to cultivate morality, intelligence, and beauty of and for themselves—or, to put it more correctly, for the sake of man, who alone among the creatures of the earth has discovered them. When we say "of and for themselves," we mean that these objects of civilized existence belong to mankind, not to anyone as an individual. The measure of an individual's grasp on them is his capacity to rise out of himself, to think and act on behalf of one or another of these objectives, not for the sake of something else, not for the sake of worldly honors, but as an ultimate end. For human beings, the end is in the striving. No man or woman is capable of achieving perfect righteousness, perfect wisdom, or perfect art. Labor toward these objects as ends, unlike labor for the sake of amassing riches or fame, is not subject to diminishing returns, except in the sense that the flesh is always weak, so that men require rest to recuperate from their labor. In the pursuit of these ends the rest itself is creative. One begins the ascent anew, not all over again from the valley, but from the point on the mountain where one stopped the day before. The higher one is able to ascend, the more wonderful the quest becomes. It is as if one were drawn upward by the sun, whose rays illuminate each day new features of a distant landscape.

Morality, intelligence, and beauty are separate and distinct from each other. Each is an end in itself. The individual can

seldom pursue them all with equal intensity. The good society must not lay predominant emphasis on any one at the
expense of the others. But as ends for mankind they are never
incompatible in the same way that the pursuit of worldly
profit, or of sensuous enjoyment, may come into fundamental
conflict with the search for goodness, truth, and beauty. The
ideal state would be one in which the material aspects of life,
together with the search for new scientific knowledge and improved technique, were so ordered as to provide for the cultivation of morality, intelligence, and beauty to the maximum
degree possible, in the lives of the people generally, as well as
in those of the prophets, philosophers, poets, and other
artists who help to show them the way.

In modern industrialized civilization, how can mankind be
guided in the direction of the ideal state? The miraculous
world which man's mind has been able to create—a world
with infinite possibilities—seems to be irreconcilable with
the finite, limited world of narrow human beings, and the
bounded territory of the earth.

> Un matin nous partons, le cerveau plein de flamme,
> Le coeur gros de rancune et de désirs amers,
> Et nous allons, suivant le rythme de la lame,
> Berçant notre infini sur le fini des mers.[1]

How can we purify ourselves of the rancor and bitterness of
which Baudelaire speaks? How can we enlarge the finite world
of land and ocean in the direction of the infinite world that, as
Baudelaire tells us in his opening lines, it is sometimes given
a little child to see in a flash in his growing mind.

> Pour l'enfant, amoureux de cartes et d'estampes,
> L'univers est égal à son vaste appétit.

[1] Charles Baudelaire, "Le Voyage," *Les Fleurs du mal*, ed. Camille Vergniol (Paris,
n.d.), p. 242.

Like many poets before him, Baudelaire saw no solution on this earth for the overwhelming problem of reconciling man's vision with the actuality. What little men can do toward its solution cannot be done quickly. Men can make suggestions; they cannot bring forward confidently bills that must be enacted. Any specific proposals that are put forward should be put forward tentatively, with great humility. If better schemes are offered, the earlier schemes should be withdrawn. It should not be our object to oppose all specific programs of reform suggested by persons who, in these days of intellectual and moral confusion, deny that there are general principles upon which men can agree or ought to agree. Men seek the good in different ways, and no man can feel certain that his own plans, if adopted, would actually bring about the results for which he hopes.

For none of the suggestions which follow is originality claimed. If one of them should prove useful, the thought spent on them would be rewarded a thousand fold. The object of setting forth some rough "means of approach" is not so much to try to remake our institutions according to a fixed pattern as to suggest the overwhelming need for all men of good will, and particularly for persons who rise to places of influence or power, to live, to speak, to write, and to act in the light of two considerations. The first is that the United States, together with the other countries created by Western civilization, is at a turning point in history, where an emphasis on material objectives for their own sake is likely to drag us into an abyss. The second, which follows both from the first and from an examination of the past wisdom of the human race, is that the object of every proposal for improvement should be judged by the contribution it would make to the morality, the wisdom, and the art of the American people and of mankind.

If we are to work toward the ultimate ends of civilized

existence, it may be desirable to make over, bit by bit, the whole educational system of the United States, by strengthening and developing all the good elements which this system contains. But schools, colleges, and universities can never be independent of the society in which they grow up. To paraphrase Pascal: "A good society is formed by education; a good society is spoiled by education. Thus a good education will form, and a bad education will spoil, a good society. It is therefore essential to know how to choose in order to form and not to spoil a good society; and one cannot make the right choice unless the good society is already formed and not spoiled. A vicious circle exists, and the society and education that can escape from it are fortunate indeed."[2]

The remaking of our education depends evidently upon the remaking of our society, just as the remaking of our society depends upon the remaking of our education. It is less the duty of education to train students to fit into the present environment than to show how the environment might be made fit for true education. Education should serve our people, but at the same time it should be recognized that the best way to serve them is to show them, through leadership, how they can serve mankind. So some of the members of educational institutions have a twofold obligation. They have the obligation to reform themselves and, if possible, their institutions in accordance with the ends of a good society, and they have the further obligation to show the persons engaged in economic, political, and social work the ways of reform that would lead toward the good society. The relation of the great majority of citizens, as well as teachers, to these reforms would consist in learning to distinguish good proposals from bad, and in rising above habit and prejudice when either obstructs the good.

It is the duty of education to inculcate in the young a love of those ends of civilization which raise mankind above the

2 "Pensées sur l'esprit," *Les Pensées*, ed. Adolphe Espiard (Paris, n.d.), I, 60.

beasts. No one in recent years has defined this objective more nobly than the late Sir Arthur Clutton-Brock. He wrote:

Education ought to teach us how to be in love always and what to be in love with. The great things of history have been done by the great lovers, by the saints and men of science and artists; and the problem of civilization is to give every man a chance of being a saint, a man of science, or an artist. But this problem cannot be attempted, much less solved, unless men desire to be saints, men of science, and artists, and if they are to desire that continuously and consciously, they must be taught what it means to be these things.[3]

The remaking of our educational system is the task not only of university faculties but of all persons who train the young. If the parents, the clergymen, the elementary-school teachers, and the teachers in the high schools and colleges fail to do their duty, there is little hope that the university professor can do his, because the number of persons who can be redeemed after the age at which they enter the university is exceedingly small. But the universities should define the nature of the duty. They should show the advantages of leadership by taking the lead. It is for them to break out from the circular course along which education and society, locked together, are rotating, in order to save Western civilization from what seems to be a downward spiral.

I. THE HIGHER LEARNING

After a century and a half as a nation, the United States has not managed to establish an independent artistic or intellectual tradition. That is partly the result of the failure of Americans as a people to husband and encourage such artistic and intellectual strength as they possess. When one reads the

---

[3] *The Ultimate Belief* (New York, 1916), p. 123. As the position that I take in my book is in agreement with Clutton-Brock's, I should perhaps explain that I came on his essay only after I had written mine! In its revision, I have been helped considerably by his. I have discussed in another place the contention that what is said by thinkers and teachers on behalf of these ultimate and abstract values does nothing to improve matters ("Philosophical Values and American Learning," *Review of Politics*, IV, No. 3 [1942], 257-70).

books and letters of earlier generations, one comes occasionally upon obscure persons whose thought on the basic matters of religion, moral philosophy, and art is in essential agreement with that of the wisest, the most saintly, and the most artistically inspired men of the past. These persons form scattered specks on the landscape of American nineteenth-century history. Their taste was instinctively good. Their writing had promise. Except in a few cases, their names are not found in books on American history. Few even got into those large volumes that purport to give brief biographies of everybody who is anybody. We meet them when we delve into the histories of families, where the public scale of values does not apply, and where some fair thought has been rescued by fond relatives from the complete oblivion to which the American scene has consigned its authors. Yet, with a small number of exceptions, the thought and taste of the Americans who have become what is called "prominent" are less elevated and discriminating, their style is less competent, than the thought and taste and style of these obscure persons.

Even today one occasionally meets, here and there, men and women with views on religion, philosophy, and art, which, if encouraged, might contribute to the formation of a genuine intellectual and artistic tradition in the United States. As might be expected from the collapse of standards and the shrinkage in the place accorded the mind during the last fifty years, such persons get no more encouragement now than others like them got a century ago when Americans were absorbed in conquering the western wilderness. So dispersed are these incipient thinkers and artists that they seldom know of each other's existence. When they do, the extreme individualism in affairs of the mind that prevails on this continent hinders them from directing their impulses toward that measure of common understanding which would be to the advantage of knowledge and art.

They seldom find a way of making a living by their activities without compromising their views or sacrificing their integrity. Even if they are financially independent, they are rarely made of stern enough stuff to face the disapproval which an uncompromising stand would involve. So they lose the confidence which the ideas they hold, if developed and enriched, would give them. As they are brought up by their companions, and usually by their parents and teachers, to suppose that nothing has value unless it can be sold, or can obtain for its possessor publicity or a substantial post of some sort, they soon abandon their instincts, for a more respectable career. If they have regrets, they take them out by grousing with their companions at lunch at the club, in the smoking-room of a Pullman car, or amid the somewhat forced merriment that prevails at a cocktail party.

Is it undemocratic to give such persons an opportunity to husband what belongs less to them personally than to humanity? If we say that it is, then we exclude from democracy the very elements which alone are capable of ennobling man. Surely it was not the object of the founding fathers, of Thomas Jefferson, to have democracy lower the stature of man.

The first step in the direction of a better society would seem to be to nourish the instincts toward goodness, wisdom, and beauty. A few centers might be created in which these instincts could be developed independently of the demands of the market place, independently of the persons and enterprises which measure artistic, intellectual, and moral values in terms of the money and the publicity which they command, or the extent to which they appear to contribute directly to material production. Might it not be possible to set up these independent centers of creative thought and art in connection with a few of the leading universities?

What is there to recommend such a course? In the natural sciences it has never been possible to measure results in terms of money, or even entirely in terms of publicity. Largely, perhaps, as a result of their special concern with the natural sciences, the American universities possess to some slight extent two elements indispensable in the cultivation of the intellect. One is the tradition of careful, impartial inquiry. The other, closely allied to this, is the tradition of freedom of thought and speech.

Neither tradition is very effective in the universities today. As Veblen suggested, the impulse of scholars to seek new truth for its own sake has been more and more submerged by the adoption within the universities of the methods and outlook associated with business enterprise. "The training given by these two lines of endeavour—science and business—is wholly divergent. . . . ." It follows from the encroachment of business practices on learning, he goes on to say, that "in many and devious ways . . . . a university man may be able to serve the collective enterprise of his university to better effect than by an exclusive attention to the scholastic work on which alone he is ostensibly engaged." Yet, "in no field of human endeavour is competitive notoriety and a painstaking conformity to extraneous standards of living and of conduct so gratuitous a burden, since learning is in no degree a competitive enterprise; and all mandatory observance of the conventions—pecuniary or other—is necessarily a drag on the pursuit of knowledge."[4] Whatever the value of the business methods in their own sphere, they are, as Veblen says, a handicap to impartial inquiry and creative thought.

It is obvious, also, that in the universities and colleges the right to freedom of speech is sometimes abused. The justification for it is that it is essential to the cultivation of the intellect. Under the guise of defending freedom of speech, some university men waste time arguing about tenure and the rights

---

[4] Thorstein Veblen, *The Higher Learning in America* (New York, 1918), pp. 77, 165, 233.

of their members to indulge in propaganda that has no relation to the intellect. They have even been known to use freedom of speech as a cloak behind which "in many and devious ways" to carry on enterprises that have little or no scholarly purpose.

Nevertheless these two traditions, which are in the keeping first and foremost of the universities, are of great value. In saving them, we will help to save our country. We may help to save Western civilization.

From the Renaissance until the French Revolution, on the Continent of Europe, artists and writers depended for their livelihood mainly upon the patronage of kings, princes, and nobles. The great centers of art and creative life were the courts. The most brilliant and important in the seventeenth and eighteenth centuries was, of course, the famous French court of Versailles. Rich men, who owed their fortunes to finance, commerce, and industry, sometimes purchased works of art. But, until the nineteenth century, it was only in England that the middle class provided many artists and writers with their means of livelihood and played a conspicuous part in the formation of taste. As Stendhal explained in the early nineteenth century, tremendous interrelated social and intellectual changes took place in France between 1785 and 1824. It became necessary for the writer to please an audience composed no longer mainly of courtiers and nobles, but of bourgeois families living mostly in Paris, each with an income of from 10,000 to 100,000 francs a year.[5] In terms of our money this means roughly from $5,000 to $50,000. Rich burgesses in the provincial towns, like M. Bruyas of Montpellier, who patronized Courbet and Delacroix, also began to influence art.

With the growth of mass production and advertising, conditions changed again. Writers and artists, especially in the United States, have been placed at a far greater remove from

[5] Stendhal, *Racine et Shakespeare* (Edouard Champion ed.; Paris, 1925), I, 91; II, 168.

the public than they were in nineteenth-century Europe. The public which is expected to buy books and patronize art has less taste or discriminating judgment of its own. Between the artist and his public, many kinds of middlemen have intervened. There are, for instance, dealers in art, publicity men, publishers, magazine editors, reviewers, members of museum staffs, etc. Such persons exercise a considerable influence in determining what the public shall see, hear, and read. But the decisions taken by many of these persons have little relation to either artistic or philosophical values, as these have been understood by past ages. Some of the critics are not much better equipped to judge values than the public. Even when they are, they nearly always have so much administrative work or lecturing to do that they cannot give their best attention to matters of taste which require time for meditation. The publishing houses care less and less for true values. One of my older colleagues has been reading books on theology and religion for the same publishing house for half a century. He has been struck by the very great decline in the interest that his employers take in his judgment of the intrinsic merits of the works they submit to him. Thus critics fall back, or are forced back, on other considerations than intellectual or artistic power. They consider, for example, in the case of a book or article, whether the subject has been recently treated, without seriously considering the value of the treatment in objective terms. They do not know that great art consists less in saying something for the first time than in saying something important better than it has ever been said before. They find it enough to ask such questions as these: Does the work contain sensational predictions, particularly concerning our economic future? Does it retail sensational stories concerning current events or contemporary men made prominent by the newspaper, the cinema, or the radio? The critics often find there is no place for some valuable article, in spite of its important message. They think the message well expressed, fundamentally right. It is one of which Americans are in need. Such an article could be published only in a serious magazine, they remark, and there are virtually no serious magazines left. There are, of course, the learned journals. But these are devoted exclusively to the results of research or to syntheses dealing with narrow fields. Even if a learned journal would take the article, it is obviously intended for a general audience, rather than for their small special groups of subscribers. The persons capable of artistic and philosophical judgments are unable, for one reason or another, to exercise them, or, if they do, they are denied by circumstances the opportunity to make them count.

What is necessary to encourage art and creative thought and to give them some influence in this country is freedom of inquiry for the artist and thinker, and an independence of sales, an independence of the whole paraphernalia that has been built up during the past fifty years for marketing books, pictures, musical compositions, and concerts. This paraphernalia may well have a place in connection with entertainment. Entertainment is desirable in the well-ordered state, provided it is not, as at present, confused and combined with art, to the damage of art, and provided it is not, as at present, given time and importance disproportionate to its value. The present confusion of art and thought with entertainment is submerging both. It does not even contribute to entertainment.

It will now be apparent why the universities have an opportunity to cultivate art and thought. Almost alone among American institutions, they retain remnants of the tradition of freedom of inquiry and of the principle that there is no connection between the value of a work of the mind and the price for which it sells or the publicity it obtains. If the universities can make room for art and thought, they may be able to affect the whole educational system and the whole life of the country for the better.

This might be done by creating at a few universities an

independent place for art and thought. It would have to be a place where artists and thinkers were free to develop according to their own inspirations. But at the same time it should be a place in which they can learn from and have influence upon the university. To make them a part of the present system of the higher learning would be to destroy the hope of their development. Some years ago, in one of the most liberal graduate schools in this country, the director began his remarks to the incoming class by telling them in no uncertain terms, "We don't want any geniuses around here." This shows how the present conception of the highest functions of graduate study is inadequate to the purposes of strengthening the intellect and cultivating art. If the director had said that he did not expect to find genius, he would merely have been making what is, sadly enough, a statement of fact. Not even a person interested in ideas could have taken exception. But, if we are to have a higher learning worthy of the name, its highest aim should be to welcome genius with open arms and to offer it every possible facility to develop.

The solution would seem to be the creation, within one or two or possibly more universities, of small faculties with entirely different objectives from those at present connected with graduate study in the United States. These faculties would be altogether independent of the departmental and divisional structure, which now covers both the graduate and undergraduate curriculum. Fields of study would have no place. The members would be chosen for their eminence as writers, artists, musical composers, or for the power of their thought as philosophers or in connection with some special subject, if it represented a contribution to moral philosophy and if their concern was with knowledge as a whole and with values, rather than simply with analytical studies.

Members of such a faculty would be paid competent salaries. Their incomes would be on a par with those of the chief professors in the present leading universities. There would be no distinction of rank between them. The terms of their employment would vary according to the length of time they found it desirable to spend each year at the universities and the nature of the work they could fruitfully accomplish there. This work should never be so arranged as to interfere with their careers as artists or creative thinkers. In so far as they earned money beyond a certain amount by their work outside the university, their earnings should either be turned over to the university or their salaries should be correspondingly diminished. The university would thus relieve the members of this faculty from all dependence on the market place. It would enable the artist or the philosopher to carry on his work with the single-minded purpose of serving mankind, of laboring to meet the needs of men for beauty, truth, and goodness, rather than to cater to their transient wants.

The number of persons holding positions on this faculty would depend on the thinkers, writers, and artists available. New chairs would be created as the opportunity arose. There might be one or two or ten or twenty. As the holders of appointments would not cover fields, there would be no question of filling chairs. The main task of the group would be to perform their functions as thinkers, writers, and artists. Lecturing would not be a requirement for membership. But those who found lecturing consistent with the fulfilment of their creative work would offer, from time to time, lecture series of a length and character suited to the nature of their subjects.

Artists and writers and university students of exceptional promise whose interests were in creative thought or in one of the arts would have the opportunity of consulting the members of this faculty and of presenting work to them for criticism and discussion. The faculty would help to bring the thought and spirit of a true university into the life of the country. For this it is not sufficient that the learned man should influence the tiny group of obscure specialists to whose suffrage he has come to be limited by the fractionizing of knowledge that has been so striking in the last fifty years. Nor can the higher learning contribute to the intelligence and culture of the American people if its only connection with the public is through professors and instructors who retail sketchy information concerning current events or who offer hastily improvised advice on current political and economic issues.

The new faculty could provide the means of enriching both scholarship and art to their mutual advantage. Such genuine scholarship as comes from the universities has something to teach the artist, the critic, and the man of letters. This lesson is now being lost. At the same time the true artist, the true thinker, and the man of letters have to show the scholar how his work can be treated in a way to make it at once intelligible, valuable, and even beautiful. That lesson is also being lost. The separation of scholarship from literature, as Archibald MacLeish has pointed out, is a relatively recent development in the Western world. It deprives both scholarship and literature of power to do good. It enables both the scholar and the artist to avoid responsibility.[6] It is to the advantage of neither. The remedy, obviously enough, is to bring scholarship and literature, along with other arts, together.

By its influence, such a faculty might help to change, in fundamental respects, the nature of ordinary graduate work for the Doctor's degree in the American universities. At the same time, standards concerning reading and study might develop that would alter the whole course of training in the colleges, high schools, and elementary schools. The standards which the new faculty might help to establish would eventually assist parents in the intellectual training of their children.

What are the other changes that are needed in the universities, if larger numbers of Americans are to be encouraged, not only in great metropolitan centers but in small localities all

---

[6] *The Irresponsibles* (New York, 1940).

over the country, to strive toward the good life? What are the other changes needed if living is to be given a purpose that it has largely lost since the struggle for existence has been mitigated and since the population, particularly the children and adolescents, have found themselves in possession of a vast amount of spare time that they have not been taught to improve?

On the eve of the first World War the late Geoffrey Scott described the condition of architecture in words that might be written today about almost every art or profession or intellectual discipline. "We subsist," he wrote, "on a number of architectural habits, on scraps of tradition, on caprices and prejudices, and above all on this mass of more or less specious axioms, on half-truths, unrelated, uncriticized and often contradictory, by means of which there is no building so bad that it cannot with a little ingenuity be justified, or so good that it cannot plausibly be condemned."[7] The only difference between conditions when Scott wrote, in 1914, and now is that traditions are scrappier than they were, that propaganda plays a larger part in discussion than it used to, that caprice and prejudice are less restrained, and that it has become so common to justify the bad and belittle the good that the words "good" and "bad," "honor" and "dishonor," "truth" and "falsehood," together with nearly all words that once had a significance in connection with the arts, have lost most of their meaning for persons who influence opinion.

For this state of uncertainty and gullibility, for this trifling with meaningful words, for this impoverishment of the language, our education is partly to blame. The tendency among teachers and scholars for several decades has been to assume that if men follow their inclinations and selfish interests in whatever directions they lead, if they speak and write without hesitating long enough to think, the ends of teaching and re-

[7] *The Architecture of Humanism* (London, 1914), p. viii.

search will take care of themselves. The belief, common not only in the Middle Ages but during most of the nineteenth century, in the existence of general principles applicable to learning and to conduct, has been weakened and almost destroyed. Discredit has also been thrown on the view commonly held by the learned in our grandparents' time that there is a limited number of great and permanent books, and that no man can call himself educated without a knowledge of some of them.

Such principles as are still taught in the colleges and universities are concerned not with learning in general, but with some particular branch of it, such as qualitative analysis, money and banking, bibliography, map-making, or historical criticism. As the number of subjects taught has multiplied more rapidly during the last fifty years than during the whole of previous Western history, such principles are the possessions of small groups of specialists, who have woven them into esoteric codes. They seldom make these codes more accessible to the general public, or even to their colleagues in other departments, than the ritual of a Greek letter fraternity or a Masonic lodge. The codes are modified so frequently that they become obsolete in a few decades, if not in a few years. The graduate student who started work for his Doctor's degree in some department of a university just after the first World War, and who returned to complete it on the eve of the second, found practically all the knowledge he had retained useless for meeting the requirements of the new instructors who had replaced his old teachers. A student is likely to meet with similar difficulties when he transfers from one graduate school to another.

Dissatisfaction with the results of recent developments in American education has been fairly widespread for some time. This is giving rise to much debate. Some of the debate has found its way into print. There have been a few constructive proposals for reform. Among them, those brought forward by the president of the University of Chicago deserve much more serious attention than they have received.[8]

One of the chief faults of education in America in the last fifty years or so has been that educators have followed the currents of their time, and have forgotten the highest moral, intellectual, and aesthetic principles, which are independent of time.[9] They have left on the student the impression that he is doing all that is necessary if he is guided by those of his instincts and desires that do not conflict with the ideas and the practices of the people with whom he associates. He is not directed by his teachers to standards of scholarly or of ethical conduct better than those to which the common run of men and women are always subject, because the flesh is always weak and it is always easier at the moment to evade and to compromise than to face issues and surmount difficulties.

At the same time, there has been an increasing disposition on the part of the teachers to belittle both the great works of the past and the serious works of the present, by debunking their authors and denying that there are such things as superior knowledge and wisdom among human beings. Of course great men of letters and other great artists have always been subject to abusive and irrelevant attacks. But now that everyone feels it necessary to be an author and assert his ego, now that the chief business of the "thinker" is supposed to be the "scientific" one of rendering obsolete the labor of his predecessors, abuse has got mixed up with instruction as well as with what passes for criticism. Many of the teachers in the universities are writers. Instead of attempting, in their teaching, the difficult task of transmitting to their students the ac-

[8] R. M. Hutchins, *The Higher Learning in America* (New Haven, 1936); *No Friendly Voice* (Chicago, 1936); *Education for Citizenship*, to be published in the near future by the University of Louisiana Press.

[9] Cf. above, chap. iv, sec. i.

cumulated wisdom of the human race, some bring their puerile controversies into the classroom, and handle great works of art and thought (on the rare occasions when they mention them) as if they were on the same level with the tens of thousands of cheap books and articles that pour every year from the printing presses. So, instead of learning to judge all men with the help of the wisdom of great men, the student learns to belittle great men armed with all the weaknesses and jealousies of small men. The student learns to conform where he ought to question, and to question where he ought to conform. He does not learn self-criticism or independent judgment. The difference between mediocrity and distinction for a considerable number of persons lies precisely in the attempt they are able and willing to make to outdo themselves. It is to Marivaux, a man sometimes charged with affectation, that we owe what is perhaps the best statement of this truth. Like Beaumarchais, Marivaux belonged to that movement in French eighteenth-century literature which has been often misunderstood because it had a lightness of touch. There is nothing frivolous about his remark in *La vie de Marianne*, "... il faut se redresser pour être grand: il n'a qu'à rester comme on est pour être petit."[10]

Yet from the cradle to the advanced age which it is now thought men and women must attain before they can venture into life, Americans are encouraged to do as they like, to remain what they are. Students are justified in concluding that there is not much value in education, if men who are called educated have nothing better to offer by way of advice than to tell them to do what they please. Even when modern education does not make a positive contribution to vicious habits, it seldom provides students with any armor against their own weaknesses. In her remarkable book, *The House of Mirth*, Mrs.

---

[10] "One must be better than one is in order to be great; to be small one has only to remain what one is" (*La Vie de Marianne* [1731–41], Part II).

Wharton has a sentence about the heroine, Lily Bart, which provides a key to the whole work. "She could not breathe long on the heights; there had been nothing in her *training* to develop any continuity of moral strength; what she craved, and really felt herself entitled to, was a situation in which the noblest attitude should also be the easiest."[11] American education in homes, schools, and churches does little or nothing to fortify those aspirations toward virtue which material advantages have made more abundant in the United States than in any other nation.

The training in colleges and universities is frequently no less aimless than that in the schools. Even the few graduates who carry off scholastic honors in their eagerness to get better teaching posts leave the universities with a warped conception of knowledge. They mistake the study of economics or chemistry or sociology, or more frequently some branch of these disciplines, for the pursuit of knowledge, and give their specialty an autonomy for which there is no justification. The best-trained graduates seldom learn more than some narrow specialty. They are usually ignorant of the general cultural and intellectual traditions that the Western world has developed from its Greek and Latin heritage. The very great majority of all graduates are without knowledge of any discipline. They find in their colleges and universities no objectives except those which are of immediate material and social interest. Their parents frequently send them to college because statistics show that college graduates earn more money than their less fortunate fellows. They frequently select the college not for the course of study it offers, or even for the eminence of its faculty, but because of the social advantages it is supposed to provide for young men and women in their quest for "success."

With what should the universities concern themselves if

[11] Edith Wharton, *The House of Mirth*, Book II, chap. viii (my italics).

they are to lead the United States and the world out of the intellectual chaos and the moral confusion which have undermined the confidence of men? Two principles which might be applied to the teaching and the study of all subjects, both in the graduate schools and in the colleges, may be suggested. In the first place, the universities might concentrate on the relations between the various branches of scholarship. While no professor can hope to know as much about the technique of banking as a good banker, he can know more than the banker about the relations between banking and ethics or between banking and politics. The study of these relationships might well become the special province of the most intelligent and enterprising university professors.

The university professor alone is in a position to examine these relationships disinterestedly, because he is not a banker or a statesman or a politician. The student should not be allowed, as he is now, to study special subjects without relation to the rest of knowledge. He should devote an important part of his time to questions such as these: How does government influence religion and how does religion influence government? What influence has philosophy upon poetry and poetry upon philosophy? In order to answer such questions professors as well as students would have to become acquainted with other subjects besides the ones they now teach. They would not be able to take refuge in the esoteric jargon of their special fields, for they would have to speak in a simple, common language intelligible to every intelligent person.

To discuss the relations between the various branches of knowledge will provide a way of discovering the relative importance of each branch. This leads to the second principle which might guide university instruction. It is to teach the student at every stage of his work that a hierarchy of values exists in relation to knowledge and wisdom, a hierarchy that has stood the test of time, in the sense that very wise men have been able to agree, in a rough and general way, upon the nature and order of the values, during some twenty-five centuries. It is frequently suggested today in American universities that there is nothing approaching agreement among ancient sages in this matter of values. Much is made of the different interpretations to which the wisdom of the past has been subject. To contend that distinctions make impossible rough and general agreement is to reveal a warped view of learning, a misunderstanding of the meaning of philosophical truth. As St. Augustine points out in the thirty-first chapter of the twelfth book of his *Confessions*, a general truth, by its nature, comprehends a number of different truths. When the interpretations to which it is legitimately subject are not entirely inconsistent with one another, they do not destroy the general truth, they reveal its fruitfulness. The greatest thinkers and the greatest poets are those who have known how to give each subject they treat a significance proportionate to its importance, according to a common view of the ends of man. Some arrangement is indispensable in carrying out research, and an arrangement directed toward important ends would give more meaning to the teaching and the written work of our universities than they now have.

Another purpose of teaching true values would be to enable each student to learn what aspect of his special studies deserves the most attention. The scholar and the advanced student who are devoting themselves mainly to economics or to political science should be taught what are the most important questions in connection with these subjects as determined by moral philosophy. All questions with which the discipline deals should be arranged according to their relative importance for the good life of society and of the individuals who make it up. The student should learn at first hand who have been the great economists and the great political scientists and why. The students of poetry, music, or history should steep themselves in the work of the great poets, the great musicians, and the great historians. They should make use of encyclopedias, handbooks, and monographs on special subjects, even if they are of no philosophical importance, but only for the sake of accurate information. They should be taught that no pain can be spared in the effort to achieve accuracy, when they make written and even spoken statements. But they should not assume that works which give reliable information are in the same class with those whose structure and content are determined by genius, and in which reliable information is introduced not simply for its own sake but as a part of creative thought or art.

At the same time, students might be taught that not all subjects within the university curriculum are equally important for the good life. They should be helped to learn that the study of the basic principles of political science, as formulated by such men as Plato, Aristotle, Bodin, Harrington, and Montesquieu, is more important than the study of public-utility administration, of ward political machinery, of labor injunctions, of sewage disposal, and other current conditions. The former study helps men to face every situation they meet in life, the latter only particular situations which have frequently ceased to exist by the time they are studied. Current problems would not be slighted by such a change of emphasis in the higher learning. If the arguments of great political thinkers of the past were treated not, as at present, as "dead," if their relevance for our own age were sought, many present-day problems would be made more intelligible than they are with only the methods of studying them now in vogue. A firmer basis than now exists would be laid for wise political action.

Students should be helped to appreciate that a knowledge of philosophy, in the ancient sense of the basic principles of justice, virtue, and wisdom, is even more important than a knowledge of political science, which may be properly treated as the most fruitful branch of it. They should be encouraged to ask themselves whether the study of economic laws, that has engaged the attention of thinkers for hardly more than two or three centuries, is likely to be as fundamental a matter for human welfare as the study of the ends of the state, which comprehend the economic welfare of its members—a study that has engaged the attention of some of the greatest thinkers since the time of Plato.

The philosophical attitude toward knowledge, in the ancient Platonic and Aristotelian sense, has a bearing on both the teaching and the writing to be done in the universities in the future. How might the present treatment of subjects be altered to help in establishing the unity of all knowledge and in showing the proper relationship of one branch to others?

Let us take the subject of economics as an example. The tendency in the work of Wicksteed, Pigou, Knight, and some others is to recognize the importance for general welfare of moral, intellectual, and artistic needs which can be satisfied only in ways that cannot be brought readily into direct or indirect relation with the measuring-rod of money. It is even denied that any human activity can be treated as separate from economics. In so far as these tendencies in economic thought emphasize the unity of knowledge and of human experience, they are to be welcomed. The danger would seem to lie not in breaking down the largely artificial barriers which scholars have erected between different kinds of human endeavors and activities, but in the assumption that ultimate judgments concerning their value can be properly made in economic terms and purely on the basis of economic reasoning, rather than in terms of moral philosophy.

There seem to be essentially two ways in which the autonomy of economics is conceived at present, and neither helps much in preserving Western culture. One is the conception of economics as a science, like mathematics, divorced from life and pursued for the sake of the elegant demonstrations that are possible. The other is the conception of economics as a body of doctrines which, if only applied by businessmen, statesmen, farmers, wage-earners, lawyers, professors, and even artists, would solve all the important problems of existence. The holders of this second conception would be inclined to substitute economics for philosophy in a manner similar to that in which Gilson has shown us Descartes tried to substitute mathematics for philosophy, Kant to substitute physics for philosophy, and Comte to substitute sociology for philosophy.[12]

If the economist adopts the first conception, he washes his hands of the difficult and dangerous world of which he is a part. He limits himself to the form of reasoning which Pascal calls "geometrical." The result of reasoning solely as a geometrician is described by Pascal in the following words: "Les géomètres, qui ne sont que géomètres, ont donc l'esprit droit, mais pourvu qu'on leur explique bien toutes choses par définitions et principes: autrement ils sont faux et insupportables; car ils ne sont droits que sur les principes bien éclaircis."[13]

If the economist adopts the second conception, he proposes to solve all the problems of the world by measures designed to increase the production and improve the distribution of commodities and services, without regard to the philosophical value of the wants which determine the nature of the commodities and services. The preoccupation with material values

[12] Cf. Etienne Gilson, *The Unity of Philosophical Experience* (New York, 1937).

[13] "Geometricians, who are simply geometricians, have therefore a true view, on condition that everything is explained to them by definitions and principles; without this they are false and insupportable; for they are only right about principles that are made perfectly clear" (*Les Pensées*, ed. Adolphe Espiard [Paris, n.d.], I, 58). Cf. above, pp. 138–40.

seems to be one of the chief sources of weakness in American education and in American life today. If, therefore, economics is to help in preserving Western culture, it should not set itself up as a substitute for philosophy. As has been suggested in the chapter on moral philosophy, economics should try to find its place in relation to philosophy. It should reveal the best roads to the satisfaction of wants which moral philosophy indicates are worth satisfying. If the economist is to contribute to the good life, if he is to help in defending democracy, he should be concerned with the production and distribution of wealth that will contribute most to righteousness, wisdom, and beauty.

When it comes to research and written work in connection with social and humanistic studies generally, such a philosophical approach might enable universities to make a more helpful contribution to the welfare of mankind than they are making at present. It should be recognized that creative thought and art, of the kind to which the new university faculties would devote themselves, are, at their best, in a higher category than purely analytical studies can ever be.

Let us take the subject of history as an example. Since the late nineteenth century, historical scholars have concerned themselves more and more exclusively, except when they were writing textbooks or popular surveys, with gathering materials and with the treatment of minute details of history or biography. The time has come, not to stop gathering materials, but to gather them more intelligently and for purposes determined by moral philosophy.[14] The time has come to lay less emphasis upon the gathering of materials and more on the use of the materials for serious syntheses, like those of Pirenne, Rostovtzeff, and McIlwain. The number of persons gifted enough to produce works of this stature will always

[14] The recent French *Annales d'histoire économique et sociale* stood for such an objective in the study of history.

be very limited. But such works could be given to advantage a much greater weight in the educational world than at present. In social and humanistic studies, research, in the sense of gathering data either for their own sake or to establish some obscure point, should not be treated as if it were equal in importance with the writing of creative histories. The sums spent by foundations and universities on analytical studies should be curtailed and, instead, some of the money should go toward the creation of special faculties devoted to genuine art and philosophy. Some should go toward the building of a better system of elementary and secondary education. Much money would still be spent on analytical studies—but it would be devoted to inquiries undertaken by scholars who have clear objectives, like A. L. Bowley, Colin Clark, and H. G. Moulton. Valuable research is done not by persons who indulge in it for its own sake, or for the sake of spending the money that accumulates on the investments of rich foundations, but by those who work under the inspiration of great historical syntheses or great works of philosophical, political, or economic thought. It is done by persons who are out intelligently "to fill the empty boxes" which creative thinkers have discovered.

As Jacques Maritain has said, we must both insure the permanence of the purely analytical historical studies of the nineteenth century and go beyond them to the writing of creative, philosophical history, which deals with the larger problems of human existence and which aims, like the histories of Herodotus and Thucydides and all great historical works, to help future generations of men in dealing with the recurring problems of existence. It is only by going beyond the purely analytical studies in this way, by incorporating some of the valuable information they contain in works of literature and human understanding, that the painstaking labor of the recent armies of fact-finders might be preserved for posterity.

In view of the preference which instructors in the junior colleges feel for modern light comedies over Shakespeare's works, it is not surprising that the students in the universities should be almost entirely devoid of a sense of intellectual and artistic values. Their lack of taste is illustrated by two of my recent experiences as a teacher in the graduate school. I gave a course in English history from 1540 to 1740, which consisted mainly of lectures. The only statement that I made which I know caused some resentment among my listeners (there were probably many others, but this is the only one I heard of) was that Shakespeare is the greatest of all English writers—that this seemed to me to be so well established that it could not be lightly challenged.

The second occurred in the examination of a candidate for the degree of Doctor of Philosophy. He was examined in the field of English history in the seventeenth century. He was asked to name the four Englishmen he regarded as the most important figures in the cultural and intellectual history of that century, to put them in the order of their importance, and to justify his selection and the arrangement he made. These were the men he chose and the order in which he chose them: Locke, Lilburne, Winstanley, and James I. The inclusion of Locke can be justified, but there was no mention of Shakespeare, who lived until 1616, or Milton, or Harvey, who discovered the circulation of the blood, or Newton, whom Addison regarded as one of the three greatest men who ever lived. And no person of discrimination, familiar with English culture in the seventeenth century, would have any doubt that, if he were concerned with political philosophers, as the candidate professed to be, Hobbes and Harrington are the only thinkers of the same stature as Locke. When pressed, the candidate said he regarded Hobbes and Harrington as less important political philosophers than Lilburne, James I, or Winstanley. But he made no attempt to justify his selection.

He had not read the works of Lilburne, James I, or Winstanley. It emerged later that he had selected them simply because
he had heard of them in a course which he had recently attended. Herein lies the danger of suggesting that the future
task of the scholar is to explore the second- and third-rate
writers of an age. No doubt much can be learned from the
obscure. No doubt much should be done to give neglected or
undervalued writers the place to which their work entitles
them. But it is the duty of scholars engaged in exploring
the hidden cupboards of history to test the quality of the
morsels they find. In teaching students, professors should be
careful not to allow the third rate to elbow out the best.

Judgment, discrimination, and taste are even more important as qualifications for the Doctor's degree than a
capacity for digging up facts. What are some of the means of
attaining these qualities? For one thing, much of the student's
time in the graduate school and the college should be taken
up with reading the great books of classical and Western civilization. Some great books of Chinese and Arabian civilization might be included, but the main matter should be the
books which have helped to form the Christian and the humanist tradition. The student of American history should
acquire a firsthand knowledge of the best books by American
writers. We are the worst educated nation of the West when
it comes to a knowledge of our own writers. Our literature
may not be as great as English, or French, or German, or
Italian literature, but it contains many respectable works and
some great ones. How can the rest of the world be aware of
this when Americans know so little about their writers that
the wife of a novelist recently asked her dinner partner, who
had mentioned *Moby Dick*, whether it was one of the best
sellers of the year?

Students should be discouraged from reading books about
great authors which attempt to expound their views at

second hand. They should be discouraged from reading text-books which are written by instructors to supersede previous textbooks and to relieve their authors from the necessity of getting along on their meager salaries. Manuals written by great masters of a special subject, like the late Professor Esmein's *Cour élémentaire d'histoire du droit français*, are in a different category. From them a student can learn much. But one would be hard put to it to find an American textbook published in recent years that measured up to this standard. There are not many subjects properly included in the higher learning which lend themselves to treatment in manuals. No matter how appropriate and well done they are, manuals should not be allowed to crowd creative works of thought out of the curriculum. It is difficult enough for most students to understand a great book when they read it. We all know men who can reel off formidable lists of famous works they have read, though their lives suggest that they got through them after the fashion of the proverbial American who boasted that he had "covered" the Louvre in ten minutes and could have done it in five if he had worn running shoes.

Another reason for avoiding textbooks is that they confuse the students about authority. I have been told that a candidate for the Doctor's degree at Columbia University attributed the Malthusian law to Professor Seligman! Writings do not even survive in the original until their authors are dead. In one of our large universities the psychological views of Watson, the behaviorist, have long been presented to the students not in his own words but through a textbook.

If great writers and thinkers are to recover the place in education to which their genius entitles them, students must be discouraged from reading commentaries upon them which contribute nothing, but simply summarize, often very badly, what the great men have said so much better. After the greatest works of an author have been read, it may often be desirable to become acquainted also with his lesser works, and with the publications of some of his followers. But the reading should be done directly, rather than through intermediaries. Unless students are sent to the sources, to the vineyards themselves, to drink the great wines of past ages, learning will sink to the position it occupied during the centuries of decaying Roman civilization. Then, if men read at all, they read commentaries on commentaries which were themselves commentaries on the works of great writers.

This leads to another important means which the universities have at their disposal of helping to cultivate the judgment, the discrimination, and the accuracy of their pupils. One thing that has raised the standards of American law schools above those of most graduate schools is the active attention paid by groups of students in analyzing cases to the weighing of evidence. Historical problems which involve the weighing of evidence should be treated by groups of graduate students in common, for the drill and discipline which such treatment can afford. The impartial study of evidence ought to be given a prominent place in the higher learning. It is closely related to the reading of great books, since one of the main objects in weighing evidence is to learn how far to trust authority. Students should be taught always to inquire into the source of any information or theory. Is the authority honest and objective? Is the information that he gives the information that is most relevant in answering the question that he is attempting to answer? What are his means of obtaining reliable information? Was he equipped to make the best possible use of his information and did he take pains to do so? All these are questions that the student should be taught to answer for himself, under the guidance of teachers who recognize their importance and insist on a conscientious and honest attempt to grapple with them. Such questions may help the student to understand that he cannot properly express an opinion about a book he has not read, or a speech he has not heard, and that he must not make use of a passage in a book without studying it, and without reading it a second and a third time, any more than a properly trained nurse will administer medicine to a patient until she has thrice examined the label on the bottle.

If the university student learns how to weigh evidence, he will be in a far better position than he is today to judge the world about him. The study of evidence will help him to retain and to enrich his common sense, and the lack of common sense among grown-up Americans today, the lack of wariness, is an important cause for their inability as parents to train their children in good moral and intellectual habits. Americans are prone to believe whatever they are told, though experience should teach them that most of the information circulating in the modern world is unreliable, or irrelevant to the arguments it is used to support. When they are constantly allowing themselves to be fooled by the wrong persons, they are not in a position to be convinced by the right ones. It is partly because persons feel free to talk about subjects they have not studied or books they have not read that the public is so confused today about learning that it cannot distinguish the authentic from the false. The sense of the meaning of knowledge, particularly outside the natural sciences, is so warped that we find members of university faculties saying they are free to talk about a subject only when they know nothing about it. Again we hear people saying that they want to hear the other side of the question when they are unwilling to take the trouble to learn about either side.

The universities should ask the student to play a much more active part in his own schooling, by writing and speaking on the subjects that he is studying, and in relation to the principles to which we have referred. Less time should be spent at lectures and conferences—many of which partake of the worst elements of textbooks—and more at hard work. The number of lectures a student is expected to attend as an undergraduate, and especially as a graduate, should be greatly reduced. Lectures should be much more formal and finished than at present. Their repetition beyond a limited number of times should be discouraged. They should be made to command the attention of the students by the importance of the subject matter. William James had some trenchant things to say about the flabby nature of the mind which spends a portion of its time every day at entertainments. Many college and university students think it is the main function of their teachers in lecturing to entertain them and to provide information which, if partly memorized, will enable them to pass examinations. They have apparently never heard of the old adage of John Dewey about the value of learning by doing.

The proportion of graduate students in American universities today who can write even tolerable English is deplorably small. The only way to learn to write is to write. The student should be required to write simply, clearly, and effectively about every subject that he studies. The principles of composition should be always in his mind, rather than remaining a separate part of the curriculum that he is free to forget when he has passed a perfunctory examination in composition. If it is true that a man can write straight only when he can think straight, it is also true that writing straight helps a man to think straight—that his thought grows as he writes. Writing is not an easy task or one in which short cuts are possible. The student should spend a large portion of his time writing and re-writing—and then in re-examining what he has written in the light of his sources and authorities. This kind of work cannot be done in a hurry, late at night after an exhausting day. It requires a great deal of study and patience; it demands the best strength a man can give. By writing and speaking, if possible to a critical audience, the student will be helped to learn that the great lessons of education are the product not of passive listening and hasty summarizing, but of active exertion, of the elaboration and development of thought contained in the serious works he is brought to consult.

The spirit of the new faculties set up by one, or two, or a few universities for the purpose of cultivating creative thought and art should permeate to graduate study. Persons throughout the country who showed genuine promise for the creative life would come naturally under the direct aegis of these faculties, if they wished to form a university connection. They would not necessarily have to reside at the universities in order to draw on the new intellectual resources.

In what directions might the new faculties and the new university spirit alter graduate study for the Doctor's and the Master's degrees throughout the country? To begin with, all course requirements and all course examinations would be abolished. The training of graduate students would not consist, as it often does at present, in committing to memory a large number of facts or theories relating to fields and courses within the department, and based on the special interests of the particular professors in charge of the fields and courses. The training would be such as to enable the student to master the facts and theories relating to any field, if and when the need arose. Teachers might be expected to play a more active part than they generally do at present as advisers, counselors, and older colleagues for the better graduate students.

A candidate for the Ph.D. would be expected to understand ideas and to acquire a sufficient knowledge of research to present material on important subjects in an intelligent and attractive way, as he will have to do if he is to teach effectively without textbooks. Graduate schools would continue to train their students for teaching and research, but they would require of the candidates for the higher degree, not simply a mastery of special subjects, as at present, but, in addition, two other masteries. One would be a mastery of the Christian and humanist traditions, as brought out in the great works of past thought and literature. The other would be a mastery of moral philosophy, in the ancient Platonic and Aristotelian sense, in its relation to the candidates' special subjects of study. Candidates would be partly prepared for these two kinds of mastery by the training they would get in the secondary and elementary schools, to which we are now about to turn. These last two requirements would be given as much importance in determining the candidates' qualifications for the degree as the present requirements.

The candidate would be expected to demonstrate his knowledge of these subjects, as well as his knowledge of the discipline in which he specializes, by his performance in several general examinations. He would be expected, also, to submit a considerable amount of well-composed written work, and to give frequent oral discourses in seminars attended by his fellow-students and his teachers. He would be encouraged to dig thoroughly into a special subject, not simply for the sake of fresh information, but in order to understand its relation both to his particular discipline and to the whole of knowledge. There would be no place in graduate writing for studies whose sole object is to dissect those elements in works of art which were not intended to be dissected, or for studies without significance for knowledge as a whole.

In the writing of theses, the candidate would be taught to think and to make an intelligent use of his materials as well as to gather them. The late Graham Wallas used to tell the story of an American graduate student in one of our leading universities, which is typical of the procedure of many. He had been at work for more than a year on his dissertation when he sent an account of his progress to a friend who had gone to England. "I have now filled five drawers of my desk with carefully filed cards," he wrote. "Tomorrow I shall begin to write and two weeks hence my thesis will be in the hands of my committee." The process of creative writing is rather different.[15] The creative writer is more likely to spend two weeks gathering materials, and a year in composition and in adding to his materials as the need for new matter is revealed to him. What is needed in American universities are fewer theses and better theses. While all prospective teachers should have training in research, and should be helped to acquire the habit of fresh exploration, without which teaching is bound to become dry and sterile, not every prospective teacher should be required to submit a full-length dissertation. The colleges seeking instructors should learn to content themselves with fewer Doctors of Philosophy. They should strive to obtain more "Masters of Creative Teaching."

The student's written work and his oral discourses, as well as his record in the examinations, would be taken into account in deciding whether he is entitled to the Doctor's degree and on what terms. In order to give the most promising candidates the recognition which might stimulate them to outdo themselves, the old practice of granting the degree, the degree with honors, with high honors, or with highest honors would be revived. The results would be published.

Such a program would not involve the elimination of the principal subjects now taught in American universities. All these subjects would be subordinated to the fundamental aims of education, the love of knowledge, art, and righteousness for their own sake. All subjects should eventually be taught according to a common plan, so that it would become apparent that neither wisdom nor knowledge is to be acquired by dividing the higher learning into a number of separate and supposedly unrelated topics. For many generations the trend in science and education has been toward the foundation of

[15] Cf. above, pp. 226–27.

new, independent disciplines. The great need in American education today is not for novelty—it is for agreement and unity. In the future the aim should be to reduce the number of disciplines by encouraging coalitions between departments and between "fields" within departments, by insisting that all departments should speak in a language that the others can understand, and by acknowledging that all departments have a common objective in the pursuit of truth. If university professors try to see their subjects in relation to other subjects and to the moral and intellectual virtues, they will stop evading the question of what ought to be by taking shelter in minute descriptions of what is, especially of what is unimportant. If a description is to have any value it must be about a subject worth describing.

II. THE ELEMENTARY AND SECONDARY SCHOOLS AND THE COLLEGES

A reformation of secondary and elementary schooling would obviously form an essential part of any plan for an improvement in the higher learning. The changes might be begun in the schools, if the teachers were prepared for them. But without standards—moral, intellectual, and artistic—teachers, parents, and clergymen are in no position to guide the worldly lives of the children and young people who are placed in their charge. Children not only need guidance; a recent statistical inquiry suggests that the overwhelming majority of them want it, at least in the home. This inquiry also suggests that the great majority of teachers, parents, and clergymen do not attempt to give it.[16] Even when they have the best will in the world, they seldom have any idea what is sound, objective advice on moral, intellectual, and artistic questions. Most of them know that it is unsafe to let children play in the street, because automobiles are likely to run over them. Many know

[16] Doris Drucker, "Authority for Our Children," *Harper's Magazine*, CLXXXII, No. 1089 (February, 1941), 277–80.

that it is desirable to put children to bed when they have a temperature, in order to lessen the risk of serious disease. But very few have any way of choosing, apart from their own predilections, which books would be best for the children to read, what subjects of study are most desirable for them, what works of art they should be taught to love, what statesmen and saints to admire, what moral habits to acquire. Whence are impartial standards on these great issues to come if not from the higher learning? The task of forming such standards rests with the American universities. If carried out successfully, the work involved in such a task would draw the universities out of their self-contained walls into touch with the life of the country. This would give learning a meaning, a vitality, and a humanity that are possible only when thought, science, and art are rooted in the life of an age.

If standards are to be built up in relation to the ultimate ends of civilization, how should the course of schooling be altered to make the inculcation of these standards most effective, and to give the children best fitted to serve the good society the opportunities to develop in the fullest measure their impulses toward virtue, wisdom, and beauty? A profound change in the methods of education in the schools, the homes, and the churches is an indispensable part of any program which aims to nourish an enduring civilization in the United States. American education will have to bear a direct relation to the economic and political order toward which it is suggested in the next chapters the United States should aim. Such an order could be adequately served only by persons trained in a variety of ways. There would be a need for persons trained primarily in the use of their minds, to serve as scientists, engineers, physicians, surgeons, journalists, lawyers, political and business administrators, teachers, ministers, professors, men of letters, and so on. There would be a need for others trained primarily in the fine arts, in music, and also in artistic manual labor, if there is to be, as it is suggested there could be to advantage, a revival of handicrafts in the United States. There would be a need for laborers to run the machines and to cultivate the soil as peasant proprietors and farm hands, in order to provide the population with the physical goods of life, and also with the implements of war which are hardly less indispensable in the world of dangerous neighbors that confronts this country today. There would be a need for persons trained to perform office work, to staff warehouses, shops, and department stores, and for others deft in housekeeping. There would be a need for trained sailors, airmen, and soldiers.

The preparation for these various types of work would differ both in nature and in length. But there would be some kinds of instruction that all would need, and that could be best given in common. Except for military training, such instruction ought to be given in the earliest stages of schooling.

The years of elementary school, in which all would have the same training, might well begin when the child is four or five. They might well continue until it is ten, eleven, or twelve. These early years are of crucial importance in the lives of most persons. Habits are formed which are never outgrown. It should be possible to give the child of from ten to twelve a better foundation than children now have when they leave the high school in such subjects as spelling, arithmetic, geometry, grammar, English composition, reading, and music, as well as in elementary history and geography. At the same time, it should be possible to provide the child with a great deal of training that has been almost entirely neglected in recent years. First and foremost should come religious and moral instruction, guidance in good moral conduct and habits. The practice of the Christian code of ethics should pervade all the other sides of education, both at home and at school.

Education in good moral and intellectual habits can be combined to advantage. Such an education could be focused around the careful, methodical reading aloud of books that have permanent value. While only a small proportion of children would be capable of getting anything out of the most advanced books, all children should be encouraged to make the attempt to understand three types of books—works of devotional literature, fables and works of fancy, and general histories.

Reading the classics of devout literature—first and foremost the Bible—would serve as the basis of the training in moral conduct both in the home and in the school. As with all reading, the children should not be excused from the study of these books just because they do not take to them readily. Most of the things that are worth while in life are in many ways distasteful at first. A love for them comes only after difficult labor, and partly as a result of it. Mature people ought to have learned this truth; they ought to be able to act upon their knowledge, though children in their early years cannot be expected to have any idea of it. The extreme modern view that it is the business of children, as a lively American columnist has written, to bring up and discipline their parents, is not likely to educate the children or even the parents, who are often too old to learn the discipline so many of them have missed. It is not necessary to be harsh in order to adopt the more normal view of education, according to which it is the duty of the older and more experienced human beings to supply the counsel and guidance. Violence in the home or the school, which is always regrettable, is even more likely to arise from a lack of leadership and example, from a lack of discipline, than from the existence of responsible authority. No mother and grandmother who has left a written record ever loved her progeny more deeply, or treated them more tenderly, than Mme de Sévigné. Yet, on this very question of the reading of Christian literature, we find her advising her daughter, in connection with the upbringing of her tiny granddaughter, as follows: "Pour les beaux livres de dévotion, si elle ne les aime pas, tant pis pour elle; car nous ne savons que trop *que même sans devotion*, on les trouve charmants."[17]

Fables and works of fancy arouse the sensitive child's imagination. They form a gateway to thought, to charm, to wit, and to art. Just as the training in good moral habits could be appropriately built around the reading of devotional books of enduring value, the training in spelling, in grammar, in taste, and in English composition could be appropriately built around the reading of works of fancy of enduring value, some of them written primarily for children. *Alice in Wonderland*, *Aesop's Fables*, *Robinson Crusoe*, *Gulliver's Travels*, *Huckleberry Finn*, *Tom Sawyer*, and perhaps specially prepared versions of the *Iliad* and *Odyssey*, of some of the *Arabian Nights*, together with selected plays of Shakespeare—this is the kind of literature to which many, if not most, children could be introduced to advantage. It is much less important to have children read many books than to have them read and re-read a few good books and so become accustomed to seeing and hearing the language of great writers.

A school child of today has to read fifteen times more matter than the average pupil of 1913, an "educator" recently told the American Optometric Association, according to the report in a Chicago paper. This report does not explain whether the conference regarded the increase as evidence of progress. For the impartial statistician there can be little doubt on that point. As the time children give to reading has certainly not increased since 1913 (many experienced school-teachers think that it has decreased),[18] the children must obvi-

---

[17] "As for fine devotional works, if she doesn't like them, so much the worse for her; because we know only too well that *even if one is not devout*, one finds them charming" (*Lettres de Madame de Sévigné*, ed. M. Monmerqué [Paris, 1862], IX, 413, letter of January 15, 1690 [my italics]).

[18] See the views of Lloyd Triplett Holden, as reported in the *Baltimore Sun* of September 29, 1939.

ously be allowed to skip and skim even more than thirty years ago. There was far too much skipping and skimming then. So the report can be regarded only as evidence of retrogression. There is faint, but deceptive, consolation in the reflection that the quality of the reading matter submitted to children has probably deteriorated so greatly that more of it is better skimmed and skipped than in the past. The report helps us to understand why fewer and fewer persons read intelligently or take joy in reading; why there is so little literary taste. The formation of a reading public, capable of providing the true artist with stimulus and valuable criticism, depends to a considerable extent on the acquaintance children make early in their lives with a few great books to which they will return later on. Even though they are too young to grasp much of the meaning of such works, association with them at an early age often makes an indelible impression, and thus prepares the ground for a true understanding. It is by the rediscovery of great books, as of great pictures and great works of music, at different ages in life that a taste for art is acquired. Every rereading reveals treasures that were hidden.

An elementary knowledge of history and geography could best be acquired by the reading of a few historical works. History provides the child with some conception of how the world has grown to be as he will find it, rather than as the works of devotion lead him to understand that it ought to be. Supplemented by the examination of maps and photographs, it can also provide him with some conception of the nature of different lands and peoples. Historical works suitable for the child are rather more difficult to select than fables and works of fancy, partly because history is a particularly difficult subject to treat artistically. But the proper principle of selection would seem to be clear. What is wanted are books which treat in a comprehensive and easily understandable way the essentials of some important phase of history, and which are

at the same time works of art. The histories that are read
should be chosen primarily for their enduring qualities as
literature. It is not important that they should embody the
latest results of historical research, for a knowledge of these
results can be acquired later, if and when the need arises. It is
not important that they should cover the whole history of
Greece, Rome, modern Europe, the United States, or China. It
is important that they should not be predigested works, composed as textbooks for the schools or for the child's reading.
Plutarch's *Lives* and the histories of Parkman, Prescott, and
J. R. Green are examples of works to which children might be
introduced with advantage.

In addition to this reading program and the studies built
about it, elementary education would include arithmetic and
geometry. It might usefully include music and poetry, which
go well together because of the importance of sound and
rhythm in both. It might also fruitfully include training in
appreciation of the fine arts. Some tests made in England suggest that young children gain considerably in taste by sound
teaching. Many examples of great works of art, mostly paintings, were paired with counterfeit art, and various school
children of different ages were asked to choose the better of
each pair. Only one of the groups of children had had the advantage of instruction from an art mistress of discrimination.
Between the ages of twelve and fourteen, after several years of
learning, the children in this group made the right choice
three times as often as those in any of six other groups.[19] The
excellent reproductions now made of great drawings and even
of great paintings should facilitate training in the appreciation
of art, if care were taken to explain to the children the in-
feriority of the finest reproductions to the originals.

Even more important during childhood than wise education in the school is wise training in the home. The formation

[19] Margaret H. Bulley, *Art and Counterfeit* (London, 1925), pp. 85–88.

of a sound character depends upon an intelligent and happy domestic life, possible only when the family circle has a spirit of its own independent of the school. But family life cannot to advantage be at cross purposes with that of the schools. The American society of the future will be well served if the level of both is raised, if their ultimate objectives are the same, and if the means employed by the one complements that of the other. Work in the elementary schools might well be combined with work in the home under the guidance of the parents. Manual tasks, designed to contribute to the order, cleanliness, and aesthetic appearance of the house and its surroundings, should be made part of a daily routine. Their performance would supplement regular periods of reading and physical exercise. Moral, intellectual, and manual education could helpfully be begun in the home as soon as the child could walk, and before it entered school.

The response of children to the various kinds of elementary instruction would differ. It would be partly on the basis of these differences that the child's parents and his schoolteachers would decide on the kind of education that the boy or girl could most suitably embark upon at the age of ten, eleven, or twelve. Children who showed an enthusiasm for, or a genuine interest in, books and other intellectual study would go on with instruction intended primarily to train the mind. Those who showed an inclination for music or the fine arts, and especially those who exhibited a genuine talent for them, would go on with instruction devoted primarily to the arts and the handicrafts. Those whose response was poor or mediocre to every variety of labor calling for an exercise of the intellect would presumably be better fitted to enter routine work of some kind. If these children showed an aptitude for using their hands it would be reasonable to assume they were especially adapted to work in the factories or on the farms. If they did not show such an aptitude, then they might embark on an education designed primarily to fit them for work in offices, shops, and department stores, and designed also, especially in the case of the girls, to prepare them to take care of homes.

There would be essentially four varieties of schooling for young Americans between the ages of ten or twelve and eighteen or twenty. They would not necessarily be carried on in separate schools. It should be made readily possible to transfer from one of the four courses of schooling to another, when it became apparent that a mistake had been made concerning a child's special aptitude.

The first course would be the shortest. It would be primarily for young men. Its object would be to train them for work as manual laborers and mechanics in the mines and factories and on the farms. It would consist, as the years went by, more and more in practical work. Apart from the training given in handling machinery and in tilling the soil, there would be three additional kinds of instruction. As in each of the four kinds of education, religious instruction and training in good moral conduct, begun in the elementary schools, would be continued and developed. It would be combined with courses in literature, history, and economic and social conditions similar to those offered by the Workers Educational Association of Great Britain. There would be regular training of the body and of disciplined habits of cleanliness and order. There would be instruction in the elementary technical and scientific matters that would be of help to miners, factory workers, and farmers.

The second type of schooling would prepare young people for office and store work of various kinds and for the administration and care of the home. It would be primarily, but by no means exclusively, for young women. Just as the students taking the first type of schooling would get practical training in the mines, factories, and on the farm, especially during summer vacations, so the students under the second type would get practical training in stores and offices. There would be courses in arithmetic, typewriting, elementary accounting, cooking, mending, care of children, and other domestic occupations. As under the first type of schooling, there would be courses in literature, history, and economic and social conditions, and there would be instruction in religion and moral conduct.

The third type of schooling would be for those children who showed gifts for creative work with their hands or a taste for music. Such schooling would be designed for painters, sculptors, and musicians, as well as for the persons who seemed fitted to engage in the artistic handicrafts. While the various arts and crafts are distinct, they have much in common. Young men and women who are receiving special training in one can usually profit by close association with those who are receiving special training in another. Courses in general culture, offered in different forms under all four types of schooling, would receive a special emphasis in connection with the arts and crafts.

The fourth type of schooling would prepare young men and women for the universities and the professional schools. It would consist of an eight-year course, covering roughly the years now spent in the final grades of elementary school, in the high school, in the junior college, and in the Freshman and Sophomore years of college. The training now offered at these stages of American education would be altered considerably. At the outset all the children, with the possible exception of those bent on careers in the physical or the biological sciences, would have from two to four years devoted primarily to the study of foreign languages. They would be expected to learn thoroughly two or three languages—one ancient tongue, either Greek or Latin, and one or two modern tongues. They would devote at least a whole year, preferably two, to each language. They would be expected to carry on all their educational work in the language. Their reading would be exclusively in it. They would be expected almost from the outset to converse in it, outside as well as inside the classroom. All their classes would be in company with other boys and girls engaged in learning it. When practicable, and in cases where it did not interfere with the home circle, the young people might live in a house where all the conversation was in the language they were learning. Language would occupy the pupils between the ages of roughly ten or eleven and fourteen or fifteen. The knowledge of literary classics, of grammar, and of composition would be obtained through the foreign tongue. The advantages of such training would come both from the discipline provided by the close study of a foreign tongue, and from the unrivaled opportunities which the study of a great classical or a great modern language affords for an acquaintance with literature, and with the perennial problems of man's relation to man as these are discussed by great writers. In order to get the most out of such training, the books read should be treated not (as is the usual practice at present) as curiosities, but as guides to life. It has been wisely said that, with a second language, a man acquires a new soul. That can be true only when his knowledge of it is intimate and profound.

At the age of fourteen or fifteen the students who had been devoting themselves to the mastery of foreign tongues would be prepared for a college course of approximately four years in general education. In this course active participation would be continually expected from the student, particularly in the presentation of written exercises of all kinds. Lecture courses in history, in the physical and biological sciences, and in the study of man would be offered. But great emphasis would be placed (particularly in the case of students who planned to devote themselves either to social and humanistic studies or to the law) upon the reading and discussion of the great books of classical and Western history and on the handling of evidence. In addition there would be some preliminary training in research, readily combined with the study of evidence—in experimental research for students planning to devote their lives to science, medicine, or engineering; in historical research for students planning to devote their lives to social and humanistic studies, to business administration, and to the law.

For as long a time as military training should prove to be necessary, the young men who emerged from the colleges and the other schools, at ages of from eighteen to twenty or so, could receive it at this time. Those whom it was found desirable to call up would remain in the service as long as proved necessary for purposes of defense against foreign enemies bent on crushing our society. After they returned from military service they would enter the universities and professional schools or embark on their life-work. But the development of Christian education in the United States would not be dependent upon military training. If the world should become saner, less ferocious, if it should be possible for the nations to understand each other better and to establish conditions of an enduring peace, general military training would eventually be dropped. Conscription can be justified only as a means of self-preservation, and it should be a primary object to abolish it by international agreement among all the great powers. If the United States were to adopt a Christian educational system, it might not only contribute to civilization at home, it might also contribute to an understanding among the peoples of the world.

III. FAMILY AND CHURCH

The success of any educational program which aims to offer all people some training in true moral, intellectual, and artistic values, and, at the same time, to maintain the high standard of living established at the end of the nineteenth century, depends upon the co-operation of the churches, the families, and the schools. Unless they agree on the ultimate objectives in training the young, family life or Sunday-school instruction is likely to undo the work of the schools and colleges, or even to make it impossible to embark on that work. Again, a school with different objectives, or with no objectives at all, can undo the work of the most intelligent family, which has brought up its children in a love of righteousness, wisdom, and beauty. Some years ago the late Graham Wallas asked a gathering of well-to-do American parents in New York whether, if they could choose, they would have a son acquire a long but curable disease which forced him to withdraw from school at the age of eight or ten, or go on in health with the kind of education offered most children. The majority of the parents voted for the disease.

It is not enough for American children to have wise parents, or to have wise priests and clergymen, if the schools undermine their work. It is not enough to have wise teachers and professors unless the parents, together with the priests and clergymen, support the teachers and the professors in their wisdom. What help can we expect from the family and the church in working toward humanistic ends of civilization?

The history of American churches and American families during the past fifty years can perhaps be summed up in the word "liberalization." Liberty is an excellent thing—as a means toward the good life. It has been advocated on the ground that it would do away with cant, secrecy, and hypocrisy. "Secrecy and hypocrisy," writes Frank Lloyd Wright, America's great architect, "both do something to the character never to be repaired. . . . . Aren't the *pretended* lives the rotten threads in the social fabric?"[20]

Hypocrisy is a blot on any character and on any civilization.

[20] *Autobiography* (New York, 1932), p. 202 (his italics).

When it comes to secrecy, a good deal depends on the definition of the word. It is obviously no more helpful for the strength of the individual or of society to have a man empty all his private affairs into the ears of everyone he meets than it is helpful for the strength of a written work to have the author empty his notebooks onto its pages. But if secrecy is another name for cant and hypocrisy, if it means concealing from someone, with design, a matter he has a right to know, if it means preaching and teaching one thing and doing the opposite—living a lie—then Wright is justified in condemning it.

In so far as the liberalization of manners and customs relating to family life has done away with artificiality, it is a blessing. There is no conspicuous benefit to humanity in high silk hats, tight-fitting corsets, or cumbersome bathing suits. There is no reason to regret the opportunity which women now have to escape from the barbaric brutality of monstrous husbands or fathers, who used to keep them in chains, and spend their fortunes. But the new freedom would be more inspiring if it had positive achievements to its credit. Each of the steps that have been taken to break down the older moral standards of the Anglo-Saxon world has been defended on the ground that it would result in a more honest, forthright way of living. Better for a man to divorce his wife openly than to visit secretly a mistress. Better to abandon all training in the moral virtues, better to stop creating a fear of hell, if teachers and clergymen indulge clandestinely in the very vices they pretend to abhor.

If such arguments were to carry weight, it was vital that the result of the new morality should have been a greater honesty in the conduct of human affairs generally, more creative relationships between husband and wife, friend and friend, colleague and colleague, employer and employee, governor and governed, nation and nation. It is hardly possible to claim that the breakdown of the older morality during the last four or five decades has been accompanied by a notable improvement in conduct, or by a growing humanitarianism, a growing spirit of comradeship between the peoples of the world. It is hardly possible to claim that modern family life has improved the moral and intellectual training of children in the home. Much evidence points in the other direction. Our courage, our sense of duty, our devotion to ideals and to each other, even our candor, all seem to have been more often weakened than strengthened. The "bright young people," with all their freedom to marry and divorce as they please, have seldom set an example capable of arousing much enthusiasm in an intelligent mind or an honest heart. The new morality has not justified the hopes that were put in it. It has not contributed conspicuously to the dignity of man or to the happiness of mankind.

No one in his senses would argue that on that account society should return, even if it could, to high hats and tightly laced corsets. The question that needs to be asked is why this experiment in freedom has proved barren. Our wisest leaders in education have already supplied a sound answer. Together with most other peoples in the modern world, Americans have sought freedom for its own sake, not for the sake of the good life. People have assumed that such virtues as kindness, courtesy, fortitude, chastity, or fidelity are of the same texture as corsets, high hats, and cumbersome bathing suits. They are to be worn only if it is convenient. What society has failed to recognize is that kindness, courtesy, fortitude, chastity, and fidelity are good things in themselves, and are to be respected and loved *for their own sake*. There is no reason for wearing a heavy suit in summer if it makes a person uncomfortable, but there are reasons for becoming and remaining loyal and faithful even when this is both troublesome and annoying, even though the reasons are not susceptible to scientific proof. Comfort may legitimately take precedence over fashion—it cannot legitimately take precedence over virtue. If that were recognized, family life would be strengthened, parents would assume a responsibility toward their children and toward each other that is now lacking. Recognizing virtue as a good thing in itself would help parents and their children to recognize that knowledge and beauty are good things in themselves. If the higher learning can give standards a new meaning and a new reality, so that parents see their value and take them on faith, then the parents will be in a position to co-operate with the teachers by giving training in the homes that will assist a wise program of education.

It may be questioned whether the liberalizing influences in recent American history have done more for religion than they have done for the family. The main problem that Protestant clergymen have had to face in recent years has been that of the empty church and the deserted Sunday school. The test of a successful minister has not been the character of the gospel that he preaches, the nature of his religious beliefs, or even his character and intelligence; the test has become the number of persons he is able to bring into his church. When a leading pastor retires, the American newspapers, upon which most of the people depend for information and misinformation, almost never ask what were his views on the dogma of original sin or the divinity of Christ. It is left for the statistician trying to determine "social trends" occasionally to "get the facts" on such matters.[21] The papers do not ask whether the pastor embodied the Christian virtues, they do not ask whether he said and did things to strengthen the faith or the morality of the community in which he lived and preached. His obituary notices tell us that after he took over a small church in Iowa he boosted the list of members from 21 to 209 in less than a year. As the crowning feature of his successful

21 See above, p. 137.

career, he raised the annual income of one of the most important churches in the Middle West from \$120,000 to \$500,-000. Recently a friend of mine listened to the dean of an important divinity school talking with much enthusiasm about one of his pupils. My friend had happened to meet this pupil, who had been given charge of an imposing church in one of the principal cities in the South. He asked the dean in what the young clergyman excelled. "Why," said the dean, without a moment's hesitation, "he's got a church with an endowment of more than four million dollars."

Accounts of religious affairs that we read or hear seldom explain how all the new members are gathered, how the formidable endowments are obtained. When money becomes the measure of all things, the need for probing deeper disappears. If curiosity persists, candor forces the outsider to the conclusion that these miracles are not always produced by instilling in the local population a deep religious faith, by persuading doubters of the truth of the gospel, or even by persuading them of the importance of trying to live in accordance with Christian ethics. In some cases, at any rate, success has been achieved by founding church golf clubs, by drawing attention to the opportunities offered by church socials for young women in pursuit of husbands, and by providing various kinds of entertainment designed to make church-going an acceptable substitute for visiting the motion pictures or listening to the radio. In extreme cases, everyone seems to applaud if the minister obtains his results partly with the help of alluring motion-picture actresses, who pose with him as hosts to some visiting celebrity. One is reminded of the remark in a recent French novel, "en Amérique la nobilité est remplacée par la publicité."

There is nothing precisely vicious in those practices. But it may be doubted whether, by themselves, they are any more likely to bring about a return of faith or a renewal of respect for Christian ethics than the discarding of high hats, long bathing suits, and corsets. If the churches are to help in a movement to restore true values in the United States, they cannot do it by making themselves substitutes for dance halls and motion-picture palaces, any more than universities and colleges can improve education, as President Hutchins has remarked, by making themselves substitutes for country clubs. The way the churches can help is by concentrating on faith, on Christian ethics, and on the development and appreciation of the liturgical arts. The way they can help is by giving men and women a sense of the ultimate ends of life, that can hardly be obtained from entertainments. Such objectives may possibly reduce the attendance. But in England and the United States during the past forty years adult attendance has been better maintained at Roman Catholic than at Protestant churches, although the Protestants for the most part have made more concessions to the world than the Catholics. Worldly wants change so fast that it is difficult to keep church diversions up to date. Spiritual needs have a greater permanence. It is doubtful, therefore, whether the repeated liberalization of dogma (encouraged by the harsh rigidity prominent in Calvinism) and the attempt to make church life fit in with the worldly interests of the churchgoers have helped to achieve for the Protestant sects generally the objective for which they were instituted by individual pastors. In any case, whatever the consequences, it is better that a church should go down fighting as a religious institution than that it should attempt a metamorphosis. If the Protestant sects are to contribute to the restoration of religious, moral, and aesthetic training in the elementary and secondary schools and in the colleges, they cannot begin by abandoning most of such training in the churches and Sunday schools.

IV. EDUCATION AND LIFE

It is frequently said that the task of all persons and institutions concerned with instruction is to prepare children and adolescents to meet life. Everyone can agree on this objective. But we make a fundamental mistake when we assume that it can be achieved by turning the schools and colleges, the churches and universities, into replicas of the practical worlds of business, of entertainment, or of politics, which exist about us. Put to such purposes, these institutions do not teach their charges to meet life, they simply leave them to drown in life. The kind of training that we have so imperfectly sketched, and that can doubtless not only be elaborated but greatly improved upon in its main lines, is what men need if they are to resist the domination of facts and events of which Emerson spoke in a striking passage. He wrote:

What is our life but an endless flight of winged facts or events? In splendid variety these changes come, all putting questions to the human spirit. Those men who cannot answer by a superior wisdom these facts or questions of time, serve them. Facts encumber them, tyrannize over them, and make the men of routine the men of *sense*, in whom a literal obedience to facts has extinguished every spark of that light by which man is truly man. But if the man is true to his better instincts or sentiments, and refuses the dominion of facts, as one that comes of a higher race, remains fast by the soul and sees the principle, then the facts fall aptly and supple into their places; they know their master, and the meanest of them glorifies him.[22]

The special achievement of American education is supposed to consist in its power to adjust itself to the needs of its victims. But, if the word "needs" is given its proper meaning,[23] that is just what American education almost never does. An adjustment to the needs of man, in the true sense of the word, would involve the encouragement and cultivation of the impulses toward virtue, wisdom, and beauty which exist in nearly all human beings. When it is denied that these elusive objectives have a reality apart from individual whim, this cultivation becomes impossible.

[22] "History," *Essays* (1st ser.).   [23] See above, pp. 220–21.

Is it not proper for education to help men to cultivate their best instincts and sentiments? The goal of the higher learning is to make man the master of his materials; the true goal of all education is to make man the master of himself. No man in modern America is suffering from lack of contact with the world about him. Men are suffering from too many of the wrong kinds of contacts, from the lack of any principles that would help them to give meaning to their experiences, and that would help them to form enriching friendships. They are suffering from a lack of moral fortitude, which many of our pioneering ancestors had to have, and which is indispensable if they are to face the disappointments and the unhappiness that life always brings. They are less likely to find such fortitude in the world about them than in the great minds of the past, and in the works that those minds have left behind. The student does not learn to meet life by being tossed from experience to experience, and from subject to subject, without the opportunity to digest his experiences and to reflect upon the subjects to which he is introduced. If men are to keep their heads above water in the sea of noise, excitement, competitive scramble, and sensational rush that the modern world has become, the schools and universities will have to teach them how to follow the good life.

If education can train men in the habits of honesty, ac curacy, and hard work, if it can teach them that there is a moral and an intellectual hierarchy, if it can help them to acquire good taste and discrimination concerning the arts, it will contribute greatly to the good life. It will serve the majority of our citizens who are concerned neither with education nor with the creative life, by teaching them the joy of doing things well. There is no occupation or activity, whether it be surgery or banking, waiting on table or living life with one's wife and children, where there are not good ways of acting and bad ways of acting. If young people have learned to discriminate between good and bad ways in educa tion, they will know that the joy of doing things well is accessible to everyone. They will not be so much concerned as at present about changing their occupations or their wives, for they will have learned the principle that everyone has open to him the fine opportunity of doing well the thing he has to do. If that opportunity is once appreciated, every task, even the humblest, acquires a dignity that none can have if it is done badly. In Paris I once picked up a taxi driven by an old chauffeur, who took me to the Bibliothèque nationale. Like many persons who drive their own cars, I sometimes feel ill at ease when I confide myself to another driver. But, before we had gone a block, I was completely comfortable, because I felt the master touch and knew that, although we were driving fast, nothing would happen to us. When I left my chauffeur, I complimented him on his driving. He admitted he was good, and he added: "In the old days I used often to drive Anatole France. One day Monsieur France said to me, 'in all the crafts there are geniuses and you are one in yours.' "

It is the central task of American education to give every American an understanding of what is good work, and a pride in doing it. If taxi drivers and cooks and small peasant farmers in France were once able to lead happy lives because of the excellence of their workmanship, although none of them supposed that what they were doing had as much significance for human welfare as the labor of a philosopher or a poet, why should it not be possible for professors of minor subjects, together with teachers in the schools and humble priests and pastors, to take an equal pride in their work? If they do, we shall have more reverence for poets and philosophers and we shall probably have better poets and philosophers.

Work is primarily a privilege, not an obligation. It is indispensable to the health of the mind and spirit even when the physical welfare of the body can be provided for without it. Now that science and machine technology have made it possible for most children and for many adults to live without work, the need for training in good working habits has become greater than ever before in history. But, at just this time, education in the United States has largely abandoned its ancient function of training young people to labor, and has left them without guidance or drill. In this way most so-called "progressive schools" have made work distasteful. Modern entertainment contributes further to the distaste for it. Most entertainment is now devised to require a minimum of effort on the part of the audience. It is served up in large measure over the radio as a sort of sauce to accompany eating, dancing, smoking, motoring, walking, reading, or what children describe as studying. When children tell us that they can concentrate better on their school work with the radio turned on, this simply shows that they do not know the meaning of concentration.

The view has become prevalent that every kind of work is an evil. A friend of mine, whose habits of labor resemble those of Trollope in regularity if not in fruitfulness, remarked to his luncheon partner that, while he did not work to excess, he found time for a long stretch of hard work every day. Over the quantity of labor my friend had been doing his partner had been showing the polite concern he did not expect to have taken seriously, a polite concern characteristic of such conversations. "Just as some people are steady drinkers," my friend said, "I am a steady worker." His partner hesitated. Then, as he thought he had caught my friend's meaning, he felt called upon to renew his pretended sympathy. My friend's lot, he remarked, was harder than that of the steady drinker, for the drinker at least "gets some fun out of it."

The luxury and loss of foregoing the labor involved in good workmanship is likely to create a nation of misfits. Some even fear that it has done so. It contributes to emotional instability, mental confusion, and incompetence of every kind. It is a luxury that would not, in the long run, contribute to the welfare of the American people even if we were living in a world without other nations, or in one where all the other nations were our friends. In a world of hostile nations, it may prove a menace to our existence.

The urgency of the case and the weakness of American education make it indispensable that university professors, together with all those who train the young, should face their great task immediately. They should bury their petty jealousies, their private ambitions, and their quarrels in a consciousness of their great mission. If the universities are to succeed, it means that no obstacles should be regarded as insurmountable, that the professors should renounce their desire for quick results, that the virtues of patience, courage, and self-discipline should be restored to the position from which they were dethroned by the American passion for getting ahead. Even if the difficulties seem insuperable, the task cannot be evaded. We shall do well to remember the motto of William the Silent: "It is neither necessary to hope in order to undertake nor to succeed in order to persevere."

X

THE ECONOMIC STRUCTURE OF SOCIETY

✣

IN NO other country has all enterprise been conducted so generally as in the United States on the principle that free competition is the mainspring behind material progress. As that has come to be regarded as the key to all progress, as economic relations have come to be treated not only as the ordinary but as the only important business of life, Americans have been intrenched in the opinion that the more it is possible to carry on every transaction by the give and take of the market place, without government intervention, the more a country is bound to prosper, and the happier its citizens will be.

I. ORIGIN AND STRENGTH OF THE LAISSEZ FAIRE TRADITION

Unlike the other great nations of the world, the United States was born and reared in the tradition of laissez faire. Throughout its history this tradition has remained the accepted ideal in economic matters. Although American history is not venerable, it is already considerable. In setting about to build for the future, no country can afford to forget its history.

When the United States became a nation, in the last half of the eighteenth century, the two European countries most powerful politically and most influential intellectually were England and France. Next to the experience of the American colonies, it was to the contemporary thought and experience of England and France that the founding fathers turned for guidance in economic and political matters when they established the Republic and wrote the Constitution. On a question that was to be of crucial importance in American history, the question of the appropriate relations between government and economic enterprise, American, English, and French experience seemed to teach similar lessons.

Before the end of the seventeenth century, England had become the foremost country in Europe in mining and heavy manufacturing. The material standard of living was higher than in any continental nation. It happens that in 1696 Gregory King made an estimate of the national dividend of England and Wales. That was before the chief purpose in writing books was to sell them or to make an impression on one's associates by their publication. A modest man, King never published his. But it was resurrected nearly a century after his death.[1] It has proved a remarkably reliable work. It enabled Mr. Colin Clark to extend his comparisons of the national income produced per head of occupied population back to the Revolution of 1688. According to his calculations, the Englishman at that time had, on the average, a somewhat larger command of economic goods to console him for life than the Italian, the Japanese, or the Russian has had in the interval between the two world wars, after more than two centuries of unparalleled economic progress.[2]

All the continental nations had begun to look to England for leadership in industrial technology in the early eighteenth century, especially in the heavy industries. "Our artisans," wrote one of Gregory King's contemporaries, a certain James Puckle, "[are] universally allow'd the best upon Earth for Improvements."[3] That was in 1697. During the next fifty

[1] George Chalmers, *An Estimate of the Comparative Strength of Great Britain* (London, 1801). Some extracts had been published earlier by Charles Davenant.

[2] *The Conditions of Economic Progress* (London, 1940), pp. 41, 83.

[3] *A New Dialogue between a Burgermaster and an English Gentleman* (London, 1697), p. 20.

years almost every visitor to England who considered the matter came to agree with him. The continental peoples, the French in particular, sent technical experts to study the English methods of manufacturing. They brought back designs and drawings of the curious new machinery and furnaces. One of these experts, who had come over from France in 1738, wrote:

I explored the shires between Monmouth and Warwick, filled as they are with iron and copper manufactures, in the company of my [English] friend. [He] was well content to show me the wealth of the workers in this district. I observed with surprise the skill of these artisans and the comforts they enjoy. Their villages seemed to me as well built as the finest towns in Flanders and I think they are richer. The prodigious consumption of provisions brought into the markets astonished me greatly. . . . . I noticed . . . . a large number of processes which are unknown to our workers, notes of which I will show you in Paris.[4]

How had England done it? This was a question that eighteenth-century mechanics, tradesmen, and financiers, economists, scientists, and even men of letters were asking themselves with increasing frequency and increasing interest. For Frenchmen the question took on a compelling importance after the death, in 1715, of Louis XIV. They were beginning to care less for the qualities cultivated, in spite of much corruption, in the age of the great monarch—good form, finish, and taste in the fine arts and in the art of living, reason and moderation in thought, high standards of moral conduct, combined with a belief in the Church and the divine right of kings. They were beginning to care more for wealth, health, freedom of economic enterprise, and the discovery of the secrets of the material world. These were objectives upon which many Englishmen had begun to focus their attention more than a hundred years before.

[4] Report of M. Ticquet (Archives nationales, Paris, 0¹1293).

The change was reflected in the changing attitude of the governing authorities toward mechanical inventors. Shortly after he came to power in 1622, Richelieu had one of them locked up as a madman in the asylum at Bicêtre, just outside Paris, for pestering him about the force contained in a jet of steam.[5] A hundred and thirty years later an expert technician, who was in fact a little mad, but who had a special gift for directing a textile factory, was put in charge of a government cloth enterprise in central France, in spite of his infirmity. The local officials arranged the routine at the factory to help him to control the aberration which led him to imagine that the workmen were deriding him whenever they coughed or sneezed, even in the depth of winter. The officials considered his mechanical knowledge too valuable to dispense with.[6]

It was natural to seek for explanations of England's material prosperity during early modern times in the special features of English public policy which differentiated it from that of France and most other continental states. The attempts made by Queen Elizabeth and her two Stuart successors to establish an economic despotism on the continental pattern had failed.[7] While there were plenty of English statutes and proclamations regulating domestic industry, commerce, and agriculture, they were seldom enforced. Their administration became particularly lax after the civil war, which broke out in 1642, and still more after the revolution of 1688. Almost all efforts to set up government-owned or controlled enterprises, resembling the French royal manufactures, were abandoned before the eighteenth century. Direct taxes, of the sort levied by the French crown, were not successfully established in England. There

[5] J. P. Muirhead, *The Life of James Watt* (London, 1859), p. 99.

[6] This information comes from a set of documents preserved in the Archives nationales, Paris. I hope to give the details in another work.

[7] Cf. J. U. Nef, *Industry and Government in France and England, 1540–1640* (Philadelphia, 1940), esp. pp. 25–57, 88–120; "Industrial Europe at the Time of the Reformation," *Journal of Political Economy*, XLIX, No. 2 (1941), 191–215, 224.

the man of wealth was freer than in France from levies on his income. He was also freer from the danger that the value of his money would depreciate as a result of governmental tinkering with the coinage.[8]

So economic thinkers in Europe and America were disposed to attribute English commercial and industrial leadership to freedom from government interference and to the absence of tolls on domestic trade. Adam Smith spoke of their absence as "perhaps one of the principal causes of the prosperity of Great Britain." Every great country is necessarily, he added, "the best and most extensive market for the greater part of the productions of its own industry."[9]

These views of economic thinkers concerning the most appropriate relation of political authority to agriculture, industry, and trade were strengthened by French history during the half-century from about 1735 to about 1785. For the first time since the Reformation the rate of industrial and commercial progress—the rate of growth in the volume of production—rivaled that in England. This progress was accompanied by modifications in the economic policies of the French government. There was a disposition on the part of public officials to disregard old regulations. Greater freedom was allowed to private individuals and companies to establish mines and factories outside the system of royal manufactures. The burdens imposed by the financial policies of the crown upon the private merchant were somewhat lightened.[10]

As the Revolution approached, progressive-minded Frenchmen were seldom, if ever, satisfied with the material advance their country had made. England was still setting the pace in

[8] Nef, "English and French Industrial History in Relation to the Constitution," *The Constitution Reconsidered*, ed. Conyers Read (New York, 1938), pp. 83 ff.

[9] *Wealth of Nations*, Book V, chap. ii, Part II, Art. 4 (Rogers ed., II, 499).

[10] Nef, "English and French Industrial History in Relation to the Constitution," *The Constitution Reconsidered*, pp. 93–97.

mining and heavy manufacturing. Many Frenchmen felt that if France was to overtake England, she would have to copy English economic policies in almost every respect.

Such was the state of dominant opinion in Europe in 1787, when the American delegates assembled in Philadelphia to frame the Constitution. Whether they consulted recent American or European experience, it seemed to justify the very policies which were favorable, as Dr. Beard has shown,[11] to their private material interests and those of the classes they represented. They were in the happy position of believing that by serving themselves they were also serving the public. The Constitutional Convention found in recent history support for one of the most important innovations of modern English thought, that by seeking one's own financial advantage in the market place one increased the general welfare—that self-love and social interest are identical.

It is no wonder that this belief found expression in the Constitution. It is no wonder that, with an undeveloped continent before the American people and with no other tradition as a nation concerning the proper relations of government to economic life behind them, this belief should have become a more influential guide to private and public conduct in the United States than in any other country. It was only in the matter of protecting inventions and of trade with foreign countries that the older conception of the value of government interference retained strength.

II. ECONOMIC FREEDOM AND ECONOMIC PROGRESS

If we set out to build the American society that ought to be, it is not enough to take for granted that a conception of economic freedom which is largely Anglo-Saxon, and in its most extreme form American, is the best for the welfare of man at all times and under all conditions. We need to inquire, in the

[11] C. A. Beard, *An Economic Interpretation of the Constitution* (New York, 1913), esp. pp. 40–42 and chaps. ii and v generally.

light of the comprehensive knowledge of economic history that has been assembled since the United States was born, how far freedom from government interference has been in fact the cause of material progress. We need to consider how much economic freedom is likely to contribute in the difficult times that lie ahead to the general welfare of the United States. Like all liberty, economic liberty, philosophically considered, is a value, not an end. As the greatest Greek philosophers might have said, the amount of such liberty desirable for happiness varies. As all economists know, there never has been and never can be complete freedom from government interference in economic affairs. Even in the thought of the Constitutional Convention and the practice of United States policy for the last hundred and fifty years, the principle of freedom was never extended to cover international trade. There never can be, on the other hand, control over every detail of economic affairs by government. The problem for the moral philosopher, and for the philosophically minded economist as well, should be to find the right emphasis. That is not the same at all times and places. They will try, therefore, to find out to what extent economic freedom is desirable as a condition of working toward the ultimate ends of civilization at the present turning-point in history. As seekers after what ought to be, we should husband what is good in the American tradition of free enterprise and discard what is harmful, either in itself or because changed conditions have made it obsolete. As practical men, we have to take account of the tenacious hold which this conception of laissez faire, historically novel in its extreme form, has over the American people.

For a historian, the first matters to consider in a rough and general way are the actual historical relations between economic liberty and economic welfare. Though the light which history might throw on this problem is perhaps less important than that which could be obtained from philosophical economic analysis, historical knowledge is essential to such an analysis. What has history to teach concerning the relation of freedom from government interference to material prosperity, to the increase in the production of goods and services "that can be brought directly or indirectly into relation with the measuring-rod of money," and to the widespread dissemination of such goods and services among the population? In so far as our present knowledge goes, periods of rapidly increasing prosperity have been, generally, periods of relatively great freedom from government interference in business. While this suggests that such freedom is favorable to prosperity, a close study of history warns us against regarding it as the primary or even the chief cause.

There have been periods of rapid increase in prosperity during which government interference was relatively great. Such was notably the case in the late fifteenth and early sixteenth centuries, at the time of the discovery of America and the passage around the Cape of Good Hope. Industrial and commercial development was striking in many parts of Continental Europe—nowhere more so than in the disintegrating Holy Roman Empire, where Germans played the leading part in enterprise.[12] German historians have studied the economic progress of the Renaissance with an intensity and an interest comparable to that taken by English and American historians in the industrial revolution of the late eighteenth and early nineteenth centuries. Economic thought in Germany never went quite so far as that in other continental countries in accepting the position of the English classical economists concerning the advantages for national welfare of freedom from government interference. But if there was one period when in theory, and also to some extent in practice, the Germans adopted liberal economic principles, it was in the late nineteenth century. This was also a period when the German

[12] See above, chap. ii, pp. 12–15.

state brought little or no pressure to bear on scholarly writers to reach conclusions that would be in accord with the dominant political authority. It is the time, therefore, when we should expect German historians to be most likely to question the benefits of political interference with private enterprise. Yet several of them attributed the increased industrial efficiency and the reduction in costs made in central Europe at the time of the Renaissance to the increase in government control over mining, metallurgy, and salt-making. The most learned of all German economic historians, Gustav Schmoller, showed, for instance, that in some cases the consolidation of salt-making enterprises in the hands of the princes was accompanied by a halving of the labor costs.[13] To collaboration between merchants and princes, the late Jacob Strieder attributed much of the prosperity in mining and metallurgy.[14] Both probably exaggerate the economic advantages of Renaissance paternalism.[15] But it would be folly to suggest that government interference and even goverment ownership and management are always incompatible with improvements in technique and a rapid increase in production.

There are, then, exceptions to the tendency which government interference has to impose a handicap on the growth of output and of prosperity. A trend toward greater freedom or toward greater political control in economic affairs, historically considered, is only one of many factors which influence the material welfare of a people. Such trends cannot properly be considered by themselves, if we are seeking for general truth; they have to be considered in relation to all the circumstances which influence prosperity. When an attempt is made to do

[13] "Die geschichtliche Entwickelung der Unternehmung," *Jahrbuch für Gesetzgebung, Verwaltung und Volkswirtschaft*, XV (1891), 660.

[14] *Studien zur Geschichte kapitalistischer Organisationsformen* (Munich, 1925), *passim*.

[15] Nef, "Industrial Europe at the Time of the Reformation," *Journal of Political Economy*, XLIX, No. 2 (1941), 200.

this, it is seen to be doubtful whether the growth of economic freedom has been in civilized history the most important cause of economic progress. It has been contingent upon other circumstances, prominent among them liberty to devote the resources of the country to peaceful pursuits. If we probe the matter further, we discover that these other circumstances have on their own account, and independently of the economic freedom they promote, much to do with the prosperity. They have possibly even more to do with it than economic freedom.

Space does not permit us to bring forward here much evidence in support of these general propositions.[16] A short demonstration of their reasonableness can nevertheless be made.

In classical times the government of the ancient Roman state became, under the Empire, and especially under the later Empire, after the second century of the Christian era, increasingly despotic. With his unrivaled knowledge of the social and economic history of the classical world, Professor Rostovtzeff has shown how the emperors imposed heavy new burdens on the landowning and financial classes, until they snuffed out most of the incentive for private initiative. They regulated enterprises more and more minutely. They took many ventures, such as mines and metallurgical plants, into their own hands and confided the management to their fiscal administration. This growing paternalism was accompanied in the late third century and afterward by a notable shrinkage in the output of mines and manufactures in most parts of the Roman Empire, and by the abandonment of land previously cultivated. There is a temptation to attribute the economic decline in large measure to the increased government interference. There is a temptation to attribute the prosperity during the

---

[16] I hope to discuss the subject in more detail elsewhere. It is touched on in essays of mine referred to in these pages, essays that I hope eventually to incorporate in a book.

first and early second centuries, in large measure, to the greater freedom which existed at that time.[17]

It is possible to argue that the rise of economic despotism was unfavorable to prosperity in late classical times, without making it the basic cause of the decay of commerce and manufacturing. Can paternalism be considered, in any case, as the principal explanation for the failure of the classical peoples to develop a mechanized industrial civilization of the sort created by the Western peoples during the last five hundred years, and particularly during the last two centuries?

Without a special knowledge of classical history it would be presumptuous to do more than offer an opinion, in the hope that it may be tested by careful research. Modern industrialism is based, obviously enough, on the widespread substitution of power-driven machinery for hand labor, and upon the use of steam, oil, or hydroelectric power in place of the force of man, beast, wind, or stream. "In the second century of the Christian era," as Gibbon wrote, "the empire of Rome comprehended the fairest part of the earth, and the most civilized portion of mankind." In that rich and highly sophisticated world, mines and quarries, together no doubt with industrial cities, "formed merely small islands in a sea of fields and meadows."[18] To understand why there was nothing remotely resembling the Ruhr district, the Black Country in the English midlands, or the Pittsburgh neighborhood, where the great factories, with their flames and smoke, blot out most signs of rural life over hundreds of square miles, is it not necessary to discover what was missing in classical times to stimulate inventions and the widespread use of mechanical energy? Why was there so little development of new me-

[17] Cf. M. Rostovtzeff, "The Decay of the Ancient World and Its Economic Explanations," *Economic History Review*, II, No. 2 (1930), 197–214.

[18] Rostovtzeff, *The Social and Economic History of the Roman Empire* (Oxford, 1926), p. 296.

chanical principles, why was little or no attempt made to use steam for power, during the preceding hundred and fifty years or so of economic liberalism, when the imperial government protected private property and encouraged private initiative? The extension of the liberal economic system of Rome to the provinces created a market, with free trade, comparable in extent to that of modern America. Under the early Empire, the capitalists of classical times had a far larger unified area in which to exploit the natural resources of the soil and the subsoil than the English capitalists had in a period of comparable length, between the late sixteenth and late eighteenth centuries. What conditions were lacking to make it possible for the classical peoples to set up steam engines, to discover cheap methods of smelting iron ore, and to work out most of the technical principles upon which the triumph of industrialism among the Western peoples has been based?

No final answer to that question is, perhaps, possible. But would an answer be adequate unless it took account of the lack of coal resources in the lands surrounding the Mediterranean, where the chief centers of classical industry and civilization were found?[19] Would it be adequate unless it took account of the special bent which the peoples of the north of Europe, and the British in particular, have shown for scientific inquiry and a philosophy of material improvement? Would it be adequate unless it took account of the relatively great security afforded the British people by their island? Their isolation made unnecessary the development of a military force, such as influenced the Roman emperors in embarking upon their policy of all-embracing paternalism.[20]

If Professor Toynbee is right, classical civilization was already doomed before the Romans dealt the other peoples of

---

[19] For the influence of coal see above, chap. iii, sec. i, and the references there cited.

[20] Rostovtzeff, "The Decay of the Ancient World and Its Economic Explanations," op. cit., pp. 207–9.

the Mediterranean area knockout blows and established the Empire. Viewed in the light of his position, the commercial and industrial collapse was a symptom of a deeper malady. It cannot be treated as a primary result of economic despotism. In any case, the collapse was accompanied by other circumstances, besides increasing paternalism, which were discouraging to agrarian, industrial, and commercial enterprise. There was the prolonged civil strife of the third century. There was the increasing cost of metal and of manufactured articles, brought about by the rise in the price of fuel and building materials, as the forests were thinned out and timber of every kind became scarce and dear. There was, finally and perhaps most important of all, the lack of any development during the late Republic and early Empire of a school of natural science such as arose in Europe—and especially in Great Britain—in the sixteenth, seventeenth, and eighteenth centuries. The Latin mind has never had, to the same extent as the British, the capacity to reopen the deal with fate; it has not the same longing to strive after comfort and health. The special aptitude of the English mind for natural science and material improvement appears even in the Middle Ages with Roger Bacon and William of Occam. In Roman times we have no philosophers quite comparable to them. We certainly have no one who took a philosophical line comparable to that taken later by Francis Bacon, Boyle, or even Descartes. All three looked forward to the conquest of nature and of disease on such a scale as no classical philosopher had ever contemplated. They looked forward confidently to a time when these conquests would greatly lighten man's labor, enormously increase production, and prolong human life. For many decades the Roman Empire had peace and a large measure of free trade. But peace and free trade were insufficient for the triumph of industrialism without the driving force of an intense belief in the possibility and desirability of material improvement. It is altogether improbable that the new philosophy, which is bound up with modern industrialism, would have developed in the later centuries of the Roman Empire, even if the relatively greater economic freedom of earlier times had persisted.

What part has the freedom allowed the private capitalists from government regulation and interference played in the triumph of modern industrialism? In order to give even a tentative answer to that question, it would be necessary to analyze industrial development with great care in relation to all the main currents of history since the Reformation. That has not yet been done. But the lack of adequate knowledge has not deterred some recent American writers from attributing all the material blessings we now enjoy (including, apparently, the great increase in life-expectancy), primarily to the creative powers of the business administrator, spurred on to become a public benefactor by a thirst for profits, with the quenching of which benevolently disposed governing authorities do as little as possible to interfere.

No doubt there has been during the past century a tendency, particularly among the followers of Karl Marx, to belittle unintelligently the part played by business enterprise, rewarded, when successful, by large profits, in the creation of material wealth during modern times in both America and northern Europe. Some socialist writers have even denied that private capital has played any creative role in increasing the national dividend. They seem to assume that, if all enterprise had been in the hands of the state and had been run by salaried officials appointed by the government, the volume of production would have increased at least as rapidly as it has since the Reformation in Great Britain and the United States. The recent experiences of Russia give little support to such opinions.

From the historical point of view, it is hardly less one-sided to attribute the great prosperity of the Western peoples in modern times entirely to the skill and enthusiasm of private businessmen, stimulated by the profit motive, than to deny to them any share whatever in bringing it about. In their enthusiasm for the business adventurer, the champions of free enterprise minimize, or forget altogether, a number of other factors. They minimize the part played in the material prosperity of Western civilization by natural resources (especially coal and other mineral wealth), by the growing area of free trade, by orderly manual labor, by invention, by the natural science behind invention, and by the philosophy of improvement behind both science and invention. They forget all about Bacon, Boyle, and Descartes, none of whom were businessmen, and none of whom were impelled to take their philosophical position by the prospect of a larger worldly income for themselves. They also forget the part played by peace in the material prosperity of Great Britain and America. Except for the civil war of the seventeenth century, there has been no serious and prolonged fighting on British soil since the Reformation. Except for the civil war of the nineteenth century, there has been no serious and prolonged fighting on North American soil since the United States became a nation. Neither of these wars lasted long enough to interfere profoundly with economic progress. Protected by the sea and united within the unrivaled frontiers which the sea has hitherto provided, Great Britain and the United States have enjoyed opportunities to occupy their energies, without the threat of destruction, with the commercial exploitation of natural resources to a degree that has never been possible on the Continent of Europe. There the various nations have been continually subject to the ravages of war, to the fear of invasion, and to frequent shifts in the frontiers which have provided barriers to trade.

In Western history, war has been a factor working to increase the scale of enterprise, as the late Werner Sombart has emphasized in his studies of the rise of capitalism. With the use of gunpowder, with the use of metal for building defenses and for hurling at the enemy, larger and larger munitions plants, arsenals, and shipyards have been required to provide for victory. So there is a sense in which war has contributed to the triumph of industrialism, by promoting the assembling of great blocks of capital. But the waging of war on a large scale, when accompanied by invasion and serious material destruction within the national boundaries, has been generally unfavorable both to the growth in the output of consumable commodities and to the freedom of private business activity. One factor that promoted the rise of economic despotism in the states and principalities of Continental Europe on the eve of the Reformation was a change in the nature of the weapons of warfare. This change was hardly less sweeping than that which is taking place in our age, with the introduction of submarines, airplanes, tanks, and motorized troops. On the eve of the Reformation gunpowder, cannon and other firearms were being introduced extensively for the first time. It seemed to contemporaries then, hardly less than now, that the technique of warfare changed overnight. The nature of the new weapons led the political authorities to declare their production state monopolies. This was done in one country after another of Continental Europe, in connection with the manufacture of saltpeter and gunpowder as well as of ordnance of all kinds.[21] The administration of the armament industries by the government encouraged state interference with and control over all kinds of enterprises in industry and commerce.

The security provided by geographical conditions both for Great Britain and for the United States has helped the two countries to exploit their great natural resources and to raise their standard of living. At the same time, this security has been an important element in reducing the need for government regulation and control over industry and commerce. In so far

[21] Cf. Nef, *Industry and Government in France and England, 1540-1640*, pp. 59-68, 88-98.

as the general industrial system of a country has to be harnessed for war purposes, a degree of unified control is indispensable. This can be supplied effectively only by the central government. It is supplied at the expense of a considerable measure of economic freedom. When an adequate defense or offense in war depends on a quick response, it is necessary to maintain a greater control over private enterprise, even in times of nominal peace, than when the danger of foreign attack and invasion is remote. So in Great Britain and the United States we owe both our prosperity and our freedom of enterprise in a measure to the security provided by our natural frontiers. In considering the services which free enterprise has rendered to material prosperity, it is important that we should not include, as is frequently done, those which prosperity owes to geographical advantages. Without these geographical advantages we should not have had anything like the measure of liberty in economic life that we have possessed.

If the danger of invasion increases, if the United States finds it necessary to meet this danger by preparing to wage war and by waging war in the air, on the seas, or overseas over a long period of time, the country can no longer continue to treat either freedom of enterprise or material prosperity as the chief objective of individual and national life. In warfare we are apparently entering a new period, which, like that of the Renaissance, involves the assembling of armament on a vastly larger scale than in the past. Unless more peaceful relations can be established between the great nations of the world, the change in the nature and scale of warfare today will bring about increasing governmental interference in economic enterprise, as in Continental Europe on the eve of the Reformation.

History suggests that freedom for private initiative in economic affairs has been less of a cause and more of a symptom of material prosperity than Anglo-Saxon, and particularly American, economic thought has commonly allowed. The amount of economic liberty that is consistent with the maximum economic well-being of a nation varies with conditions. Warfare is the most readily recognized condition, but it is by no means the only one, which may make increasing interference with the free play of individual wants in the market place desirable in the interest both of the general happiness of a nation's population and even of their material standard of living.

III. ECONOMIC FREEDOM AND GENERAL WELFARE

With the decline of moral and intellectual standards, and with the exaggerated emphasis placed by most Americans on the economic side of life, materialism threatens to become its own worst enemy.[22] Now that material welfare seems to be dependent upon an improvement in the moral, intellectual, and artistic life of mankind, upon a greater measure of common belief than exists in the United States today, it is no longer helpful to regard material welfare as separate from the ultimate ends of civilization. Even if it were our sole object to increase the output of goods and services that can be brought into relation with the measuring-rod of money, and to improve the material standard of living, we should have to consider the influence of economic freedom upon noneconomic as well as economic welfare. In the present age, the latter seems to be even more contingent on the former than the former is upon the latter.

Up to a point, increases in the national dividend of material goods and services—and particularly a rise in the standard of living of the poor, who are always the most numerous class—together with reductions in the manual labor required to produce a given quantity of physical wealth, do contribute to the love of virtue, knowledge, and beauty. But it is not true that by focusing all the attention of a people upon the production of

---

[22] See above, chap. iv, secs. i and iii.

physical goods and entertainment, upon methods of producing them at a lower cost in manual labor, and upon the transportation, the advertising, the sale, and the consumption of goods in the largest possible quantities we shall approach as close as possible either to happiness, in Aristotle's sense, or to justice, in Plato's. Justice, as Plato might have said, is brought about by the most harmonious possible balance between all the needs of men, their desire for physical goods and entertainment, their yearning for faith, and their love of righteousness, wisdom, and art. Such a balance in any state—certainly in a vast state like the United States, with its hundred and thirty million people sprawled over a continent—can be produced only with the help of wise advice, good government, and many independent units, each capable of performing economic or noneconomic functions which contribute to the common welfare.

What seems to have come about with the triumph of industrialism, and with the moral and intellectual crisis of our time, is this: The disproportionate emphasis laid by our institutions and our social and economic life upon material values is depriving the American people of the opportunity to cultivate for their own sake the needs of the mind and spirit. The mechanized nature of physical work in mines and factories, and the almost equally mechanical mental chores performed in most large stores, shops, and offices which sell and advertise the products of industry, give the people who labor in them almost no room, while working, to exercise their reason. The work of housewives, as well as of men, has been lightened. But many of the synthetic objects produced and sold by the new methods clutter up the increased leisure hours —at home, on the way to and from work, and in vacation time—in ways that provide little more scope for the exercise of reason than does the labor of making and selling the new products. Without reason, there can be no religion. There can be no ethics. There can be no art. Ultimately there can be no science. As the opportunity to seek righteousness for its own sake disappears, selfishness blots out the altruism and the sense of responsibility that existed to some extent during the great age of laissez faire. As the opportunity to seek knowledge for its own sake disappears, there is a steady decline in the zest for work that was fairly widespread during that age. As the opportunity to seek beauty for its own sake disappears, disorder and untidiness obliterate the wisps of taste that persisted among the middle class and even the workmen during that age.

Responsibility, orderliness, and pleasure in steady and even hard work are all necessary—not only to create a good society but to maintain a wealthy one. In so far as economic liberty raises the standard of living, it provides comfort and leisure which help men to cultivate the goods of the mind and spirit. But, by the ways in which it has worked to raise the standard of living in recent decades, it has often deprived men of the training and experience which are indispensable if they are to cultivate these higher goods. In a country where there are few private institutions which effectively stand for goods of life other than material wealth or publicity, it is doubtful whether a return to the economic liberty which prevailed in the United States in the late nineteenth century would contribute as much to happiness as it would destroy, even in the unlikely event that the immediate result should be a great increase in the material well-being of the population.

Material well-being is an important means to the good life; it is not the only one. Freedom of economic enterprise is an important means to material well-being; it is not the only one. Just as extreme materialism seems to have become its own worst enemy, so the extreme economic individualism which worked for the material welfare of all the Western peoples in the nineteenth century, would probably not contribute today to that of American society, now that such welfare seems to have become contingent upon the recovery of a love for the higher goods of life and of opportunities to participate in them.

The more we consider either history or philosophy, the more apparent becomes the danger of regarding material well-being and freedom for private business as ends in themselves. In our history as a nation we have given both places of special importance. From the point of view of national welfare the emphasis upon both, especially in the early decades of the Republic, did much to husband the energy and promote the prosperity of the United States, though throughout American history the disproportionate attention paid to them has inter-fered with the cultivation of thought and art. Since the Civil War, and especially during the last fifty years, Americans have discarded most of the other values embodied in the religion and the general culture that we derived from Europe and from classical antiquity. Yet, in spite of the changes that have made material objectives and economic individualism less desirable for the national happiness than they were in the nineteenth century, the attachment of the American people as a whole to the former is even greater than it was, and the at-tachment of powerful and influential elements among them to the latter is no less tenacious.

The United States is at a parting of the ways. Even if the country is able to survive in a world of dangerous neighbors without a fundamental change in its scale of values, it will not succeed in offering light for other people without such a change. The hope of building a great American civilization lies in emphasizing the needs of the mind and spirit. Such a change in emphasis cannot be brought about either by leaving the future to private initiative or by substituting a government bureaucracy for free enterprise in economic life. It can be brought about only by providing institutions independent of both the private businessman and the politician, devoted to the cultivation of righteousness, knowledge, and beauty for their own sake.

The trouble is not that we have too many material goods. The trouble is that we lay too great a store on material goods which cater to comfort rather than to intelligence and the love of beauty. But it is doubtful whether a reduction in our supply of material goods will be a tonic of the kind that will restore the old values which are so greatly needed. Selfish and irresponsible as we have grown to be, compared with our Victorian ancestors, and above all lacking in the conviction that our grandfathers had that the more humane civilization we have built up, for all its faults, is worth defending, a reduction in the standard of living is fraught with serious dangers for the freedom of thought and speech, the kindly physical treatment of human beings, and the rough equality of opportunity that still command the outward support of this nation. These are values we must strive to save. So a reduction in the standard of living is not to be welcomed for its own sake. That kind of economic order which will do most to prevent such a reduction is the one we should seek, provided it is also an economic order which will permit us to build a civilization worth defending, a civilization that our people will defend even at the cost of serious sacrifice in their standards of living.

The development of institutions independent of both politics and business need not diminish our material prosperity. Machinery and cheap power make it feasible to produce plenty of economic goods for the entire population without the continuous labor of a large portion of it. If it is possible to bring about a change in values, so that work for nonmaterialistic ends is treated as no less respectable than labor which increases the volume of goods and services that can be sold at a profit, might not the problem of starvation in the midst of plenty disappear? There need be little or no unemployment.

Work for the highest ends of civilization would constitute a claim on the national dividend, as well as work for purposes that our economists have been erroneously assuming bring with them all the other goods of life. The labor of producing and the trouble of selling machine-made products and synthetic entertainment might be seen in their proper proportions. Freedom, in the sense of the liberty of men to seek good ends, and to choose the means most likely to lead toward them, might increase in spite of the curtailment of economic liberty that has taken place in all countries since the nineteenth century.

A true democracy worthy of a new and higher civilization than any yet achieved on earth must be based upon love of one's neighbors, upon love of the distinctively human ends of civilization, rather than upon a desire to get all one can for one's self. When, therefore, we find a conflict between an increase in the national dividend of material commodities, such as automobiles, electric refrigerators, and cigarettes, and a strengthening among our people of faith, goodness, wisdom, and beauty, we should as lovers of the ideal state favor those measures and cultivate that economic order which will contribute to faith, goodness, wisdom, and beauty. These are the scarce commodities today. It is for them more than for physical comfort that the scholar who loves his country and humanity should work.

With this broad principle as a guide, to what extent and within what spheres would freedom of business enterprise be desirable? The lessons of history suggest that, from the point of view of social welfare, freedom from state authority and control is helpful, on the whole, to certain kinds of enterprise and harmful to others. The lessons of history suggest that such freedom is favorable under certain conditions and harmful under others. As almost everyone recognizes, economic individualism is both more readily possible and more desirable in a state that is not faced with the necessity of waging war on a great scale than in a state that is faced with such necessity. Great freedom for private initiative in economic matters is also better suited to the exploitation of new and rich natural resources than to the conservation of the economic wealth of a settled and generally developed country. Private enterprise, dependent for success upon profits obtained in a free market, is better suited to the development of heavy industries, such as coal-mining, iron-making, and automobile manufacturing, than to the artistic industries, where quality is of more importance than quantity.[23] The need to please the general public, the need to sell his wares in competition with chewing gum, cigarettes, and pulp magazines, is not a great inspiration to the artist. Freedom to develop his art according to aesthetic needs is the fundamental matter. This liberty can be destroyed by the demands of a market place devoid of taste, as well as by a despotism. This does not mean that the solution is to put all art in the hands of the democratic state. It does mean that independent institutions, such as the universities, the churches, and private foundations devoted to the cultivation of the arts, are necessary if art is to be preserved and cultivated. Otherwise all art will degenerate into commercial art and entertainment. If architecture and the making of furniture, for example, are not undertaken mainly for artistic purposes, they will be developed eventually for the provision solely of comfort and utility.

IV. THE ENDOWMENT OF NONECONOMIC INSTITUTIONS

From these general considerations, one fundamental conclusion would seem to follow. The sphere within which business enterprise, conducted for private profit, came to dominate at the end of the nineteenth century is much wider than is

[23] Cf. Nef, *Industry and Government in France and England, 1540–1640*, pp. 139–40, 146, and *passim*.

desirable for the happiness of the people of the United States in the twentieth. It is much wider than is desirable for the future of civilization. Signs are not lacking that even in the sphere in which economic freedom is most appropriate—the heavy industries and the industrial and commercial establishments that cater to comfort and entertainment—private initiative is working somewhat less in the interest of the general welfare than was the case in the eighteenth and nineteenth centuries. For one thing the American people are beginning to have a surfeit of some of the commodities produced under private competition and pushed onto the public by advertising, instalment selling, and other high-pressure methods. At the same time, what economists have frequently called "financial capitalism" has largely replaced the industrial capitalism of the nineteenth century.[24] The businessmen who control much of the capital of industrial and commercial enterprises are less interested than they were in the future of a particular industrial unit, in building up an efficient and reliable firm. They are more interested in profits divorced from the actual output and distribution of goods and services. So the creative element in business, which makes demands on the intellectual and scientific capacities of the owners, is less prominent now than it was in the nineteenth century. In the third place, private savings are no longer available as readily as they used to be for investment in new and daring economic ventures. Much of them is tied up in trust funds of various kinds. Often they can be invested only in seasoned securities, the purchase of which is not likely to lead to the building of new types of plant and to the production of new kinds of goods in large quantities. The situation of the private individuals who control large blocks of capital today resembles in some ways that of the ecclesiastical foundations at the end of the Middle Ages. The wealth of the Church and its extensive possession

[24] Cf. N. S. B. Gras, *Business and Capitalism* (New York, 1939).

of property had been useful to the development of the type of economic civilization that grew up in Europe in the eleventh, twelfth, and thirteenth centuries. But the power of the Church over wealth was much less useful for the progress of the type of economic civilization developed since the Reformation, especially in the north of Europe and in America.[25] It is therefore possible that the great freedom of economic enterprise which prevailed in Great Britain and the United States, which served the Western world well in the eighteenth and nineteenth centuries and which served the English people well ever since the Elizabethan Age, is less essential to the nobler civilization that might be built in the twentieth and twenty-first centuries than it was to the triumph of industrialism.

The solution is not the control of all enterprise by the state. Still less is it the abolition of private property. Churches and other ecclesiastical foundations were not deprived of all their estates in the modern world. It is at least arguable that there might be an even better civilization in the English-speaking countries than exists if the churches had retained more property, if fewer institutions and values had been sacrificed for the sake of material improvement.

The remedy for one extreme is never to rush to the other. Recent events suggest the country is in danger of doing exactly that. It is well to remember that one extreme is as bad as another and that justice in the state consists in cultivating the greatest possible harmony between all the needs and all the necessary desires of human beings.

Among the legitimate wants are the desires for private property and for freedom to pursue business enterprise for the sake of profit. If it ever came in the United States, communism would be even worse than in Russia. All but the most blind among our citizens are beginning to realize how bad that is. We shall renounce all hope of a future American civilization

[25] Cf. above, chap. vi, sec. iii.

worthy of the name if we guide the ship of state to the port of Leningrad. Laissez faire is part of our national heritage. The danger that its complete abandonment would constitute to political and moral stability is increased by the disposition of Americans to magnify their disagreements and to neglect opportunities for agreement when they present themselves. What is important for the United States is the recognition that private property and economic individualism are means rather than ends, and that, as with all means, it is possible to have more of both than is desirable for the general welfare. The sphere of private business enterprise can no longer fruitfully be as extensive as it was in the nineteenth century. We need to redefine the sphere within which private enterprise can work for good. An even more important task is to build up, outside the realm of private enterprise, another realm in which the best values of nineteenth-century Western civilization and thirteenth-century Western civilization can be revived and developed. We must try to combine equality of opportunity, freedom of thought and speech, and the humane physical treatment of our fellows with a new spirit of self-sacrifice, a love of our country and our fellow-men which can come today only if Americans have opened to them the chance to build together, millions strong, a society nobler and more enduring than that ever achieved by earlier peoples.

If we are to work for such a society we should strive to avoid the concentration of wealth or power either in the central or local government, or in the hands of private businessmen, or in the hands of labor-union leaders. The central government will have to exercise, as it already does, greater economic authority than it exercised in the United States during the nineteenth century, but it should exercise this authority with restraint on behalf of the highest ends of civilization and not in order to make the state dominant in the life of the nation. An important step in the direction of this goal would be a redistribution of the economic resources of the country in the interest of a better society, devoting its energy less exclusively to economic objectives. The national government might use its power over wealth both to create new institutions and to strengthen some of those already in existence—institutions which could conduct their affairs independently of both political authority and economic influence. The churches, the endowed universities and colleges, and the private schools offer us examples of such institutions. They are dependent for further development upon gifts from private individuals or from the foundations created by wealthy men in the past. With the course which interest rates have taken during the last decade they may become dependent even for continued existence upon these sources. It is doubtful whether the sources will prove adequate. Yet the future of religious faith, of moral philosophy, and of art in the United States may well depend upon the maintenance and extension of independent endowed institutions.

It will depend no less, of course, upon a change in the objectives and methods of these institutions. Unless they devote themselves to faith, righteousness, wisdom, and beauty, as well as to natural science, unless in social and humanistic studies methods derived from science are made the tools of reason (instead of substitutes for it), unless the universities and colleges work toward the unification of knowledge, the provision of fresh endowments out of public money will not improve the general welfare of the United States. Public support of endowed institutions involves great risks. It involves a communal act of faith. But the condition of life is the acceptance of risks. Does it not follow that this is also the condition of a life of the mind? Unless there are strong institutions, independent of both economic and political pressure, there will be no chance to cultivate faith, righteousness, wisdom, and beauty, each for its own sake.

How can we make such institutions at once more numerous, more secure economically, and more independent of private interests than they are at present? There would seem to be only one way—for the government to take part in endowing them. Instead of increasing the scale of state education by setting up further schools and colleges dependent upon the income voted annually by the national government or by state and local governments, the political authorities would make the gifts that wealthy private men are now either unable or unwilling to offer. The electorate should encourage the political authorities to vote these gifts. As the institutions would be founded or developed by public money, they would belong to the people. The people would have to recognize their own need for the guidance and the spiritual food which can be supplied only by moral, intellectual, and artistic leadership.

Under such a plan, the national government would make gifts to endowed universities, colleges, and schools concerned with teaching good moral and intellectual habits and a love of beauty. It would make gifts to churches concerned with the cultivation of faith and good moral conduct. It would create by gifts in various parts of the country a series of establishments devoted to the arts and handicrafts. They would be concerned with music, painting, architecture, and the fashioning of beautiful objects of decoration. Decisions concerning the allocation of public funds for endowments would rest with a commission of scholars and creative artists, chosen partly by the national administration and partly by the privately endowed institutions already in existence. While political authorities might have a share in selecting the trustees for the newly endowed institutions, with the advice of the best writers and artists the country affords, they should not control the policies. Those should be decided by the independent needs of the institutions themselves.

Such a plan might do much to encourage in our educational

institutions a less businesslike and more philosophical treatment of learned subjects. It might even lead to the emergence
of a philosopher or two. Plato suggested that the ideal state
could never be achieved "till philosophers are kings, or the
kings and princes of this world have the spirit and power of
philosophy, and political greatness and wisdom meet in one."
If the independence of the mind could be encouraged in the endowed institutions of learning so that the spirit and power of
philosophy extend to government, then the sovereign people
who permitted their representatives to perform for them this
act of faith would have an adequate return for the gifts they
had made.

In a similar way, the churches endowed by the government
might be gradually relieved of the necessity for developing
programs likely to suit the tastes of their parishioners for entertainment and amusement. They might be relieved from the
necessity of competing with motion-picture houses, dance
halls, hotels, and sporting clubs. They might concern themselves with religion, with religious art, and with the great
problems of Christian theology. In this way the gifts of the
government might contribute to the restoration of faith and to
the cultivation of the virtues for which Christ lived and died.
If such a result were achieved, the sovereign people of the
United States would have no reason to regret the gifts they
had made.

In a similar way, the new establishments devoted to the arts
and crafts might be free to develop independently of the current demands of the market place for cheap machine-made
products and for all synthetic works which are made, not according to the requirements of beauty as they develop in the
inner life of the artist, but according to the requirements of
persons with little or no taste and little or no knowledge, who
depend for their livelihood upon sales. Such establishments
might then contribute to a revival of genuine art. They might

help to create in the United States an American style. With such a style, our cities and villages could be gradually rebuilt on aesthetic principles. If this result were achieved or even approached, the sovereign people of the United States would have no reason to feel that their investment in the arts and crafts had been wasted.

There would remain an immense sphere within which private business would be free to operate. The demand for food, heat, conveyances, and materials of all kinds would hardly diminish if all the population of the country were employed in useful or creative tasks, though the nature of the demand might change. Time and energy would no longer be wasted in private drives designed to raise money for worthy causes. The life of the community would no longer be dominated as completely as it is today by the business or the labor-union view of life. Industry, trade, and finance would exist to serve man, not man to serve industry, trade, and finance.

XI

THE FUTURE OF DEMOCRATIC GOVERNMENT

*

THE future of constitutional government has become so precarious that its defense concerns every American who cares about the future of civilization. It is hardly possible for any scholar who is deeply interested in his work as an economist or a historian, or even as a philologist, a chemist, or a geologist, to ignore the challenge. The survival of creative scholarship depends upon the maintenance of democracy, upon the maintenance of the rights of free intellectual inquiry and artistic expression which have been kept alive among the Western peoples, in spite of an occasional eclipse, ever since the little group that was to form the University of Paris began to meet on the banks of the Seine and those wonderful Gothic cathedrals began to appear in the north of France in the twelfth century. With the eclipse of the liberty essential to intellectual inquiry in every country on the continent of Europe, the survival of Western thought and art is coming to depend on America. As the guardians of Western culture, the American universities have a duty to keep democracy alive.

Many persons who read or hear the words of American university professors and college teachers who denounce the dictators for their latest barbarities assume that they are aware of the dangers that beset them. Even if this were true, it would not follow that they are doing all they can to meet these dangers. It is not enough to recognize evil, it is necessary to work constructively against it. Denunciations of dictators are not enough in a world where the dictators themselves are not lacking in the power to denounce, and where they alone have ready access to an audience in every country. In a world flooded with propaganda and counterpropaganda, talk has become the cheapest of all commodities, words have become emptier of meaning and belief than ever before in Western history. If American scholars, writers, and artists are to face the present threat to constitutional government with any hope of meeting it successfully, they will have to deal with more basic issues than those they generally touch on in newspaper interviews and articles and radio talks.

During the last two years the world has watched with astonishment the Germans demonstrating on the continent of Europe that the advantages in war have passed from the defense to the offense. In the last war, when the armies in the north of France hurled tons of steel at the enemy and followed the steel with men carrying guns and bayonets, they generally lost two men for every one lost by the defenders. Even at that cost, the gains made by armies with hundreds of thousands of soldiers were generally small and unimportant. Today, in so far as the figures of casualties are to be trusted, the situation is reversed. In the Battle of France it was apparently the defenders who had two casualties for every one of the offenders. And the net result, instead of being negligible, was, we know, total victory. As Mr. Hoover put it picturesquely, the defenders have lost everything except their carving knives.

Is it not possible that, in the struggle to preserve our constitutional liberties, we can learn a lesson from the new methods of warfare? Is it not possible that, in the sphere of government, changes have taken place during the last thirty years parallel to those that have taken place in military tactics? It is no longer enough to preserve democracy by defending the status quo. It is no longer enough to clamor for free speech, for the importance of voting on every issue. By trying to save too much, by extending the voting principle to matters for which it was not intended and where it does more harm than good, we run a grave risk of losing all. The way to save democracy is not to make a long Maginot Line out of the old precepts of universal suffrage and laissez faire. Such precepts are valuable as means—not as ends. Voting and doing what you please are good in so far as they contribute to the dignity and the strength of the individual and to the justice of the state. They are good no further. They are good only in so far as they contribute to the ultimate ends of civilization.

New precepts are needed if men are to realize the best that is in them in the twentieth century. We should recognize that democracy itself will have to be reconstructed in order to survive. We must try to rescue out of the democratic creed of the past the passion for justice and for the dignity of the human being which the constitutional form of government at its best supported as no other political regime has done.

In order to rescue these values in the twentieth century, we cannot afford simply to cling to ancient democratic rights. These rights must be made to stand for something. Individualism can no longer be construed simply in the sense of the privilege of a man to enjoy comforts. It must be construed as an opportunity to fulfil obligations on behalf of the common good. Democratic government should be built up in such a way that it helps to create among the people of this country a desire to serve their fellows as well as themselves.

How is this to be brought about? What political reforms are needed? Is it not possible to find in connection with the recent weaknesses of democratic government clues that may enable us to put forward some tentative suggestions for strengthening it, imperfect though the suggestions are bound to be?

I. IN DEFENSE OF DEMOCRACY

The world into which was born the generation now assuming the responsible positions in politics was a world where government was carried on, in varying degrees and with varying success, with the consent of the governed. The sovereign authority, at least in Great Britain, France, the United States, most of the smaller countries of Europe, and at the moment even in Italy, rested not in a monarch or a dictator or an oligarchy but in representatives chosen at specified intervals by a vote of the people. We have lived to see the democratic principle of government placed on the defensive. Whether the attack on it succeeds completely, or whether again, in President Wilson's fine phrase, the world is "made safe for democracy," our descendants centuries hence, if they are allowed to study the past impartially, are likely to regard the establishment of democratic government in states with populations running into tens of millions as one of the remarkable achievements of Western civilization.

In order to prove that democracy is worth saving it is not necessary to prove that it is the best form of government ever devised. It is enough to show that it is superior to the alternative confronting us. That alternative is despotism. Whether we adopted some form of national socialism or fascism or communism, we should be adopting a more absolute form of government than any which has existed in Europe since the eighteenth century, and a government in which the ruler is under less restraint than the ruler of any despotism that Western civilization has known. In a famous book written a century ago a Frenchman of genius warned his readers that if democracy was replaced by any other kind of government, it would be by an extreme form of despotism. "Are you going to read Tocqueville?" I once asked a student whose thesis dealt with economic conditions on the eve of the American Civil War. "No," he answered, "he is too early for me."

Even if he had been concerned with conditions at the outbreak of the second World War, *Democracy in America* should
have been put on his list of required reading. Like Stendhal,
Tocqueville might have insisted that the course of history
would oblige men to read him long after he was dead.

It is a favorite pastime nowadays, in some circles that pass
as learned, to deliver discourses intended to show that no two
thinkers can possibly agree on any abstract matter. This is
frequently done by ignoring what is vital and important and
emphasizing what is unessential—by ignoring the spirit of
thought and making mountains out of unimportant details.
One is reminded of Harrington's comment at the expense
of some English seventeenth-century scientists. "The University Wits," he remarked, in referring to the group of
learned men who were about to form the Royal Society, "are
good at two Things, at diminishing a Commonwealth and at
multiplying a Louse."[1] While a concentration upon the infinitely small may contribute greatly to an understanding of
matter, when hairsplitting over small points is made the principle of inquiry in human relations, it is likely to increase confusion, suspicion, and misunderstanding. Our modern "university wits," who have carried the procedures of the natural
scientist, ridiculed by Harrington, into the study of man and
society, would be hard put to it to show that Tocqueville's
view of the dangers to which democracy can lead was fundamentally different from that of another out-of-date author,
Plato. In the later books of the *Republic* we are shown how
readily democracy can disintegrate into tyranny, the worst of
all forms of government. One principal source of danger is
made plain by Plato, as well as by Tocqueville. Tyranny is
brought about because the pursuit of wealth becomes for most

---

[1] James Harrington, *Prerogative of Popular Government* (London, 1658), as cited by
Dorothy Stimson, "Dr. Wilkins and the Royal Society," *Journal of Modern History*, III,
No. 4 (1931), 548.

of society an end in itself—the only important end of existence. Men's physical appetites get the upper hand and control
their minds and their spirits, thus destroying the proper
harmony which makes for justice in the individual and in the
state alike.

If we are to decide as reasonable men between despotism and
democracy, our decision should depend upon a comparison of
their ends. The end of despotism is power. In the despotic
state of the present time every other objective is pursued only
in so far as it promotes the power of the leader and of the nation he leads. Thus the interests of the people—their art, their
virtue, their religion, their philosophy, their science, the
most private aspects of their family relationships, and even
their economics—are subordinated to the strengthening of
the leader. If it is felt necessary to destroy art or religion in
order to strengthen the leader, then art and religion must be
destroyed, or so modified that they lose the independence essential to both. Herr Hitler is reported to have said, "The
art of a national socialist era can be only national socialist."
We are told that even some of the works of Rembrandt—regarded by many excellent painters and critics for generations
as perhaps the greatest Western painter—have been taken from
the German museums whose walls they used to ornament.

The interests of other peoples in the world are also subordinated to the power of the people personified by their leader.
It becomes the mission of the leader and his people to gain
adherents for their state and to add territory to it all over the
world. There is no limit to the objectives of expansion and
power.

Are the ends of democracy any better? The fascists and national socialists taunt the democracies by telling them that
they care for only one thing, material wealth—that their
statesmen are willing to sacrifice everything else so long as they
can increase or retain their dividends and their salaries, and

those of the supporters who keep them in office. The taunts of the communists are of a similar nature. They suggest that all would be well if only the wealthy were disappropriated so that the poor could pursue material ends unimpeded by the rich.

The charges of materialism leveled against Great Britain, the British dominions, and the United States are in part the result of envy of our material prosperity. Yet, when we have made allowance for jealousy, the charges against the democracies are not without substance. If, as the great philosophers of the past have argued, material wealth is not properly the ultimate goal of man, if the ultimate justification for wealth is the contribution which it makes to righteousness, wisdom, and beauty, then Americans are bound to ask themselves whether civilization in the United States is really worthy of the great wealth that the country possesses and that the people enjoy. The psychologist whose researches into the civilization of American cities were cited in an earlier chapter, measures the goodness of life for good people by the material comforts they enjoy and their per capita wealth.[2] How can he be sure the people are good or are becoming better as a result of the "general goodness of life," when he is unable, as he admits, to measure "personal qualities." A preoccupation with material wants and with selfish interests is characteristic of our time. Materialism and individual selfishness are America's greatest weaknesses. Unless the Americans react against them, as the English to some extent seem to be doing, democracy will almost inevitably degenerate into despotism. To be effective, the reaction against materialism and individual selfishness will have to be something more than a temporary expedient called into being by the exigency of war. If the struggle is between material selfishness and power, power is almost certain to win in the end, even if a particular tyranny that

[2] See above, pp. 47–49.

threatens materialism should collapse. The most important difference between democracy and despotism is not that democracy is committed to free enterprise in business and to private property, but that it is also committed to freedom of intellectual enterprise, to freedom of thought. Democracy holds in its hands not only the future of private property but the future of religion, philosophy, and art, and of the virtues with which religion, philosophy, and art, at their best, are always associated. Religion, philosophy, art, economic thought, and even natural science could hardly flourish without an independent existence within the state. While the materialistic temper of democracy makes difficult the creation of the permanent works of art and thought in which civilization consists, the institutions of democracy, unlike those of modern despotism, permit their existence. While freedom of thought is a means and not an end, it is an indispensable means if society is to approach the ends of civilization. As long as democracy survives there is hope for a revival of what is best in Western civilization. There is even hope for the discovery of a new type of civilization, nobler and more altruistic than any of the past. For the discovery of such a new type of civilization there is no hope under totalitarianism.

II. THE RECENT WEAKNESS OF DEMOCRACY

So democracy is worth saving. It will not be saved merely by wishing. No magic carpet, such as existed to some extent in the nineteenth century, is at the disposal of the Western peoples in the twentieth. Nor can democracy be saved merely by fighting the totalitarians. How, then, can it be saved? One way of working toward an answer to that question is to consider why democracy has been disintegrating, why it has been first on the defensive and then on the decline in Europe, at least since the first World War.

The peoples of Europe were told that the war was being

fought to save democracy. When the war ended with a victory for the champions of democracy, the representative form of government was established temporarily in nearly all the states of Europe, great and small. Its success depended upon the use statesmen made of it and upon the kind of return the people expected from it. For the most part they looked upon the freedom they were offered not as an opportunity for service but as an opportunity for material improvement. Everyone was anxious to take, no one was anxious to give. Under the circumstances it was inevitable that the new governments should be judged almost exclusively in terms of the material prosperity of the individuals whom they governed. If the national dividend increased from year to year, then the government might be tolerated.

The first World War coincided roughly with a turning point in the economic history of Europe. After decades and even (in the case of Great Britain) centuries of rapid industrial and commercial progress—during which the volume of output had been increasing at a continually accelerated rate—the Western world has entered a period when the rate of increase in output is diminishing.[3] In a number of European countries the material standard of living was lower in the 1920's than before the war.[4] These new economic conditions were caused by a combination of forces that no government could have controlled. While national policies are not without their influence upon prosperity, they are only one of many factors which govern it. Even if most of the statesmen after the first World War had worked with the greatest intelligence to bring about an increase in the national wealth, they must have disappointed the returning soldiers who had been promised homes for heroes, the wage-earners who expected continuous im-

[3] See above, chap. iii.

[4] Cf. Colin Clark, *The Conditions of Economic Progress* (London, 1940), chap. iv.

provements in their standards of living, and the shareholders and *rentiers* who counted on an increase in their incomes from stocks and bonds and real estate. In fact, the responsible political leaders were not always as intelligent as they might have been. So the people could plausibly blame their disappointments on their government. Democracy had been expected to bring light to the world. It was not bringing the material improvement that everyone counted on, and that nearly everyone with influence mistook for the only form of light.

The weakness of democratic government in the face of economic difficulties arose partly out of this preoccupation of the governed with material improvement. Governments have always been held responsible to some extent for economicde pressions. But the disposition of the people after the first World War to judge governments exclusively in terms of material improvement was novel.[5]

Democratic government can be no better than the elements which make up the state. If these elements are healthy, they will produce wise leadership. The influence of great leaders within a democracy might have done much to revitalize representative government and to strengthen the confidence of the people in it during recent years. But after the first World War no such leadership appeared among the generation who had fought in the trenches. Such effective leadership as existed came from their elders, men whose age prevented them from keeping the torch of democracy lighted for any length of time. They represented an old democratic creed that was strong but insufficient in the face of the breakdown of moral and intellectual standards which has accompanied the material crisis of the twentieth century. While their successors, who were elected to represent the people, had no deep belief in that creed, they had nothing effective to offer in its place.

[5] Cf. above, chap. iv, pp. 65 ff., 87 ff.

They rarely understood the historical forces that produced the tension of the present age better than the older men whom they succeeded. Those men had grit without insight. The new politicians lacked grit as well as insight.

Without leadership, without faith, without confidence in themselves, without the rapidly increasing income which had taken on an importance out of all proportion to its value, the nations of Europe were at the mercy of the strong man who could secure enough force and power to turn guns on them unless they conformed to his will. The strength of the new leaders lay not only in the power that they gained over arms, but in the weakness of the appeal of their democratic rivals. These rivals were forever making promises of better material things—promises they were never able to fulfil. The strong man talked less about wealth than about the importance of order, discipline, and sacrifice. Men look forward with hope to more wealth, but none attain happiness by wealth alone. They distrust leaders who offer them wealth and then fail to deliver it. So some of them mistook the strong man's talk of order and discipline for the higher voice of the spirit they had missed. When they discovered their error, they could turn back only by entering the concentration camp or by facing the firing squad. Order, discipline, and sacrifice are qualities that a tyrant can always demand, but in a tyranny there is no opportunity for wise men to help direct these qualities to good ends.

The weakness of those countries which retained the representative form of government in the face of the dictators lay partly in the existence within their boundaries of the same kind of opinion that facilitated the rise of despotism in other states. Long before the triumph of national socialism in Germany, many of the upper class and upper middle class in France had begun to talk of the need for order and discipline. "We want a dictator," they were always saying. Men without genuine enthusiasm for democratic government, men who prefer a despot to a constitutional ruler, are not likely to make democracy into a dynamic creed capable of winning the enthusiastic support of the nation. It became difficult for the democratic countries to make a stand against pan-Germanism or even to recognize it before it grew strong and dangerous, since so many of their citizens sympathized with the despotic form of government.[6] Under the circumstances it was natural, perhaps inevitable, that, in foreign policy, the victors in the last war were firm when they should have been conciliatory, conciliatory when they should have been firm. They failed to see the danger of giving away under threats of force the things they had refused to give in peaceful negotiations.

What lessons can Americans draw from the collapse of constitutional government on the continent of Europe? The principal lesson would seem to be this: The threat to democracy arises from within the state to an even greater degree than from without. If democracy seems to be more firmly established here than in any other nation, is it not mainly because of America's geographical isolation and because of the long history of constitutional government in this nation? This isolation would offer the United States greater protection than it does were it not reduced every year and almost every month by new mechanical devices designed to bring death-dealing engines nearer these shores and by the new engines of propaganda which sow antagonism and contempt for the democratic form of government within our frontiers, as well as in the neighboring states to the south. The long tradition of constitutional government in the United States would provide a stronger bulwark than it does against both propaganda and foreign invasion if Americans had inherited a respect for tradition. But what respect for tradition can be expected from a

[6] See the excellent analysis of these conditions in France by Yves Simon, *La grande crise de la République française* (Montreal, 1941).

people inclined to agree with Henry Ford that history is bunk, from a people taught that modern society is dynamic as contrasted with all past societies, which were static, and that all rules which might have been of value in past societies are irrelevant in ours? What respect for tradition can be expected from a people, some of whose social scientists teach them that in "the society of the future . . . . morality, as it is generally conceived, will have no place"? What respect for tradition can be expected from a people who are brought up with so little knowledge of their own history that, for many who pass as cultured, the difference between Herman Melville and Margaret Mitchell consists in their never having heard of Melville.

Were it not for the blessings of Providence, might we not have been more vulnerable in the face of despotism than the English? We have possessed security from the strains imposed on nations whose frontiers border, and whose coasts are near to, those of many other nations. We have not possessed the same security from the other elements that have been undermining constitutional government abroad.

More than Europeans, Americans in the nineteenth century were exposed to the unsettling influences of changes in living conditions and circumstances which work against stability in all things, including government. Throughout the nineteenth century Americans were concerned more single-mindedly than most Europeans with trade, finance, and manufacturing, all of which tend to divert men's minds from the permanent and the spiritual to the unstable and the material. We may pride ourselves on the opportunity afforded by the American way of life, with its "three generations from shirt sleeves to shirt sleeves," but we cannot claim that this is the most successful way ever devised for promoting social or intellectual stability. Down to the eighties our people were always moving on into new areas. When the frontier was finally pushed as far as it was possible to push it, the movement did not come to an end.

Men and women continued to move, no longer to uninhabited areas but from the country to the town, from one town to another. They continued to tear down old buildings to build new ones, so that the lack of permanence in their houses and their furniture, which struck foreign observers like Tocqueville a hundred years ago, is not less characteristic of our own time.

It is not the unsettling forces which lost strength with the crossing of the last frontier, but the stabilizing ones. The great waves of immigration from southeastern Europe and the east have produced a more complicated mixture of people, with different traditions and habits, than is to be found in any European country. No less unsettling have been the changes in the training of children and young people, whether the children of immigrants or of parents who can trace their lineage back—without the help of paid record searchers—to the landing of the "Mayflower."

The same process of disintegration in institutions and conventions concerned with virtue and wisdom rather than material wants has been going on in America as in Europe since the last decades of the nineteenth century. A similar slowing-down in the rate of economic progress set in here a little later. Here, as in Europe, people with political influence have come as never before to subordinate all other values in life to material improvement, at a time when they can no longer look forward as a matter of course to a rapid increase in the national dividend from decade to decade. Here, as in Europe, constitutional government has been blamed for a lack of stability and a weakening of confidence, the causes for which are not to be sought primarily in government policies, and not exclusively in economic conditions. After the present crisis is over, constitutional government, if it should survive, will be blamed again unless something more fundamental is done to strengthen democracy than waging war or staying neutral and getting rich.

III. TOWARD A STRONGER CONSTITUTIONAL
DEMOCRACY

The survival of constitutional government in the United States, and its revival in other countries, seem to depend, above all, upon the reassignment of economic objectives to a subordinate place in the order of goods, to a reaffirmation of the ancient belief that there are principles of right conduct which remain always essentially the same. While it may not be given to men to discover these principles in their most perfect form, and while it is certainly not given to men to administer them perfectly through institutions like the church, the school, or the family, it is only by acknowledging the existence of these principles and striving to live by them that men can fulfil their highest purpose. No form of government whose claim to survival rests exclusively, or even primarily, upon material improvement can hope to justify itself in the century that lies ahead. If it is to survive, democracy will have to appeal to men as an opportunity for service, as an opportunity for cultivating those values in art and religion, philosophy and science, which have nothing to do with material advance and with material advantage. So long as men believe that ethical problems will take care of themselves if the death rate is reduced and the national dividend increased, the democratic state will be unable to take its stand on the ethical principles that alone can provide it with a firm foundation. No government which, like that of a democracy, does not coerce its subjects into supporting it can hope to maintain itself unless it finds among the governed a belief that there are general truths independent of circumstances and private interests. As long as men believe that each problem is unique, and set out to solve it by fresh experiences without the help of tradition, they will fall easy victims to the coercion of dictators. The lack of inner conviction in the people concerning truth and right conduct helps to give the despot his strength.

How are men to gain convictions when they suppose that all truth and all conduct must bend to circumstances?

The future of democratic government rests, therefore, not only in the hands of statesmen, generals, and admirals, political scientists and economists, as we frequently assume. It rests also in the hands of the persons who determine the curriculums of our schools and colleges, the nature of religious instruction, and the ideals of family life. It is up to these people to re-establish the permanent, unifying, nonmaterial values in education, in religion, and in the family, which the last two generations undermined in their excessive zeal for a kind of freedom that only those rare persons capable of the greatest self-discipline can exercise to the general advantage.

The first step in defense of democracy should be to persuade our political leaders to stop making their main appeal to the voters by promises of material prosperity. It is not necessary or desirable that government should cease to be concerned with increasing wealth and with keeping up the standard of living, but questions of wealth should be made subordinate to questions of justice, of true liberty, of philosophy, and even of art. When candidates for the presidency, the Senate, or the House of Representatives ask the electors to judge them in terms of their success in reducing crime, in reducing waste both within the government and outside it, in diminishing the influence of propagandists and other self-seekers, when they ask the electors to judge them for their skill in fostering a love of genuine art and literature, in providing better opportunities for the virtuous, the intelligent, the deserving, and the honorable, whatever their station in life, they will perform an important service for constitutional government.

The best government is the one which gives all the citizens an equal opportunity to realize their potential powers to cultivate righteousness, wisdom, and beauty, each for its own sake. That is the sense in which a state should be dedicated to the proposition that "all men are created equal." The best government is not one which treats all grown men as equally honorable, equally wise, or equally gifted artistically, so that the only distinctions between them are those of income or of the space they obtain in the organs of publicity.

Statesmen should make plain to the people that the material prosperity of the state, like that of the individual, may suffer through no fault of the men in control. They should ask their constituents to face the fact that a sacrifice of material wealth may sometimes be necessary in the interest of justice and intelligent understanding, or of the beauty of the surroundings in which they live.

A statesman must not neglect, of course, to deal with the difficult problems of the needy and the unemployed. But it is certain that the proportion of the people who die from actual want is smaller in the United States than in any other country at this time or at any other. If material comfort made for political contentment, the people of the United States, even since the depression of 1929–33, ought to be more contented with their form of government than any people who ever lived. The fact that discontent has been so widespread indicates that the remedy of material improvement is an inadequate remedy. It indicates that the so-called crisis of our time is less an economic than a moral crisis.

In the economic sphere it is right, of course, for statesmen to promote agrarian and industrial prosperity, to provide for old persons, for cripples who are destitute, and for the able-bodied unemployed when they cannot find work. But these should not be a statesman's only objectives, nor should they invariably be given precedence over others. He must also promote social stability, provide interesting and useful work, and encourage the widespread ownership of property in order to give the common man a stake in the government of the country similar to that of wealthy businessmen with large holdings in industry and finance. Harrington's statement concerning the relations between the form of government and the distribution of property has never been seriously refuted. "If the whole People," he wrote, "be Landlords, or hold the Lands so divided among them, that no one Man or number of Men . . . . overbalance them, the Empire (without the interposition of Force) is a Commonwealth."[7] Tawney has recently used his great powers as a historian to demonstrate, in a fascinating article, the truth of this connection between changes in the distribution of landed estates and changes in the form of government, by a study of English social history from the Reformation to the civil war.[8] Land is not the only form of property that needs to be considered. The endowment by the government of private institutions for educational, religious, artistic, and craft purposes would help to produce the balance of wealth that is needed for the future of democracy. The maintenance of our form of government depends not upon the indiscriminate granting to the needy and the non-needy of income without work, as is suggested in the numerous share-the-wealth schemes, but upon the granting to as many men as possible of the property and the conditions necessary for absorbing, useful work and creative leisure. The maintenance of our form of government depends less upon granting people facilities for moving from one part of the country to another than upon encouraging them to make the most of the opportunities provided within the region where they have already settled. A growing stability, a growing attachment of men to the soil of the particular region in which they were made to feel they had, through local institutions, a stake of their own, would help to create those common bonds which have been

[7] *The Oceana of James Harrington and His Other Works*, John Tolland, ed. (London, 1700), p. 40.

[8] R. H. Tawney, "The Rise of the Gentry, 1558–1640," *Economic History Review*, XI, No. 1 (1941), 1–38.

lost in our age of specialized work and constant migration. It would help to divert men's minds from the fleeting to the permanent.

"Perhaps never in its long history has the principle of constitutionalism been so questioned as it is questioned today," writes one of the greatest living students of political thought. "The world is trembling in the balance between the orderly procedure of law and the procedures of force which seem to be so much more quick and effective. We must make our choice between the two, and it must be made in the very near future."[9] Professor McIlwain does not conceal his own overwhelming preference for constitutionalism. On several occasions he has brought his almost unrivaled knowledge of constitutional history to bear on the great crisis of government in the twentieth century. A principal cause for this crisis, he has said, "is the feebleness of government. It must be strengthened. The present danger is despotism. It must be prevented and by legal limitations on government. . . . . We must preserve and strengthen those laws beyond which no free government ought ever to go, and make them the limits beyond which no government whatever can legally go."[10]

These words offer a key to a fresh conception of democracy which may enable us to decide for the orderly procedure of law rather than for the disorderly procedures of force. Such a conception might place constitutionalism on a more permanent basis than any in history. If the United States could take the lead in developing a constitutionalism the value of which would be apparent throughout the world, this new form of government might gradually be adopted by other countries of their own free will, as the British conception of government was adopted in essentials to a considerable extent at the end of

[9] C. H. McIlwain, *Constitutionalism, Ancient and Modern* (Ithaca, 1940), p. 3.

[10] McIlwain, "The Fundamental Law behind the Constitution of the United States," *The Constitution Reconsidered* (New York, 1938), p. 14.

the eighteenth and during the nineteenth centuries. Nothing could do so much to lay the foundations for an international order based on righteousness as a conception of national government based on righteousness.

What would be the nature of the righteous government that we are seeking? There are three aspects of government in the United States that call for re-examination. There is, first, the form of government. This is determined by the manner in which the rulers obtain their authority. There is, second, the effectiveness of their power to act (within the sphere where they may legitimately exercise authority) and to carry through a program of reform in the interest of justice and the common good, a program involving changes in connection with education and with economic and social life. There is, third, the reinforcement of certain old limits on the powers of rulers and the creation of new limits, to insure righteousness and legality and to protect the individual from arbitrary arrest and from persecution of the kind that has grown to such monstrous proportions in Russia, Italy, and Germany, and that now threatens to spread to the entire world.

When we began our discussion of the possible means to the attainment of a civilization better than any in past history, we drew attention to Pascal's vicious circle and suggested that a higher conception of education depended upon a higher conception of social and political life.[11] It is equally true that a higher conception of government depends upon improvements in education and in the economic order. These improvements can be made only if there is a recognition by the people that too much emphasis has been laid upon the function of man as voter, and above all as talker, and too little upon his function as a human person. What government at its best has to do is to provide protection for what is best in man, to encourage men to shoulder their responsibilities as citizens in the spheres

[11] See above, p. 264.

where they have special capacities for assuming such responsibilities—in their families and their occupations.

All the moral and economic reforms that are needed could be carried out within the framework of our government as it is at present constituted. Their initiation and their successful completion would depend upon a change of heart among the governed and their governors. The power of the executive during the term for which it is elected must not be so hedged in that it cannot successfully take vigorous initiative. The test of the desirability of a statesman's action under the constitutional form of government must always be the free vote of the people when he stands for re-election. During the interval the President, the other executive officers, the members of the Senate and the House, in their appropriate spheres, should be expected to lead public opinion on current issues, not to follow it. If they are intelligent, they will nearly always be in a better position to make decisions than equally intelligent outsiders, but they should be willing to consult experts and competent persons on technical matters. The basic philosophical position behind the decisions and acts of statesmen, legislators, and judges cannot properly depend upon prejudices that they have picked up here and there in the course of their lives. They should turn to moral philosophy, in the Platonic and Aristotelian sense, as interpreted and augmented by the wisdom which it is hoped may emerge from the leading American universities. Statesmen, legislators, and judges should be encouraged to make decisions based on a high sense of justice and intelligence and in accordance with a conscience schooled in the Christian virtues. If they do this they will always be in a stronger position to appeal to their constituents than if they bend with every wind set in motion by the bellows of propaganda and of special private interests.

The inability of post-war government in the democratic states to deal with instability and moral disorder, or even to formulate the problems which instability and moral disorder have created, has brought constitutionalism into disrepute. American statesmen must not show the same weaknesses. If they are to avoid such weaknesses, they must not have to justify every small act, for it is possible to arouse against almost any act a chorus of propaganda that is the result not of intelligence and conviction but of chicanery, frequently of the most sinister kind.

What positive action has the United States government to take in the decades before us? It has the task of maintaining our integrity as a nation, if need be by force of arms. In order to do this it must prepare armaments on a colossal scale to meet the threat to our independence that obviously exists. Until that threat has subsided a large part of our national income each year will have to go to the building up of our navy, of a great air force, and of a highly mechanized army, as well as a home guard. In order to carry through such a program the government will have to collect enormous taxes.

The present crisis has led inevitably to an increase in the powers of government. The future of constitutionalism depends in a great measure upon how our rulers use their increased powers—whether they are able to use them in such a way as to create confidence in democratic leadership divorced from the old economic principle of laissez faire. How could such confidence be obtained? It could be obtained partly by improvements in the administration of public funds in the direction of greater efficiency and thrift. The American people are in much need of examples of both. Such confidence depends partly upon a limitation of military and naval tasks to objectives which are consistent with the cultivation of a righteous state in this country. Such confidence depends mainly upon the creation of a nobler conception of citizenship among Americans, such as will give their ancient right to freedom a meaning that has been lost now that the word has come to be confused with license.

The program of educational and economic reform, set out in

the two preceding chapters, should go forward now, in so far as this is consistent with the national defense. In any case, that program should go forward if and when the present military crisis is surmounted. The success of the reforms hinges on the maintenance of a strong but constitutional government. It hinges also, perhaps even more, upon a self-denying government, acting not in the interest of power as such but in the interest of the welfare of the citizens.

A redistribution of property, such as would be involved in the endowment of schools, universities, churches, and establishments devoted to the arts and handicrafts[12] would not destroy private business enterprise. It would leave private business enterprise a large measure of freedom, but would limit the sphere in which it operates to the kinds of work to which it is best suited. It would create a sphere devoted to training in good moral and intellectual habits, to art, craftsmanship, religion, science, moral philosophy, and studies relevant to moral philosophy. All the persons engaged in work independent of the ordinary give and take of the market place would be subjects of the government, just like workmen, managers, technicians, employers, and investors in private enterprise. Like private businessmen, they would have rights and functions of their own independent of the government.

A fairly widespread disposition to regard all money taken by political authorities as little better than theft has been characteristic of the American, and to some extent of the British, people in modern times. In the United States this has been brought about in a measure by the widespread corruption and inefficiency in the collection and the spending of public money—particularly by the local authorities, state and municipal. If we are to have anything approaching righteous government in the future, honesty and efficiency in

[12] See above, chap. x, sec. iv.

the collection of public money will have to replace corruption and inefficiency. Our opposition to taxation arises, also, from the traditions of free enterprise which have been so much stronger in this country than in any other. But economic and political conditions in the twentieth century make any return to the kind of economic freedom that existed in the United States in the nineteenth century out of the question. The choice is not between a nineteenth-century kind of economic freedom and dictatorship, as we have been frequently told. The choice is between a fresh form of democracy and dictatorship. The choice is between an unrighteous state and some approximation to that righteous state envisaged by the wisest philosophers of the past—a state in which industry and free enterprise have an important but not a dominant place, a state which aims to increase the wealth of the citizens, but only in so far as this is consistent with the cultivation of righteousness, knowledge, and beauty. As Maritain has argued with wisdom, moderate Machiavellianism cannot provide an effective bulwark against absolute Machiavellianism. The final reply to absolute Machiavellianism is absolute righteousness.[13]

The endowment of independent institutions would help in establishing limits upon government. But the mere existence of these independent institutions could not create, define, or maintain these rights. Institutions, like governments, should exist for man at his best, and not man for governments or institutions. Effective and wise limitations on governmental authority could be developed only in so far as these institutions performed their functions of working for the good of man. The breakdown of religion and philosophy in recent

[13] Maritain stated his position fully in a paper recently read at the symposium on "The Place of Ethics in Social Science," held in connection with the Fiftieth Anniversary Celebration of the University of Chicago. I understand that this paper is to be published in the January, 1942, number of the *Review of Politics*.

times has been accompanied by the weakening of those ancient principles of natural law which, throughout Western history, had imposed some limits on the power that any sovereign
could exercise at the expense of his subjects. It should be the
main task of the independent institutions to cultivate righteousness, wisdom, and beauty, and thus to establish the
rights of men as human persons—rights which no government
can ever transgress. "Remove righteousness," wrote St.
Augustine, "and what are kingdoms but great bands of
brigands?"[14] In this world righteousness will always wither
unless it is nourished. The command obtained by the Western
peoples over the material world provides them with an opportunity unique in history to guide mankind toward the
ultimate ends of civilized existence.

The rulers in the state should be chosen by vote of the whole
people at periodic intervals. The rulers would be imbued
more and more as time goes on with the importance of service,
with the importance of emphasizing now the sphere of private business, now that of the endowed institutions, now
that of national defense, in accordance with the needs of the
whole people. The check upon the rulers would be the freedom to reject them at the polls, together with the growth of
principles based on natural law and administered by the courts.

There is no use in having an executive power unless it is
given authority. If the function of the executive is merely to
be ornamental, then he should be dressed up in a costume and
treated as a master of ceremonies. No ship can be efficiently
governed by a crew. No ship of state can be effectively
governed by the people as a whole. But a ship of state is
obviously a bundle of infinitely more complicated rights and

[14] *The City of God*, iv. 4. I have used Professor Ernest Barker's translation of this
passage. Cf. the paper delivered by Professor McIlwain, with St. Augustine's words
as text, at the symposium on "The Place of Ethics in Social Science." I understand that
his paper is soon to be published in the *American Political Science Review*.

obligations than a ship, and the executive in a state is the servant of the people in an exclusive sense in which the captain of a ship, with his obligations to the passengers and to the company which employs him, can never be of the crew. Therefore, a need for limitations upon the powers of the executive arises. It is plain enough what some of these limitations should be. No change should be permitted in the system of elections or in the right of free speech and of every citizen to a legal trial. No change should be permitted in our form of government except through constitutional channels. In case laws are passed which do in fact alter the form of government or the system of free elections, or which do abridge the right of free speech or interfere with the rights of all citizens to a fair trial in the courts, then the Supreme Court should annul these laws.

The rights of groups within the state—the rights, for example, of the schools and colleges, of the churches, of the family, of endowed institutions of all kinds—to an independent existence should be affirmed. It is no more desirable for the state than for private donors to determine the nature of the curriculum in the schools and colleges or to influence their administration. It is no more justifiable for the state than for wealthy parishioners to determine the content of sermons and the ways in which the churches shall spend their money. It is no more justifiable for the state than for the neighbors to determine the nature of instruction within the home—to decide what books the children should be encouraged to read or what political doctrines they should be taught. The school, the university, the church, the institutes for arts and crafts, and the family have all important functions to perform in the defense of democracy and civilization. Each of these institutions should be given privileges and responsibilities in the hope that it will be able to use them on behalf of knowledge, art, and right moral conduct. It is up to the school, the church, and the family to instil in youth a passion for righteousness. It is up to the new faculties that would be created in the universities to define and explain the nature of righteousness. These institutions cannot perform their functions properly if they are subject to pressure from without or coercion from above.

Finally, it is plain that the properly elected government of the United States, faced with the threat of despotism, should possess the strength to deal with the enemies of constitutional government within the United States and to meet the threat of aggression from without. Come what may, the Bill of Rights must be maintained. But there are in this country laws against spying. If representatives of totalitarian governments come to the United States for the purpose of weakening our people in their resolve to oppose the expansion of despotism at the expense of other peoples, and eventually at the expense of this country, they can do more damage to the future of constitutional government than any number of ordinary spies. The laws against spying should be extended to cover their activities.

There are in this country laws against advocating the overthrow of our government by force. If Americans set out to advocate a revolution in this country which would replace our present constitutional government by a government under which the people would be denied the right to free elections, free speech, and a fair trial in the law courts, they are in effect advocating the use of force to undermine our principles of government. People cannot be denied the right of free speech or fair trial without the exercise of force. Herr Goebbels is reported to have said in 1935: "We, national socialists, have never stated we were democrats. On the contrary, we publicly stated that we only used democratic means to win power but after the seizure of power we would ruthlessly deny our opponents the facilities that were granted us when we were in opposition." Could the danger that confronts the constitutional government which tolerates the advocates of despotism be put more plainly? To talk about the importance of fair play in the face of such a challenge is like advising an army to adopt tennis rules when it goes into battle with the enemy.

It is difficult to determine the exact place at which the government may properly intervene against the advocates of despotism. While the rights of freedom of speech and freedom of assembly must be preserved, the boundary drawn around these seditious activities and intrigues should be adjusted to cover the new forms of propaganda that have been devised during recent decades. The laws against the overthrow of our form of government by force should be extended to cover the activities of persons, whether citizens or not, who scheme to deprive us of our liberty. In addition, libel laws similar to those in England should be enacted, making it possible to punish by fine in the court persons who spread lies in print or on the public platform concerning our statesmen or any of our citizens. With despotism knocking at our door, democracy has the right to defend itself.

Many well-meaning persons who detest despotism, and who still believe there are such things as truth and right, think that if events are left to take their course, truth and right will take care of themselves. The despotic governments, with their formidable weapons of propaganda, find it convenient to have their agents exploit this idea among Americans. But the price of retaining the democratic form of government is the recognition that nothing worth while has ever been obtained by a people except through collective effort. The price is the establishment of a democracy in which the standards of justice, honor, truth, and art are much higher than at present, of a democracy in which the people place justice, honor, art, and truth above material advantage. If we cannot discipline ourselves, powerful men whose objectives are not those of Christianity or Western culture will discipline us.

The defense of democracy rests in the hands of every

American. If men today could find the same fortitude in dealing with the problems of their daily existence that the early pioneers of this country had in meeting physical hardships and dangers even more terrible than any we have to face, democracy might be saved. When propagandists suggest that these pioneers were no less imperialistic than the agents of the totalitarian states today, we should not forget that the pioneers were expanding at great physical risk into the uncivilized wilderness, which Parkman has described so vividly, bringing with them the principles of Christianity and of human rights, while the totalitarians propose to expand at the expense of the most highly civilized countries, and do not intend to allow the principles of Christianity and human rights to stand in their way. Our past is not so bad as the future which the totalitarians have in store for us. If we cease to identify all the goods of life with a rapid increase in the volume of material goods consumed, might it not be possible to construct a future better than our past?

XII

THE FUTURE OF INTERNATIONAL JUSTICE

✵

THE difficulties in the way of improving the character of government and civilization in the United States would be great if the country were completely isolated from the rest of the world, or if it were in a world by itself. The difficulties are tremendously increased by the fact that it is part of a world which contains many countries and peoples. The information available to Americans concerning other nations comes largely from foreign correspondents, radio commentators, diplomats, and other professors of current events, whose knowledge is superficial. When the information comes from scholars, it comes from specialists who not infrequently make a virtue of avoiding the attempt to see the world as a whole or of examining the meaning of what they find in relation to moral philosophy. As a result even the responsible political leaders understand far too little that is of importance in dealing with foreign nations. Americans know almost nothing of the essential nature of foreign countries. They are bombarded with a host of ill-assorted, ill-digested facts, many inaccurately presented, about the events of yesterday. If these facts are interpreted for us, or if we try to interpret them for ourselves, the interpretation is generally made without any real understanding of the history and traditions of foreign nations, which would give the facts a meaning different from the one they now have for us. Many Americans in responsible positions of authority, together with most of those who speak on matters of foreign policy, are in a much worse case than if they were simply ignorant. They have mistaken their ignorance for knowledge.

In the nineteenth century the ignorance of Americans was, perhaps, no greater than it is today. There are various reasons for our failure to improve our understanding of Europe. Until the rise of progressive education, during and after the nineties, the introduction to Christian learning offered in the schools and colleges gave Americans a common bond in culture with Europeans—a bond which has been weakened.[1] The attention of most European nations was directed to ends similar to those which the young American civilization was seeking. The goals of scientific and technological progress and improved living conditions were pursued by most of the European peoples only less single-mindedly than by ourselves. So we were in a position to understand each other's ways rather better than we are now, when these goals are losing their attraction for many European peoples.

In any case, the ignorance of Americans about Europe did not matter much then. However inaccurate were their opinions about the other great world-powers, however much they misunderstood the intellectual and cultural forces of history, their misunderstanding was not a serious danger when the prospect of a mortal conflict with any of these powers was remote. The only first-class nation with an important foothold on this continent was Great Britain. No other great country had a conception of the objectives of civilization so much like our own as Great Britain. To a greater degree even than the British, we regarded economic progress and commercial and industrial prosperity as the chief purposes of human existence. Both in Great Britain and in this country the

[1] Cf. above, chap. iv, pp. 67–69.

cultivation of progress and prosperity was proving consistent with greater physical gentleness in the relations between man and man. It was proving consistent with constitutional government and with an extension of the suffrage. The two countries were in essential agreement on the position in military matters adopted by the English ever since the late sixteenth and seventeenth centuries. The British conquests, like those of the United States, have been carried on mainly at the expense of primitive peoples rather than at the expense of the civilized nations of Western European stock. After the loss of Calais in 1558, England never attempted to acquire sovereign authority over a substantial block of territory in Continental Europe. She intervened in continental wars only for the purpose of preventing any single power from gaining absolute political control over the Continent. As Great Britain and the rapidly growing United States regarded each other as on the whole civilized, in spite of the strictures at the expense of Americans by writers like Mrs. Trollope and Dickens, and in spite of the traditional antipathy of Americans toward the patronizing "mother-country," it was not difficult to reach peaceful agreements when issues arose between them. No love was lost; but both countries long ago abandoned the view that the best way to settle private or public differences between civilized peoples is to fight. Since the battles of 1812–15, notwithstanding some serious friction, the two countries have never been at war with each other.

I. GROWING WEAKNESS OF THE MERCANTILE CONCEPTION OF CIVILIZATION

As long as the conceptions of civilization and government developed in the north of Europe, and above all by the British and Americans, were accepted by the other great states, as long as no other state with fundamentally different conceptions grew strong enough to challenge Great Britain or this country, both nations remained secure from any serious threat to their existence from abroad. In the seventeenth and eighteenth centuries, the cultivation of industrial and commercial prosperity by the British came to be regarded as a sign of as great a virility and enterprise as the military qualities of some other European peoples. The old Germanic conception, expressed by Georgius Agricola in his great sixteenth-century treatise on engineering, that the calling of the soldier and even the calling of the miner were superior to that of "the merchant trading for lucre,"[2] lost strength even on the Continent. In eighteenth-century England men had begun to put the soldier and the merchant on a par. Soldiering had become a profession in all the Western countries. During most of the eighteenth century, wars threatened the lives of great nations hardly more than duels in France in the early twentieth century threatened the lives of the participants. According to Dean Tucker, writing about British social standards in 1751, "the Profession of a Merchant is esteemed full as honourable as that of an Officer."[3] Even earlier, Defoe had claimed that "the descendants of tradesmen here [in England], for gallantry of spirit and greatness of soul, are not inferior to the descendants of the best families."[4]

During the last fifty years the mercantile conception of the end of life has been placed on the defensive for a variety of reasons. It has been challenged in all countries by the workmen and their leaders. They have claimed that the profits arising from free enterprise, and the interest paid on capital, are received for little or no service rendered. At the same time, the material advantages of our industrial civilization have become less apparent as the output of manufactured com-

---

[2] *De re metallica* (1556), eds. H. C. and L. H. Hoover (London, 1912), p. 24.

[3] Josiah Tucker, *A Brief Essay on the Advantages and Disadvantages which respectively attend France and Great Britain with regard to Trade* (2d ed.; London, 1750), p. 34.

[4] *The Complete English Tradesman* (London, 1745), chap. xxv.

modities for private consumption has ceased to increase as rapidly as the population.[5] The growing disposition to measure everything by material standards, by mere quantity, has destroyed the balance that was maintained to some extent until the end of the nineteenth century between the physical wants of men and their needs for faith, virtue, beauty, and intelligence. At the very time when men are beginning to recognize that they can hardly hope for an unending improvement in their physical standard of life, they find themselves without spiritual, moral, intellectual, or aesthetic resources to fall back on. However much men are the children of darkness, as long as they are civilized they will miss the goods of the mind and spirit, if these goods are not shown them. They will feel an incomplete satisfaction in all mechanical contrivances and comforts that do not help them to find at least a trace of light.

As the British Empire and the United States have been the citadels of the mercantile conception of life, the weakening in the prestige of that conception has helped to create a new position for them in the world. They have been slow to recognize the change. Their ignorance of the true conditions in other nations hindered them from seeing that they were being placed on the defensive. They were accustomed to measure a nation's strength in terms of national output or in units of economic income per capita. Statisticians showed that their position, measured in these terms, was superior to that of other great nations. So they assumed that they were in no danger of attack. Often in the last two decades we have heard businessmen say it was unthinkable that Japan would ever go to war with the United States, because a nation does not go to war with its best customer. If they are right about Japan (and let us hope that they are) they will have been right for the wrong reason. Germany has demonstrated that it is

[5] Cf. above, chap. iii, pp. 50–51.

possible to prepare for war on a great scale while trade with the best customer nations shrinks. Germany has demonstrated that it is possible to go to war with one's best customers.

At the same time that men and women were encouraged to measure everything in economic terms, they ceased to ponder over old books that contain lessons relevant to every age. They did not observe, for instance, that, if Herodotus was right, the strength of the Persians, in their early period of conquest, lay more in their poverty than in their wealth. Americans did not observe that at a later time, when the Persians set out to conquer the Greeks, when the Persians were no longer "a poor people with a proud spirit" to the extent they once had been, the confidence of the Greeks was founded on their indifference to wealth. The famous foreboding of one of the Persian leaders is no longer seriously considered. He learned from deserters, in the presence of the great Xerxes himself, that there were many Greeks who trained and labored to cultivate their bodies for no reward other than an olive wreath. "Good heavens!" the leader exclaimed, ". . . . what manner of men are these against whom thou hast brought us to fight?—men who contend with one another, not for money, but for honour!"[6]

Few Englishmen and fewer Americans realized that their mercantile conception of life was losing its ascendancy in the rest of the world. In its place there arose the conception of military despotism in a new and more uncompromising form than any known to Western history. Military despotism arose in the same countries that had been foremost in the development of despotic rule at the end of the fifteenth and during the sixteenth centuries—the decaying Holy Roman Empire, Italy, and Spain.[7] The new relations of the governing authorities to economic life in these countries were similar to those of the

[6] *The History of Herodotus*, trans. Rawlinson, i. 89, 153; viii. 26.

[7] Cf. above, chap. ii, pp. 15–17.

princes and kings in early modern times. Their paternalism does not involve, as with Marxian communism, the elimination of nearly all business for profit. But it subordinates all private business to the ends of political policy. It assumes that the most effective way of conducting industrial and commercial ventures is to have them either under the direction of the state or subject to detailed regulation by codes and administrative orders. The rising military despotisms now claim a virility and resourcefulness for their conception of life such as the British and Americans since at least the eighteenth century had claimed for theirs.

As the prestige of wealth and private economic enterprise shrank, the nature of warfare changed. The development of the submarine and then the airplane robbed first Great Britain and then the United States of much of the protection they had possessed against the danger of foreign attack. The development of propaganda through the newspapers and magazines, the motion pictures, the radio, and through clubs devoted to the discussion of current affairs made it easier than in the past to sow discord within the borders of these states to the advantage of warlike despotisms. This was particularly true in America, where a homogeneous civilization and homogeneous cultural traditions have been lacking. The greater physical protection which the United States possesses by virtue of her geographical position, as compared with Great Britain, is partly offset by the gullibility of her people to more insidious forms of attack than those of overt warfare. Unlike Great Britain and the United States, the new military despotisms feel no scruples about conquering civilized peoples, either with physical weapons or with propaganda. As most of the primitive parts of the earth had been pre-empted before the twentieth century, conquests can now be carried on, if at all, only at the expense of civilized or at least semicivilized peoples.

The immunity from war possessed by Great Britain and the United States—largely by virtue of their geographical situations—has been lost. Geography has been challenged by the natural science and invention bred in the seventeenth and early eighteenth centuries especially in England, and utilized for practical purposes increasingly since the middle of the eighteenth century all over the world. Great Britain and the British dominions, and even the United States, are now threatened by other powerful nations. Wars on the grand scale engulf the Western and Oriental peoples. Unless one side wins a total victory, or both sides succeed in virtually exterminating each other (which is unlikely), the world is faced with the possibility of serious and recurring wars for many decades to come.

II. STANDARDS OF RIGHTEOUSNESS AND WORLD-PEACE

How is the United States to meet this new situation? We are concerned not with the immediate issue of peace or war. We are concerned with the development of a wise foreign policy that will help us in facing war or the threats of war that may recur for a long time. What is the wisest general policy for the United States to adopt in the decades that lie ahead? How can the country strengthen itself at home to face the ordeals that it will have to meet?

It is paradoxical that, in the twentieth century, at the very time when movements to outlaw war became more numerous and vociferous than ever before in history, the Western peoples have entered anew on a period of wars. The new wars are conducted upon a scale without precedent. They draw upon a larger proportion of the material and human resources of the nations engaged than any past wars of Western civilization. How has it come about that, when so large a portion of the civilized population of the earth have voiced their desire to live in peace, not only with their fellow-countrymen but with foreigners, they should find themselves drawn, in spite of themselves, into battle?

Never before have there been so many peace societies as in the twentieth century. Never has the subject of international law been studied so assiduously in universities and colleges. Never has so much machinery been devised for settling disputes between nations without recourse to war. Why have all these movements and all this machinery come to nothing?

One obvious explanation for their failure is that the very prevalence of the desire for peace among the peoples of the earth offered an unparalleled opportunity for conquest to martial nations prepared to use war as an instrument of policy. With the rise of despotism such nations could send their agents to encourage the pacifist movements in other countries, while they prohibited all pacifist expressions of opinion and exterminated all pacifist movements in their own. By exploiting at once the fears, the martial ardor, and the sense of frustration of their own people, they were able, with the help of modern science and technology, to build up striking forces of such tremendous power that they cowed their immediate neighbors. At the same time they were able to risk war with any of the chief pacifistically inclined powers.

What is the deeper meaning behind this history? Hardly anything could illustrate better that machinery for settling international disputes is powerless unless there is behind the machinery a will and spirit on the part of the peoples of the earth to enforce righteousness and international justice. Hardly anything could illustrate more perfectly the danger of relying too much on means and thinking too little of ends. The efforts of pacifist societies often made peace less, not more, probable than it would have been without them. The societies had the support of persons who were already converted to the cause of peace. For the most part they made no impression on the persons or the nations that needed to be converted, unless it was to satisfy them that they were in a position to advance their interests by war. Political leaders in the countries where constitutional government prevailed were always devising new schemes for keeping the peace between nations. These schemes reassured their peoples that peace was likely to last, and so further convinced the totalitarian leaders, who were prepared to risk war for the sake of conquest, that they stood to gain by taking chances.

In our desire to get at the reasons for the failure of the efforts toward peace we should not belittle the importance of means. Machinery is obviously indispensable for the settlement of international disputes. The machinery hitherto devised has been far from perfect and, if a measure of tranquillity is again restored in the warring world, efforts should be made to improve on the League of Nations. No provision was made in it for the peoples of the various nations to choose their representatives by voting, as the late Professor F. J. Turner suggested to President Wilson on his departure for the Peace Conference in Paris.[8] Turner had hoped this might help to establish political ties stretching across national boundaries, as he thought the American parties had helped to bind together the different sections of the nation. What was still more serious for its success, the League of Nations did not create effective means for bringing about peace when an independent sovereign nation defied it. No international police force was created to enforce international justice.

With all its technical shortcomings, the League offered more adequate machinery for the peaceful settlement of international disputes than had existed at any time between 1815 and 1914. Why, then, did it prove more difficult to keep the peace than during the hundred years between the Napoleonic

[8] MSS of Professor Turner, preserved in the Huntington Library, San Marino, California. Turner gave the paper to Professor Charles H. Haskins in the autumn of 1918 to show the President on the voyage to France. A copy was published in the *American Historical Review* for April, 1942.

wars and the first World War? Even with the League, the enforcement of justice depended ultimately, as before 1914, upon
the policies of independent nations. So the success of the
League depended ultimately upon the will of democratic
peoples to resist aggression by force of arms. Its success depended on the maintenance among the democratic peoples of a
belief in values worth fighting for. Success depended upon the
acceptance of the thesis, hardly embodied in the Kellogg Pact,
that the use of war as an instrument of policy is an evil so
great that the nations of the world should agree, if the need
arises, to combine in the use of a strong armament against any
nation which breaks the peace for the sake of conquest. As
Tawney has written:

> What matters most is not what men say, and the language in
> which they say it; it is what they mean to do, and the intensity
> with which they mean it. The important point is not that they
> should express—or even hold—opinions as to policy which attract
> attention as "extreme." It is that they should show extreme sense
> in reaching them, extreme self-restraint in keeping their mouths
> shut until the opinions are worth stating, and extreme resolution in
> acting on them, when stated.[9]

The words seem appropriate to the history of international
relations between the two great wars. The richest nations can
hardly be said to have given a conspicuous example of the kind
of self-restraint and determination that Tawney suggests is
indicative of strength.

Even with the League, the maintenance of peace depended
upon the power of the belief that the way to get peace is to enforce right, that the object in international relations is, in the
words of Pascal, to make justice strong and force just. That
can be done only when people are taught that righteousness
and justice are something more than matters of opinion.

During the last fifty years or so the belief in the value and

[9] R. H. Tawney, *Equality* (3d ed.; London, 1938), p. 265.

even the existence of such a thing as righteous conduct, independent of private advantage or personal idiosyncrasies, has waned again and again throughout the world. It is this more than anything else that has given the despot his power. The improved machinery for settling disputes provided by the League was more than offset by the deterioration in the strength of belief. When the Western peoples cease to care for truth and virtue, when they even deny that truth and virtue exist independently of the whims of individuals, they pave the way for the triumph of evil. We shall do well to remember the words of one of the greatest English poets:

> . . . . sometimes Nations will decline so low
> From vertue, which is reason, that no wrong,
> But Justice, and some fatal curse annext
> Deprives them of thir outward libertie,
> Thir inward lost. . . . .

The lesson of *Paradise Lost* is a lesson that mankind had forgotten, but is learning again to its cost amid a hail of bombs and steel.

The generation now in middle life grew up to regard the Victorian Age as an age of hypocrisy. We have freed ourselves from much of the hypocrisy for which our ancestors are famous, but along with it we have thrown away most of the residue of belief in the value of righteous conduct which our ancestors possessed. We have made the error of assuming that it is better to deny the existence of truth and virtue than to affirm a belief in them when human nature makes their attainment, in forms invulnerable to criticism, impossible. It is shocking to find persons who talk of goodness straying away from it. But as long as there are persons who can be shocked by that, there is still hope of recovering a measure of goodness. Remove the belief in goodness, remove the capacity of men to be shocked by lapses from goodness, and there remain few obstacles to impede the advance of evil.

During a large part of the nineteenth century, the Western peoples had high ideals of righteousness, however far away from them they drifted in practice. The happy industrial and commercial developments which poured material riches into the lap of every Western nation gave their peoples an opportunity to develop a code of justice in international relations higher in many ways than had prevailed at any earlier time in Western history, unless it was to some extent in the reign of St. Louis in the thirteenth century. In the nineteenth century there were fewer pacifist societies than in the interval between the first two world wars. There was no League of Nations. But there was more peace. What was the strongest factor working for the maintenance of peace? It seems to have been a common belief in righteousness, independent of the private ends either of the individual citizen or of the individual nation. This sense of righteousness created a bond between the great powers of the world. Fragile though the bond was, it was an important factor in preventing a major international disaster. As long as this bond existed there were limits beyond which the political leaders of nations felt it unwise to go in trifling with their country's pledged word. There were also conventions of international decency which had to be adhered to. There were bounds to the territorial aspirations of even the most warlike state. No European nation was free to step beyond these limits, conventions, and bounds. To do so, they knew, would arouse the general will to war among the rest of the European peoples. They knew they would encounter the spirit of resistance, expressed on the eve of the first World War by one of righteousness' great champions and one of the most powerful French poets of modern times. Charles Péguy died in the first Battle of the Marne when he was forty-one, as he had shown himself willing to die in the lines he had written some years before.

> Heureux ceux qui sont morts pour la terre charnelle
> Mais pourvu que ce fut dans une juste guerre
> . . . .
> Heureux ceux qui sont morts dans les grandes batailles
> Couché dessus le sol à la face de Dieu.[10]

These were lines such as were not to be written in the interval between the great war that cost Péguy his life and the great war that cost France her army.

As long as 'righteousness remained an ideal, it was impossible to outrage righteousness too far with impunity. The differences between the limited objectives of Bismarck, the far wider but still limited objectives of the Kaiser, and the almost limitless objectives of Adolf Hitler are a measure of the debasement of the conception of righteousness without which all treaties, pacifist societies, and leagues of nations are bound to be impotent. It is not accidental that Hitler felt free to declare openly his policy of conquest. In the nineteenth century such a declaration by the head of a state, even if he had made it before he came to power, would have put the other peoples of Europe on the alert instead of leaving them cringing in fear or averting their eyes from unpleasant dangers. It is not accidental that Hitler was able to tear up treaties and make several moves on the European chessboard before 1939, any one of which would have precipitated a general war in the nineteenth century. A less serious move, the declaration of war by Austria on Serbia, did precipitate a general war in 1914.

Since 1914, the value placed by the Western peoples in America and Europe on the pledged word has diminished hardly less than the gold content of the standard coins of the major continental nations. What good is a League of Nations if the representatives of the countries which founded it treat it as a joke? In central Europe during the 1920's one used to listen to the diplomatic representatives of Britain and France

[10] "Heureux ceux qui sont morts," *Souvenirs* (Paris, 1938), p. 124.

heaping ridicule upon this excellent institution. "The League of Notions" was a favorite nickname for it at a time when it was still functioning much according to the plan of its founders, at a time when it was still regarded as an important arbiter in disputes between the various world-powers. For these diplomats it was already dead. They had buried it long before Hitler directed his representatives to secede from it in 1933. What wonder was it, then, that the secession caused little more than a murmur among the great powers of Europe. In their hearts a growing proportion of the political leaders no longer recognized such a thing as international righteousness. Cynicism concerning international relations increased. It was a reflection of the decline in moral and intellectual standards that was taking place among the Western peoples everywhere.

What good are pacifist societies when their aim is not to promote righteousness in international relations but to protect the bodies of the young men of their own nation? Apart from a few leaders, of whom the late Jane Addams was an outstanding example, the great majority of persons who organized for peace were interested in peace less because it was righteous than because it was comfortable. War had proved horrible beyond measure, especially to men and women brought up to suppose that the infliction of intense physical cruelty was a thing of the past. Meanwhile, the sense of moral obligation to one's fellow-men, which had played a great part in the decline of cruelty, was being lost. Responsibility to others was giving way to license to do whatever one pleased for one's self. So the citizens of unwarlike nations recoiled from war as never before. They failed to recognize that peace can be obtained more by the exercise of positive virtues than by negative organizations. What is the good of a peace oath if all oaths are losing their binding force throughout the world? It is of little help to dwell upon the destruction that war brings to property and life and to the physical fitness of the younger generation, unless something is done to strengthen the standards of morality among the peoples of the earth. Of what good are property and long life and physical fitness if men do not use them to improve the better sides of their natures? Man can be, as Aristotle says in his *Politics*, "the noblest of all animals." But, Aristotle goes on to say,

apart from law and justice [man] is the vilest of all. For injustice is always most formidable when it is armed; and Nature has endowed Man with arms which are intended to subserve the purposes of prudence and virtue but are capable of being wholly turned to contrary ends. Hence if Man be devoid of virtue, no animal is so unscrupulous or savage, none so sensual, none so gluttonous.[11]

The weapons are vastly more destructive today than Aristotle ever dreamed they could be. To him the building of a vessel as long as a modern battleship seemed the height of folly. Yet the very scientific and technical progress that has made obsolete some of Aristotle's scientific and technical opinions has made his comments concerning law and justice even more relevant to the present than to his time. Truth does not always grow rusty with age.

The peoples of the world will not have peace by wishing for it, by declaring their hatred of war. Such wishes and declarations are perfectly natural. It is right to hate war. But, by themselves, such wishes and declarations are neutral. They may even prove harmful to the maintenance of peace between nations.

The world has now become more of a unit than ever before in history. Standards of wickedness and (let us hope) standards of righteousness spread from one country to another almost as rapidly as mechanical inventions. If there is any truth in the view of Aristotle and other great sages concerning the importance of justice in the state, then a lack of harmony is created when righteousness is not given its proper place

[11] Book I, chap. iii.

above riches in man's hierarchy of values. That lack of harmony begets strife. It begets war no less than a lack of harmony between the foods we eat—as, for example, the drowning of pheasant in an internal bath of fizz water—can be a cause for war in the stomach. The establishment of peace between the nations depends upon the establishment of proper proportions between the various objectives of life within the nations, as well as upon a revival of international machinery for settling disputes. Just as the improvement of our own state depends upon an improvement of the standards in education, in statecraft, and in the arts, so an improvement in the moral condition of the world depends upon an improvement in the moral condition of the various states that make it up. "There can never be peace on this globe," the Archbishop of Westminster said in a broadcast summer before last, "till men of good will everywhere strive to rule by moral and religious principles and determine to uphold the triumph over hell on earth."[12]

The United States is confronted with two tasks in its international relations if it is to reject totalitarianism. The first is to resist any attempt at conquest. The second is to build up within this country a love of righteousness that will make the nation a model for other nations throughout the world. It is an error to suppose that modern states are strengthened for war by changing over to the totalitarian form of government, as the experience of Italy shows. Germany was a great military state on many occasions before she became a national socialist state. The military strength of the modern United States in a death grapple with a major foreign enemy has still to be tested. This much is probable. The strength of the country will not be increased by modeling the form and spirit of government on that of the present German state. Americans

[12] Talk by Arthur Cardinal Hinsley, delivered over the N.B.C. Red Network, August 4, 1940.

have much to learn from Germany in efficiency. But unless Americans work toward a renewed belief in good ends for the state and for the individuals who make it up, efficiency will not enable the United States to preserve the democratic form of government.

The country has no totalitarian traditions in its political background. If it is to remain a great power in the world of the future it will have to evolve a constitutionalism of its own and defend this against all assailants. The chance of defeating Germany if the United States were to become as totalitarian and ruthless as she is would be less than if we were to strike out along a path of our own. In any case, if the United States became totalitarian, a victory would be empty.

III. STRATEGY AND WORLD-PEACE

The problem of defense has become in large measure a matter of military and naval strategy and diplomacy. It should be the object of Americans to place their country in such a position that, if and when she fights, she fights on the best possible terms, with a view to a victory such as will preserve her integrity and enable her to survive as a great constitutional state. This means that she should strive to have as many other countries as possible actively or passively on her side and as few as possible actively or passively against her. This means that our statesmen should strive so to command events that they can use our weapons with the most telling effect against our enemies and on behalf of our friends. This means that they should conduct policy in such a way as to create as much spirit and enthusiasm as possible among the persons who will have to do the fighting and suffering.

Let us take up, first of all, the matter of defense, which has become so urgent. Diplomacy, armed strategy, morale—these are the weapons the country has to use. The conditions pertaining to all of them change frequently, though the basic principles which govern them remain much the same. One of these principles is this: Alliances between states are fragile. They frequently turn into enmity. Unless in the near future one nation conquers all the others, the changes in alliances are likely to continue. The United States should do all she can, therefore, to show other nations that she is determined to deal with them justly and on a basis of equality. At the same time she should show them that she wishes to preserve the integrity and independence of states threatened by aggressors. In these ways the United States can make it plain to the world that nations prepared to live within their ancient boundaries, and willing to accept the principle that new territory shall be acquired only by peaceful negotiations, have nothing to fear from America. The United States should make it clear that she is prepared to make concessions to peaceful requests which she will not make to armed threats.

Diplomacy and military strategy raise problems which are primarily for experts to solve, though they cannot meet these problems without studying the essential factors that have governed diplomacy and strategy in the past. If the morale of the American people is to be strengthened, three things would seem to be of great importance. In the first place, the government should call in for advice and consultation leaders whose positions on the great issues differ from its own. In the second place, it should explain to the people at frequent intervals its ultimate objectives and the reasons for its course of action. In the third place, it should strive toward an ever increasing efficiency, and toward the elimination of waste, in both military and industrial matters. The country must have adequate weapons. It must have the means and the will to use them effectively when the need arises. This calls for force and drive, and, above all, for the intelligence to co-ordinate the various defense industries and the various branches of the armed forces. On the eve of our entrance into the first

World War, Brooks Adams referred, in his private correspondence, to the experience of the King of Jerusalem before the army of Saladin.[13] That experience showed, Adams wrote, that a kingdom based on "individualism" with the "cross" thrown in is no match for a unified social organism without the "cross." The United States is confronted today with perhaps the most powerfully co-ordinated military organism the world has ever seen, an organism far more dangerous than the German military organism that alarmed Adams. In case it decides to strike, the United States will have to employ her industrial and military power with a skill far greater than was needed in 1917–18. But it is of paramount importance that, in striving for a unified social organism, the country should not relinquish the remnants of the Christian ideals which have been the chief glory of Anglo-American civilization. Let us contrive to combine efficiency with righteousness; but, when there is a conflict between the two, let us put righteousness first. That emphasis may save us in the end; the other is certain to lead down the road to tyranny and barbarism.

The intelligence and the morale indispensable to adequate defense cannot be developed without a deep and widespread belief that our cause is just. That belief will grow only if the United States has something better to offer her people and the world than have the totalitarian powers, which already control so large a portion of the civilized part of it. What is of paramount importance is that the nations of the earth should be won over to a new and better way of life, founded on peace and agreement rather than on war and on conquest. This cannot be done by trying to conquer the world and then to police it in the interest of the maintenance of a high material standard of living, primarily for Americans. In this country today there are some mild-mannered men, gentle with their wives,

[13] I owe my knowledge of this letter to Dr. Max Farrand, to whom it was written on January 2, 1916.

their children, and their friends, who assume that the proper way to deal with the international situation is to prevail by armed might over all other countries. This is to be done, of course, in the interest of peace and prosperity. When it is accomplished, the United States will maintain peace by denying weapons to all other nations.

Whatever may be thought of our capacity to carry out such a program, it is an error to represent it as an appeal to reason. The peoples of the European countries that have been conquered would not, if freed, choose to live under the rule of Germany. It is equally clear that they would not, if freed, choose to live under the rule of the United States. They would not even be likely to wish the United States to select their form of government for them. In spite of the lower standards of living which prevail in the various countries of Europe and the Orient, the peoples of those regions do not feel themselves inferior in character to Americans. They find little or nothing in our present conception of civilization to inspire them to follow us. Whether unjustly or not, they regard the material advantages of the United States as the result of her good fortune, especially of her endowment in natural resources and ocean frontiers. The riches by which Americans have been accustomed to measure merit are everywhere at a growing discount. The material goal as a driving force is being questioned everywhere, except, possibly, in the United States. Other states can hardly be made to swallow present American standards of success, except by force. "War, as we have remarked several times, has its end in peace," wrote Aristotle.[14] Such could hardly be the result of a war undertaken to Americanize the world. All that Americans can properly do is to defend the right to work out, with the help of the Christian and the humanist traditions, a new and better civilization than the one which has made such vast conquests during the past few

[14] *Politics*, Book IV, chap. xv. By "end," Aristotle means "object."

years. To accomplish that task would require all the energy and all the good will of every one of us. Each of us would have to strive to be ever so much better than he is.

We cannot appeal as a leader to other nations unless we reform ourselves, unless we cultivate in a new, better, and more enduring form the cultural values which these ancient European and Oriental states regard as civilized. However bitter the various European peoples feel toward their conquerors, they have no special sense of gratitude to the British or the Americans. During the last two decades, first the United States and then Great Britain withdrew step by step from the task they assumed during the war of 1914–18. That task was to protect the continental nations, France in particular, from German aggression, because it was then believed that such aggression constituted a threat to Great Britain and the United States and to the civilized values for which those two great countries stood, however unworthily. If they succeed in surviving as independent countries, the Americans and the British can regain the confidence of other nations only by an example of economic altruism without precedent in history. Once the threat of German hegemony in the world is overcome, and until the more serious suffering caused by the war is at an end, they should be prepared to share their food and resources with the nations of Europe without exacting in return any payment or any control over their internal affairs. They should not oppose an economic union of the European states, such as Germany now holds out to them under her domination. All they can ask for in return is a world-league of states pledged to keep the peace.

If there is to be a world-state in which the American people play a leading part, it can be brought into being only by a long process of building. It can be brought into being only if Americans work toward the highest goals set forth by the wise men and the saints of the past. The nature of these goals and possible means of approaching them have been the subject of two of the three parts of this essay. A recapitulation of the main argument should therefore point the way toward a better international order. That order can be constructed only in peace. But whether as a nation we are at peace or at war, we should strive unceasingly to keep these goals before our eyes. Upon a recognition of them depends our success in war as well as in peace.

IV. CONCLUSION

For good or ill, the United States finds itself a part of the civilization of Western Europe, whence came most of the ancestors of those persons who now populate it. There was a time when Americans thought of themselves as a new people, free from the trials and strains of the Old World, free to ignore the laws of history, free to ignore European experience. These were not views which most of the founding fathers shared. They were developed as part and parcel of the pioneering movement to the West, into largely unpeopled country, full of fabulous natural resources. They were views developed as part of that spirit of the frontier which influenced every aspect of American life during the nineteenth century, as Turner showed.[15]

The influence of the frontier has become so much a commonplace among Americans that a country which has not been profoundly interested in ideas, and which has found it hard to remember its dead, has almost forgotten how much of a debt it owes to Turner. When we read him now we find that (making all allowances for the differences in creative stature) Turner is, like Shakespeare, full of quotations. The late Virginia Woolf once remarked that most people forget that *Robinson Crusoe* had an author. We are in danger of forgetting that the theory of the frontier had an author. That is not an

[15] F. J. Turner, *The Frontier in American History* (New York, 1921).

altogether good omen for the future of the mind, if Americans are in danger, as they seem to be, of forgetting its power to work for good. One is almost led to fear that the time will come when Americans will claim that *Robinson Crusoe* and *Twelfth Night* were the products not of human minds but of animal reflexes.

If the country is in danger of forgetting the author of the theory of the frontier, it is, paradoxically enough, also in danger of failing to recognize that the conditions which created the frontier spirit among Americans no longer exist. The last frontier was crossed more than fifty years ago. In the meantime the development of old inventions, together with the discovery and development of new mechanical devices, has brought the United States within fighting range of the nations to the east and west as well as to the north and south. America, one of our poets has told us, "is neither a land nor a people."[16] That is a great danger now when we have no longer the freedom to work out our destiny by ourselves, as a race of men armed with gunpowder could have done if they had peopled the whole country at the time when Columbus visited it with his fragile little wooden sailing vessels.

Gunpowder and other explosives have now provided weapons capable of destroying civilization. They no longer provide, as Gibbon supposed they always would, the means of assuring it perpetual life.[17] The voyages of Columbus and the Reformation which followed marked the beginning of an epoch. The passing of the frontier in the eighties of the nineteenth century and the striking diminution in the rate of growth in the world-demand for energy, which began in the second decade of the present century,[18] mark the end of this

[16] Archibald MacLeish, "American Letter," *New Found Land* (Paris, 1930).

[17] Cf. Robert M. Hutchins, "The Next Fifty Years," *Science*, XCIV, No. 2441 (1941), 334–35.

[18] Cf. above, chap. iii, pp. 38–41.

epoch for the United States as well as for Europe. From the point of view of traditions and intelligence, the United States seems to be less well prepared than any other great nation to solve the problems of the new epoch.

Why do we say this? Even if peaceful relations should be re-established, the world, including the United States, is faced in the decades that lie ahead with a much slower rate of growth in its industrial production than the rate which prevailed throughout the nineteenth century. If the twentieth century should prove to be a century of great wars, the chances are that industrial production will increase little if at all. Yet of all the countries in the world the United States is the one in which the most people take it for granted that economic progress, in the sense of a rapid growth in production and a rapid rise in the material standard of living, will go on in-definitely. We are more accustomed than any other people to measure all values in terms of income and physical produc-tion. Compared with ourselves, Great Britain absorbed indus-trialism in small doses. While Germany absorbed industrialism much more rapidly than Great Britain and almost as rapidly as the United States, the authority of the state in Germany and the strength of the military tradition prevented the eco-nomic measuring-rod from ever becoming the common de-nominator of German civilization to the same extent that it has become the common denominator of ours.[19] French natu-ral resources and French civilization (with its balance, its finish, its reason) were in such disharmony with modern in-dustrialism that, after a century of adaptation that began long before the French Revolution, France may be said to have ceased trying to keep up with the other great nations as an industrial power. French population hardly grew after the middle of the nineteenth century. In the early nineteenth cen-

[19] Cf. Thorstein Veblen, *Imperial Germany and the Industrial Revolution* (New York, 1918).

tury, France was the most populous Western European state, as she had been for centuries. Today she has a smaller population than any other great power in the world.

The United States sets a more exclusive store by the economic side of life than any other nation, at the very time when hopes measured in economic terms are more likely than ever to meet with disappointment. We have as yet little in the way of other values to fall back on. It has been common to assume that the United States is more progressive than any other nation, ahead of all the others in ingenuity and enterprise. This is only true, if at all, in the spheres of science, medicine, commerce, and finance. In thought and art we have always lagged behind the great European countries. In this country all our artistic movements, with one or two notable exceptions, like Frank Lloyd Wright and his architecture, have followed in the wake of similar European movements. At a time when it is of compelling importance for us to think for ourselves, to work out a destiny that differs from that which circumstances and military despotism seem to be forcing on Europe, we are without experience in this great task. What is perhaps even graver, most of the persons who occupy posts in universities and other institutions ostensibly devoted to thought or art do not recognize our want of experience. They have neither the taste nor the sense of tradition which are essential to creative life. They are not only incapable of practicing the creative life; they go so far as to deny that there is such a thing as the creative life—or, more frequently, they call something the creative life which has no real connection with it. In an age when words have largely lost their meaning it is not remarkable that they can do this with impunity. The few voices raised so imperfectly on behalf of taste and tradition are either drowned in a storm of verbal abuse and chicanery—which is miscalled criticism—or are interpreted in such a way that their authors' meanings are lost to the minds of the persons who might profit by them.

This state of affairs is partly the result of our early history as a nation, and even as a set of colonies. The kind of development the country underwent in the heroic age of pioneering was not conducive to the cultivation of the art of thought or of any of the other arts. It is a state of affairs that has been aggravated now that we have "come of age." The moral and intellectual crisis of Western civilization, which has accompanied the material crisis, is common to all the Western nations. Far from escaping it, the United States has been to a considerable degree a leader in those movements (such as pragmatism) which, in spite of the intelligence and character of some of the leaders, have helped produce a decline in the integrity and the freedom of the mind and spirit during the last fifty years. It is ironical that, up to the present, the one conspicuous sphere in which we should have taken the lead in connection with thought should be in the undermining of it. The result has been that the standards of learning that still had a hold in American education down to the eighties and nineties of the last century have been almost completely submerged.

What can be done about it? If Americans do not believe in the mind and spirit, nothing. Again, if the vast majority of persons who seem to be working, either consciously or unwittingly, to destroy the mind and spirit, and to attach the names "mind" and "spirit" to elements that have little in common with either, succeed in burying the persons who are striving, however imperfectly and unworthily, to grope toward truth and toward beauty—again nothing can be done.

Whatever happens, Americans are in for a long testing-time of struggle, suffering, and disappointment. In this sense it is true that past history—but past history including the past history of the mind—has determined the immediate future for us. There is little reason to think that our people, any more than the British, can look forward to aught save "blood, toil, tears, and sweat." What the United States will be like after this period of turmoil, when this period will end, are questions no man can answer. Certainly no historian, who, by his studies, is made only too well aware of the incalculable elements that rule the affairs of men, would try to answer these questions in detail. But if history is any guide it suggests the chances are strong that, after the worst is over, we shall find a continent between the Atlantic and Pacific oceans! The chances are hardly less strong that this continent will be populated by men and women not so very unlike ourselves in the essentials of their physical makeup. If they are human beings, and if civilized living survives, they will still need to cultivate the mind and spirit.

Many of our contemporaries are fond of saying that you cannot stop a tank with philosophy. Of course that is a great truth. But it is only part of the truth. It is a statement that will appeal especially to persons whose minds do not range beyond very restricted limits. The mind that is concerned with the ultimate nature of historical forces will probe deeper. If there is any truth in our analysis of the relation between the decay in moral and intellectual standards and the recent conquest of Europe by military despotism, one is led to wonder whether the tanks and motorcycles would have run so wild if there had been more true philosophy—if, by the power of his mind, man had succeeded in maintaining in a new and better form the standards that existed in the nineteenth century. One is led to wonder whether, in the period of struggle and suffering that lies ahead of us, we shall not come out better than otherwise if we learn from our past mistakes in the realm of morality, intelligence, and art. One is led to wonder whether we shall not be better off if we cultivate philosophy. One is led to wonder whether we may not serve humanity by refusing to accept the defeat of human integrity, no matter how many setbacks it meets with, no matter how many insults and how much scorn is poured out upon it and how much intrigue is practiced at its expense.

We should have the faith to discard two preconceptions of our time, though the discarding of either appears superficially to add to the difficulty of discarding the other. One is the view that immediate worldly success is a test of the merit of a work of thought or art. The other is the view that whatever a man does with his mind is without influence for good or ill upon the course of history. That view has always been held by some people, but it has become especially prevalent in the last fifty years. The best answer to it was given over a hundred years ago by Tocqueville. In ending his great book on *Democracy in America*, he wrote:

I am aware that many of my contemporaries maintain that nations are never their own masters here below, and that they necessarily obey some insurmountable and unintelligent power, arising from anterior events, from their race, or from the soil and climate of their country. Such principles are false and cowardly; such principles can never produce aught but feeble men and pusillanimous nations. Providence has not created mankind entirely independent or entirely free. It is true that around every man a fatal circle is traced, beyond which he cannot pass; but within the wide verge of that circle he is powerful and free; as it is with man, so with communities. The nations of our time cannot prevent the conditions of men from becoming equal; but it depends upon themselves whether the principle of equality is to lead them to servitude or freedom, to knowledge or barbarism, to prosperity or wretchedness.

The task of churchmen, scholars, teachers, and artists is to hold out to man the vision of a better world, here on earth as well as in the hereafter. Their task is to provide mankind, with the help of reason, of natural science, and of the research of all kinds done in the past, with a pattern of that better world. Their task is to re-create a faith in the absolute values of righteousness, truth, and beauty, in spite of the impossibility for mere man to attain to a complete and perfect knowledge of these values. These tasks are not community tasks. They must be carried out by individuals of genius. But every common man, in so far as any trace of human good exists within him, can do something to facilitate their accomplishment in a simple, common-sense way. So can the scholars, the artists, and the religious leaders in the practical life which they share with common men, and by the institutions which they should maintain and develop for the benefit of common men.

Here a lesson could be learned from the recent past. We have left the world of the nineteenth century, where an attempt, however imperfect, was made to see that honor was rewarded, where men were able to say with a semblance of truth that honesty was the best policy. There is little attempt now to see that honor is rewarded, or even to admit that honor exists. Honesty, in the deeper sense, is the best policy less frequently than in the nineteenth century. Therefore, if men are to work for honor, truth, and beauty, they must be willing to lose by the work. In the nineteenth century, especially in England and the United States, for almost the first time in Western history men supposed that in this world the good were rewarded. They began to forget that behind many actions, even in the realm of scholarship and learning, lay ulterior and even sinister motives. Many reasonably honorable men of the older generation persist today in the idea that there is some connection between worldly rewards and virtue, when this is much less true than it was fifty years ago. In the meantime the bad men and the evil elements in man have taken advantage of the persistence of this nineteenth-century idea. They have found that it is no longer necessary for them to play the game of life according to the nineteenth-century rules. Since every man is supposed to be equally good, there is no disposition to distinguish between one man and another on moral or even on intellectual grounds, and the two are closely related. The good men go on playing the game according to the nineteenth-century rules. They go on assuming that goodness and truth will automatically come up on top, at least in the

United States. As things have turned out, to play the game in that old nineteenth-century way is to play the game for the destruction of what is best in man. The good men and women do little to strengthen each other. They do little even to rescue their fellows when they are in trouble. They do not recognize evil when they see it or when it is practiced. They do not even recognize each other.

Is it not at just this point that it might be possible to break away from the vicious circle of Pascal, according to which a weak society encourages a weak system of education, and a weak system of education, a weak society? If it is possible, then all honorable men should work ceaselessly to find the good in the world that lies about them, much as the placer miners scour the streams for gravel containing gold. Righteousness, wisdom, and beauty are scarce. Truth is difficult to distinguish from falsehood. Good is difficult to distinguish from evil. If the distinctions are to be revived the United States will have to employ that fine instrument, man's mind, which has been discarded and forgotten for other more mechanical instruments which serve the natural scientist and his imitator, the social scientist. How can man's mind be revived? Some of John Donne's lines suggest that the only path is the long and difficult ascent of that steep mountain which he describes in one of his finest poems.

> And the right; aske thy father which is shee,
> Let him aske his; though truth and falshood bee
> Neere twins, yet truth a little elder is;
> Be busie to seeke her, beleeve mee this,
> Hee's not of none, nor worst, that seekes the best.
> To adore, or scorne an image, or protest,
> May all be bad; doubt wisely; in strange way
> To stand inquiring right, is not to stray;
> To sleepe, or runne wrong, is. On a huge hill,
> Cragged, and steep, Truth stands, and hee that will

Reech her, about must, and about must goe;
And what the hills suddennes resists, winne so;
Yet strive so, that before age, deaths twilight,
Thy Soule rest, for none can worke in that night.[20]

These lines of Donne suggest the basic lesson, the first principle, that lies behind an attempt to save civilization from destruction and build a better nation in the United States. Some years ago MacLeish described Americans as, "Many of one mouth, of one breath, dressed as one—and none brothers among them." If the United States is to become what MacLeish said it was not, "a land and a people," equal to the task of meeting aggression from abroad, dissension and evil from within, there is only one way. It is for the good and the just, the lovers of honor, truth, and beauty, to find their brothers. They need to rephrase and make over two famous and enormously influential passages in Rousseau and Marx. In their original form, these passages have been leading several generations of men away from truth. They might help to guide mankind toward truth if they read: "Wisdom, goodness, and beauty were born free, but everywhere they are in chains. Truth-loving, good people, beauty-loving people of the world unite. You have nothing material to gain for yourselves; but you have the opportunity to serve humanity. You have the opportunity to bring about a rebirth of the human mind and spirit."

[20] "Satyre III," *The Poems of John Donne*, ed. Herbert J. C. Grierson (Oxford, 1912), I, 157.

INDEX

INDEX

✲